Federico Fellini
as Auteur

FEDERICO FELLINI AS AUTEUR

SEVEN ASPECTS OF HIS FILMS

JOHN C. STUBBS

SOUTHERN ILLINOIS UNIVERSITY PRESS

CARBONDALE

Portions of chapters 1 and 4 were previously published as "The Fellini Manner: Open Form and Visual Excess," *Cinema Journal* 32, no. 4 (Summer 1993): 49–64 (© 1993 Board of Trustees of the University of Illinois), and "Fellini's Portrait of the Artist as Creative Problem Solver," *Cinema Journal* 41, no. 4 (Summer 2002): 116–31 (© 2002 by the University of Texas Press, P.O. Box 7819, Austin, TX 78713-7819), and have been reprinted with permission from the University of Texas Press. Portions of chapter 5 were previously published as "The Mime and the Method: The Working Relationship Between Fellini and Masina," *Literature/Film Quarterly* 30, no. 4 (2002): 264–70, and have been reprinted with permission of *Literature/Film Quarterly* @ Salisbury University, Salisbury, MD 21801.

Library of Congress Cataloging-in-Publication Data
Stubbs, John Caldwell.
  Federico Fellini as auteur : seven aspects of his films / John C. Stubbs
    p. cm.
  Filmography:
  Includes bibliographical references and index.
  1. Fellini, Federico—Criticism and interpretation. I. Title.
  PN1998.3.F45S78 2006
  791.4302'33'092—dc22   2005024126
  ISBN-13: 978-0-8093-2689-1 (cloth : alk. paper)
  ISBN-10: 0-8093-2689-2 (cloth : alk. paper)

To June

*ispiratrice, moglie e tifosa
di Federico e Giulietta*

CONTENTS

FIGURES

PREFACE

This book is an auteurist study of the films of Federico Fellini. I hope it is, however, an enlightened auteurist study. Certainly, it is written with the awareness that Roland Barthes, in his celebrated essay of 1968, has declared the author dead. Of course, looking back at his essay from our vantage point today, we will very likely find it a modest attempt to dislodge the author from a position of authority over the "meaning" of a text and to open up the text or the film as a field of play for meanings. If this is the case, then I want to take up the challenge here and play with the possibilities offered by Fellini's oeuvre. I have little desire to proclaim Fellini a "great man" and discuss the chronological growth of his "genius" in the romantic sense of those terms, as indeed traditional auteurists have already done. Rather I want to discuss Fellini's movies as something of a genre, called the Fellini films, not unlike genres we might call Hitchcock films, Welles films, or Oliver Stone films, and then I want to break down this body of work into seven groupings that I think can be discussed usefully in separate chapters.[1] There are, as I hope to demonstrate in my book, certain advantages to gathering the films of Federico Fellini together and looking at them in terms of various groupings, especially since we can now consider the body of work complete after Fellini's death in 1993.

My overview of auteur criticism is informed by the works of certain scholars who have laid out the problematics of the criticism clearly. The most basic of these is, of course, John Caughie's edition *Theories of Authorship*, which presents the basic documents and offers telling criticism of the essays themselves.[2] Three later works are indispensable overviews of where auteur criticism stands today and the strengths and weaknesses of each stage of its evolution: Pam Cook and Mieke Bernink's *The Cinema Book,* Virginia Wright Wexman's *Film and Authorship,* and David A. Gerstner and Janet Staiger's *Authorship and Film.*[3] The final and perhaps most important book is David Bordwell's *Making Meaning.*[4] Bordwell asks and answers the basic question, What is it we do when we criticize? My debt to these scholars sometimes will be apparent and sometimes will lurk beneath the surface of my criticism of Fellini's works.

Auteur criticism has passed through at least five stages. I have drawn on or quarreled with all five of them, some certainly more than others, as the reader will discover. The first stage is the classic one associated with the *Cahiers du cinema* critics in the 1950s and the 1960s, particularly François Truffaut and André Bazin. It equates the film director with authors of novels or plays. This stage was clearly an attempt to gain for film the status of respectability already held by the two literary genres. These early auteur critics asserted that a director's body of works possessed a unity and offered a means for grouping films for study, and they implied that the author's "intention" was crucial to understanding the "meanings" of the body of works. In so doing, they were urging what Bordwell has called "explicatory criticism," with which the critic searches for "implicit meaning" put into the work by its author, whether consciously or unconsciously. The author, therefore, becomes the *agent* who creates meaning and is a prime source of help for the critic in uncovering the meaning. In this book, I continue to see the author, Fellini, as the agent who begins the work of filmmaking. I view the author, furthermore, as a useful means for grouping films, although I consider the oeuvre best studied when broken down into subgroups or clusters. And finally, although I don't regard Fellini as an unimpeachable source to the "meanings" of his films, I do value his observations made in numerous interviews.

The second phase was auteur structuralism, associated in the late 1960s with British critics Geoffrey Nowell-Smith and Peter Wollen.[5] This group drew loosely on the models of structural linguistics and structural anthropology. The critics tried to replace the idea of a biological author with the notion of the author-in-the-text, that is, a group of themes, conflicting dichotomies, and visual mannerisms associated with the author. The structural critics, of course, ran the risk of being reductive in their readings, reducing all films of an author to certain issues or patterns, and they lay themselves open to charges of confusion between biographical authors as conscious or unconscious creators of the films and authors-in-the-text who can be discovered only after the films have been completed. Despite the very real difficulties in structuralist criticism, my debts to this group are substantial. I am attracted to their so-called "work-in-the-field," that is, their close readings of the films they treated, and to their use of one film to shed light on others by the same author. I hope to avoid their reductiveness not by concentrating on *the one body* of film work but by insisting instead on a division of at least seven aspects of Fellini's oeuvre to be explored in separate chapters and by suggesting that other critics will surely discover other divisions or issues to take up almost endlessly.

The third stage of auteurism, in fact, runs parallel to auteur structuralism, although it has seemed to pass strangely unnoticed by European critics, perhaps because of its commonsense, nontheoretical nature. Yet it is an important stage. It is collaborative auteurism. This stage may be considered to have begun with Pauline Kael's 1963 article "Circles and Squares," in which she threw down the gauntlet and attacked auteurism by arguing that films, especially Hollywood ones, are made by a group rather than an individual author.[6] This stage is perhaps best illustrated in the ongoing debate about the authorship of *Citizen Kane* conducted by Kael, Peter Bogdanovich, and Robert L. Carringer in the 1970s and 1980s concerning Orson Welles's indebtedness to his screenwriter, his cinematographer, his film editor, and others.[7] The debate ended with the assertion by Carringer that the director is an "author" only in a carefully defined "collaborative" sense, perhaps as a "leader" of a team. Here, in this book, I have tried to learn the lesson well taught. The idea of collaboration is particularly important in chapter 1, where I discuss the "Fellini manner." His style is, of course, the result of work done by various teams he brought together at various points in his career.

The fourth stage is the one mentioned at the outset in reference to Roland Barthes's declaration of the death of the author. Barthes's point, as noted earlier, was to open up the text and to shift emphasis in the communication model *AUTHOR > TEXT < READER* from the author end of the diagram to the reader end. He states, "The birth of the reader must be at the cost of the death of the Author."[8] His wish is to free the text from the "tyranny" of the author. As Caughie has put it, Barthes sought to open the text up "to the play of its meanings, rather than tying it down to an authorized interpretation of closed meanings."[9] Barthes's work has, indeed, changed the face of criticism. No longer is it possible for critics to argue for a "definitive reading," although I still hold steadfastly to the notion that some readings are more insightful or more interesting, in some senses of those troubled terms, than others. In *Federico Fellini as Auteur,* I would claim for the critic the same right Barthes asserts for the reader—the right to choose aspects of a text or an oeuvre and muse on those aspects that please me the most and about which I feel most competent to write.[10] I hope to open up the oeuvre of Fellini rather than to "tie it down" or reduce its possibilities.

The final stage of auteur criticism, the one that currently holds sway, is the poststructuralist one, with Michel Foucault taken as its intellectual mentor and a later group of *Cahiers* critics, such as Jean-Pierre Oudart and Jean-Louis Comolli, taken as representative practitioners. As early as 1969, Foucault argued the need to keep alive and reexamine the "author-function" in his essay "What Is an Author?"[11] However, as his ideas and those of other poststructuralists have evolved and merged with speech-act theory, Lacanian psychology, and revised Marxism, the concept of the author has become that of the "discursive subject," one who "enunciates" a discourse or a network of discourses, perhaps psychological (concerning individual or collective unconscious), perhaps ideological (embodying regressive capitalism or transgressive Marxism), or perhaps intertextual (related to other films or literary works). The poststructuralist approach, then, focuses on the middle unit of the communication model, the TEXT, and the author vanishes into the text he speaks.[12] The role of the author at this stage is summarized by Staiger: Poststructuralists "redefine the author as contradictory, a tablet upon and through which culture writes its historical discourses. This is the final poststructural subject, devoid of knowing intention and without coherence or continuity."[13] It is at this point that I pull back and cling stubbornly to a "somewhat" knowing author who initiates and guides, to some extent, the film projects, although I admit that some of the more interesting aspects of his films may be unknown to him or unrecognized by him and must be discovered by viewers and critics. In most cases in this book, I have tried to "conceptualize" each of the seven aspects of the Fellini films I take up, but I stop well short of a poststructuralist argument that the "contexts" may have "written" the films.

Looking at the Fellini films as a genre, drawing the oeuvre together and then dividing it into clusters, has certain benefits. One of the most obvious is the attention it draws to various pleasures of the body of work. Further, we may use one film to shed light on another. What may be clear in one work may be murky in another, and the juxtaposition of the two may prove extremely useful. Or we may use the informing ideas of the clusters to illuminate various of the individual films within a given cluster. More than these things, however, we as active viewers may recreate "new movies" by combining in our minds parts of various different movies into a new entity—say, the "Fellini film of adolescence" taken from parts of different movies; or we may construct new categories—such as the "Fellini ending"—which we may enjoy as much as any of the traditionally released films in their entireties.

I have chosen seven groupings to write about. I do not, however, consider my choices to be definitive ones that *must be* treated. The seven aspects are those that interest me the most and that I feel most qualified to discuss. I don't try to give "complete readings" of films. Rather I use "readings" of sections of the films to support and illustrate my generalizations. My hope is that readers can cut into this book at the beginning of any of the seven essays that comprise the book, although it seems to me that chapters 1 and 2 are more global than the others and that the material of chapter 3 logically precedes the subject matter of chapter 4. I wish, then, to invite the reader to enter this book with something of the same spirit I had when I entered the body of Fellini's films, going first to the films or sections of films that interested me the most and proceeding from there to the rest of the oeuvre and further discoveries.

ACKNOWLEDGMENTS

This project is one I have worked on and thought about for a number of years. Many people have aided me or encouraged me in a variety of ways. I am indebted to my colleagues in the Unit for Cinema Studies at the University of Illinois who helped me launch the project. This list of colleagues includes John P. Frayne, Robert L. Carringer, Edwin Jahiel, Richard Leskosky, David Desser, and several others. Similarly I thank the students in my courses on Italian film, movie directors, and special topics at the University of Illinois and at Virginia Tech, where I was able to try out my ideas on (especially) live audiences. Particularly I thank Alexander Doty, Kim Worthy, Lynn Traugott, and Stefan Hall for the range of ideas they provided in those courses.

My research was aided greatly by two extended stays in Italy: a Fulbright lectureship in Rome and a visiting professorship at the American Academy in Rome. I received valuable assistance from Cipriana Scelba and Luigi Filadoro at the Fulbright Agency and from Adele Chatfield-Taylor, Caroline Bruzelius, and Pina Pasquantonio at the Rome Academy. The staff at the Cineteca nazionale of the Centro sperimentale di cinematografia in Rome helped me gather materials. And in my visits to Studio 5 at Cinecittà, Gianfranco Angelucci, Fellini's assistant director at that time, was always an expert guide and wise counselor. My stays in Italy were supported in large measure by research grants from the University of Illinois and from Virginia Tech. I am grateful to the Trustees of the University of Illinois and to the Board of Visitors of Virginia Tech for this support.

Portions of this book have appeared previously in print. Chapters 1 and 4 are expanded versions of the articles "The Fellini Manner: Open Form and Visual Excess," published in *Cinema Journal* in 1993, and "Fellini's Portrait of the Artist as Creative Problem Solver," published in *Cinema Journal* in 2002. Chapter 5 is an expanded version of "The Mime and the Method: The Working Relationship Between Fellini and Masina," published in *Literature/Film Quarterly* in 2002. My thanks to the University of Texas Press and to *Literature/Film Quarterly* for permission to reprint this material. For the illustrations in the book, I thank Erica Maurer of Diogenes Verlag AG, Simone Potter of the British Film Institute, Ron Mandelbaum of Filmfest, and Dan Albright of the Dan Albright Studio. Saundra Taylor of the Lilly Research Library at Indiana University was also helpful in giving me access to their collection of Fellini-Pinelli manuscripts. I am grateful to the anonymous readers at Southern Illinois University Press who advised me where to revise and expand my manuscript and to my editor, Karl Kageff, who, in turn, advised me where to condense and tighten it. The book has surely benefited from both processes.

Finally, my appreciation must go to Federico Fellini himself and to his wife Giulietta Masina, who gave up valuable time to answer my questions and to encourage me to continue the project until the end. Their kindness, wit, and intelligence were inspirational.

Federico Fellini
as Auteur

1

FELLINI'S MANNER:
THE OPEN FORM AND THE STYLE OF EXCESS

Perhaps the most salient fact about Fellini's work is that viewers who have seen two or three of his movies feel confident they can identify any other of his films or can correctly designate films by other filmmakers as Felliniesque. They believe, in other words, that they can recognize Fellini's particular way of putting together his movies. This identification involves both the kind of subject matter he treats and the manner in which he treats it.

A filmmaker may be considered to have a narrative manner and a visual one. Narrative manner refers to the filmmaker's way of playing out to his viewers his story material. Contemporary formalist critics would call the story material simply "story" and the manner of playing it out "discourse."[1] The study of a filmmaker's discourse would involve asking questions like the following: Does he or she pursue a strictly chronological order in telling the story, or does the filmmaker begin in medias res and allow the past to unfold, through flashbacks, for example, as the work drives toward its conclusion in the future? Is there a cause-and-effect pattern between the sequences that leads us from one initial problem through its complications to a final solution (a discourse of *resolution*), or are the sequences linked more loosely according to some other principle, say, the desire to investigate a diverse range of material with a common theme holding them together (a discourse of *revelation*)?[2] Is there a single hero whose development as a complex human being or whose progress toward a defined goal gives the work its focus, or is the hero rather a group whose diverse types are played off against each other or whose interactions give the work its focus? And since no work can give equal time to all elements, what elements are presented at length and in detail and what elements compressed or elided? Finally, what sense of closure does the filmmaker want to attain in the endings of the works—does the filmmaker solve all the problems he or she created earlier in the work or merely offer a summarizing view of a dilemma or mystery the filmmaker has gradually built up in the work?

The visual manner of a filmmaker is more often called his or her style. It may involve the mise-en-scène, that is, visual elements such as costumes, sets, lighting, and character movement that he or she puts before the camera; it may involve the filmmaker's use of the camera itself in terms of how he or she composes for the frame, how he or she moves the camera, and how long he or she holds the shots; and it may involve the filmmaker's method and rhythm of editing the shots within a sequence and his or her method and rhythm of editing the sequences within the entire film.[3] For an element to be important in a filmmaker's style, it, of course, has to be something the filmmaker repeats characteristically from film to film to make visual impact, but it does not have to be unique to him or her. Uniqueness may very well come from the particular bundle of stylistic elements a filmmaker uses, even while any particular element may also be a part of another filmmaker's arsenal of weapons.

There are further complications. As I have maintained in the preface, the filmmaker is not the author of his or her films in the same sense a novelist is author of his or her novels. The filmmaker, even when he or she is the prime originator of his or her works, is much more dependent on the efforts of other people to bring films into being—collaborating screenwriters, set designers, musical composers, cinematographers, and, most obviously, actors. Auteur criticism now recognizes the director as author only in the sense that he or she is a kind of leader of a team. Here I consider Fellini as the leader of a team that answers finally to him, but I must admit at once that the team, although consistent by most movie standards, has changed almost completely over the span of Fellini's fifty-year career.[4] And, of course, Fellini himself has grown and changed somewhat. This development is inescapable if for no other reason than that he began making his films in black and white in the 1950s and then changed over to working in color in the mid-1960s. But there is more involved than this. His films have grown more complicated, longer, and more thickly layered over the years.

It might make good sense to talk about an evolution of Fellini's narrative and visual styles as he and members of his team changed and grew. We might be able to trace a curve—and a fairly familiar one at that—from simplicity to complexity to self-reflexivity. However, I think it is more interesting and more useful to hypothesize a manner that is perhaps never perfectly attained in any particular film but is approached from one angle or another in most of Fellini's movies.

Almost all of Fellini's films are informed at some level by the idea that life is ineffable.[5] The idea does not frighten Fellini; rather it intrigues and stimulates him. The normal and the rational, on the other hand, seem to bore him. They are too easily grasped. His interests in spiritualism and in Jungian depth psychology testify to his attempts to approach a something— not necessarily religious—that is beyond what is rationally perceived. It is this tendency that links Fellini with the surrealists Salvador Dali and Giorgio de Chirico. In interview Fellini has said, "The deepest meaning of film is its magic, ironic, mysterious meaning. When you take it away, you take away from film its obscure fascination."[6] Not that Fellini has mastered a "mysterious meaning" that he wishes to spell out for the edification of his viewers. It is rather that he encourages us to look for such things and to share with him the excitement of pushing ourselves imaginatively for the something more. Admittedly, it may be the romantic process of pushing ourselves that he celebrates more than the notion of our ever attaining a goal.

Fellini's aim is to "defamiliarize" us, as formalist critics would put it, with our world and have us see it afresh as something exciting and mysterious.[7] To do this, Fellini plays against our conventional expectations. Whereas the classic Hollywood studio film offers a tight, closed narrative, with all story elements determined by their relevancy to a central, cause-effect plot line,[8] Fellini tends to follow a more episodic, open narrative form, like the films of Jean Renoir and some films in the Neorealistic movement in which Fellini served at least a part of his apprenticeship.[9] Whereas the classic Hollywood studio film may be said to compose its visual images toward the center of the frame, to balance its compositions carefully in an uncluttered, mannerly way from left to right, and to keep the action on a single plane, all for purposes of quick comprehension, Fellini often uses a kind of layered composition, similar to those composed in deep space by Orson Welles, William Wyler, Stanley Kubrick, and Jean Renoir but more teeming with elements and contrasts. He also often emphasizes tactile elements, intrusive sound, and constant motion in the manner of Josef von Sternberg and Max Ophuls. His visual manner taken all together can only be called a style of excess. It seems deliberately to exceed the classic Hollywood norms at every turn.

The chief elements of the Fellini manner, then, are the open narrative form and the visual style of excess. Their common denominator is Fellini's desire to defamiliarize us with our world and to make it again stimulating to our imaginations. In this chapter, we look closely at the elements that make up Fellini's open form and those that make up his style of excess.

The Open Form

The basic element of a Fellini film is the sequence. Like a short-story writer or a lyric poet, Fellini excels at rendering a single event and teasing from it all its richness. His forte is the ten-minute, self-contained episode, which becomes a kind of story within the main story. This gift is a fortunate one in that it serves well Fellini's aim of pushing against the grain of conventional filmmaking. As his career progressed, Fellini tended more and more to privilege the individual sequences, the parts, over the whole. In retrospect, the tendency is apparent in embryo form even in his early, highly plotted comedies, but by the midpoint of his career, say *La Dolce Vita* (1960), it is a dominant aspect of his films.

The form that he follows we may call the open form. The term is perhaps best known to us through the work of Fellini's fellow countryman Umberto Eco in his book *The Open Work,* in which Eco cites the examples of baroque art, modern music, Alexander Calder's mobiles, and James Joyce's *Finnegans Wake* and speaks of a deliberate "indeterminacy of effect" and an increased role for the spectator-performer-reader in creating meaning.[10] Perhaps more useful here, however, is Leo Braudy's elaboration of the ideas Eco put in play. In *The World in a Frame,* Braudy distinguishes between closed and open forms as follows:

> In a closed film the world of the film is the only thing that exists; everything within it has its place in the plot of the film—every object,

every character, every gesture, every action. In an open film the world of the film is a momentary frame around an ongoing reality. The objects and the characters in the film existed before the camera focused on them and they will exist after the film is over. They achieve their significance or interest within the story of the film, but, unlike the objects and the people in a closed film, the story of the open film does not exhaust the meaning of what it contains.[11]

Braudy's distinction is worth expanding. In the closed film, we might add, the emphasis is on narrative tightness. Usually as the story is laid out for us through its discourse, a conflict is established in the opening minutes. This conflict is expanded in the middle; that is, we encounter story elements that help us move toward a solution or elements that retard us. At the end, some sort of a solution to the initial conflict is achieved. Such a work is a film of *resolution*. A classic Hollywood studio example would be John Huston's *The Maltese Falcon* (1941) or indeed almost any detective movie. But there is also another kind of closed film that is a standard kind of studio film. This is a film in which a character is defined in the opening minutes, undergoes a series of experiences that give him opportunity to grow or test him in some way, and finishes the film either significantly changed or thoroughly entrenched in his earlier ways. This, too, is a film of resolution, although of character, not of events. An example of such a film is the 2001 romantic comedy *The Family Man*. In this movie, Jack, the protagonist played by Nicholas Cage, begins as an arrogant investment banker, becomes a "family man" through the intervention of a mysterious angel, and emerges as a more humanized person at the end. What these two types of movies—the detective film and the romantic comedy of character—have in common is the central unifying drive forward through the three Aristotelian sections of beginning, middle, and end, by means of a chain of cause-and-effect relationships. What makes them both closed types, though, is that all other elements contribute directly to this central drive. Anything extraneous is cut away. If a minor character is introduced, for example, the character is present only for what he or she can do to influence the central drive. Objects, in turn, like Chekhov's gun, are introduced only if they will prove important to the forward rush of the discourse. The appeal of such films is, at least on the surface, its streamlinedness but also, perhaps a little deeper down, its unspoken assumption that events and characters can be reduced to a single line of cause-and-effect relationships.

In the open form, on the other hand, the main emphasis is on looseness and diversity. Its unspoken or deeper assumption is that life cannot be reduced; it is too various; it overflows the frame that the movie "momentarily" puts around it. Following the lead of André Bazin, Braudy has told us that open form in movies has its roots in the work of the Europeans— Jean Renoir, the Italian Neorealists, and the French New Wave—but has spread also to America after the demise of the studios. If a minor character appears in an open film, he or she may well play a role in the forward push of the discourse, but the character may also present us with traits that tell us something about his or her past and make us wonder about his or her future. Digressions from the main action are not merely permitted, they are virtually mandated. Thus, in Stanley Kubrick's open film *2001: A Space Odyssey* (1968), for example, we digress for a lyrical interlude on weightlessness as a space satellite station spins sedately to Johann Strauss's "Blue Danube" waltz. The open film tends to be *revelatory,* then, rather than concerned with *resolution.* It pauses to show us a variety of things about its subject matter.

To this definition of the open form, we need to add the notion, mentioned earlier, that the individual sequences tend to be privileged over the central structure of the whole. This idea is implicit in Braudy's definition but must be spelled out if we are to understand Fellini's version of the open form. The idea is implicit, because emphasis on individual episodes provides yet another way for the open form to diverge from strict adherence to a central line of cause-and-effect relationships. It sets up a counterpull.

Before proceeding to an analysis of the overall structures of Fellini films, we might do well to inquire into his organization of a representative sequence. Generally speaking, his organization of a sequence is tighter than his overall organization of a film. A problem or mystery will be set up in order to be solved, or a character relationship will be set up in such a way as to call for some resolution. This closed form aspect will provide the overall organization of the sequence. But on the way to its resolution, the sequence will usually reveal a rich diversity of materials that constitute its real appeal to viewers. A perfect illustration is the *Rex* sequence in Fellini's *Amarcord* (1974).

The Rex *Sequence*

The sequence begins with the establishment of a mystery and an accompanying mood of expectancy. The first shot reveals a townsperson in the street calling to someone above him an invitation to witness an event that will take place shortly before midnight. Tracking shots then follow various groups from the town as they make their way to the shore and put out to sea in boats of differing sizes. We may suspect that the townspeople are setting out to see a ship, since we overhear a group of boys exclaim to each other, "It's thirty stories high and has sixteen smokestacks. . . . Think what a pirate could do with a ship like that!"[12] But this information makes the event more mysterious, rather than less, and as if to underline the sense of mystery for us, Fellini has Giudizio, the town fool, look back over his shoulder directly into the camera and ask, "Where are all these people going?"

One of Fellini's aims in the sequence is to poke fun at some of his type characters from the town. Accordingly, he gives us a brisk series of moments when certain of his characters respond to the situation according to type. Gradisca, the town beauty whose function is to delight an audience of males, uses the occasion to wear a delightful sailor suit and walk bouncily across the beach to a boat that an admirer has waiting. The mayor begins an impromptu speech: "This is certainly a very important day for our country. . . ." A science teacher with his telescope on the hotel verandah attempts to show off his scientific apparatus to the school principal and to convince him they will see the mysterious ship, "bigger than life," from the verandah. Best of all, perhaps, is the portrait of the town's self-proclaimed macho male, Lallo. He is hauled up over the side of one of the boats. "The water is freezing. My nuts have shriveled to the size of two dried beans," he announces. When asked whether he swam out, he replies proudly, "Sure, I did the Australian crawl." But his heroic feat is undercut by the rings of flab that hang over his bikini trunks and his sprawl of exhaustion on the deck.

At this point, the tone and the narrative strategy of the sequence shift. The boats ride in place, waiting. We see the sun setting and darkness coming on. Instead of the tracking shots of the earlier part, we now get still compositions from a stationary camera. The *Amarcord* theme, played earlier by a full orchestra, is taken up now by single instruments, a mandolin and an accordion, and done at a slower tempo. And at this point, Fellini gives us more extended scenes about two of his characters: Aurelio, the bricklayer whose family we follow throughout the movie, and Gradisca, the town beauty. The portraits are still satiric, to some extent, for both Aurelio and Gradisca are hopelessly naive and sentimental, but the portraits are not *just* satiric. The portrait of Aurelio reveals a certain capacity for wonder in the man and a gentleness, and the portrait of Gradisca, a sadness at the passing of young womanhood. The scenes balance each other. Aurelio, sitting on the left side of the frame in medium close-up, speaks to his family, and Gradisca, on the right, also in medium close-up, talks with her sisters and her admirer known as "Ronald Colman," who owns the movie house. In both scenes, there is a gentle, slightly artificial rocking motion to the boats, as if the two characters are being lulled into a comfortable, drowsy state in which an admission might slip out unguarded.

Aurelio looks up at the stars above him and murmurs, "Look how many there are. Millions and millions and millions of stars. Jesus Christ, I wonder how the whole lot stays up there in place!" His sense of wonderment is real enough, but the only terms he has at his disposal, his only frame of reference, are the terms of the construction business. "It's pretty simple for us," he continues. "If we have to build a house, so many bricks, so much lime. . . . But up there, Jesus Christ, where do you put the foundations? They aren't just confetti, you know!" Certainly, we are invited to find Aurelio naive and his language amusing, but we can also recognize the genuineness of his wonder and appreciate his difficulty in finding words for it. We may smile, but we probably do not laugh. In any case, the scene in *Amarcord* shows us a gentler, more reflective side to Aurelio than we have been accustomed to seeing earlier in the film, when he has been most often the irate father of bad little boys. Here, to conclude his scene, he offers his coat to his wife to protect her from the evening's chill.

Gradisca's scene may be less innocent and more staged, for she leans back at precisely the right moment to permit her audience to sense her languidness and brings a catch to her voice in time to prepare them for the tears that will follow, but here, too, there is a certain genuineness. Apparently her thoughts about the glamorous ship and the possibilities for a romantic encounter on board have prompted her to consider her own situation. She tells "Ronald Colman" that she is thirty years old. For a town beauty this can be, of course, a dangerous transition point. In her thirties, she will no longer be a *signorina,* a young woman. Earlier in the film, we have seen her in a movie house watching her idol, Gary Cooper. Now she seems to have scaled down her romantic aspirations to the level of a "good husband," but even here she has fears: "I want a family, children, a husband to chat with in the evening after supper and maybe to make love with now and then. . . . I am so full of affection. But who can I lavish it on?" Beneath the sentimental clichés of home, hearth, and an overflowing heart, we can detect the presence of a hard principle of reality: After thirty, Gradisca's chances for a good match, a wedding to capture the imagination of the town, will diminish. This she senses, and the scene is a poignant one. Later, when the ocean liner passes, Gradisca wipes her eyes and tries to smile and blow kisses to it, but she is not entirely successful in joining the elation of the other people around her.

Up to this point, we have considered the sequence as a series of individual character portraits. A series of shots running through the sequence suggests, however, that it is also about shared experience. These shots include tracking shots of the townspeople walking to the shore, long shots of all the boats leaving the harbor, and a long shot of the boats riding in place, waiting, as the sun begins to set. All of these shots prepare us for the final event of the sequence: the coming of the *Rex* (its name being called out here for the first time) and the reaction of the group to its sudden appearance. We see the ship over the shoulders of Aurelio's family and other townspeople, and then we scan the reactions of the townspeople in two tracking shots. All are waving excitedly and even joyously at the ship that looms over them and then passes by. What is significant here is that the town is acting almost as one. They are, in effect, experiencing a moment of community through shared experience.

In interview Fellini has criticized the people of the town in *Amarcord* for their childlike credulity and sense of naive wonder that make them vulnerable to the Fascists and the spectacles staged by that group.[13] Such vulnerability we witness in an earlier sequence that depicts a Fascist rally. Some of our negative reaction to the earlier spectacle must almost certainly carry over to this sequence, for the *Rex* is a product of Fascist-controlled industry and is, to some extent, a symbol of the kind of mechanized power and glamorous elitism that Fascism aspires to. But to read the last moment of the sequence solely as an exposé of the vulnerability of the townspeople would be falsely reductive. Again we should acknowledge that the treatment is not *just* satiric. If the townspeople are credulous and naive, they also have the capacity to respond spontaneously and joyfully to a glittering, mysterious object that delights them. That they share this capacity gives them, in turn, a moment of sheer exhilaration beyond the initial delight. The sequence as a whole, then, moves toward a final celebration of shared experience.

Another aspect of the sequence must be mentioned: the obvious artificiality of the mise-en-scène in the later sections. The gentle rocking of the boats of Aurelio and Gradisca, mentioned earlier, is obviously artificial in that the two boats sway only from side to side, not up and down, and in that the other boats sit completely motionless in the background while the two boats in the foreground rock. The *Rex* itself is clearly a stylized, painted model, lit from behind, with spray for the bow and smoke from the stacks added in too great a profusion. And the sea on which the boats of the townspeople float, we notice in the final shot of the sequence, consists of wet plastic sheets blown up into billows by wind machines below. As the night draws on, the sequence becomes more obviously illusionist. The result is that the last part of the sequence, particularly the arrival of the *Rex,* stands out, or is defamiliarized, from the earlier part. Critics have claimed variously that the shift to obvious artificiality is a way of creating a heightened magical world like that of musical comedy, a way of undermining Fascist spectacle as merely fake illusion, and a way of calling attention to the medium in which the film is made as a part of a self-reflexive stance in the postmodernist manner.[14] But, for our purpose here, we need simply notice that the shift in mode makes the final section stand out from the rest as worthy of more consideration by viewers. From a formal point of view, the sequence is organized by the question of what the townspeople are setting out to look at. This question is resolved at the end of the sequence when the *Rex* appears. The sequence, then, might be taken as a discourse of resolution. Throughout the sequence, however, we receive an extended series of brief, satirical portraits, a balanced pair of scenes that allows us to explore the mixture of sentimentality and genuine feeling in two of the characters in more detail, and a final rendering of the shared experience of the townspeople. The movement, here, is toward more and deeper revelations about the townspeople. This movement, it seems to me, takes over the organization of the sequence and makes it finally a discourse of revelation. And because of its emphasis on such a variety of different revelations, each with an independent claim on our attention, we are clearly involved with open form. The series of portraits that comprise the middle of the sequence could go on longer or could be reduced. Yet we must admit also that the sequence does have a sense of closure to it in the shots of the *Rex* and the shared reaction of the townspeople. We end our discourse of resolution with a view of the *Rex* and our discourse of revelation with a final generalization about the townspeople as a group.

Nights of Cabiria

What we have seen in microcosm with the *Rex* sequence, we can see in macrocosm with Fellini's films taken as narrative wholes. Some of the organizing principles of the closed form will be present, but the deeper principles, the more important ones, will be those of the open form. This will become increasingly true as Fellini's career progresses. To illustrate this notion, we can examine the structure of an early Fellini film using a central character as the unifying factor to hold together the series of episodes and then discuss briefly a later film with a similar structure but with a different emphasis. Both films are discourses of revelation, that is, they set out to reveal the central character to us, but they cleave to that goal in unequal measure.

Nights of Cabiria (1957) is our first example. The central character is Cabiria, a small, gamine-like prostitute. Fellini seeks to demonstrate, among other things, her wondrously resilient spirit. The film consists of five major parts, each a separate adventure of Cabiria. The major sequences may be described briefly as follows:

1. *The Giorgio section* (twelve minutes). In a field outside Rome, Cabiria and Giorgio embrace by the Tiber. Suddenly Giorgio grabs Cabiria's bag and shoves her into the river. Cabiria is rescued by a group of boys and goes back to her cinder block home, hoping to find Giorgio there. When she discovers the house empty, she burns Giorgio's belongings and hurls a rock at the streetlight.

2. *A night with a famous movie star* (twenty-six minutes). While walking the streets near the fashionable Via Veneto, Cabiria is picked up by a famous movie actor, Alberto, who has had a fight with his glamorous blond girlfriend, Jessy. He takes Cabiria to a nightclub where she basks in her situation. Then they return to Alberto's villa. He signs a photograph, certifying

their relationship, and they begin to dine. The sudden arrival of Jessy, however, forces Cabiria to spend the night concealed in the bathroom.

3. *The pilgrimage to the shrine* (thirteen minutes). Cabiria attends a church festival. Included in the crowd is the crippled uncle of one of the pimps in Cabiria's group. At first, Cabiria scoffs at her friend Wanda's seriousness about the religious ceremony, but soon Cabiria enters into the religious feeling, too, and prays to the portrait of the Madonna, "Help me change my life." The uncle then tries to walk without his crutches and crumples ignominiously to the floor. Later, outside at a picnic, Cabiria sulks and then announces, "We haven't changed."

4. *The vaudeville performance* (eleven minutes). Cabiria enters a theater in which a magician is performing. He calls for volunteers, and Cabiria somewhat unwillingly goes up on the stage. The magician hypnotizes her and introduces her to an imaginary suitor named Oscar. In her trance, Cabiria picks flowers and waltzes with the imaginary man. Then she asks, "Do you honestly love me?" Seeing that the performance is going too far, the magician snaps Cabiria out of her spell.

5. *The Oscar section* (thirty-five minutes). After the vaudeville performance, Cabiria meets a polite young man at the stage door. He takes her to a cafe table, tells her that his name is Oscar, and begs to see her in the future. They meet several times, and eventually Oscar proposes. Later, Cabiria announces to Wanda that she will marry him and sell her house so that they may buy a shop in the country. We see Cabiria packing, giving up her house to the new owners, and bidding Wanda good-bye. At supper at a restaurant overlooking a lake outside Rome, Cabiria shows Oscar her "dowry" from the sale of her house. He invites her to see the sunset from a vantage point by the lake, and there he robs her.

As brief as this summary is, it is enough to demonstrate the narrative organization of *The Nights of Cabiria*. The film might be described as five short stories, and we might diagram the movie as in figure 1.1.[15]

In a classical, closed narrative, the five segments would be linked to each other by a chain of cause and effect that grows out of an initial mystery to be solved or a question to be answered. That is not the case here in *Nights of Cabiria*. Only in the most general way could we argue that the loss of Giorgio in the first episode creates a void in Cabiria's life that she tries to fill in a variety of ways in the rest of the movie. In fact, each segment seems to give us a kind of fresh start. What holds the episodes together, essentially, is the notion of parallelism. Each segment contains some moment of happiness or self-fulfillment for Cabiria that she attains briefly only to have it quickly slip away. In each episode after the first, she approaches the moment with a good deal of skepticism before giving in eventually to its lure. Cabiria is thus presented to us as skeptical and gullible, as a feisty battler and a woebegone loser. Fellini, though, chooses to emphasize Cabiria's ability to bounce back from the disappointment of each sequence with fresh vitality in the next. The point of her resiliency will be underscored by the movie's ending.

It is time now to admit the incompleteness of our initial description. We need to add the movie's four-minute coda. It is one of Fellini's best endings. In this scene, Cabiria walks along the road away from the lake. She is overtaken by a group of festive young people who circle her and cheer her up. Cabiria looks into the camera and smiles softly. Thus Fellini ends with the upward turning of a new cycle, just as he conversely began the film with the downward turn of the first cycle.

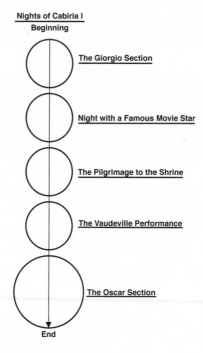

Fig. 1.1. The five segments of *Nights of Cabiria*

The film is further held together by a series of four short scenes wherein Cabiria plies her trade of prostitution on the Passeggiata Archeologica outside Rome. These scenes serve various functions. The first two are resting places between major episodes, and the other two provide punctuation for the long section 5. All are scenes in which Cabiria reflects on preceding events, and several of them give indications of what is to come. All serve to underline some character attribute of Cabiria: high-spiritedness, combativeness, curiosity, vulnerability, or wistfulness. Accordingly, we must add to our description the following:

Cabiria at Her Station

A (four minutes). Cabiria arrives in the rear of a motorcycle-truck. She inspects a new car bought by another prostitute and her pimp. Cabiria dances a mambo to a tune on a radio. She then fights an Amazon prostitute in a leopard-spotted dress, who taunts Cabiria about the loss of Giorgio.

B (four minutes). Walking in the rain, Cabiria is teased by the other prostitutes about her story of a night with the movie star. The crippled uncle of one of the pimps arrives and discusses the festival at the shrine of the Madonna that he will attend.

C (two minutes). Cabiria passes out chocolates from Oscar to the prostitutes and pimps and tells them about a gladiator movie Oscar took her to. Wanda questions the motives of the man. Cabiria responds that she does not care what they are, as long as Oscar is the one who pays.

D (one minute). Cabiria stands in the rain beneath her umbrella. She smokes a cigarette and appears lost in thought.

And we can now expand our diagram to a much more complete version (fig. 1.2).

Perhaps the most important function of the four short scenes is to provide a continuity to the work through repetition. The similarity of the four scenes is assured by the similarity of place and the similarity of Cabiria's "uniform," which she wears in all of the scenes (a ratty fur jacket, a tight black skirt, a cinch belt, bobby socks, and saddle shoes, with a collapsible umbrella as accessory). The four scenes tend to reassure viewers that they are following an orderly work, one that is not out of control. Yet, as much as we have stressed ordering devices, the fact remains that without a tight chain of cause and effect growing out of an initial mystery to be solved or a question to be answered, the narrative is a loose structure. The beginning and end cannot be changed. They bracket the work in a symmetrical way. But the middle could be expanded endlessly, or it could be contracted. We could, for example, remove episode 2, and the narrative would still make perfectly good sense. By the same token, we might add several more episodes. Here, we need only be bound by the rule of making the episodes parallel to the others in terms of moving Cabiria toward a moment of happiness or self-fulfillment and then snatching the moment away. In theory, this could be done endlessly. In practice, of course, an audience will tolerate only so much repetition before it demands a break in the pattern. Still deeper lies another concern. If the movie were to be expanded and if the characterization of the central character were not to be made more com-

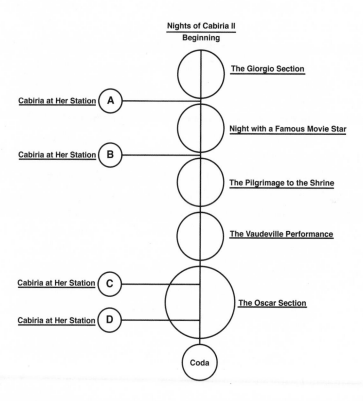

Fig. 1.2. The five segments, four short scenes, and coda of *Nights of Cabiria*

plex, one of two results would follow. Either the film would become tedious in its repetitiousness or the attention of the audience would begin to shift from the central character to the worlds of the separate episodes or to the other characters in these episodes. There is, in other words, a law of parsimony at work in loose, open forms united by a central character. The viewers will watch until they have learned enough about the character, and then the filmmaker must stop, which is what Fellini does in early films like *Nights of Cabiria,* or he must develop other aspects systematically throughout the work to absorb the viewers' residual attention.

The later film *Fellini's Casanova* (1976) falls into the second category. This movie will be discussed in more detail in chapter 7, which deals with Fellini's adaptations of works written by others. Now we should notice, however, that the film traces Casanova's career as he leads us through the various courts of eighteenth-century Europe—Venice, Paris, Parma, London, Rome, Dresden, Württemberg, and Dux in Bohemia. Like several other Fellini heroes, Casanova will try to define himself through his love relationships with women. However, because there is a certain emptiness in Casanova and because his love affairs never quite satisfy his expectations, there is only so much he can learn about himself. The movie's focus gradually begins to shift to the worlds Casanova travels though. These worlds are, as we shall see in chapter 7, interesting vestiges of old feudal societies in their last stages of overripeness. The movie thus becomes a double film.[16] Our attention is claimed both by the central character and by the various societies he visits. In some cases, Casanova will seem to us the most important aspect of the movie to attend to, but in other cases, Fellini's depictions of the societies will dominate our attention. This is particularly true for the sections in Paris, London, Dresden, and Württemberg. Such a double movie seems a logical outgrowth of the structure of a film like *Nights of Cabiria.* But this is not to say the development will necessarily be for the better. At some point, the open movie may become too loose in form, and viewers may no longer have the all-important sense of a controlling principle at work. And worse, the two strands, as we have in *Fellini's Casanova,* may compete with one another and, to some extent, negate each other. The open form, then, is not without its difficulties, and *Fellini's Casanova,* despite the beauties of many of its episodes, might be a film that has crossed an invisible line.

Closure

Because Fellini's films follow an open, episodic form, we might assume that he would have trouble creating appropriate endings for his movies. After all, he does not have at his disposal the conventional possibilities of a closed plot in which a question is posed at the beginning and resolved at the end. Somewhat surprisingly, however, Fellini's final scenes tend to be among his most memorable and to give the sense of completeness we expect from a narrative. It may be that without the conventional ending to fall back on, Fellini has particularly felt the need to extend himself with his last scenes and make them haunting.

Certainly this is the case with both of the movies just discussed, *Nights of Cabiria* and *Fellini's Casanova*. In *Nights of Cabiria,* the ending doubles back on the beginning and shows us Cabiria again coming out of the experience of being robbed and abandoned by a lover. Since the final act of robbery and abandonment seems the more severe (we have seen more of the love affair; the money lost is ten times as much; and Cabiria has lost her home), we can measure accurately the high cost of Cabiria's final smile and consider whether she has gained a quieter maturity at the end.

With *Fellini's Casanova,* the ending is perhaps less open. As an old man, Casanova dreams of Venice and himself in his young manhood. He walks on the frozen canals. The head of the goddess Rèitia appears beneath the ice. Many of Casanova's former lovers come to him and run off. Then a mechanical doll appears. She takes his hand and they dance. The scene is a summary revelation of character. We see, and Casanova sees, a final image of himself as mechanical lover. It is hard, nearly impossible, for us to reject a harsh reading of this final image, for the mechanical doll sums up various motifs of mechanicalness developed throughout the movie. However, we may also want to admit that there is a certain cold gracefulness to Casanova's dance that is not without appeal and maybe even a certain pathos in the various separations within the scene. The summary image, the final moment of character revelation, is thus not without its own trace of ambiguity.

Before we go any farther with this consideration of Fellini's endings, it will be useful to review some of the things movie endings can do. The list below, while certainly not definitive, is intended to call attention to a rather wide range of possibilities.

1. *Closure of resolution.* The ending solves mysteries or plot questions begun early in the work and delved into in the middle.
2. *Closure of revelation.* The ending shows the final state of a character or a character relationship, or it offers a summary overview of either.
3. *Poetic closure.* The ending creates a final mood, as when the camera passes over a landscape that has been significant in the work.
4. *Symbolic closure.* The ending offers a final image representative or symbolic of a final state of affairs.
5. *Affective closure.* The ending relaxes or "lets down" the audience after a dramatic or suspenseful climax.
6. *Closure of peripeteia.* An ironic or frightening twist occurs, especially after an apparently happy solution. A final shock.
7. *Theatrical closure.* The actors pass in review for a final bow.

Of this list of seven possibilities, only the first seems outside the range that Fellini draws on, and even this one can be found in some of his early comedies.[17] Of course, we should expect categories to overlap. There is nothing to stop, say, a poetic ending or a symbolic one from relaxing or "letting down" an audience, too, and nothing to stop an ending of character revelation from involving a theatrical finale with many of the characters returning on screen. In fact, so charged and so dense are most Fellini endings that the rule seems to be that he will draw on two or three of the possibilities at the same time.

A justly celebrated ending is the conclusion to *I Vitelloni* (1953). In effect, there are two endings. The first one is a fairly conventional closure of revelation showing the final state of the marriage of characters Fausto and Sandra. Their relationship and especially Fausto's infidelity have been major threads of interest holding the episodes of the film together. We look to the ending to provide us with a last statement on the relationship, and we get it. Fausto discovers Sandra in the home of his father, where she has gone presumably to complain of Fausto's infidelity. Fausto has already suffered a good deal of anxiety over Sandra's whereabouts. Now the father takes off his belt and spanks his son, causing him physical pain as well. The act is a perfect example of *contrappasso:* the punishment fits the crime. Fausto has acted like a child, and he is punished like one. Furthermore, we must acknowledge that Sandra now sees her husband more clearly and is prepared to act on her new knowledge. "If you ever get me mad another time," she tells him, "I'll do just like your father. . . . Even worse! I'll beat the hell out of you!"[18] She will play the parent to his role of child.

The second ending is more interesting. It involves the departure of the protagonist Moraldo to seek his fortune in the big city. If the first ending closes the narrative, the second opens it again and insists on a quality of ongoingness in the work.[19] Early in the morning, at the train station, a young boy who looks something like Moraldo, asks him why he is leaving, and Moraldo responds, "I don't know. I must." The leave-taking, however, is scarcely heroic. As the train pulls away, Moraldo looks back, thinks of his friends, and then falls slowly back from the window into his seat. To show us more precisely Moraldo's thoughts as he looks out the window, Fellini intercuts to moving shots of the *vitelloni* sleeping, with the noise of the clicking train wheels remaining on the sound track. Slowly, the camera dollies back from Moraldo's friends Leopoldo, Riccardo, and Alberto, each in his separate bed, and then it moves in on Fausto, Sandra, and their baby— as if to give Moraldo a better look—and then veers away. This brief montage, of course, constitutes a kind of theatrical finale, recalling the major players to the screen for us, but it also emphasizes the friendships Moraldo is giving up. A final symbolic image underscores the point. After Moraldo has sunk into his seat away from the window, we continue to look back at the town. We see the boy who looks like Moraldo playfully try to walk balanced on one of the rails as he returns to the station house. In this scene, the boy seems a youthful alter ego for Moraldo. The image is apparently intended for us and not Moraldo, who has given up his angle of vision. We see, in effect, a symbolic farewell to Moraldo's youth. We cannot doubt that Moraldo must leave town if he is to reach full adulthood. In the course of the movie, we have encountered no real opportunity for him in the small town. But the ending, emphasizing as it does the things left behind, is finally a mood piece or what I have called poetic closure. With music that extends the mournful but inviting call of the train's whistle, the ending is a bittersweet leave-taking. The second ending of *I Vitelloni,* then, involves four kinds of closure at work at the same time: revelatory, theatrical, symbolic, and poetic.

A simpler but no less striking example of closure is the ending of *Fellini's Roma* (1972). The problem of closure is particularly acute in this movie.

Fellini has defined the film as a subjective documentary in which the eternal city is seen from three points of view: the viewpoint of those in a provincial village; the viewpoint of a young man who arrives in Rome from the provinces; and the more mature viewpoint of the film director.[20] Essentially, these are the three points of view Fellini has held at the various stages of his life. He is, however, unwilling to privilege any one of the three at the end. His ending must be something other. His solution is to give a final poetic evocation of the city's mysteriousness, its inexhaustibleness. His means is to picture a helmeted motorcycle gang speeding through the city late at night. Perhaps Fellini thinks of the city at night as being taken over by spirits or demons, and perhaps these masked cyclists are embodiments of such spirits. What makes the ending haunting, though, is the contrast between the cyclists' modernity (the roar of their engines, the flaring effect of their headlights, and the speed at which they move) and the ancient grandeur of the city they move through (they pass in rapid succession the Castel Sant'Angelo, the baroque facade of Sant'Andrea della Valle, the Bernini fountains in the Piazza Navona, the statue of Marcus Aurelius on horseback on the Campidoglio, the Roman Forum, and, finally, the Coliseum glowing with lights). The monuments we see are, of course, familiar postcard representations, but discovered late at night, haunted by the demonic cyclists, they become defamiliarized. The effect allows Fellini to end his movie with a view of Rome that suggests that although he has told us many things about the city, it remains an inexhaustible mystery.

The Style of Excess

The most important aspect of Fellini's visual style is the sense viewers have frequently that they are receiving images of life that are highly charged with movements, contrasts, textures, colors, and, above all, surprises. The term most often associated with Fellini's style has been *baroque*.[21] The term is useful up to a point, but because it refers most often to certain specific uses of sinuously curving lines in painting and sculpture that play only a small part in Fellini's repertoire, I prefer the more general term "style of excess" that suggests a wider range of stylistic possibilities. If, as I argued earlier, Fellini wishes to defamiliarize the world and make it new, startling, and mysterious again, the visual strategy he has followed is that of giving viewers more than they are accustomed to receive in a movie. The strategy is most obvious in his later color films in which costumes and artificial sets have become extravagant, but it is no less at work in subtler fashion in his earlier black-and-white films.

Layered Compositions

Fellini often likes to compose his images in deep space. To do this, he will arrange figures or elements in the foreground and another set in the far distance with appropriate perspective cues to let us know that the composition exists on two planes. He will, in effect, layer his composition. To be sure, any movie maker who wants to give his film a "realistic," three-dimensional feel will do this. The usual strategy of such films, however, is that once the location has been established, the audience will continue to assume it is there ("the et cetera principle" of visual perception), and the filmmaker can turn his or her attention and the audience's attention to the principle action without the interference of other elements. But in the Fellini film, the interference of other elements is not only tolerated, it is actively sought. Fellini will hold the deep-focus, layered shot for a long duration or else return to it several times in an established rhythm.

A simple but interesting layered composition occurs toward the beginning of *Nights of Cabiria,* when Cabiria returns to her cinder block home and complains to Wanda about Giorgio's abandonment of her. Three times we detect in the background a free-form construct of pipes near Cabiria's house. The composition cannot simply be relegated to the Neorealist category of character shown in his or her environment. The free-form construct is too whimsical for that. It is a scene stealer, or more precisely, it vies with Cabiria in the foreground for our attention. Finally in a fourth shot, with Cabiria not present, we see children climbing on the form and understand that it is a homemade set of monkey bars for them. Up to that point, however, the construct of pipes has been a mysterious object that created a certain tension in competing for our attention. Similarly, later in the movie, when Cabiria is hypnotized at center stage of a variety hall, she must vie for visual dominance with a considerable amount of backstage activity (fig 1.3). Because the camera is set at oblique angles, we can see into the wings. On the left, we see a clown with a derby, overalls, and sneakers converse with a woman in a harem costume. One or both appear in the background ten times. The clown, in particular, stands out when he fans himself with his derby. Deeper on the left is a female singer in an evening gown who appears six times and draws attention by adjusting her long gloves and her gown. To the right is a man in tails and a female dancer in tights. One or both of them can be seen in the background of eight shots. He smokes a cigarette, and she straightens the seams of her stockings and adjusts her plumes. All this while Cabiria is making her most intimate revelations in the foreground.

Of course, Fellini can use the layered composition as a means to joke about the action that is taking place on one of the shot's planes. In *8 ½*, a pan following Guido's movement to the confessional in the deeper plane also moves more slowly (because the camera is nearer) from the feet to the head of the chalky skeleton of a martyr on display in the church, commenting wittily on the antilife stance of the institution Guido must battle. The principle, however, remains the same as in the other examples. Fellini insists we deal with a conflict between planes that vie for our attention.

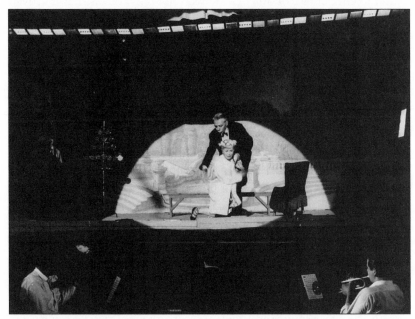

Fig. 1.3. Cabiria performing on a vaudeville stage in *Nights of Cabiria*. A publicity still illustrates the principle of layering the composition, with Cabiria in the middle ground on the stage, the orchestra in the foreground, and the clown in the wings in the left far distance. BFI.

A final example, this one from *Amarcord,* may suffice to illustrate the principle. In the *Rex* sequence, Fellini uses a tracking shot to follow some of the townspeople to the beach. The shot lasts only fifteen seconds, but much is injected into it. As the shot begins, the camera tracks from right to left, showing a line of schoolchildren on the far side of a street. The camera moves at approximately the same speed as the schoolchildren. Into the frame from the right, on the near side of the street, come a horse and buggy, a woman on a bicycle, and another woman with a large straw hat. They, in effect, overtake the camera. As they pass out of the frame on the left, still traveling faster than the camera, the camera itself overtakes a portly gentleman in a two-piece bathing suit. With his overblown form, he is the comic surprise of the shot. Unconcerned with the movement around him, he strolls at his own pace, slower than the schoolchildren and slower than the camera, down the middle of the street. A car whizzes between him and the camera for a moment. And finally, the camera slows and stops, allowing the bather to remain in the frame and indeed to approach its left edge. Technically difficult, the shot owes its effectiveness to the different speeds of the figures on their different planes in relation to the speed of the camera on its plane. The camera makes discoveries by overtaking and by being overtaken. We can scarcely anticipate which edge of the frame or which depth plane to watch.

Grotesque Character, The Moving Camera, Pairing, and Expressionistic Devices

Grotesque is a term used in art to describe a certain style of distortion. Wolfgang Kayser, in his landmark study *The Grotesque in Art and Literature,* traces the style back to ornamental art in the Roman Empire around the time of Christ in frescoes and on pillars. The style either intermingles animal, vegetable, mechanical, and human qualities to form unnatural, monstrous beings (say, a man with the head of a fish) or uses caricature, which involves selective exaggeration of normal proportions (say, a man whose nose is too long and whose visual presentation is dominated by this distortion). The religious art of Hieronymous Bosch (1450–1516) seems to Kayser to embody the first kind of grotesque, which Kayser calls demonic, and the more satirical art of Pieter Brueghel, the elder (1529–69), to represent the second kind, which Kayser labels comic (fig. 1.4).[22] Both kinds, however, tend to amass many figures and to defy laws of gravity or realistic perspective in the composition of the figures. Grotesque art, Kayser argues, is subversive. Both strands work against a mainstream art that demonstrates the world as orderly, stable, and rational.

Given the choice of Kayser's two strands of the grotesque, we would obviously place Fellini's work in the second category, the comic grotesque tradition that depends on caricature, and indeed, this is precisely what William J. Free has done in a brilliant essay on Fellini's *The Clowns*.[23] We should add at this point that Fellini is a caricaturist of considerable skill. As a boy, he earned money by drawing caricatures of the tourists on the beaches of Rimini, and as a young man, he worked as a cartoonist for the satirical magazines *420* and *Marc' Aurelio*. In planning his movies, he frequently drew caricatures of his actors to help him and his staff visualize how the actors will appear on screen. And in some instances, he drew versions of his character and asked the actors to conform to the drawing. (Compare the caricature of Casanova [fig. 1.5] with the photograph of Donald Sutherland [fig. 1.6]). But the division of grotesque art into two types may be at base a false distinction. Surely there are comic juxtapositions in the work of Bosch,

Fig. 1.4. Pieter Brueghel's *Mad Meg* (1563), which demonstrates a tradition of grotesques in the visual arts. Museum Mayer van den Bergh, Antwerpen © collectiebeleid.

and the odd, bent caricatures of Brueghel can have a disturbing, if not demonic, quality. In Fellini's work, the grotesques are usually comic, but sometimes in their freakishness they are genuinely disturbing. The strange, frightened child with the oversized head, Oswaldo, in *La Strada* and the
hunchback DuBois, who mimes the part of a devouring praying mantis in
Fellini's Casanova, are two examples of grotesque figures who are disturbing. The important point to make about Fellini's use of grotesque figures,
however—indeed, Kayser's most important point about grotesques in general—is that his figures defy the notion of a rational, harmonious norm and
suggest that life is more rich, more various, and even more mysterious than
the endorsement of norms implies.

Giants, dwarfs, hunchbacks, large fleshy women, transvestites, characters with large noses or hollow socket eyes, these are Fellini's "freaks." They
can appear at any time in a film, keeping viewers off balance. But quite frequently Fellini uses galleries of one sort or another. The teeming quality of
the paintings of Bosch and Brueghel is also a part of his visual strategy. A gentle
version of a gallery of grotesques is the photographic portrait scene of the
schoolchildren in *Amarcord* (fig. 1.7). Here Fellini simply draws on the odd
proportions that adolescents caught in the throes of irregular growth spurts
are doomed to exhibit. There are those who have not lost their baby fat and
those who have; those who have shot up in height and those who have not.
Irregularity is the rule. But, in the main, the gallery of grotesques in Fellini
movies comes in sequential order as a protagonist passes among the grotesques or as the grotesques parade by the protagonist. Our view often coincides with that of the protagonist and we are often uncomfortably close.
This is certainly true when Guido and the camera move among the elderly, overdressed guests at the spa in *8 ½,* or in *Fellini Satyricon* (1969) when
Encolpius, the hero, and his boy lover Giton walk along a street in the prostitution area of Rome's Suburra, with the camera tracking with them, and
catch glimpses of wizened procurers and prostitutes, sometimes beautiful
and sometimes overblown, trying to attract the attention of the young males.

A fairly representative Fellini gallery comes in a scene in *Fellini's Roma*
(1972), when the young protagonist arrives in Rome for the first time and
is shown through the pensione in which he has arranged to live.[24] He meets,
in rapid succession, a Chinese man cooking spaghetti who bows to the young
man, a little boy wearing glasses and sitting on the toilet, a tiny grandmother

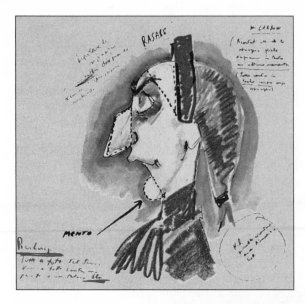

Fig. 1.5. Fellini's sketch of the profile of Casanova as a model for the look of Donald Sutherland in *Fellini's Casanova*.
Federico Fellini Copyright © 1982 Diogenes Verlag AG Zürich.

Fig. 1.6. Donald Sutherland as the eighteenth-century courtier Casanova, his profile modeled on Fellini's sketch. BFI.

Fig. 1.7. Schoolchildren arranged for a class picture, providing a "gallery of grotesques" with their differing sizes, shapes, and characteristics, in a publicity still from *Amarcord*. Courtesy of Photofest.

hunched in her rocking chair in the attic, a ham actor with tinted glasses and a very broad-rimmed hat, an overweight former beauty drying her long black hair, an old man with the bald head and jutting chin of Mussolini who recites the doctrine of Il Duce, and the enormous, block-figured mistress of the pensione who lies abed with inflamed ovaries and is eventually joined by her sunburned, grown-up son in an odd parody of an oedipal relationship.

Contrast is also important. Fellini likes to pair large characters with small ones for the jarring effect produced. The giantess in *Fellini's Casanova* is attended by two midgets, and the extremely tall Uncle Teo in *Amarcord*, by a midget nun. The short, underdog figures played by Giulietta Masina are contrasted with the hulking Zampano (Anthony Quinn) in *La Strada*, with large fellow prostitute Wanda (Franca Marzi) in *Nights of Cabiria*, and tall, voluptuous Suzy (Sandra Milo) in *Juliet of the Spirits*. Fellini's young Guido in *8 ½* and Titta in *Amarcord* are overwhelmed by the large, overpowering women, Saraghina and the tobacconist. And the entire movie *The Temptation of Dr. Antonio* (1962) turns on the size disparity of the giant poster figure played by Anita Ekberg and the small, frantic censor, Mazzuolo, played by Peppino De Filippo. There are, of course, issues of power, fear, and attraction involved in some of these pairings that we will come back to in later chapters. Now, though, we may recognize that the pairing of the very large with the very small is a visual means of calling attention to deviations from the norm at both ends of the scale.

Similarly, Fellini uses the old expressionist devices of projected shadows and extreme camera angles from the German silent cinema to increase or decrease the sizes of his characters, or to make them, in effect, grotesques. Guido, in his harem fantasy in *8 ½,* has his magnified silhouette projected against the wall as he cracks his whip in domination over his women; the tobacconist, in *Amarcord,* is magnified also in shadow form as she advances on young Titta, who sits beneath the shadow; and the female gladiators of *The City of Women* are made terrifying through large shadow representations. On the other hand, the Cardinal of *8 ½* has his frail body represented as a stick silhouette when his shadow is projected onto a sheet behind which he stands, and Casanova, toward the end of his film, has his figure foreshortened by his shadow behind him, cast by a light from above, as he stands in a privy complaining of his treatment by the servants of his patron. The uptilted camera makes Saraghina seem to loom over us at one moment when she dances in *8 ½,* and the camera placed near the feet of the recumbent black sorceress in *Fellini Satyricon* makes her appear elongated and distorted. The down-tilted and distant camera makes Antonio of *The Temptation of Dr. Antonio* appear foreshortened and puny. These distortions are, of course, old "tried and true" effects, and Fellini can scarcely be given credit as an innovator in using them. Yet we should not pass over them too lightly. The expressionist shadows and extreme camera angles give him useful means for the kind of distortion the grotesque requires.

Disjunctions and the Surreal Effect

A large measure of Fellini's style depends on surprise. Fellini enjoys startling viewers by putting together images that are in some way disjunctive. This principle appears in its most obvious manner in the small shocks with which he frequently begins sequences. After a fade-out, Fellini often begins his next sequence with an unknown or peculiar object or with the close-up of a face in shadows. As the camera pulls back to reveal the context of the puzzling object or as the concealed face is revealed by a change in the lighting, we become able to orient ourselves in the new situation, but not before we have received a little shock of uncertainty. A sequence in *I Vitelloni*, for example, begins with the shot of a child in a sultan's costume being walked by two adults as if he were a pet monkey. The camera then pulls back to reveal that the three are figures in a parade, and the narrator's voice tells us that we are at Carnival. In *8 ½*, a sequence begins with the shot of a puzzling silhouette against the background of a window. Suddenly a light is turned on, and we see that the form is Carla, Guido's mistress, with her head wrapped in a scarf. The two characters, Guido and Carla, are in Carla's hotel room and engaged in a love game. This kind of disjunctive editing runs throughout Fellini's work, whether his editor is Leo Catozzo or Ruggero Mastroianni, but its most concentrated use comes in the middle of Fellini's career with such films as *La Dolce Vita, 8 ½,* and *Juliet of the Spirits,* which are more open than previous films and perhaps show his desire to mark off more definitively the major episodes from each other.

Along the same lines, Fellini likes to inject surprise by having a character rise from beneath the frame to confront us suddenly. A striking example is the French actress with hornlike barrettes who rises up close to the camera in the harem fantasy of *8 ½* to declare Guido's treatment of a dancer unjust. Her appearance is particularly surprising in that there was no reason for her to have been beneath the relatively normal sight line of the camera (at eye level) prior to her appearance. Also striking is the slower rise of Juliet's silhouette in *Juliet of the Spirits* from beneath the frame as she takes her departure from viewing a film of her husband's infidelities. There is, of course, a logical reason for her to have been beneath the frame, since she was sitting to view the film. But to the extent we as viewers have become absorbed in the film-within-the-film as a reality unto itself, her intrusion will startle us. More whimsical than either of these two examples and perhaps more to be expected is the masked reveler in the Carnival sequence of *Fellini's Casanova* who pops up like a jack-in-the-box from below the frame to gesture at us mockingly throughout the opening sequence of the film. As with the disjunctive editing, Fellini's aim here is to surprise.

Similar in effect is the appearance of what I will call a "surreal object" or "surreal figure" in a scene where it does not logically seem to belong. This is an object like the cafe table with three glasses on a tile floor in the middle of the desert in Dali's *The Sun Table* (1936; fig. 1.8). The purpose of such an object is to break down our assurance that reality is rationally predictable. Such objects or figures in surreal art are virtually impossible to account for. In Fellini's films, such objects are simply difficult to account for or puzzling for a moment until we concoct a rational explanation for them after the fact, but at the moment of initial impact, they, like their counterparts in surrealistic painting, create a moment when the assumptions of the rational world seem suspended. Perhaps the best-known example of such a moment is the sudden appearance of the White Sheik on his trapeze in the woods to his admirer Wanda[25] (fig. 1.9). We have been led to expect actors in exotic costumes, but the Sheik's appearance on the trapeze is never explained. (He does not seem to be on the set where the photographing is being done.) Important to the impact of the shot is the contrast between the Sheik's costume and Wanda's utterly practical, tailored suit. Equally unexpected and arresting is the appearance of three musicians who march along a field playing their instruments and lead the delighted Gelsomina into town in *La Strada*. After the fact, we may explain to ourselves that they are musicians for the festival in town and have been hired to lead in festivalgoers from the country, yet this explanation does little to diminish the sense of strangeness we feel initially on seeing musicians playing to an empty field.

A sequence in *Fellini's Roma* seems designed to set up a series of surreal moments when an object or figure appears that seems inexplicable or momentarily startling in its context. The sequence is a depiction of the traffic jam as Fellini and his crew drive into Rome on a modern autostrada. It is hard to imagine a more mundane contemporary situation. But in the course of the scene there appear objects or figures that startle. One is a dappled, riderless horse in the midst of the traffic, calmly making his way along with the cars. Another is a man on the back of a truck who appears to be flying as he holds upright a mirror reflecting the sky. And perhaps almost magical is a lamp shop along the highway as it appears at night with all its various hanging chandeliers turned on.

The reverse of this use of the startling object in the realistic setting is the use of real characters, that is, real actors, in a setting that is obviously artificial. We have already noted that Fellini used this device toward the end of the *Rex* sequence of *Amarcord,* in which the townspeople ride their boats on a plastic sea and salute a ship painted on a backdrop. Suffice it to say that the effect is not limited to *Amarcord,* although it does seem an effect confined to Fellini's later, color films. The plastic sea, for example, in *Fellini's Casanova* takes up even more space in the frame than it does in *Amarcord,* and the setting aboard the *Gloria N.* in *And the Ship Sails On* features a

Fig. 1.8. Salvador Dali's *The Sun Table* (1936), which shows a cafe table with three glasses on a tile floor in the middle of a desert for a startling, disjunctive effect. © 2005 Salvador Dali, Gala–Salvador Dali Foundation/Artists Rights Society (ARS), New York. Museum Boijmans Van Beuningen, Rotterdam.

painted sun that draws comment from a traveler. Here, though, if the effect of the painted sun has a surreal quality, we need not go to painting for a source. The effect seems precisely the same as that in American musical comedies when Gene Kelly danced in a make-believe Paris or Fred Astaire on a make-believe ocean liner. The result in Fellini, though, is somewhat different from that in the American musicals in that the artificial sets are not just fanciful "softeners" but are in fact part of a more thoroughgoing program on Fellini's part to bring the shock of disjunction into his films.

Fig. 1.9. The White Sheik appearing to Wanda as a romantic figure on a trapeze swing in a publicity still from *White Sheik*. BFI.

Costumes, Overflowing Forms, Texture, and Color

Unusual costumes are of major importance to Fellini. In his historical films—*Fellini Satyricon* and *Fellini's Casanova*—they are required. But in addition, virtually all his films set in the twentieth century have scenes in which the characters are given the opportunity to dress up in extravagant ways. Such occasions include variety shows on the stage, circus performances, Carnival festivities, a fashion show, display rituals in houses of prostitution, strolls on public thoroughfares, and, of course, parties at which the guests put themselves on view for other guests—in short, in various Fellini spectacles. A primary function of the dressing up is to give us insight into the characters. What they choose to wear usually tells us something about who they are. Beyond this, however, the dressing up gives Fellini yet another way to make his films more visually and tactilely extravagant, to once again exceed normal expectations.

Fellini is fond of overflowing forms. In particular, he likes to use winged shapes. These appear in the headdresses of nuns like the one in *I Vitelloni* and those in the ecclesiastical fashion show in *Fellini's Roma*. The shape is picked up in hats of secular characters such as Juliet's sister Adele in *Juliet of the Spirits* and the two daughters of Dr. Moebius of Berne in *Fellini's Casanova*. Suzy, the seductive neighbor of Juliet in *Juliet of the Spirits*, even wears wings of tulle on her gown. But we need not confine ourselves to specific lines or shapes. The basic principle often at work in Fellini designs is that the characters, especially the women, will wear costumes that make them overflow the lines of their bodies. The women wear feather boas, large, oversized hats, enormous wigs, and ruffled dresses. Stage performers are plumed and feathered. And the males, when costumed as the White Sheik and Casanova are, wear capes.

The element of texture is also important to Fellini. Many of his scenes have a tactile quality. In painting, this quality is produced mainly through the rendering of light on surfaces—its opaqueness or luminosity. Fellini uses this possibility, too, but given the medium of films, he is also able to use the element of movement. He gives a sense of how much a fabric weighs and how flexible it is by showing us how it moves. Thus, as we watch the figures move, we know at once how heavy and stiff is the brocade gown of the mechanical doll in *Fellini's Casanova* and how light and flexible the dress of the lady in white in *8 ½*. But texture is not confined to costumes alone.

Often in the background of Fellini shots are fabrics that rustle in a breeze or lie limply and fabrics that absorb light or transmit it luminously. Most striking in this regard is a scene near the end of *La Strada* when Zampano questions a woman about Gelsomina. The woman is hanging her wash, and as she talks, it flutters and glistens around her. We can almost feel the warm, pleasant breeze, which contrasts with the sadness of the message she gives to Zampano about Gelsomina's death. A more artificial version of this effect occurs in the harem sequence of *8 ½* when an unseen person waves a gauze veil in front of the camera, perhaps recalling to Guido the breeze on the day he saw Saraghina at the beach with the veil over her shoulder or perhaps just adding a note of lightness to the scene.

Yet another weapon in Fellini's arsenal is his use of color in nonnaturalistic ways. He bathes scenes in certain lights for the psychological effects they can produce. Generally he follows the accepted notion that the cool colors (blue, green, and violet) produce moods of serenity and pleasantness, if given in a light hue, and the warm colors (red, yellow, and orange), if given in a dark hue, produce more intense moods. Pleasant memories and fantasies, such as early memories of Rome in *Fellini's Roma* or early memories of women in *The City of Women,* are shot in blue light. Suzy's party, mentioned above, is done predominantly in reds of various hues from scarlet to pink that are influenced by the somber juxtapositions of blacks. (Here I refer to the costumes of the women as well as to the silks and the set decorations.) Many of the interior shots in *Amarcord* are lit with soft, diffused yellow light, which gives them an unreal and perhaps nostalgic, golden look. There is, then, about many of Fellini's scenes a painterly quality, in which he uses color not just for representational purposes but for an effect in itself.

All of these practices are, of course, employed by other directors. Indeed, such is the case, as I have said earlier, for most of the stylistic practices discussed in this chapter. But what makes certain scenes clearly Fellini's or at least Felliniesque is the use of many of the elements simultaneously to create an impression that is strong to the point of excess. An example of a scene that uses in a pronounced way all the elements of costuming, overflowing forms, texture, and color (as well as the play of the large against the small) is the walk through the forest by Juliet and her family in *Juliet of the Spirits.*

In this scene, Fellini plays Juliet off against her two sisters and her mother, all of whom dominate Juliet in one way or another. Giulietta Masina in the role of Juliet is a short woman. The costume she wears makes her look even shorter, for her hat tends to diminish her to the level of its low brim. Her plain, white pajama suit makes her seem colorless and maybe even unfeminine in that her figure is completely hidden. By contrast, her two sisters, Adele, played by Luisa Della Noce, and Sylva, played by Sylva Koscina, and her mother, played by Caterina Boratto, tower over Juliet (fig. 1.10). Their size is increased by the hats they wear. Adele and the mother wear winged-shaped hats, and Sylva a large, ornate disk shape. In color and texture, also, they dominate Juliet. Adele wears a pink maternity dress that glows in the sun. Sylva has on a turquoise dress with several light, overlapping layers that flutter as she moves, and she carries a luminous, turquoise parasol that she opens, twirls, and closes. The mother wears a heliotrope cape, a string of pearls, and a large, airy, white veil. Each is more "feminine" than Juliet in a different way. Adele is more maternally fruitful, Sylva more playful and girlishly seductive, and the mother more elegant. When Fellini puts Juliet in the same frame with Sylva, Juliet is dominated by the height of her sister, the color of her dress and hat, and the busy textures of layers and flowers on her sister's costume; Juliet is almost crowded from the frame. We might even also go so far as to say that Juliet is dominated by the landscape. As the camera tracks the family group walking through the woods, we see luminous yellow leaves close to the lens and bright green foliage in the distance. (The color of the woods is artificially enhanced. At one point, we see quite clearly a stand erected to hold plastic vines or branches.) Against this background, Juliet's plain, stiff costume seems dull to the point of comic absurdity. In both color and texture, she is the least interesting object in the scene. Fellini has employed his stylistic visual devices very successfully to create an underdog figure for whom we must have sympathy. It is worth pointing out finally that his mannerisms here are not ends in themselves but effective means to the end of creating character. When Fellini is at his best, there is no separation between his style and his discourse.

As we have seen, the Fellini manner involves the open form of revelation and the visual style of excess. On the level of storytelling and character presentation, each of Fellini's movies may be relatively different. But at the deeper structural level of manner, his strategies in organizing discourse and presenting visual material are strikingly similar. The strategies, in turn, are directed at defamiliarizing the material presented and at exceeding boundaries. I would argue that Fellini has gravitated to this kind of manner out of belief that, at base, life is mysterious and ineffable. By definition, the mysterious and the ineffable cannot be described clearly. They can, however, be suggested. One very good way to suggest the mysterious and ineffable dimensions of life is to show an art form straining at its limits, fretting with them, as it were, to get something that cannot quite be contained. The filmmaker or artist may not show us the thing itself but may very well convince us of his or her effort to push the art form out toward it, and that effort in itself may be enough to persuade us that the thing is there, at least for as long as we are engaged with the work. In this way, by means of the Fellini manner, the films of Federico Fellini make the same assertion over and over.

Fig. 1.10. Juliet dominated visually by her mother and sister Sylva as they walk in the woods in a publicity still from *Juliet of the Spirits*. BFI.

2

FELLINI, JUNG, AND DREAMS

"I believe I am naturally religious," Fellini has commented, "since to me the world and life seem wrapped in mystery."[1] As we have seen, Fellini's art rests on the assumption that life is ineffable. He finds an almost mystical dimension that stirs in him something akin to religious response, and he attempts to insert a sense of his wonderment at the mystery of life into his movies. At the same time, however, for all Fellini's interest in the suprarational dimension of life, he is clearly a filmmaker in opposition to the institution of the church. In *La Dolce Vita* and *Nights of Cabiria*, Fellini depicts sham miracles that raise hopes in worshippers, only to disappoint those hopes. In *8 ½, Juliet of the Spirits,* and *Amarcord,* he presents scenes in which his protagonists encounter harsh admonitions of one sort or another from church figures against human sexuality; admonitions that prove finally to be life-denying. And, along the same lines, a religious procession in *Fellini's Roma* that is at first a kind of superficial fashion show, turns into a funeral procession or a dance of death at its conclusion.

Despite his antipathy for the church, its severity, and its inflexibility, Fellini has clung to his sense of religious mysticism. As his career progressed, he linked that sense with the creative force of the artist and with a source inside the individual. He puts it this way: "Even if I hadn't been fascinated as a child with that mystic feeling that penetrates existence and makes everything unknowable, I think the profession I practice would have led me naturally to religious sentiment. I create a dream, or rather with open eyes

I abandon myself to imagining something. . . . Who guides us through the creative adventure? How could it happen? Only faith in something, or someone, hidden within us, can inspire the mysterious work of creation—someone little known, a wise and subtle part of us, working within us."[2] On a more secular level, Fellini has also demonstrated an interest in the mysteriousness of life beyond the rational and the normative through his filmic and personal use of mediums, magicians, spiritualism, dreams, and visions.[3]

The major thinker who has given Fellini a belief system to draw on is the Swiss depth psychologist Carl Gustave Jung (1875–1961). Indeed it seems apparent that Jung's writings provided Fellini with intellectual support for attitudes Fellini had arrived at on his own and with an iconography that Fellini could put to work in his movies, particularly those with dreams in them or with dreamlike qualities. In short, Jung's writings seem to have taken the place that orthodox religious doctrine might have filled for someone less disaffected from the church.[4] The basis for Jung's appeal lay in the emphasis the psychologist placed on the mysteriousness of life and of the individual's inner self. For Jung these mysteries could be explored and, to some extent, described but could not be solved. In his autobiography, for example, Jung writes,

> Reason sets the boundaries far too narrowly for us, and would have us accept only the known—and that too with limitations—and live in a known framework, just as if we were sure how far life actually extends. As a matter of fact, day after day we live far beyond the bounds of our consciousness; without our knowledge, the life of the unconscious is also going on within us. The more critical reason dominates, the more impoverished life becomes; but the more of the unconscious and the more of myth we are capable of making conscious, the more of life we integrate.[5]

Jung, then, urges us to look beyond reason and consciousness into the mysteries of the unconscious. This is exactly the kind of urging Fellini wants to follow, for he, like Jung, finds in his unconscious self the basis of his creative impulses and of his fascination with life's limitlessness. In interview, Fellini has made this point emphatically by means of contrasting Jung to Freud:

> Freud wants to explain to us what we are; Jung accompanies us to the door of the unknowable and lets us see and understand by ourselves.

Jung's scientific humility in confronting the mystery of life seems more likable to me. His thoughts and ideas don't pretend to be doctrine, only suggest a new point of view, a different attitude which can enrich and evolve our personality. . . . Freud with his theories makes us think; Jung on the other hand allows us to imagine, to dream and to move forward into the dark labyrinth of our being. . . .

For Jung a symbol expresses an intuition better than any other expression of it. For Freud a symbol substitutes for something else which should be done away with and therefore is better forgotten than expressed. For Jung, then, a symbol is a way of expressing the inexpressible, albeit ambiguously.[6]

Fellini's statement seems to suggest that Jung's ideas gave him an intellectual credibility in his own eyes. After all, Jung was someone who saw life almost exactly as Fellini did and was someone of vast learning who could defend his vision of life with evidence from cases in his own psychoanalytical practice and with evidence from world literature and myths of diverse cultures.[7]

Fellini discovered Jung after the film director had already achieved a large measure of success. The impact was exhilarating. It came at a time of midlife when, according to the Jungian system, an individual should look inward to ensure further growth. Fellini has described his discovery of Jung this way: "The reading of several books by Jung, the discovery of his vision of life, took on for me the nature of a joyous revelation, an enthusiastic, unexpected, extraordinary confirmation of something that I myself seem to have foreseen to some small extent. I owe this providential, stimulating, fascinating discovery to a German psychotherapist named Bernhard."[8] The psychotherapist he refers to is Dr. Ernst Bernhard, a Jungian analyst living and working in Rome. The encounter took place in 1960, after the making of *La Dolce Vita* (1960) and prior to the making of *8 ½* (1963).[9] The circumstances of the first meeting have been worked up by Fellini into an anecdote that would have pleased Jung, who reveled in the notion of "synchronicity" or meaningful coincidence. Fellini has related to biographer Hollis Alpert that fellow director Vittorio De Seta told him about Bernhard and aroused Fellini's interest in meeting the man. The meeting itself, however, came by chance. Fellini explains:

One day I dialed a number that I thought belonged to a very beautiful lady. A man answered. "Who is speaking?" I asked him. "This is Bernhard," he answered. "Bernhard who? Who are you? I am trying to reach the number of a beautiful lady." "I'm sorry," he said, "but I'm an old man." I discovered he was the very Ernst Bernhard De Seta had told me about, and I told the doctor I wanted to meet him.[10]

Fellini insists that he did not "undergo analysis" with Bernhard but talked frequently with him about Jung's ideas, read several books by Jung suggested to him by Bernhard, and even gained some relief from "a depressed state of mind."[11]

Clearly Fellini found in Jung, through Dr. Bernhard's help, an intellectual mentor. Jung, like Fellini, was fascinated with the occult and magic and with the abilities of spiritual mediums. More important, Jung was fascinated with the interior world of the psyche and with the mysterious force within it that Fellini has called the "wise and subtle part of us" and that Jung calls the "self." Finally Jung, like Fellini, thought dreams were the surest way to the "wisdom" of this interior source. Because Jung's system gave Fellini a framework within which to work, the system is worth a brief exposition here.

Jung's Phenomenology of the Psyche and the Role of Archetypes

Perhaps the most pleasing aspects of Jung's system are that the system is a self-regulating one and that it urges us toward an inner growth. Although Jung treated deeply disturbed people for much of his career, he was an extremely positive theorist and felt that neurosis, or an imbalance of the psychic system, could in fact prove to be a useful warning to an individual. Different from Freud in that he did not view the sexual drive as the prime motivating factor of an individual's psyche, Jung insisted on a drive toward balance as the most important impulse of our psychic system. The drive is controlled by a center or a "complex" that, as we have noted, Jung called the "self."[12]

To understand Jung's concept of psychic balance, we need first to consider his notions of "functions" and "types." Jung argues that the conscious psyche has four main functions. These four psychic activities he called "thinking," "feeling," "sensation," and "intuition." Thinking and feeling, he felt, were rational functions: Thinking tells us what a thing is, and feeling tells us whether it is "pleasant, desirable, and beautiful, or . . . unpleasant, disgusting, ugly, and so on."[13] The other functions are irrational: sensation perceives the thing in all its details (but does not categorize it or judge it) and intuition foresees the "possibilities inherent" in the thing or situation.[14] In addition to these functions, Jung defines two kinds of attitude types, the introvert and the extrovert. "The introvert's attitude is an abstracting one," Jung explains.[15] This type turns experience inward. The extrovert, on the other hand, constantly affirms the importance of the external and defines himself or herself in terms of his or her relation to the external world. This distinction between introvert and extrovert is certainly one of Jung's best-known ideas. So deeply ingrained in our minds is it that we probably accept it uncritically as fact. For Jung, however, it was a hypothesis to work with. The distinction could be used as a means for furthering the notion of the functions. When we combine function with type, we come up with eight rather carefully defined personality types ranging, say, from the extroverted-feeling type to the introverted-intuitive type. At a given moment in life, an individual may have a predominant personality type with some associated secondary functional characteristics. Jung considered that a usual pattern for a person might be to live the first half of life as an extrovert, when finding one's place in the external world is of primary importance, and then to live the second half as an introvert, when the individual has more opportunity to look inward and consider the metaphysical question *Who am I?* However, there might also be other possibilities of type and function that the individual does not have available at a particular stage. If those possibilities are, in some sense, crucial to the individual, it will be the regulating function of the unconscious within the individual to signal the problem to the individual's center of conscious, which Jung calls the "ego." The means through which the unconscious speaks to the ego are primarily, at least for our purposes here, dreams, fantasies, and visions. The ego must, in turn, subject the unconscious's warning to a critical evaluation and perhaps mediate the advice in some way before assimilating it. Change or transformation never comes easily in the Jungian system, but it is a necessary thing for the individual who would develop to fullest potential.

At this point, it may be helpful for us to look at a map or diagram of the Jungian psyche. The diagram demonstrates Jung's elaboration of the schema he inherited from his mentor Freud, with the primary (but not the only) difference being Jung's claim of a "collective unconscious" as well as a "personal unconscious."

Persona

Consciousness
(Ego)

Personal Unconscious

Collective Unconscious
(Archetypes)

First, if we begin at the outside of our psyche and work inward, there is our *persona,* or social mask that we present to the outside world to function competently.[16] The mask of the courteous, attentive waiter might be an example, or the mask of the swaggering, streetwise tough guy might be another. At a somewhat deeper level is the private, interior area of *consciousness.* This is the area in which we are aware of our thoughts and feelings. The center here, as noted above, is the ego. Beneath this level is the *personal unconscious,* an area of psychic activity where, in Jung's words, "forgotten, repressed, subliminally perceived and felt material of all kinds" reside.[17] The materials at this level are elements that the individual has absorbed during the course of his or her life up to that moment but has not retained in the consciousness. At the deepest level is the *collective unconscious.* It is, as I have implied previously, Jung's most original contribution to our conception of the psyche. Jung distinguishes it from the personal consciousness as follows:

> The collective unconscious is a part of the psyche which can be negatively distinguished from the personal unconscious by the fact that it does not, like the latter, owe its existence to personal experience and consequently is not a personal acquisition. While the personal unconscious is made up essentially of contents which have at one time been conscious but which have disappeared from consciousness through having been forgotten or repressed, the contents of the collective unconscious have never been in consciousness, and therefore have never been individually acquired, but owe their existence to heredity.[18]

This area is universal. It is the individual's tie to human beings in other cultures and other historical periods. The collective unconscious is made up of primordial images that Jung called *archetypes*. He elaborates:

> The primordial image, or archetype, is a figure—be it a daemon, a human being, or a process—that constantly recurs in the course of history and appears whenever creative fantasy is freely expressed. Essentially, therefore, it is a mythological figure. When we examine these images more closely, we find that they give form to countless typical experiences of our ancestors. They are, so to speak, the psychic residue of innumerable experiences of the same type.[19]

These images we share. They frequently instruct us with the time-tested wisdom they embody. Indeed they may force our ego to confront certain lackings in our psychological make-up if, as I discussed earlier, our psychic system is inappropriately out of balance. The archetypes come to us primarily in our dreams, fantasies, and visions, but we may recognize them as comparable to figures in various cultural myths, fairy tales, and religious rituals.

Especially in the second half of an individual's life, Jung felt it possible for the individual to move toward maturity or self-realization in terms of a balance of psychic qualities—a realization of a relatively full range of the possibilities for the person. This process he called "individuation."[20] It is an inward journey, or in terms of our diagram, it is a journey from the top down. Jung found that this journey was guided in many cases by certain archetypes. These include the shadow or darker side of the individual, the anima-animus, or the feminine aspect of the male and the masculine aspect of the female, the old wise man or magician who frequently represents spiritual wisdom, and the great mother who usually represents natural cyclical forces of life and death. An archetype of balance that Jung found often to be a part of the process was the image of the mandala.[21] This is generally a magic circle. It may be also a circle that contains a box within it. Sometimes the circle is bisected by two axes whose four ends, according to Jung, represent the four functions of thinking, feeling, sensation, and intuition. The circle often has at its center a symbol that may stand for the self. The mandala represents a goal toward which the individual struggles.

This Jungian system provided Fellini with a framework he found congenial. Moreover, it provided him with a set of ideas and images he could play with in his movies. The operative word here, however, is *play*. It would be a mistake to attempt to reduce Fellini's movies to Jungian concepts.[22] We might consider certain of his post-1960 films, those after his study of Jung, to bear more overt reference to the personal unconscious and the collective unconscious and to certain Jungian archetypes and to the general notion of an interior journey than his earlier movies had, but we ought not to expect all elements to fit together in quite the same way as they did for Jung. Fellini is too experimental or playful a filmmaker for that. And furthermore, we are able to discover certain anticipations of these elements in Fellini's earlier movies of the 1950s, too, for the attitudes that brought Fellini to his study of Jung seem to have been present from the start of his career. For now, however, we must turn our attention to the medium by which the unconscious, personal and collective, speaks to us, the medium of dreams.

Drawings and Images for Films

About the time Fellini began to discuss Jung with Dr. Bernhard, he started also to keep a series of dream notebooks in which he would draw major images from his previous night's dreams with colored pencils. He would add captions to the drawings that would set clear the context in which the image appeared. To collect his dreams in this manner was, in effect, to gather material for a Jungian analysis. In therapy sessions, Jung would often have a patient describe or draw key images. The patient would supply interpretative glosses from his or her personal memories for the personal level, and then Jung would supply analogies from myths, folktales, artworks, and pieces of literature from a wide range of cultures—in short, archetypes from the collective level. Analyst and analysand would work together to determine the message of the dream. They would not "translate" the symbols as in Freudian analysis but would try to discover the "direction" in which the self was trying to urge the analysand to move. We do not know whether Fellini discussed his drawings with Dr. Bernhard or simply mused over them himself. We do know, however, that he kept up the practice of recording his dreams until 1980.

Several of Fellini's drawings have been published, an early batch edited by Ornella Volta in the journal *Positif* in 1974 and a somewhat fuller collection edited by Lietta Tornabuoni in *Dolce Vita* in 1987.[23] Tornabuoni's collection shows a drawing dated as early as 1960 and another as late as 1980.

While it would be difficult to analyze any of these dreams without the context of other dreams dated from the same period and without the personal observations of the dreamer given in detail, we can note at least a few interesting preoccupations.

Perhaps the most Jungian of the dreams is an undated but clearly late sketch that depicts the balding Fellini on a beach looking out at a figure of a large, buxom Asian woman. The figure of the woman seems to rise from a stormy sea. The Fellini figure calls out, "I don't understand you. Come back to the beach." Two small, feminine figures on a promontory to the left offer the advice, "As long as you talk to her from the shore, she will never hear you. On the other hand, her place will remain where it is." This dream is what Jung might refer to as an invitation dream. Generally, in Jungian analysis, figures that rise from the sea are chthonic representations of the collective unconscious who are inviting the dreamer to recognize an aspect of the unconscious self not yet discovered, in effect to "dive deeper."[24] That the woman is "other" in the sense of ethnicity would reinforce this kind of interpretation, and so too would the fact that she resembles the archetype of the anima mediatrix, a guide figure such as we will discuss later in the chapter, who beckons the dreamer further into the unconscious. The clincher, however, is the advice of the two women on the promontory, who urge the Fellini figure, in effect, to go out to the woman. The dream, then, would be an invitation to set out anew on an inward journey.

This dream late in Fellini's career seems to echo, on the basis of how he represents himself, a 1967 dream that Fellini recounts in his autobiographical essay "Rimini, My Home Town." In this dream, the Fellini figure in fact swims out from the port of his hometown toward the sea. He does not go toward a gigantic figure but is himself such a figure. This is a bolder dream in that the dreamer actually does set forth, yet it is a dream that speaks to the same invitation:

Last night I dreamt of the port of Rimini opening onto a green, swelling sea, as threatening as a moving meadow, on which low clouds ran close to the surface.

I was a giant, swimming out to sea, starting from the port, which was small and narrow. I said to myself: "I may be a giant, but the sea's still the sea. Suppose I don't make it?" But I wasn't worried. I swam with great strokes through the little port. I couldn't drown because I was touching bottom. I might drown out at sea; but I swam on, just the same.[25]

Fellini calls this dream a "sustaining" one, "an invitation to overestimate myself; or else to underestimate the small protective conditions of departure that might hold me back." This dream came at a point in Fellini's career when he was summoning up his courage to break up his old, tried-and-true filmmaking team and to start out in a new direction, for better or worse, with his new crew in films like *Toby Dammit* (1968) and *Fellini Satyricon* (1969). It may well be that the later dream of the Asian woman is another call to explore further with more self-analysis or creative projects that deal with yet more reverberations of elements from the collective unconscious—a film like *City of Women* (1980). And it may be that such invitation dreams have recurred in Fellini's life as markers of those moments when he felt he had done enough in a certain area and needed to push on further.

An image from a Fellini film that most resembles the dream image of the Asian woman rising from the sea, however, is certainly that of the gigantic head of the statue of Reìta that rises from the Grand Canal in *Fellini's Casanova* only to sink back down. Here the statue's invitation is extended to both Casanova and the viewer. It asks all parties to be prepared for a descent into the self in the film that follows. In all of these—the dream sketch, the verbal recounting, and the film image—the impact comes to the same thing. All are an invitation to explore the collective unconscious.

An interesting cluster of drawings from the dream notebooks among those published by Ornella Volta in 1974 involves sexual encounters. Fellini represents himself in these sketches as a slim young man with a double pompadour. The situations seem to depict him as a naïf newly arrived in the city, or in other words, the situations seem to echo possible occurrences from Fellini's memories of the time he left Rimini in 1938 to make his way to Rome and to seek a career in the late 1930s and early 1940s. The women of the dreams are threatening to the young man in some way. The power they generate is part of their attraction for him—perhaps the main part. The women do not invite him to explore the "feminine side of his nature," as we might expect from popular interpretations of Jungian anima figures, but as anima figures and even sirens they "lure" him to explore the stranger passions of male sexuality inside himself, passions outside the boundaries of propriety and correctness. As I discuss in chapter 3, this situation is essentially an adolescent one in which the inexperienced male is fascinated and awestruck by the more experienced female. That the situation is adolescent, however, should not lead us to dismiss it. The situation is, in fact, one of great intensity, and it can work very well as a symbolic scene for the male dreamer (if not the female one), inviting him to explore the powerful and frightening aspects of his sexuality.

The adolescent aspect of the sexual situation is most clearly demonstrated in the sketch of a train encounter. Here a powerful figure of a woman seems to loom over the Fellini figure. She is both sexual and adult in terms of her huge breasts and thighs and her pubic hair. A hat and a fur wrap give her both tactile and adult qualities. The Fellini figure, a model of propriety here, is fully clothed. Humorously, his stature is a diminished one not just in terms of scale: He seems reduced almost to the role of serving as end post to the train seat where he sits. The encounter in the dream depicts the power and fascination that the experienced woman holds for the young Fellini.

Another dream sketch of a similar situation depicts the young Fellini figure in a town street looking at the large, exposed buttocks of a woman walking near him. To the right of the sketch are two smiling and somewhat sinister male figures, perhaps pimps, watching the situation. This dream seems to draw on the difference in size between the woman and the Fellini figure of the first sketch and on a sense of a criminal activity. Furthermore, someone watches the Fellini figure from behind a barred window. This silhouette person resembles the main Fellini figure in that his head is cast down at a similar angle. This figure in the window may be an embodiment of Fellini's "conscience," a "disapproving" side of him, or a side of him longing to "break out," but, whatever our interpretation, this figure who watches the Fellini figure seems to be a "shadow" who turns up the intensity level of the situation.

We might be tempted to say that such dreams are relatively normal expressions of male curiosity, like those we might expect from an adolescent or a young adult setting out on his own for the first time. But the dreams are those of Fellini in 1960 or 1961 when he was a married man in his forties. As such, the dreams seem a reaching back to a previous time for imagery, and in Jungian terms this imagery would seem to urge the dreamer to explore his sexual feelings more fully than he has done earlier in order to become a more nearly whole individual. The dreams do not offer specific directives; rather they indicate a direction for exploration.

One of Fellini's movies, *The Temptation of Dr. Antonio* (1962), could be seen as an expanded reenactment of this Jungian situation in which the protagonist is invited by the inner self through a series of fantasies to explore forbidden sexual emotions. This movie is discussed in detail in chapter 6 as an example of comic pairing. Here, however, we can note that the central situation, the coming to life of a giant billboard representation of actress Anita Ekberg to tower over a tiny protagonist, reconstitutes an adolescent experience in which Antonio, the protagonist, claims to have covered his eyes to avoid watching a mature woman disrobe.[26] As we will see, Antonio is a prude who needs a comic comeuppance, but the charm of the movie for viewers may also lie in the gradual recognition of Anita, the billboard star, as an archetype who seeks to "educate" the protagonist.

Two final images from the dream notebooks that we might consider here involve the notion of floating in a free space. One entry depicts a parachutist who has jumped from an airplane and drifts suspended in air, and the other, a deep-sea diver who has gone over the side of a boat and hangs suspended near the bottom of the sea. Fellini has glossed these dream images as "solutions" to the problem he was having in completing the film project *The Voyage of G. Mastorna* (circa 1967). Generally, in Jungian analysis as in Freudian analysis, the urge to fly or to dive is the expression of the urge for power or potency—to be godlike. Here, however, the wish seems less assertive; it seems more the urge to escape to a kind of free zone where the anxieties of everyday life cannot reach the dreamer, at least for a while. The dream is a relatively common "escapist" wish for those who feel the pressure of their lives closing in on them, as Fellini apparently did with his *Mastorna* project, and we hardly need the apparatus of Jungian psychology to explain it. However, in the context of other Jungian imagery and the idea of the journey into the self in Fellini's movies, the image of floating seems to be often a precondition for the journey of the hero. It seems often a moment of stasis during which he or she shakes clear of limiting or debilitating forces and prepares to undertake new exploration.

While many images of floating abound in Fellini's movies,[27] it is in *Juliet of the Spirits* where such images seem most prominent. Juliet, the heroine of the film, encounters at least three situations or images that seem to promise the kind of release from the entrapments of her life that she both desires and fears. All involve the figure of Iris-Fanny-Suzy (played by the same actress, Sandra Milo) who represents versions of freer sexual attitudes for Juliet. Iris is a spirit voice who urges Juliet to seek love; Fanny is a beautiful circus performer who ran off with Juliet's grandfather; and Suzy is the next-door neighbor who runs a house of exotic delights. The three dreamlike images of floating that Iris-Fanny-Suzy presents Juliet are all seductively attractive. When Fanny first appears to Juliet in an apparition at the beach she swings gracefully on a circus trapeze swing, clad in a white tutu and white veil—almost a bridelike figure. Then within a memory, which is more fantasy than reality, Juliet envisions Fanny and the grandfather flying off in an old-fashioned circus biplane and hovering above the pursuing figures of Grandpa's family and school where he taught, all clamoring for the pair to return. And finally, Suzy uses a strange forest elevator, shaped like the basket of a hot-air balloon, to transport Juliet and herself up to a tree platform where they can sunbathe and talk candidly of Juliet's attitudes about her marriage and about love. None of these three images—trapeze, biplane, or elevator—offers a solution to Juliet, any more than Fellini's dream visions of flying offered him a lasting solution beyond momentary escape. Each, however, seems to hold out in an extremely seductive way the lure of a free zone where Juliet can shake clear of her limiting entanglements and consider the possibilities of a new (and perhaps arduous) journey of self-exploration.

The Mage

The figure of the mage is an important one in Fellini films. It is one of the archetypes from Jung that Fellini has adapted to his own particular uses. The mage is not a figure about which Jung has written extensively. He was, however, fascinated with the sixteenth-century physician and alchemist Paracelsus who experimented with amulets, spells, and talismans and saw no conflict in this with his traditional religious belief or with his other "scientific" experiments.[28] Jung, indeed, seems to have thought of the mage finally as a version of the wise old man, more important for his wisdom in spiritual matters than for his prowess to perform feats of magic. In his essay "The Phenomenology of the Spirit in Fairytales," for example, Jung states, "The wise old man appears in dreams in the guise of a magician, doctor, priest, teacher, professor, grandfather, or any other person possessing authority."[29] The figure, however, is an important one for post-Jungian analysts and scholars. In *The Magician Within,* Robert Moore and Douglas Gillette, for example, stress a more proactive role for the mage: "The Magician urges us on into the unseen. He is the mediator and communicator of hidden knowledge, the healer, technologist, teacher, and contemplative— he is behind our insatiable human curiosity."[30] They describe the mage as a figure who "would rather study a problem than solve one" and who brings the logic of the "left brain" into contact with the visions and intuitions of the "right brain."[31] The mage is then an initiator, one who starts a quester on an interior journey but does not necessarily foresee the outcome of the quest or the solution to a problem. Perhaps for this reason, there is generally an ambiguity about the mage: The gender may be indeterminate in some instances. Is he or she a force for good or evil?[32] Moore and Gillette, for instance, point to the range of attitudes toward the legendary English wizard Merlin. They conclude, however, that the mage is generally a positive force who leads us into the self in psychological terms or into a sacred space and time in religious terms: "The Magician is the master of spirits, though, and he holds the keys to the initiatory gates at the thresholds of sacred space and time. He can help us keep our wits about us. He helps to insulate us from the power of the other archetypes, but uses their energy resources to aid us in life-enhancing ways."[33]

The definition of the mage that Moore and Gillette offer is more grand than Fellini's conception of the figure, but the role of Fellini's mages is, at bottom, the same. They are ambiguous figures, perhaps strange characters or tacky entertainers. Their gender may be uncertain. And they may or may not point the heroes or heroines toward useful goals. They are, however, clearly figures who introduce the major characters to their interior worlds. For better or worse, these gatekeepers open the gates.

Perhaps the best example of Fellini's use of the mage figure is the magician Maurice who is teamed with the telepathic Maya in *8 ½* (see fig. 2.1). Maurice, dressed in the traditional top hat and tails of a stage magician, starts Guido off on his inward analysis by transmitting Guido's recall of the magic phrase from his childhood, *Asa Nisi Masa,* to Maya. (The phrase is a coded version of the word *anima* as well as an incantation like *abracadabra.*)[34] That Maurice is teamed with a partner puts him in the position of being a mage who initiates but does not completely understand the mystery he is sending the protagonist into. When Guido asks him, "But tell me . . . what's the trick? How do you transmit?" the magician, an old friend of Guido, tells him candidly, "There are some tricks, but there's also something true about it. I don't know how it happens, but it happens."[35] The result is that we feel we are encountering something more mysterious, something deeper, than the magician can describe or even know. The magician mystifies, in other words, rather than demystifies the dreamlike memory he is about to usher in. The figure of Maya, the magician's partner, is one that interested Jung greatly.[36] She is the spinning woman of the Hindu religion. Her dance of the veils is thought to be an enticement of the senses that the spiritual seeker must pass *beyond.* In *8 ½,* however, she seems just the opposite, for she helps Guido begin his journey into his memories, fantasies, and dreams that he must pass *into,* if he is to gain insight into himself. The motif of hanging white sheets and gauzelike white veils that appears in so many of Guido's memories, fantasies, and dreams, almost as an indicator that we are looking at an "interior" scene, may surely be traced back to the idea of Maya's dance of the veils.[37] It could be said, in fact, that Guido's inward journey is an entry into the world of the veils. Fittingly enough, then, at the end of *8 ½,* when Guido begins to make sense of, or become comfortable with, the figures of his inward journey, Maurice, the magician, serves again as master of ceremonies for the affirmation scene, telling Guido, "We're ready to begin," and leading Guido from his car back to the movie set on the beach.[38] Also fitting are the white veils, curtains, and streamers blowing in and out of view, which contribute to our sense that the scene is part of the journey into a magic world.

More ambiguous are the two mediums who appear in *Juliet of the Spirits,* Genius and Bhisma. Both are sexually complicated. Genius appears to be a gay male with feminine gestures and inflections. Bhisma seems of indeterminate gender, male or female by turns. The actor Genius is a real-life medium who was a part of Fellini's circle of friends. In the film he is an entertainer invited to the party in Giorgio and Juliet's home mainly to provide a game for the guests to play.[39] Once Genius's seance begins, however, the consequences for Juliet are serious. He holds a pendulum over Juliet's head and pronounces her "very receptive." She had visions of castles, dark forests, streets, and faces with sparkling eyes when she was a child but has since lost this gift. Now, at midlife, the time at which Jung finds inward

Fig. 2.1. Fellini's sketch
of Maurice the magician
as a Jungian mage in *8 ½*.
Federico Fellini Copyright © 1982
Diogenes Verlag AG Zürich.

exploration often becomes necessary, Juliet discovers at Genius's seance that spirits wish to contact her again. The first voice is that of Iris, who, as we noted before, also appears as the circus performer, Fanny, and as the neighbor, Suzy. Iris's voice is seductive and encouraging: "Love for everybody" is her message. The second voice is that of Olaf the Turk. His voice is aggressive and attacking: "Who do you think you are? You're nobody to anyone!" As different as the two voices are, they seem to be pushing Juliet in the same direction, that is, toward an exploration of her emotions and her sexual drives. Iris's method is to coax her on, and Olaf's is to frighten her into proceeding. Simply put, Iris seems to use what the movie takes to be a "feminine" approach and Olaf, a harsher "male" approach. This duality is borne out by the two sets of dreams Juliet has on the beach. Iris appears as Fanny, dressed in white tights and a veil, on her trapeze swing. Olaf appears on a raft with his sword raised, holding captive a closed barge of naked, emaciated prisoners and towing another raft of horses, one dead, with feet in the air, and two others, gaunt and swaybacked. Iris demonstrates the attractiveness of sexuality, and Olaf, the consequences of repression.

The ambiguous figure of the medium Bhisma, part female and part male, is ideally suited for the role she-he plays in the movie.[40] Apparently a teacher of Buddhism, she-he is, in fact, a medium through whom spirits may speak. During a consultation in her suite, which is draped with white gauze curtains reminiscent of the various kinds of "veils" in *8 ½,* Bhisma's body becomes the site of a power struggle between the spirits Iris and Olaf. The first to speak is Iris: "You remember me? I was born this way. A woman of passion. Am I not beautiful? . . . You've seen my hair? I never comb it; I caress it. I love to caress myself. . . ." But when Juliet objects that Iris's advice is for Juliet to behave like a prostitute, Bhisma goes into convulsions, and the spirit of Olaf attempts to take over and frighten Juliet, perhaps as punishment for her objections. Bhisma speaks what is apparently a two-part dialogue: "Who is it? Olaf. Olaf, go away. Iris!" The two spirits then seem to struggle for control of Juliet's visions. We see Iris again as Fanny on the trapeze, but she is spinning dizzily out of control. Next Fanny is astride a dark, plumed circus horse, and then she stands, legs spread above Bhisma's sleeping physician on a bed in the suite—two blatant sexual images involving Iris-Fanny but imbued with the aggressiveness and assertiveness associated with Olaf. "The spirits can be dangerous," remarks Bhisma's assistant, and he adds, "They like to play tricks." The badly shaken Juliet has now passed from the first mage, Genius, to the second, Bhisma, and her sense of entering into a fearful mystery has deepened appreciably.

The Shadow

"Man needs an opposite to concretize his experience," writes the Jungian analyst Jolande Jacobi.[41] For Jung, this opposite is the archetype of the shadow. This archetype usually exists at the level of the personal unconscious, although Jung also posits a deeper (and generally darker) version that can reside in the collective unconscious. The shadow is the other, a double or *doppelgänger.* It is always of the same sex as the individual concerned and represents what is latent in the individual but underdeveloped. If the individual is a virtuous, moral person, the shadow is his or her darker side, as the vicious Mr. Hyde is to Robert Louis Stevenson's highly respectable and honorable Dr. Jekyll. Jung states, "The shadow is the moral problem that challenges the whole ego-personality, for no one can become conscious of the shadow without considerable moral effort. To become conscious of it involves recognizing the dark aspects of the personality as present and real."[42] Such recognition of an opposite side to one's self is a major step in the process toward individuation. But the opposite need not always be "darker." If the individual is a selfish, dissolute person, as Edgar Allan Poe's William Wilson is, the shadow will be a high-minded, idealistic figure, as is Wilson's double. Or if the individual is an introvert, the shadow will be an extrovert; so if the individual is one given to analytical thought, the shadow will be a figure of strong feeling. The notion of the shadow is ideally suited to literature, for it can serve as a foil to point up the traits a character has as well as those he or she lacks. In a Jungian frame of reference, however, the shadow is more than a device; it demonstrates characteristics the protagonist must recognize and assimilate or recognize and defeat. "To confront the shadow," Jacobi tells us, "means to take a mercilessly critical attitude towards one's own nature."[43]

Shadow figures in *Juliet of the Spirits* function as educative forces for the protagonist Juliet. These figures are Fanny and Suzy, the two personifications of the spirit Iris.[44] Juliet is a person with virtually no life. She is an introvert, but her interior world of feeling is stifled by the moral conventions of the church, which emphasize martyrdom, and the social conventions of marriage, which emphasize propriety and decorum. Fanny, the circus performer, and Suzy, the neighbor, are both booming extroverts and advocates of sexual freedom. Fanny's primary scene is Juliet's memory of her visit to the circus. Juliet's encounters with Fanny are pleasant and encouraging: Fanny swings on the trapeze, as we noted earlier; she greets Juliet and tells her she is pretty; and she flies off with Juliet's grandfather in the biplane. Fanny is, thus, an embodiment of liberation for Juliet.

A darker form of the shadow is the neighbor Suzy who is more earthy and overtly sexual. She first appears in a yellow bikini on her barge at the seashore. The prim Juliet finds her not quite respectable and calls back her two nieces who have run to meet the new lady on her arrival. Later, Juliet joins her husband, Giorgio, to watch the neighbor through his telescope and pronounces Suzy beautiful, but she does so circumspectly, perhaps so as not to disturb the social veneer of the moment, for the guest Jose is present.

Gradually, however, through three visits or, we might say, "trials," Juliet moves more deeply into Suzy's world and learns a good deal more about her own sensual and sexual appetites. Each visit ends with a temptation for Juliet, and although she gives in to none of them, she does finally have to admit to herself the appetites. On the first visit, as Juliet returns Suzy's cat, Juliet is caught up in the fantasy of Suzy's house, which bears resemblance to an enchanted castle, with its bright gauze harem tents and canopies and its stained-glass interior windows. She tours the private chambers of the house and ends in Suzy's own chamber, with its mirrored ceiling and its chute into the pool of warm water. Juliet sprawls playfully on the bed and looks at herself in the ceiling mirror, but she refuses the temptation of a nude swim in the pool.

The second visit involves the trip into the forest to Suzy's tree house discussed earlier. Here Juliet, comically covered up in hat, scarf, long pants, and sweater, refuses Suzy's invitation to sunbathe, and yet she does give in somewhat to the intimacy of the situation to talk about her feelings about her husband and about love. A new element is added to this second "trial," however, when two young men who, aided by clues from Suzy, have been following the women wish to join them. The situation has become too improper for the married Juliet, and so she makes a hasty departure.

The third trial is more severe. Juliet has learned of her husband's infidelity from a private detective, and now she returns to a party at Suzy's house with an almost grim resolve to seek out and give into a temptation of the flesh. She takes a turn in descending the stairs as a woman on display, an act that ends with Juliet in tears, crouched on the steps. Yet Suzy, the shadow figure, does not allow Juliet to remain there. She beckons Juliet to her chamber again and sends to her Suzy's young, faunlike godson on the bed beneath the mirror. Juliet is about to give in to her sexual feelings for the young man when a vision of her martyred friend Laura calls her back from the temptation. The point is not that Juliet escapes the third temptation as she had escaped the earlier two but that she felt it in a clear and unequivocal manner, as opposed to the previous two, and must recognize the sensual and sexual longings she harbors within her. The shadow figure Suzy has done her office, and Juliet is now ready to move on to further stages of interior development or, indeed in her case, to think about beginning a life outside the various restrictions she had imposed on herself at the start of the film.

The shadow figure in *8 ½* serves a rather different function. This role is played by Daumier, the harsh, analytical critic with ideological concerns whom Guido has hired to advise him on his film project.[45] Daumier is an opposite to Guido in at least two senses. Whereas Guido is concerned with exploring his feelings, Daumier is concerned with thinking in the Jungian sense of logical reasoning, and whereas Guido is concerned with his own inner development, Daumier wants an impact on the external, social fabric. Jungian analyst Marie-Louise von Franz has noted, "To a person who lives out his natural emotions and feelings, the shadow may appear as a cold and negative intellectual."[46] This is precisely the role Daumier plays in *8 ½*. For example, Daumier responds to Guido's memory of his childhood encounter with the prostitute Saraghina, so important to Guido's sense of mystery about sexuality, maternalness, play, and women, with utter incomprehension and yet with a certain validity, given Daumier's point of view. "And what does it mean?" Daumier asks. "It's a character from your childhood memories. It has nothing to do with a true critical consciousness. No . . . if you really want to engage in a polemic about Catholic consciousness in Italy . . . well, my friend . . . in this case, believe me, what you would need above all is a higher degree of culture, as well as, of course, inexorable logic and clarity."[47] Daumier would have Guido be a Suetonius for his age, that is, an analytical examiner of a social institution, and he would have Guido bring more intellectual rigor ("logic and clarity") to the task. This, however, is not what Guido is about. Guido wishes to look inward into those things that have marked his emotional life and to do so by measuring the intensity of the experiences, not by applying analytical skills.

Why, we might ask, has Guido invited Daumier to work with him in the first place? Daumier himself raises the same question early on when he says, "I'm really surprised you thought of me for a collaboration that, frankly, I don't think would work out." It must be, if we are right to consider Daumier a Jungian shadow, that Daumier raises questions that Guido has inside himself and that run counter to Guido's current enterprise. Bringing Daumier onto the set would then become a way for Guido to confront his self-doubts or his rational questioning of the value of what is emotionally intense for him. Daumier is thus a test for Guido. He cannot defeat his opponent with logic; he must defeat him in spite of logic; he must defeat him with the intensity he feels for the elements of his inner development. And this is essentially what Guido does at the end of *8 ½*. In his imagination, Guido orders his assistants to hang the critic during the screening of the auditions in the theater, but this is only a means to stop Daumier's incessant carping for the moment. The final defeat comes when Guido hears Daumier out fully in his car as the critic praises the artist who can "educate himself to silence." It is at this point that Guido turns to the figure of the magician Maurice and the dream figures he conjures up for Guido and elects to treat these figures in a film simply because their attraction is irresistible. The function of the shadow in this film is that he is there to be overcome. That he is overcome is then, in turn, a measure of the strength of those figures in Guido's memory and unconscious who pull him deeper into his emotional life.

The Anima

Women. Fellini's films abound with women. Yet to many female viewers, the women often seem male fabrications of women rather than accurately drawn, multidimensional human beings of the real world. "We are all women created out of his imagination," says one of the characters in the harem of *8 ½*. She is, of course, speaking of Guido, the film director within the movie, but at the metalevel of the film, she is also speaking accurately about Fellini himself. His women are often like figures from the male psyche. More properly in Jungian terms, they are frequently Fellini's versions of the archetype of the anima, the figure who takes up the journey for individuation where the shadow leaves off.

To Jung, the anima is the "woman within" the male. Jung states, "Every man carries within him the eternal image of woman, not the image of this or that particular woman, but a definite feminine image. This image is fundamentally unconscious, an hereditary factor of primordial origin engraved in the living organic system of the man, an imprint or 'archetype' of all the ancestral experiences of the female, a deposit, as it were, of all impressions ever made by woman,"[48] and Jung's disciple Marie-Louise von Franz adds succinctly, "The anima is a personification of all feminine psychological tendencies in a man's psyche."[49] Fellini follows this definition of the anima almost exactly in discussing the women of his films. In a 1966 interview mainly concerned with *Juliet of the Spirits,* he states, "We don't really know who woman is. She remains in that precise place within man where darkness begins. Talking about women means talking about the darkest part of ourselves, the undeveloped part, the true mystery within. In the beginning, I believe that man was complete and androgynous—both male and female, or neither, like the angels. Then came the division, and Eve was taken from him. So the problem for man is to reunite himself with the other half of his being."[50]

The problem of what this "woman within," this missing part of the male, represents is, however, a complicated matter, for Jung's considerations of the anima vary over his career. There are at least three different kinds of roles he has assigned for her, all of which Fellini seems to have taken over and used.[51] The first of these is the *contrasexual* role, in which the woman supplies things the male lacks, as suggested by Fellini in the interview statement above. For Jung, though, the contrasexual role of the anima is tied to Jung's late-nineteenth-century notions of gender roles, wherein the male is associated with Logos, rational thinking, and patriarchal law and the female with Eros, feeling, and matriarchal nurturing. As von Franz puts it somewhat archly, the anima can represent for the typical male such feminine tendencies as "vague feelings and moods, prophetic hunches, receptiveness to the irrational, capacity for personal love, [and] feeling for nature."[52] However, the contrasexual role need not be so stereotypical. It need only be different from or opposite to the male's chief qualities. Jacobi elaborates this opposition:

> Since the soul-image coincides with the function that has been least elucidated and still rests in the unconscious, it is antithetical to the main function, and this contrast will be manifested in the figure symbolizing it. Therefore in principle an abstract scientist's anima will be primitive, emotional, and romantic . . . and it is no accident that effeminate emotional men usually bear in their hearts the image of an Amazon. . . .[53]

What is particularly interesting about Jacobi's remark is that it accounts very nicely for the image of the amazon as she appears in so many of Fellini's movies. Characters such as Guido in *8 ½,* Encolpius of *Fellini Satyricon,* young Fellini in *Fellini's Roma,* and Snaporaz in *City of Women* all have in common the trait of indecisiveness and have about them in their different ways a certain softness. Also, all of these male characters are enamored of female figures who are their sexual opposite—the amazon. This begs, for the moment, the question of so many large, powerful women in Fellini's own drawings. It is beyond the range of this book to "psychoanalyze" Fellini himself. My focus is on his works. However, the large threatening figures among Fellini's sketches do suggest a certain kinship between Fellini and his protagonists, especially the more autobiographical ones, in terms of a basically introverted male (whatever contrary public persona he may present) who is guided by feelings and intuitions longing to develop more forceful, aggressive capacities to act with influence in the external world. But there are other possibilities for us to muse upon, also.

The second role the anima plays is that of a figure of Eros, or sensual love, in its varieties. The emphasis here is not so much on the women figures themselves but on the "erotic" longings they evoke from the males who pursue them. Jung elaborates on four kinds of Eros, represented by the figures of Eve, Helen of Troy, the Virgin Mary, and Sophia, or *sapientia aeterna,* of the Gnostic cults.[54] The Eve figure for Jung is "the personification of a purely instinctual relationship." It is uncomplicated. Its end is physical gratification and self-reproduction. The figure Helen is one of complication and intrigue. Jung describes the love she represents as "sexual Eros, but on an aesthetic and romantic level." Clearly, the psychology of the longing and of the pursuit is important here. The third figure, Mary, "raises Eros to the heights of religious devotion and thus spiritualizes [it]." The fourth figure, Sophia, "represents something which goes beyond the almost unsurpassable third stage: *Sapientia* (Wisdom)." The fourth figure, then, seems to merge with the kind of wisdom and experience of the wise old man and the earth mother of the final stage of individuation and, in effect, ceases to be an anima figure and becomes something more. The first three figures, however, present a range of possibilities that seem to have captivated Fellini. In his interview cited earlier, Fellini remarks, "Man is not basically a monogamous animal. . . . The tragedy of modern man is that he needs a multiplicity of individual relationships, whereas, at least in the culture in which I live, he is still forced into a single-mated mold."[55] If we take his statement as something more than an attempt to excuse philandering, we can see it as an endorsement of pursuing on the fantasy level a range of anima figures that can show us much about the Eros within the male. The first three variations of the anima as Eros seem to have captivated Fellini, and in his films he seems to have splintered and reflected the categories.

The women of *La Dolce Vita* are strikingly like those of Jung's first three categories. The peculiar thing about this similarity is that the movie was made before Fellini began his program of study with Dr. Bernhard. Fellini, therefore, seems to have anticipated what he would soon discover in his reading of Jung. The most basic figure is Marcello's fiancée, Emma, She offers him sexual gratification when she asks him to come home from the press conference because she "want[s] to make love"; she feeds him a picnic lunch in the car as they drive to the field of the pseudomiracle; and during their visit to Steiner's apartment after Emma has seen Steiner's two children, she whispers to Marcello, "One day we'll have a home like this, you and I. We go well together, you and I, don't we? We are made for each other."[56] However, Marcello finds this kind of love insufficient and tells Emma later during an argument, "You talk of nothing but the kitchen and the bedroom. . . . I don't believe in this aggressive, sticky, maternal love of yours. I don't want it! I can't use it! This isn't love, it's bestiality."[57] He sees this traditional, marital love as a limitation, and he wants to explore other possibilities of Eros. Yet it is worth noting that Marcello returns to Emma again and again in the movie as if she is a secure base he is not willing to give up.

A more sophisticated, even kinky, level of love comes to Marcello in the figure of the wealthy socialite Maddalena. When we first encounter her, she is masking a black eye behind her dark glasses, and she soon involves Marcello in lovemaking in the basement apartment of a prostitute they pick up together. Later, at a party of aristocrats, she leads Marcello to a chamber of whispers in the villa and speaks to him clearly but in a low voice from a concealed spot rather far from him. She tells Marcello what he wants to hear—that she is in love with him and that she would like to be both a faithful wife to him and a whore who amuses herself—but she adds that she has lost the power to make a choice. As she talks, she begins to embrace another man who has come to her hiding place, and she steals off with this new man, leaving Marcello to search for her unsuccessfully. Certainly, Maddalena is the elusive one-from-whom-the-lover-is-parted. She tantalizes and then disappears, schooling her lover in the erotic play of the chase.

A similar and yet somewhat different figure is the movie star Sylvia. She seems a transitional figure between Jung's second and third levels. As a movie star, she is the very queen of commercial sexuality who seems to function in a world of "photo opportunities." Yet at the press conference, she tosses off her sexual one-liners with a splendid sense of humor, and at the party held for her in the Baths of Caracalla, she dances with an energy and spontaneity that indicates a refreshing naturalness. When Marcello has the opportunity to dance with her, he tries to proclaim her a goddess—a pre-Christian one, to be sure, as befits the setting—and he tries to make of her an archetype from the collective unconscious and, of course, an anima figure of the third level. He says to her, "You are everything, Sylvia. . . . You are the first woman on the first day of creation. You are the mother, the sister, the lover, the friend . . . an angel, devil, the earth, the home."[58] Later, in the evening, it would seem Marcello will capture just such an archetypal figure when he wades into the Trevi Fountain basin to receive a baptism from the hand of Sylvia. But the jokes are many: Sylvia does not understand Marcello's words in Italian; the fountain's waters cease running at a moment that breaks the spell of the baptismal scene; and Marcello must take Sylvia back to a surly husband who gives him a sound beating for his attentions to his wife. The fantasy fails to hold up, and yet, for an evening, Marcello experiences the erotic pull that the anima figure has for him.

The young girl Marcello encounters at the seashore is a clear figure of the anima at the level of the spiritual, Jung's third level, represented by the Virgin Mary. While trying to write, Marcello sees the girl in the soft, dappled light through the lattices of an outdoor restaurant and tells her, "You remind me of one of those little angels in the churches of Umbria." He is quite struck by her youth and her innocence. At the end of the movie, she appears again as someone on the beach, separated from Marcello and his group of friends by a small channel of water. She beckons to Marcello, and he indicates in return that he does not understand what she is trying to tell him. We will never know precisely what she wishes to say to Marcello. Perhaps she just wishes to go for a walk with him. But in the symbolism of the movie, she seems to be offering some alternative to the companionship of the jaded revelers he is with—something more innocent and simple. Marcello turns from her and walks back to the revelers, but maybe more significant than his choice to walk away from her is that he has felt the attraction of what she represents, even if for only a moment. Through her, he has the opportunity to recognize something about himself, and this time Fellini does not joke or disclaim.

La Dolce Vita is a movie of parties. As the movie progresses, the parties get larger, and the behavior becomes more bizarre. This is, of course, Fellini's way of commenting on the society of contemporary Italy during the affluent 1950s and of exhibiting its decadent qualities. We might also consider, however, that the parties provide a way for surrounding Marcello with a variety of women and a variety of erotic possibilities.[59] Not all of the possibilities attract Marcello, although many do. Even so the parties do give him the opportunity to test his reactions to a very wide range. The party with the aristocrats and the final orgy, actually a celebration of an annulment, with show business people offer Marcello glimpses of two groups who do not have to "play by the rules." We see casual sex, sadistic slappings, and examples of the gay lifestyle and transvestism. At least part of the strategy here seems to be for Fellini to present Marcello with as many kinds of Eros as possible so that he can explore the Eros within himself, and when Fellini does this, he goes well beyond the Eve, Helen, Mary, and Sophia of Jung.

The final role that Jung assigns to the anima, in addition to her roles as *contrasexual* figure and representative of Eros, is that of *mediatrix* to the unconscious. In a letter to Count Herman Keyserling in 1931, Jung asserted, "The anima emerges in exemplary fashion from the primeval slime, laden with all the pulpy and monstrous appendages of the deep,"[60] and then more clearly in his 1958 essay "Flying Saucers: A Modern Myth of Things Seen in the Skies," he states, "The anima plays the role of the mediatrix between the unconscious and the conscious."[61] Jungian psychologist James Hillman reflects interestingly on the anima's role as mediatrix:

> That is what "unconscious" means: both unknown *and* unknowable. What is unknown can become known, but what is unknowable remains fundamentally unable to be known; and it is precisely this psychic unconsciousness, beyond the reach of insight and knowledge, that the anima mediates. She makes us unconscious. . . . "With the archetype of the anima we enter the realm of the gods. . . . Everything the anima touches becomes numinous—unconditional, dangerous, taboo, magical."[62]

The job of the anima may be to show what is knowable in the unconscious, but it is also to show us that there is more. This "more" is what I have called the "ineffable" earlier, and it is perhaps the most important aspect of Jung's appeal for Fellini. It is not necessary to group or understand the ineffable. By definition, that is impossible. But what is important is to know that it exists. The mediatrix can offer such assurances.

The role of the mediatrix to the unconscious is played best in Fellini's films by the giantess of *Fellini's Casanova*. This figure is one invented by Fellini for inclusion among the tales from Casanova's memoirs. Fellini cloaks this figure in mystery. Casanova first sees the giantess while he is in the process of attempting suicide in the Thames. She, in effect, gives him new life. She appears in the mist on the bank of the river, accompanied by two dwarves who serve to call attention to her height in contrast to theirs. Casanova sets out to follow her and comes to a street fair. There he decides to enter the interior of an embalmed whale, one of the attractions of the fair. The descent is archetypal. The whale is called "Mouna" which biographer John Baxter tells us is a term from the Romagnolo dialect of Fellini's youth for the vagina.[63] One of the barkers announces, "Out of Mouna has flowed the world, with its trees and its clouds, and at one time, all the races of men. And Mouna has come out of Mouna as well. So praise be to Mouna."[64] In effect, Casanova, led to the fair in pursuit of the giantess, descends into a version of the collective unconscious. He sees what we must assume is only a very small part of a vast realm. In a magic lantern show within the whale, Casanova sees several versions of the *vagina dentata,* in particular, slides of women's genitals containing a scorpion, a vortex, and a devil's face. The show presents, then, the dark fearful side of sexuality— with possibilities of castration, venereal disease, and loss of one's soul all attributed to the sexual woman. The barker also tells us, "Mouna is an open door who leads who knows where. She is a barrier, a wall, that you must breach." Clearly the descent into Mouna brings Casanova to a frightening confrontation with a part of the mystery of sexuality that a Jungian would believe exists "within," at least for males. But, again, more important than the specifics of the mystery is that the mystery exists—the unconscious exists. To know this is to know much. When the descent is over, Casanova refinds the giantess. She defeats him at arm wrestling and seems the contrasexual partner to the introverted male of feeling or intuition; and she plays with dolls and takes a bath with her two dwarves all with a surprising gentleness. But her most important role is that of a mediatrix who tries to lead Casanova to a discovery of the unconscious. If Casanova benefits little from her instruction, the failure is his own. She has done her office.

The Last Journey

"With each night, the great adventure begins," we are told by the ancient female servant in the home of Xavier Zuberkock in *City of Women*. She refers not to amorous adventures—those have ended—but to the great adventure in dreams. The last half hour of *City of Women* consists of a dream journey of the protagonist Snaporaz to find the ideal woman and the kind of wisdom this anima figure can lead him to. Snaporaz's journey resembles the Jungian journey of individuation. It is Fellini's fullest treatment of the subject and his last.

The dream journey is actually a dream-within-a-dream. It takes place within a story space dreamed by Snaporaz during a two-hour nap on a train. This dream-within-a-dream begins when Snaporaz hears voices beneath his bed and crawls under only to discover an entrance to a toboggan slide and three elderly vaudevillians in top hats and tails inviting him to descend with them. The three vaudevillians are, of course, mage figures such as we have discussed earlier, and their invitation is a call to descend into the unconscious. The toboggan seems at once a carnival roller coaster and, because of its pink interior, an entrance to a vagina. The first phase of the journey takes the protagonist through a series of sexual encounters in his conscious ego (his memory) and his personal unconscious. On another level, the encounters allow Fellini to reprise material from the films *8 ½, Amarcord, Fellini's Roma,* the unrealized film treatment *A Journey with Anita,* and his somewhat fictionalized autobiographical essay "Rimini, My Home Town" so that the journey will seem to knowledgeable viewers as a metafilm about Fellini, and Snaporaz will seem perhaps one of the most autobiographical of Fellini's heroes. The encounters with women, moreover, take us through the variety of anima figures we have come to expect. The first women are nurturing figures. One is a maid. Young Snaporaz creeps under a table to touch her legs and perhaps look up her skirt while she irons. She discovers him, drives him off, and then calls him back to smother him to her large bosom. In his essay, Fellini has described a similar experience with a nursery school teacher: "When I was at nursery school, there was a lay sister with black curls and a black apron, and a face red with spots that burst out because of disorders in the blood. . . . Certainly her femininity was explosive, as they say. Well, she used to hug me and stroke me, all in a smell of potato peel, the stink of rancid soup and nuns' habits."[65] In both cases, the situation seems an initiation into the sensuousness of the female body for the little boy. Next as the toboggan ride continues, Snaporaz sees the introduction of two leather-clad female motorcyclists who are presented as daredevil performers in a carnival event called the "Circle of Death." These two women are the amazon figures we are familiar with. They represent the more daring and challenging side of Eros. Then there is the exotic German female vacationer, such as those we encounter in *Amarcord, A Journey with Anita,* and "Rimini, My Home Town" whom Snaporaz and his childhood friends spy on as she changes into her bathing suit during a visit to the beach. There are also various movie stars on the screen before whom Snaporaz and other males masturbate in a bedlike movie theater. Finally, there is Snaporaz's visit to a brothel, where he pursues the notion of "sinful sex" and announces himself a man with a fetish for large buttocks—an "assophile." All these are Fellini's own versions of Jung's Eve and Helen animas, however far Fellini may have strayed from the original examples. And the descent on the toboggan into the unconscious, with a child's song as musical accompaniment, is so far a pleasant one for Snaporaz.

The next stage is a dramatic turnaround. Here we seem to be in an intermediary space, where the personal unconscious overlaps with the collective unconscious. In this part of the journey, we are in the antechambers of a coliseum where male gladiators await their turns to do combat with amazons. For Snaporaz, the antechamber is a place of sexual fear not unlike the belly of the whale in *Fellini's Casanova.* One of the male gladiators is carried back from the coliseum on a stretcher, and another makes out his will before going forth. A man being examined in the clinic of the antechambers is pronounced "limp." Snaporaz is tended to in a fussy manner by two gay males, much to his annoyance, indicating perhaps a certain anxiety on Snaporaz's part about his own gender orientation.[66] (It is after all his dream-within-the dream.) The most threatening aspect of this section of the journey, however, is the board of feminist inquisitors who interrogate and mock Snaporaz as he sits on the ground before them in a near fetal position. The scene is, of course, a reworking of the harem sequence of *8 ½,* wherein the women of Guido's fantasy attack Guido for his inadequacies, only to have him rise to his feet with a bullwhip and a cowboy hat and retake control of the harem. There is no such rise to power by Snaporaz here. The best he can muster is an occasionally jaunty mimicry, for he is essentially at the mercy of the women. If the harem sequence of 8 ½ is an ultimate macho fantasy, the inquisition scene of *City of Women* is an ultimate male nightmare of castration and humiliation.[67] The women fire charges at Snaporaz in rapid succession. Some of the charges are quite valid, and others are nonsense charges, but none can be rebutted. Snaporaz is charged with being unable to offer a woman sexual fulfillment, with being unable to define his feminine component, with being hairy, with taking himself too seriously, with deceiving himself by imagining one ideal woman, with believing women are mentally inferior, and finally with peeing standing up. While many of these charges ring true in this movie and in many other Fellini movies—putting aside the matters of body hair and urination—it seems that one of the major functions of the inquisition scene is to provide Snaporaz with a test. When the inquisition is over, Snaporaz is free to leave, that is, free to wake up. But he chooses to go on. To do this, he must enter deeper into the collective unconscious, and he must step into what appears to be a Jungian mandala.

The mandala as we have noted earlier is the archetypal image of balance. It is a circle or a circle with an enclosed square. In *Fellini Satyricon,* a mandala appearing near the end seems merely to represent a hoped-for state that is not achieved. Groundskeepers sculpt a series of circles within circles in the sand floor of the Garden of Delights where Encolpius will try to recover his "manhood." He fails ignominiously in the garden, and, at the end of the movie, Encolpius will need to continue his journey into middle life before he can even approach the kind of wisdom represented by the mandala. The situation in *City of Women* seems to closely resemble the situation in *Fellini Satyricon,* even though Snaporaz is an older, more troubled hero than Encolpius. The mandala of *City of Women* is a hoped-for but not achieved state of well-being. Specifically, Snaporaz enters the circle in an arena, with a squared boxing ring mounted on a tower within the circle. This is Jung's notion of the magic circle with a square within it—an image of perfect geometric symmetry. This is the longed-for goal of the quest of individuation. Unfortunately, the state it represents is not attained.

As Snaporaz walks around the ring, women in the stands of the arena throw him flowers, and one throws a hand grenade that explodes behind him. The ring is full of images of anima figures: a recumbent fertility goddess on the arena floor; a sculpted stone medallion of a Greek or Roman goddess, perhaps Athena, leaning against the base of the tower; a Byzantine Madonna in mosaic further up the wall of the tower; and other portraits of women in Renaissance and nineteenth-century dress—in short, a visual history of the anima figure in art. The task of Snaporaz is to climb the tower to find the last, the most perfect anima figure to take him to a final state of well-being as prefigured by the mandala. In the Jungian system, there can be no dearer wish in the collective unconscious, beyond the terrors of the unconscious. Snaporaz is looking for a figure like Jung's Mary to lead him to the final stage of wisdom. On top of the tower, in the square within the circle, Snaporaz discovers an ancient female servant (a female equivalent, perhaps, of the wise old man archetype) who prepares him for the final segment of the journey.

This segment takes place in a hot-air balloon in the shape of a giant woman. We have returned to the image of flying from Fellini's own dream notebooks, where the act of flying stood for both freedom and power. Snaporaz revels in both. He grips the cables that hold the passenger basket suspended from the balloon and hoists his feet in a joyful half somersault like a child on a jungle gym. He is removed from the torment of the feminist inquisition below and is flying away toward the kind of wisdom or harmonious state prefigured by the mandala. The female figure, comic in that she is, after all, a hot-air balloon, is a composite of the anima figures we have seen so far in this movie and in Fellini's works as a whole. Her large breasts and buttocks establish her as a nurturing, maternal woman; her bright red lipstick, high-heel shoes, bra top and garter belt, as the prostitute or the sexually "enticing" figure; and the halo around her head, her tiara, and her white veil, as the Virgin Mary and the bride. Moreover, her face is that of Donatella, the young lady who has served as Snaporaz's mediatrix, sometimes helpful and sometimes mocking, throughout earlier portions of the movie. Hence Snaporaz's joy. This is one figure who can fulfill all the roles. She is the appropriate one to transport him to the last stage of his spiritual journey.

This is not to be, however. The "real" Donatella, wearing the ski mask of a radical and carrying an automatic weapon shoots down the giant balloon. What are we to make of this state of affairs? The politically correct reading of the movie's ending would be that Snaporaz has been pulled out of his fantasy world by Donatella. Indeed she has destroyed the fantasy world in a most dramatic way. Snaporaz can now put such fantasies behind him and begin to get to know flesh-and-blood, autonomous, and complex women of the real world. There is much to support this reading. In the final scene of the movie, Snaporaz, awake from his dream, sits in his train car with a group of "real" women who have peopled his dream as fantasy figures—his wife, the lady on the train who started his fantasy, Donatella, and Donatella's female friend. If ever he wished to learn about the "real" equivalents to his fantasy figures, now would be the time. Further, the train pulls into a tunnel as it did at the beginning of the film, but this time we see light at the end of it as if there were the possibility of emerging into "real" daylight. On the other hand, there is a sly smile about Snaporaz's lips as he sits back to think about what has befallen him. The smile may say much. It is legitimate to wonder whether Snaporaz is not thinking, "The journey did not work this time, but maybe. . . ." To support such a reading, we might note that Snaporaz has broken the right lens of his glasses while dreaming but still has the left one intact. In one of the entries of the dream notebooks, Fellini has described a dream in which someone surgically removes his right eye; he comments that the loss is not serious, for he can depend now on his left eye, which is the one associated with fantasy.[68] It may be that Fellini is drawing on this folk belief to signal that Snaporaz's power of fantasizing is still alive and well. The ending of the film seems sufficiently open that we will have difficulty choosing between the two readings.

What we may agree on, however, is that Snaporaz's fall with the bullet-riddled balloon figure marks the end of Fellini's self-conscious and overt treatments of Jungian materials. It is no coincidence that in 1980, after completing *City of Women* Fellini gave up keeping his dream notebooks. His study of Jung seems to have ended at this point. Probably Fellini felt that he had carried his treatment of the Jungian journey as far as he was prepared to go. Indeed, this may be one reason for his bringing Snaporaz down at the point he does. To have Snaporaz go farther would be to force Fellini to show a final truth or to solve the "mystery within."[69] This, Fellini was not prepared to do and almost surely had no interest in doing. His initial attraction to Jung was that "Jung accompanies us to the door of the unknowable and lets us see and understand by ourselves." There is no reason to believe that Fellini ever intended to go beyond his mentor. To attempt to do so probably would have seemed false. Yet for the twenty years from 1960 to 1980 when he kept his notebooks and read Jung's works, Fellini seems to have found a vision and archetypes that helped shape his films. We might also agree that some earlier films, in the 1950s, demonstrated an anticipation of Jungian materials, and some of his films of the last years of his life, after *City of Women,* show a gradual, lingering falling away.

3

AUTOBIOGRAPHY, CHILDHOOD,
AND ADOLESCENCE

"I have invented myself entirely: a childhood, a personality, longings, dreams and memories, all in order to enable me to tell them."[1] This statement uttered by Federico Fellini in 1971 seems intended as a chide to critics and interviewers to pay more attention to the imaginative shaping in his films than to the so-called autobiographical "facts" from which several of his more interesting films take their beginning. Ironically, though, no statement he might have made could have been more near the center of modern debate on the genre of autobiography. Critics as diverse as the Russian formalist Boris Tomashevsky, the French poststructuralist Roland Barthes, and American genre critics Elizabeth Bruss, James Olney, and William Spengemann all would have nodded their heads sagely in affirmation had they been present when Fellini spoke.[2]

Modern criticism of autobiography has concerned itself far more with the interesting relationship of the author to the protagonist he creates than with the "factualness" of the work. "Factuality," indeed, has been called into question. An author may shape the way a "fact" is perceived by arranging the context around it, and, of course, the author is always putting forward his or her memory of the "fact," not the "fact" itself. For a work to be considered autobiography, we seem generally to want two things from it: a flesh-and-blood author who purports to be giving an account of his or her own life and events that can, to some extent, be verified with historical inquiry.

When these two elements are present, we may feel a particular kind of intimacy between author and audience that is imitated, but not quite duplicated, by other forms of first-person narrative. But modern critics have pointed out that we are usually willing to accept a certain amount of liberty with the events—the so-called "facts"—because our more profound interest lies with the real flesh-and-blood author and his or her projection of himself or herself, the protagonist, even if the protagonist is to some extent fictionalized.

One of the most interesting critics of autobiography, William Spengemann, describes two types of relationships between author and protagonist that are relevant to Fellini.[3] The first type of relationship he calls "historical self-recollection." Two models are St. Augustine and Dante. The teleological aim of *The Confessions of St. Augustine* and *La Vita Nuova* is to reconcile the autobiographer's past life with a present enlightened state of being, that is, to trace the path by which the autobiographer comes to be what he or she is at the time of writing. The writer's present state is the justification for the work. The second type of relationship Spengemann calls "philosophical self-exploration." Models are Rousseau and Wordsworth. The romantic assumption in Rousseau's *Confessions* and Wordsworth's *Prelude* is that the narrator in the present has fallen away from some enlightened state in the past. His or her movement now is backward. The author returns nostalgically to previous moments of his or her life to analyze them and to recapture something that may have been lost.

Both of these types of autobiographical tendencies seem to be at work in Fellini's autobiographical films, often at the same time. It would certainly be too much to claim that Fellini attained an "enlightened state." But he was a successful artist. Some or indeed many of the early autobiographical episodes in his films can be seen as moments in his growth toward becoming a filmmaker. The presence of the successful director may be said to give the episodes a defining goal to move toward in the future. Additionally, the return to some autobiographical events in the past may often seem to us an attempt to seek out and perhaps find again a capacity or an energy source that has decreased or changed. Perhaps Fellini himself would not have been consciously aware of such motivation. Yet it does seem inherent in the privileged status given to childhood and adolescence in his films as opposed to the relatively fitful, anxious states of the adult autobiographical personae.

There is more. In *I Vitelloni* and *Amarcord,* two of his best autobiographical films, Fellini goes beyond the depiction of a single protagonist to a more general group portrait. *Amarcord* becomes a general portrait of early adolescence, and *I Vitelloni,* one of late adolescence. In these films, Fellini is able to treat a range of aspects of adolescence that interest him. These movies are, then, about the Fellini protagonist and about adolescence in general. They are, in other words, a mixture of intimate confession and generalized portraiture. Indeed, if we range through Fellini's autobiographical films, taking scenes from them and rearranging them in chronological order, we could assemble a new movie that traces the Fellini protagonist from childhood to middle age and allows Fellini to comment broadly on general aspects of each successive stage.

The Legend

In "Literature and Biography," Boris Tomashevsky writes, "The biography that is useful to the literary historian is not the author's *curriculum vitae* or the investigator's account of his life. What the literary historian really needs is the biographical legend created by the author himself. Only such a legend is a *literary fact.*"[4] His statement amplifies Fellini's assertion that he has invented a self to use it as a basis for movies. With Fellini, we get a flesh-and-blood author who gives us a "legend" about himself and then makes movies from the legend. Indeed, the making up of the legend seems a necessary stage in the creative process for Fellini's autobiographical films.

The sources of the legend are interviews, autobiographical essays, and, of course, previous autobiographical films, for Fellini movies are, to some extent, self-referential. Particularly important to Fellini's creation of his version of his childhood are an interview, "Confesso Fellini," he gave to Camilla Cederno for *L'espresso-mese* in 1960[5] and an interview he made for Belgian television in 1962.[6] Both were given prior to the release of *8 ½* in 1963, a film that they inform. The fullest presentation of Fellini's version of his adolescence is his essay "Rimini, My Home Town," published first in 1967[7] and providing a basis for *Amarcord,* released in 1974. We must assume that Fellini's autobiographical legend is a mixture of fact and invention. Early in the process, the biographer Angelo Solmi undertook the difficult task of trying to separate the one from the other by seeking corroborative testimony about the major incidents of the legend and achieved only the kind of moderate success we might expect.[8] More recently, John Baxter undertook the challenge and has succeeded better in several notable instances.[9] The legend that deals with Fellini's childhood and adolescence, this mixture of fact and invention, is worth reviewing here, however, for it is the raw stuff of the scenes, sequences, and movies we consider in this chapter.

As Fellini makes clear in his essay on his hometown, Rimini, a small resort on the Adriatic, is the site of both his childhood and his adolescence. He was born there in 1920. Fellini has described it as a town with two distinct seasons. In the summer, tourists come to visit the beaches, the Roman ruins, and the medieval churches. In the winter, with the tourists gone and with cold drizzles and fogs in from the sea, Rimini becomes a quiet provincial town.

During his youth, Fellini was drawn to those things that stimulated his imagination and his capacity to fantasize. In "Rimini, My Home Town," he describes his discovery of an acting troupe at rehearsal of a Grand Guignol production in a theater next to a house where Fellini lived as a boy. One of the actors brought Fellini onto the stage. He comments: "I saw the gilded boxes, and, right over me, the belly of a railway engine hanging from the flies, among red, white, and yellow gels."[10] Two evenings later, his parents took him to the play, and he was even more entranced: "My mother says I never moved throughout the performance. The train came forward from the darkness, about to run over a woman tied to the tracks, until she was saved, and an enormous soft, heavy red curtain fell on her. My excitement lasted all night."[11] Fellini's first view of the circus struck him with as much or even more force. It was a traveling one directed by the clown Pierino. Fellini has commented on Pierino: "From that first moment, I was totally fascinated by the clown. For he embodies, in a fantastic character, all the irrational aspects of man, the instinctive part of him, the touch of rebellion against the established order which is in each of us."[12] In telling his legend of himself, Fellini has given various accounts of running away to this circus when he was approximately ten years old.[13] Fellini's mother, however, has adamantly denied to Solmi that any such incident ever took place.[14] The running away seems merely to have been a wish.

In his childhood, Fellini enjoyed putting on puppet shows, and at a somewhat older age, he was attracted by the fantasy world of the comic strips. He went frequently to the movies at the town's Fulgor Theater. And as an adolescent, his imagination was fired by the spectacle of summer dances at the town's resort hotel, the Grand: "On its terraces, curtained by thick rows of plants, the Ziegfeld Follies might have been taking place. We caught glimpses of barebacked women who looked marvellous to us, clasped in the arms of men in white dinner-jackets, a scented breeze brought us snatches of syncopated music, languid enough to make us feel faint."[15]

The legend emphasizes a certain distance between Fellini and his parents. The family was solidly in the middle class. His father was a salesman in groceries, preserves, confectionery, and coffee. He traveled in his job and was often away from home. Fellini has commented, "My father had an eye for women, and this led to many bitter quarrels between him and my mother."[16] His mother Fellini has described as "a good housewife who has had too much cause to worry over me," and she, in turn, has commented to an interviewer, "Federico and I have never had a talk. Oh, he's played tricks on me, and he's always made me laugh—we're good friends!—but I don't feel as if I really know him."[17] Fellini has described himself as a child who liked to draw attention to himself by means of staged "scenes." In the interview for Belgian television, he recounted that he used to crouch immobile for long periods on a high window sill in his home to puzzle the adults, and he claimed once to have stained his forehead with red ink and arranged himself at the foot of the stairs in a position designed to arouse alarm.[18]

Fellini obtained his education at the primary level from a school run by the nuns of San Vincenzo. For the next level, he claimed that he was sent to a small boarding school run by the Salesian Fathers at the nearby town of Fano. Fellini describes the school at Fano as a enormous building with long, dimly lit corridors.[19] Discipline, he said, was severe. Students were rapped on the hands and made to kneel on kernels of corn. Fellini has stated that the strong sense of guilt that he carries with him has come from his education at Fano. This story provided Fellini with a body of material he could put to good use in *8 ½,* but it is something of a fabrication. Baxter discovered that Fellini did not attend the school in Fano. His brother Riccardo did. As Baxter has put it, "Fellini simply co-opted [Riccardo's] experiences."[20] For his education at the levels of the *Ginnaseo* and *Liceo,* Fellini attended the public school Giulo Cesare on the Corso d'Augusto in Rimini. He speaks of this phase with good-natured affection. He describes a headmaster nicknamed Zeus as a man with "a foot as big as a Fiat 600, which he aimed at us children, giving kicks that could break your back,"[21] and he recalls, "We were the despair of the teachers, especially . . . the scripture teacher, whose life we certainly shortened."[22] At this stage, Fellini participated in the public activities of the Fascist youth groups—parades and ceremonies—as did the others of his age group. He insists, however, that he held himself back from commitment: "At Fascist meetings, I never had a complete uniform: I always lacked something—black shoes, grey-green shorts, the fez. This was a sort of lukewarm sabotage, to stop me looking wholly Fascist."[23]

Some of Fellini's time in the summer was spent at his grandmother's house in the small country town of Gambettola in the Romagna area. Fellini admired his grandmother. He says of her, "My grandmother always carried a cane and made the men jump with it; it was just like a cartoon film. The men were day labourers she employed to work the land, and she certainly kept them at it."[24] Gambettola, the town itself, was a place where gypsies and strange itinerant workers passed through, and these figures made an impact on Fellini. He remembers in particular the gelder of pigs who would appear suddenly in town each year wearing a black coat and an old-fashioned hat. According to the Fellini legend, the man once left pregnant a poor idiot girl, and it was said by the people of the town that the baby was the devil's child.[25]

Fellini claimed that he made the discovery of the existence of sex in his eighth year when he and a group of friends paid a prostitute to reveal herself to them on the beach. She was a prostitute who offered her services to fishermen and was known as "la Saraghina." Fellini has described her as "an unbelievable mountain of white—a kind of Moby-Dick that didn't scare me at all, even though I couldn't talk for at least fifteen minutes afterward."[26] As an adolescent, he was infatuated with "Gradisca" ("Please do"), the town vamp. She was the first to wear false eyelashes and the first to have a permanent wave in her hair. Her walk past the Cafe Commercio, in her black skirt, was an event eagerly awaited by the male customers of the cafe. Fellini explains her nickname as the result of an evening she once spent as a semi-official ambassador for the town to a prince who visited Rimini: She was said to have bade the prince, "Please do." Fellini also tells an anecdote of his approaching Gradisca in the movie theater:

> When I reached the seat next to her, I put out my hand. Her opulent thigh, up as far as her garter, felt like mortadella tied up with string. She didn't interfere, just went on looking at the screen, magnificent, silent. My hand went further, up to the white, soft flesh. At this point, Gradisca turned slowly round to me and said kindly: "What are you looking for?" I was unable to continue.[27]

Fellini has used this anecdote to great effect in *Amarcord*. Baxter, however, has discovered that the event, if it happened at all, happened to Fellini's good friend Titta Benzi, a boy more outgoing and aggressive than the relatively shy Fellini.[28] Again Fellini appropriated the material for his legend and put it to good use.

In contrast to these introductions to sex, Fellini's first love affair seems to have been polite and almost courtly. It involved Bianchina Sorianis, a girl two years younger who lived in the house across the street. "The first time I saw her," Fellini said, "she appeared at the window, or else—I can't remember—she was wearing her Fascist youth movement uniform, with fine heavy, already motherly, breasts."[29] Many years later, Bianchina told Solmi about the relationship: "Our greatest escapades consisted of a few romantic walks outside the Porta d'Augusto, a few bicycle rides—with myself on the crossbar whilst Federico pedalled around the outskirts of the town."[30] The love affair ended when Bianchina moved to Milan.

The legend is a streamlined one. Another filmmaker telling and inventing his roots would have stressed other elements if he had lived through Fellini's experiences. The legend itself reads like a Fellini movie, with each experience making a nicely fashioned sequence, complete with a final punch line, and revealing just a little bit more about the central character. The legend is too perfect. But its shaping is interesting. Fellini has selected essentially those elements that stimulated the imagination of a young artist. The incidents tend to be those that challenge, intrigue, or bedazzle the senses, or else they tend to stress the capacities of the young Fellini to respond to such stimuli. Furthermore, this engagement of the young Fellini with these elements is presented in the relatively safe, experimental territory of Rimini. To be sure, at least three potentially harsh elements intrude—Fascism, religious disaffection, and a certain distancing from the parents. These things are not swept under the carpet in the legend, but neither are they allowed to intrude too far. The central issue must be—the repetition is almost obsessive—the young person in a situation where he can extend his imaginative capacity.

Childhood

In Fellini's presentation of childhood, essentially three dramas unfold. The first involves the depiction of the child's sense of wonder at a show or a magical situation. The second, not unrelated, involves the presentation of the child's wonder before the mystery of sexuality. And, the third, more troubling, deals with his sense of distance from his parents. The first two clearly present portraits of a young artist, for they show the sensitivity and openness of the boy to incidents that stimulate his imagination. The last also might be considered to bear on the portrait of the artist in a covert way, if we accept the Freudian notion of artwork as a partial solution to neurosis, or, to put it another way, artistic creation as a means to force admiration from parents. "When we are children," Fellini has said in interview, "we are much more open to everything. We are not protected by the quality of the mind that we call rationality. We are more open in every sense, more open to be made to wonder, to be surprised, to be amazed, but also to be scared."[31] He continues, "I wanted [several years ago] to make a [film about] a big building in which different families live and of the relationships of all the little kids—two years old—and even smaller—and of the kinds of relationships between one floor and another. . . . [It would have been an attempt] to go inside of the craziness and fantasy of little human creatures, until the first day of school, until the first day when they lose . . . this capacity of naiveté, of ingenuity, of fantasy, and they become what we might call huddled or enclosed beings."

Although Fellini did not make his movie about the children in the large apartment house, he did, in at least two striking instances, try to show his autobiographical hero at this particular stage. One instance comes at the beginning of the movie *The Clowns*. The young protagonist is awakened by sounds he probably cannot comprehend: calls, creakings, and groanings. The sounds are those of a circus tent being raised, but he doesn't know that at the moment. The child goes to the window and looks out. A bonfire is flickering and casting shadows. We can make out the circus tent, but the young protagonist is apparently still puzzled. The next morning, dressed in a sailor suit (appropriate for exploration), the boy asks the maid what is happening. Her answer explains the event but at the same time adds to its fearfulness: "The circus is here. Be good or those gypsies will carry you away." The child visits the tent during the day and finds it a red, cavernous space with a network of ropes and curtains. The boy stands frozen—perhaps overwhelmed as Fellini claims to have been, in his legend, on going to the stage of the Grand Guignol production near his house. Later that night we see the acts of the circus, and we detect the back of the boy's head, from time to time, in the left foreground. He doesn't move: He sits frozen in a pose of alertness. Several of the acts seem directed at the boy. The barker for a pair of conjoined twins, for instance, speaks to him, "You see them, little boy? Aren't they nice?" Then the clowns take center stage and perform their routines. The boy begins now to cry, and his mother carries him out. The final shot shows the boy again in his bedroom in his nightgown at the window. In voice-over, Fellini narrates, "That evening ended badly. The clowns didn't make me laugh. No, they frightened me."

The other instance comes in *8 ½*. It is the Asa Nisi Masa sequence. The sequence is presented as a memory of the mature filmmaker Guido. Participating in a mind-reading act with the magician Maurice and the clairvoyant Maya, Guido thinks of the magic words "Asa Nisi Masa," discussed previously. This, in turn, reminds him of the night he learned the words. The event took place in his grandmother's farmhouse. In a flashback, we see the young Guido bathed in a wine vat with his young cousins and then tucked into bed by a loving and maternal nanny. He is in a room with several of his cousins, and as soon as the adults withdraw, a somewhat older girl tells him, "Guido, don't go to sleep tonight! It's the night the portrait's eyes move. You're not scared, are you? You have to be quiet! Uncle Agostino's eyes will look into a corner of the room, and the treasure will be there!"[32] As the girl chatters, we see the attentive young Guido in the left foreground of the frame, facing the portrait.

These two sequences have much in common. Both are given a kind of dreamlike status. The circus sequence is bracketed by bedroom scenes as if it could have been dreamed, and the part of the *8 ½* sequence that interests us here takes place in the bedroom with the lights out, within the musing reminiscence of the mature Guido. Furthermore, both sequences are also given a kind of magical status, such as we have discussed in chapter 2. The

8 ½ sequence is, of course, about a magic portrait, and we are led back to the memory by a magic act on the stage. But so, too, is the circus sequence enfolded in the notion of magic with the strange sounds in the night that lead the hero to a puzzling vision. These elements put frames around the moments and defamiliarize them. In both instances, the boy comes face to face with something that "scares" him and stimulates him at the same time. We might even say he comes face to face with mystery, if we mean by that an intimation that there are things he can't and won't be able to reduce to rational explanation and control. This is obvious enough with the magic picture, but it is also true of the clowns for Fellini. He has remarked, "A clown for a little boy is, yes, funny, but it is always a little bit monstrous. It is like a ghost, like something he recognizes as a phantom of his fear when he is alone in bed in his obscurity."[33] The similar positioning of the boy in the frame and the similar pose of stark rigid attention ought to suggest to us that the two experiences are similar. What is perhaps most striking in the two experiences, however, is the intensity of the boy's reaction. Most children, we might agree, are intrigued by clowns and magical portraits. But the young Fellini protagonist is more than intrigued; he is transfixed. In the boy's intensity, then, may lie the beginning of the portrait of the artist.

Much the same thing could be said of the next drama to be played out in Fellini's depiction of childhood, the child's discovery of the mystery of sex. This occurs in the Saraghina episode of *8 ½*. The young Guido is older here. He is now in private school, modeled on Riccardo's school in Fano, and is beginning to feel the weight of Catholicism. Throughout the sequence, he wears his uniform to remind us of these things. But he still has his curiosity and his sensitivity. At the conclusion of a soccer game in the school yard, a group of boys invites Guido to come with them to see Saraghina. Guido seems to know the invitation is illicit, for he looks around to see if anyone is observing him before running off with the boys. (He is, ironically enough, standing beneath the statue of a pope whose hand is raised in benediction.) There is no indication that any of the boys expects to have sexual relations with the huge prostitute who lives on the beach. Their purpose is simply to watch the sexual woman as she dances a rumba for them. This is infantile curiosity as opposed to adolescent wish. Saraghina is shot often in a manner that emphasizes her power. At one point, she looms over the camera as she bares her shoulders, and at another, in a shot discussed earlier in chapter 1, her enormous hips in the foreground dwarf the figure of Guido in the far distance watching her (see fig. 3.1). But not all the shots emphasize power. There is also a gracefulness about Saraghina that is revealed when she dances against diffused sunlight in a long shot and a genuine kindness to her when she notices Guido's uneasiness, invites him to dance with her, and picks him up as if he were her child. After Guido is caught by the priests, he is shamed in a variety of ways: He must stand before his mother who has been informed of Guido's transgression; he must wear the placard that reads "Shame"; and he must kneel on kernels of corn in penitence. At confession, Guido is told that Saraghina is the devil. Largely passive until now, Guido chooses to go back alone to see Saraghina again—this creature so powerful yet gentle, sexual, illicit, even called the devil. He finds her on a chair, looking out at the sea and singing a lullaby, with a veil over her shoulder that streams in the wind. The mystery is complete. She does not appear to be the devil. She no longer even seems frightening. How is he to understand her? Unable to, Guido falls to his knees as he had fallen to his knees earlier for penitence.

Saraghina's size and her mysteriousness embody adult sexuality as it might be perceived by a child. It is certainly possible to imagine that Saraghina would not have seemed as big nor as puzzling if Guido had encountered her when he was an adult. But given Guido's small size at the time and his lack of knowledge, she appears enormous to him and mysterious beyond comprehension. The movie, then, gives us Guido's subjective view of Saraghina. Thus we might expect that the encounter on the beach will be one of the most intense moments of his life. The older he becomes, the less awesome will be other encounters. The later encounters can never have about them the same mystery or the same force. Here it is important to reiterate the gentle qualities of Saraghina. She is not so frightening that she drives Guido away from sexuality. She is just frightening enough to make the boy fall to his knees and wave to her from a safe distance. Other filmmakers might emphasize other qualities in sexual encounters, but for Fellini, who seeks always moments of maximum feeling, his privileged moment is the first one, in which the contrasts are the greatest and the feelings the strongest. And again we might compare Guido waving to Saraghina with Guido staring at the magic portrait or the young Fellini protagonist watching the spectacle of the circus. In all these instances, the child is presented as one who responds intensely.

Fig. 3.1. Publicity still from *8 ½* showing Saraghina dancing on the beach for Guido and his young friends. Courtesy of Photofest.

The third drama that unfolds in the autobiographical films is less positive than the other two. This drama has to do with feelings of estrangement and guilt that the child feels toward his parents. The child is not as close to his parents as he would like to be and does not please them. There is the sense that the child would like to make things right, and it may be that in this sense lies the beginning of artistic ambition, for artistic success would be something the parents would have to accept and admire.

Particularly interesting is the tension between father and son. In *8 ½,* Guido dreams about meeting the ghost of his dead father at a cemetery. Guido, although played as an adult by Marcello Mastroianni, wears his schoolboy uniform and clearly stands next to his father as his little boy. The father even adjusts Guido's cape and pats his head at one point in the scene. The dialogue between the two males begins with a plea for communication from Guido, as he catches sight of the father moving among the tombstones.

"Pappa, wait," he cries. "Don't go away! We've talked so little to each other. Listen, Pappa! I had so many questions to ask you."[34] There follows then a series of conversational gambits on the father's part that serve, either intentionally or unintentionally, to show the son's inadequacy or lack of dutifulness. "Do you see how low the ceiling [of the tomb] is here?" the father complains. "I would have liked it higher. . . . Could you take care of it, Guido?" Then, when Guido's producer arrives to pay his respects, the father asks hopefully, "How is my son doing?" as all fathers have asked all employers of their offspring. But when he gets only a noncommittal shrug in response, he intones lugubriously to his son, "It is sad to realize that one has been so mistaken!" Clearly that Guido has not lived up to his father's expectations.

The fact that Guido dreams the encounter with his father is important. The father may not actually have maneuvered his son in the ways just described; rather Guido may have imagined him doing so. The memory of the father may have become a masochistic means for Guido to attack himself about his failures and his deviations from conventional moral standards and familial responsibilities. In short, Guido may have done what any contemporary child psychologist would expect him to do. He has "internalized" the father and made a conscience figure of him. What may be unusual here, though, is the extreme pain Guido feels over the lack of closeness between father and son and over his failure to meet the father's standards of behavior.

Two further instances of the tension between father and son may be worth considering here. They occur in *La Dolce Vita* and in a story Fellini wrote for the screen but did not film, *A Journey with Anita* (1957). In *La Dolce Vita* the father visits his son, the autobiographical protagonist Marcello, in Rome. (Both father and son are played by the same actors who play the roles also in *8 ½*, Annibale Ninchi and Marcello Mastroianni.) Marcello is now a successful journalist–feature writer, and he seems genuinely pleased to receive a visit from his father, perhaps hoping to be able to demonstrate his sophistication and achievement to him. At a nightclub where he takes his father, Marcello explains to his photographer assistant, Paparazzo, "When I was a little boy, my father was never home. He'd go away for a week, and he'd go away for twenty days. Yes, and it seemed he'd never come back. Oh, how my mother cried, how much she cried. Me—I'd see him only rarely and sometimes when he came back I wouldn't recognize him. How happy I was tonight to see him."[35] The possibility of a rapprochement between father and son seems good. However, at the nightclub, the father has a flirtatious encounter with a chorus-girl friend of Marcello and leaves with her despite Marcello's uneasiness over the turn of events. Later that night, when Marcello goes to the girl's apartment to retrieve his father, he discovers that the father has had a mild heart attack and wants to take the next train home. Not only does the rapprochement between father and son fail to take place, but the breach has surely widened. Marcello has now seen the way his father must have acted on his sales trips in the past, and the father, almost certainly realizing the poor figure he cuts in front of his son, wants only to creep away as soon as possible.

Rapprochement between father and son does occur in *A Journey with Anita,* but only after the death of the father. This story describes the return home of a successful writer, Guido, in his late thirties, from Rome to the small provincial town of Fano, to be at the bedside of his ill father. Guido travels with his mistress Anita, and at one point late in the story, he defines his relationship with his father for her:

> With sincerity and his usual bluntness, he tells her the long story of his relationship with his family. It is a story of a lack of understanding between father and son, begun in Guido's adolescence. Maybe it was like the usual lack of understanding between fathers and sons, but in the case of Guido and his father it was probably made more severe by the intensity of feeling on both sides. . . . When Guido was not quite seventeen, on bad terms with his family and fed up with life in a provincial town, he ran away, almost like a fugitive, to seek his fortune elsewhere.[36]

At the root of the problem was a battle of wills, with the father wanting his son to prepare for a conventional and respectable career in a town like Rimini and the son longing to pursue other, less conventional, more literary ambitions in the larger world.

The rapprochement comes after the father dies and the battle of wills ends. The son approaches the deathbed and, in effect, discovers a sense of continuity between his father and himself:

> At first, held back by an obscure fear, Guido contemplates his father from a distance. Then he moves forward, drawn by the calm, mysterious smile

fixed on his father's face as if a mask had fallen away and the man were revealing defenselessly now an intimate secret he had concealed all his life. All at once Guido has the strange sensation that he sees himself in the body of his father. The feeling of complete detachment or estrangement from his father that he has always felt in the past vanishes.[37]

From this moment on, Guido can make discoveries about his father's life without prejudice and accept the way the man was admired, even with his shortcomings, by the townspeople. "Everywhere [Guido] went," we are told, "he encountered old friends and acquaintances. All of them were genuinely saddened by his father's death. They said over and over like a refrain, 'He was so cheerful he made everyone feel good.'"[38] And Guido discovers the attractiveness of the life in the provincial town that his father had mapped out for him—an attractiveness that lies in the reassuring stability of the town's rituals and the sincerely expressed emotions of its citizens. It is too late for Guido to make over his life and return to his father's town, but his acceptance of the town's values is an extension and solidification of his act of "making peace" with his father.

The mother-son relationship in Fellini's autobiographical films mirrors the father-son relationship in some respects. In *A Journey with Anita,* we are told of the mother, "His mother has always been a woman of few words. She has always shown a great deal of restraint about her children and their private affairs, a restraint that could have been construed as indifference or inability to understand."[39] In this story, however, Guido becomes relatively close to his mother, because it is his task to comfort her in her grief and, as the man in the Italian household, to manage the affairs of the funeral. He is, it must be admitted, somewhat puzzled by the extent of his mother's grief for he lost husband.

> Without knowing the details, Guido has always been aware of a serious dissension between his mother and father involving the repeated, flagrant infidelities of the husband and the jealousy of the wife. Yet now all this seems blotted out in the memory of Guido's mother. . . . She describes the marriage in terms of eternal characteristics—births, domestic problems and joys, companionship, and reciprocal affection lasting all the life of both parties together. It is as if death had wiped out the dissension between them.[40]

But puzzled or not, he performs the role of dutiful son and stays with his mother through the loneliness of the first night after the father's death.

The mother's restraint or distance is much more evident in *8 ½*. She appears in the Saraghina episode after the priests have caught Guido and returned him to the school. The mother, in fact, constitutes part of Guido's punishment. He is made to face her, and when he begins to run to her, she stops him with an up-raised arm and declares melodramatically, "Oh heavens, what a disgrace. . . what a terrible blow!" There is more than a little hypocrisy in her performance. While she dabs at one of her eyes with a handkerchief, we notice that she takes in the impact of her performance on her audience with her other, very clear, dry eye. Later when Guido prepares to end his life in a fantasy, the mother reappears, not to voice concern but to raise her arm again and despair, "Guido, Guido, where are you running to, you naughty boy?" The mother, then, is restrained and, like the father, judgmental.

She also plays a part in the dream about the father's sepulcher in *8 ½*. She begins and ends the sequence. At the beginning, we see her polishing the glass window of the sepulcher, and at the end she says, perhaps asking for sympathy, "Guido, I do the best I can. What more can I do?" Guido goes to her to comfort and embrace her. The embrace, however, becomes a fierce, passionate kiss from which Guido struggles to remove himself. When he steps back he sees that his mother has become Luisa, his wife, who invites him to return home with her. The dream may tell us something of Guido's oedipal wishes (it is *his* dream, after all), but his linking of his mother with his wife tells us more about the mother as an internalized conscience figure, for throughout the movie, Luisa is one of Guido's harshest and most accurate critics insofar as his honesty with people is concerned. If Guido has married Luisa as a substitute for his mother, the quality he sought in Luisa would seem to have been the mother's harsh judgmental aspect.

There is, of course, a warm nurturing woman in Guido's childhood. It is not his mother, however; it is the nanny at his grandmother's farm who carries Guido from the wine vat where she bathes him to his warm bed and croons over him, "My little sweetheart, aren't you my little sweetheart?" We might argue that because Guido does obtain a certain amount of affection from his nanny, the judgmentalness and distance of his mother lose some of their sting. He does have his compensation. But it is probably more valid to argue that the mother suffers in Guido's eyes and ours in comparison with the ideal represented by the nurse.

Both the mother-son and the father-son relationships are striking in their deviation from ideal relationships. The Fellini hero, even as a mature man, seems to reflect on these deviations and, perhaps immaturely, brood about them. He seems to want to earn the approbation of his parents and a closeness to them, and it may well be that artistic achievement is the route he follows to this end. But this is, of course, a route he chooses, not they.

Early Adolescence: *Amarcord*

Writing at the turn of the century, the psychologist G. Stanley Hall, who is considered by many to have "invented" our modern conception of adolescence, stressed the importance of adolescence in the development of the range of mind of the adult. "It is certainly one of the marks of genius," he stated, "that the plasticity and spontaneity of adolescence persists into maturity."[41] For Erik Erikson, perhaps the most noted of post-Freudian psychologists to deal specifically with young people, adolescence is a period of "moratorium" between childhood and adulthood where the individual has time and opportunity to try many roles before settling into a lasting "identity."[42] And for the literary critic Patricia Meyer Spacks in *The Adolescent Idea,* it is a period of "exploration, becoming, growth, and pain."[43] These writers and virtually all other writers who take up the subject describe adolescence as a time for expanding the curiosity of childhood into the transactions of a more complicated social world that resembles but is more protected than the adult world.

Fellini exists well within this tradition. From a certain point of view, we might expect the child, not the adolescent, to be more important in the Fellini scheme of things. After all, Fellini has said of the relationship between the child and the artist: "The artist is someone . . . who remains, lives . . . between the conscious and the unconscious and in that vague territory he tries to operate the transformation of the unknown essence [into the known]. To be able to carry out this kind of operation, to create this magic operation, it is psychologically necessary for him to maintain some of the innocence of a child who is completely and deeply involved in the unconscious atmosphere."[44] But, in fact, Fellini has devoted more time to the adolescent in his films than he has to the child and may well have more interest in this formative stage. The Fellini adolescent is more inventive than the child: He creates situations and he fantasizes about them. In short, he brings his curiosity into a broader field of action.

Fellini is a celebrant of adolescence in his two movies *Amarcord* and *I Vitelloni*, let us make no mistake about that, but he seems almost a sheepish one, as if a little embarrassed by such a romantic stance. In an interview with Valerio Riva on *Amarcord*, Fellini has stressed that the "blocked" adolescent qualities of the adults in the film have, in a sense, permitted the Fascists to take power, for the adults are all too willing to cede responsibility and accept dependency.[45] However, the adolescent qualities of the boys of the film, who take up much of the screen time, seem more positively presented, since their qualities are unarguably right for their age. With *I Vitelloni*, a similar dialectic occurs. On the surface, the film is a denunciation of the overage boys who shamelessly exploit their parents and relatives who support them, pursue immediate gratification for themselves, and selfishly disregard the pain they may cause others. On the surface, the movie is a homily about the importance of growing up and accepting responsibility. But a subtext shows us the joy and inventiveness in the lifestyles of the *vitelloni*, and these qualities, in comparison with the relatively joyless and routine aspects of the adult lives we see in the film, force us to raise the subtext to the level of dominant statement before the film ends.

Before proceeding, we need a clear sense of the normal qualities of adolescence. A 1973 study by Gisela Konopka and a team of psychologists at the University of Minnesota, under the auspices of the Department of Health, Education, and Welfare, supplies just such a composite listing. (The study is contemporaneous to *Amarcord*.) The Konopka group defines adolescence, generally speaking, as the period from the onset of puberty to the completion of bone growth and then goes on to list five key elements in adolescence and some of their emotional results.[46] Many of these elements and emotional results are used, with varying emphases, by Fellini. The elements are as follows:

1. *The experience of physical sexual maturity.* The maturing of the sex organs creates in adolescents a great wonderment about themselves. Biologically, this is a new experience, but perhaps more important are the increased societal expectations that surround the event. The sense of wonderment about this change suggests there may be other new areas of exploration

ahead. *Enormous mood swings* from exhilaration to depression may be related to the physiological upheaval in the body of the adolescent.

2. *The experience of withdrawal from benevolent adult protection.* Because of growth in size, the adolescent is asked to assume, or begins to assume on his or her own, a position of less dependency on the parents and other parental figures such as teachers. Related to this is the "generational conflict" that takes place as the adolescent may "rebel" against the control of parental figures. In addition, the removal of benevolent, adult protection may contribute to a sense of *emotional vulnerability* on the part of the individual and a need for a *peer group* and *older role models* to supplant the function of the parents.

3. *Consciousness of the self in interaction.* The development of a sense of self begins in childhood, but a sense of the self in interaction with others or as perceived by others becomes acute in adolescence.

4. *Reevaluation of values and ideas.* The adolescent reexamines values and ideas that he or she has either accepted or rejected earlier on the basis of authority figures telling him or her to do so. Coupled with this is the adolescent's need to be *argumentative* as a means for testing out ideas verbally.

5. *The necessity of experimentation.* The adolescent needs to try things for himself or herself physically and emotionally. He or she needs to find the limits of what he or she can do, and therefore *risk taking* is an important element of this stage. So, too, is *fantasizing,* which is a form of mentally trying out possibilities.

To this list we should add the notion of *play* as a subheading under experimentation, perhaps equal to fantasizing, since the kind of acting out of roles in the games Fellini adolescents play is surely a means for them to try out new possibilities of behavior. And certainly we must make some cultural distinctions. The Konopka group studied American adolescents of the post–World War II era; in *Amarcord,* Fellini treats Italian adolescents before the war. The Italian parents of *Amarcord* seem far less willing to surrender "adult protection" than the Konopka group suggests happens with American families. Also the Catholic church is a force in the Italian adolescent's life. It is another form of authority for him or her to deal with.

In *Amarcord,* sexual experimentation is one of the chief concerns of the adolescent Titta, who is modeled to some extent on Fellini and to some extent on his friend Titta Benzi.[47] We see Titta's curiosity about sex in his confession scene. When the priest asks if he "commits impure acts," if he "touches himself," Titta thinks to himself, "Can you avoid touching yourself when you see [Lucia] at the tobacconist's, stacked as she is, when she says, 'Export brand'? And the math teacher who looks just like a lion! Madonna . . . how can you avoid touching yourself when she looks at you that way!"[48] He tells the priest that Volpina, a beautiful but retarded "wild" woman, has kissed him with her tongue and asks incredulously, "Did you know people kissed that way?" This kind of intense curiosity is the basis for many of the risks Titta takes and for many of his fantasies.

The most obvious risks involve Titta's approaches to the woman tobacconist Lucia and to Gradisca. Both of his approaches end in humiliation for Titta, and, in both cases, it may be said he "luxuriates" in the emotion. With the tobacconist, Titta makes his approach at night, as Lucia is closing her shop. He tells her he wants to buy a Nazionale cigarette, offers to help her move a large sack, and then boasts he can pick her up. Everything about the tobacconist bespeaks power. Lucia is an enormous woman. When she closes the metal safety door of the shop, it echoes with a loud thud, and as she walks toward Titta, her footsteps, exaggerated on the sound track, crack like gun shots. Lucia's stature is magnified even more by her gigantic shadow cast on the wall above the seated boy. She bares her breasts and moves the boy's face from one to the other. "Don't blow! Suck! . . . You have to suck, you idiot!" At one point, Titta's head becomes lodged comically between the two large breasts. He gasps, "I can't breathe!" She pushes Titta back from her and dismisses him by giving him the Nazionale he said he came in for. And further humiliation awaits Titta. He cannot lift the heavy safety door and must wait for the tobacconist to do it for him before he can leave the shop. There is something archetypal about the situation of the boy locked in the confined space with the large, forceful, sexual creature. The experience is more than an attempt to find out what the sex act consists of: It is also a moment of daring when the boy takes on the challenge of adult power as well as adult sexuality and then suffers adolescent humiliation.

Similar cycles of risk and humiliation in sexual experimentation occur with Titta's pursuit of Gradisca. She is the "withheld object of desire" of most of the males in town. The boys walk behind her and her sisters when they take their evening *passeggiata,* with the adolescent named "Naso" (Nose) imitating her feminine hip swing. They are desperate to attract her attention. Titta, in particular, is smitten with a crush. In the opening sequence, the festival of the burning of the witch of winter, Titta stares at Gradisca as she pauses to straighten the seams of her stockings and then stammers a denial that gives him away completely: "I wasn't looking!" He can hardly believe his good fortune, then, when he finds himself virtually alone with Gradisca in the balcony of the movie theatre. She is watching her idol, Gary Cooper, on the screen. As Fellini claims falsely to have done in his legend, Titta moves closer and closer until he is next to her, and then he attempts to put his hand on her thigh. Haughty and not particularly alarmed, she asks, "Looking for something?" Titta's comment in voice-over narration completes the cycle: "I felt like an asshole. I could have jumped in the harbor."

In fantasy and play, however, Titta imagines himself masterful and sophisticated, the very opposite of how he is in his performances with Lucia and Gradisca. At one point, he pictures himself the winner of the thousand-mile auto car race. He drives his bright red car up to a cheering crowd, which consists entirely of women, beckons Gradisca to join him in the driver's seat, and with a roar, speeds off with her. He has captured his "prize" and has an audience to witness his moment of triumph. He wears the accoutrements of a flying ace: goggles and a streaming scarf. His gestures are quick and sure: a brief smile, a slight nod to the seat beside him, and a practiced adjustment of the goggles. For once, in a moment of sexual encounter, Titta thinks of himself as in control.

Mastery and sophistication are the qualities Titta and his friends admire in Titta's Uncle Lallo and White Feather, the two "Latin lovers," who wear their crisp, white summer jackets well, dance gracefully on the terrace of the Grand Hotel with attractive female tourists, and end their evening with a conquest of one sort or another. "It's always a pushover with Germans. She's really fallen for me. And to prove it, she even offered me posterior intimacy," brags Lallo to the bandleader. Titta and his friends watch the proceedings on the terrace from behind the arbor. "My uncle dances very well!" Titta exclaims. When the headwaiter chases the boys away, they stay away only for a moment and then creep back. The show is too good to miss. Later in the film, during the fall when the tourist season is over, the boys return to the deserted hotel and imagine themselves old enough to take on the roles of sophisticated adults. Naso plays a make-believe sax; Ciccio, the chubby boy of the group, pretends to play a violin; and Titta dances with an imaginary German tourist, whispering "Danke schoen" to her. Again Titta wants very much to think of himself as having the kind of control that as an adolescent he really can't have.

It would be appealing to argue that the Fellini protagonist, Titta, displays the most intense feelings of humiliation in his scenes with women and compensates for these feelings with the most glorious or intricate fantasies and make-believe roles of any of the boys in the group. The argument would be appealing because it would set Titta off from the others in the group as the one who will grow up to be the artist. This argument, however, simply won't work. As we have already seen, many of the boys take part in the make-believe dance on the steps of the Grand Hotel. Naso, furthermore, demonstrates a rather good ability in other scenes to imitate Gradisca, which, in turn, implies a certain inventive ability. And then there is the chubby Ciccio. He goes through the same cycle of humiliation in real life and wish-fulfilling mastery in fantasy as does Titta. At a gathering for a class photograph in front of the school, Ciccio tries to attract the attention of his tall, pretty classmate Aldina, who may resemble the Bianchina of the legend, but she spurns him and looks up at a handsome, aristocratic, privately taught student sitting in one of the windows above them. Later we learn that Aldina has torn up a poem Ciccio has written for her. And at the thousand-mile race, when Ciccio calls to her the name of the driving team in the lead, she, sitting comfortably on a balcony with the aristocratic student, responds that "we" already know the team in the lead. Ciccio's immediate response is to imagine himself winning the race and pulling up his car beneath Aldina's balcony to give her a brusque arm gesture and a raspberry. His most extravagant fantasy, however, comes earlier at the Fascist rally. Ciccio dreams that the rally turns into a wedding ceremony for Aldina and him, with the gigantic head of Mussolini fashioned from red and white carnations pronouncing them man and wife. Ciccio's fantasies are no less intriguing than Titta's. If anything, the dream of the wedding surpasses Titta's imaginings. What we have to conclude, then, is that the ability to fantasize is a quality that Fellini prizes among adolescents in general. The artist will, of course, be the one who can hold on to the quality.

Another quality that Fellini cherishes in the adolescents of *Amarcord* is their delight in challenging authority. The school sequence seems to be included in the film mainly to provide the boys opportunity to demonstrate their rebelliousness and, in some cases, the inventiveness that goes along with it. In science class, the teacher holds up a stone on a string and asks the class to identify the object. The answer he expects is a pendulum. The answer he receives from Ciccio, however, is, "an elephant's testicle." In Greek class, when the teacher tries to get a student to pronounce the word *emarpzamen,* the student produces a string of raspberries that delight the class and unsettle the teacher. In the class on religious studies, when the priest Don Balosa discusses the Holy Trinity and closes his eyes in rapture, the boys tiptoe from the classroom one by one until only a few dutiful students are left. Of course, there is scatological humor. The most elaborate prank takes place in math class. The teacher, the statuesque "lioness," who wears a tight sweater, calls to the blackboard a neat, well-groomed student with hollow eyes. As the well-groomed student and the teacher concentrate on a math problem, a tall, skinny, and somewhat scruffy student, Gigliozzi, pieces together sections of rolled-up maps and pisses through this long "pipeline," leaving a puddle of urine near the feet of the well-groomed student for the math teacher to discover. In school, then, the boys seem to be relentless in their rebelliousness, but there are, we should note, limits beyond which they won't go. They won't tempt the anger of their fiery headmaster Zeus, and they won't, unfortunately, challenge the authority of the Fascist leaders. These waters, they seem to sense, are too deep.

The adolescents perform primarily for each other within the peer group. Fellini has called such performances exhibitionism.[49] When we learn that Titta has pissed from the balcony of the movie theater onto the hat of a certain Signor Biondi, we probably assume he did so to gain the admiration of his friends. And when Naso imitates Gradisca, he does so certainly with the hope of getting appreciative chuckles from his friends. But there is more involved than exhibitionism. The boys enjoy the same things, and they support each other in these interests. Together they trail Gradisca, set off firecrackers at the festival, watch the dances on the veranda of the Grand Hotel, masturbate in a parked car in a garage, stare, fascinated, at the count's peacock as he spreads his tail in the snow, and, of course, defy the authority of the teachers. Their camaraderie in these things is one of the most attractive parts of the movie. We can see that it is a kind of emotional buttress against the various humiliations they suffer when acting singly. Further, the kind of friendly competition involved in the boys seeing who can amaze the group the most is additional encouragement to each member to use his imagination to the fullest. Delighting the peer group could be considered, of course, an unsophisticated version of the later filmmaker trying to astound his movie audience.

The generational conflict, that continuing theme in Fellini films, has its place also in *Amarcord*. The father, Aurelio, however, bears little relationship to Fellini's father; he is modeled more on Titta Benzi's father. Aurelio is a bricklayer, not a salesman, and he is never far from home and an active role in running the affairs of the family. Aurelio is also a comic stereotype of the provincial, authoritarian father who explodes like a volcano at the actions of his mischievous children.[50] His wife Miranda also bears little relationship to the somewhat distant mother Fellini has reported his own mother to have been. Miranda is the stereotype of the overly dramatic Italian mother who will lock herself in the bathroom and wait to be coaxed out or who will threaten to poison the family with strychnine in their soup for wrongs she will never explain. Her mission is to pamper her younger brother Lallo and defend her two sons from Aurelio's wrath.

The conflict between generations is, at first, played for comedy. The early sequence on the family dinner is a classic in its use of the comic formula of having stereotypical characters face a crisis situation in type. The father and son, for example, wage a continuing battle of adult authority versus adolescent self-assertion. Titta will reach for a piece of chicken on the serving plate. The father will block his reach with a brandished fork and serve the boy himself. Then when the father leaves the room to speak with a caller at the door, the son will quickly grab a second piece. The major crisis of the scene involves the father's discovery (from the caller) that Titta has pissed from the balcony of the movie theater. During the comic chase that ensues, the father yells to his wife, "You have to tell me who fathered this piece of shit! At his age, I'd been working three years," and the son, not very diplomatically, prompts him further in the speech, which must be all too familiar to Titta, "And you gave all the money to grandma."

As the movie progresses, however, the portrait of the family grows gentler and more attractive. We see a certain capacity for kindness in the family as a group when they organize an outing for Aurelio's brother Teo from the asylum where he stays. Also we see a gentleness in Aurelio when he puts his coat around the shoulders of Miranda in the *Rex* sequence, and we witness concern and gentleness in Miranda when she waits for Aurelio to return from his inquisition by the Fascists and then helps her husband wash the excrement from his body after the Fascists have force-fed him castor oil. For much of the movie, however, these things seem lost on Titta, wrapped up as he is in his own concerns. When Titta comes out of his room to find his father washing off the excrement, he can only hold his nose and tell his father, "What a stink!" And when Miranda tries to tell her son about her courtship by Aurelio in response to a question from Titta as he lies ill in bed, he can only murmur his self-absorbed complaints about the tobacconist and his rejection by her.

There is room, then, for growth in Titta in terms of learning to see beyond his own adolescent self-interests and understanding others outside his generation. A certain amount of this kind of growth does occur toward the end of the movie. The first sign appears when Titta and his father visit the gravely ill Miranda in the hospital. Titta begins a cheerful litany of charges about his father's unfairness to him, but his voice gradually runs down and the scene ends with Titta listening attentively as his mother tells him, "He is tired, poor man, when he gets home. You shouldn't answer back. You're grown up now." Then when Titta learns of his mother's death, he goes to her room alone and cries. Later, after the funeral procession, he sees that his father's grief is similar to his own. He watches his father sitting alone, his head down, at the kitchen table, that hub of family life earlier. Without speaking, Titta goes out to stare at the sea. He seems to understand the father's need to be alone. There is an unspoken sympathy from the son for the father. This is not to say that Titta has grown up completely. *Amarcord* is not a coming-of-age film. In the last scene of the film, Titta is tipsy and giggly at the wedding of Gradisca. But it is to say that he has moved further toward late adolescence.

Late Adolescence: *I Vitelloni*

The five heroes of *I Vitelloni*—Fausto, Alberto, Leopoldo, Riccardo, and Moraldo—are in a period at the end of adolescence and prior to adulthood. They have finished their schooling but have not gone on to a university or to a profession. They are in a moratorium period where they can, theoretically, weigh possibilities and try out future roles, as Erikson has suggested.

In fact, the five boys are, for the most part, holding on to their adolescence with all their might. They appear to be in their mid- to late twenties, and at one point, Fausto claims to have reached his thirtieth year. They have been able to hold out against adulthood as long as they have because parents or relatives support them. There is middle-class affectation involved here. They are being permitted to live like young princes (i.e., without responsibilities) for a certain period of their lives. But there is also condemnation. Their nickname *vitelloni* is usually translated as "lazy good-for-nothings." (Literally, the word means large, overgrown, milk-fed calves raised to provide veal.) Fellini's official stance in the movie, as I suggested earlier, is to condemn the *vitelloni* for their irresponsibility and their foolish pursuit of amusement or unrealistic attainments. But the film's subtext, its most interesting part, is the counterdemonstration that their lifestyles contain much that is lively and attractive, especially in comparison with what we see of adult life in the film. This point has been made emphatically by Suzanne Budgen in her 1966 monograph on Fellini. "In a sense," writes Budgen, "the *vitelloni* are right not to want to settle down. Whatever Fellini may have been aiming at, what he has in fact shown is the unnaturalness of living by the clock, tied to an uncongenial occupation, merely in order to survive."[51] In short, the overage adolescents have qualities that Fellini values. The fact that time is running out on the period of late adolescence in which the qualities are nurtured gives the movie its poignancy.

First we must consider the various kinds of irresponsibility the *vitelloni* exhibit and the opportunities to grow up that they ignore. Then we can examine the various kinds of qualities that flourish in their adolescent world and see how the appeal of the qualities takes over the movie.

Fausto is described as "the spiritual leader" of the group by the film's narrator (Fellini himself). The narrative about Fausto provides the central thread that holds the movie together. He is an adolescent fantasy figure, the "Latin lover" who lives to make conquests, and he is one who wishes to maintain *la bella figura,* that is, he wishes to look stylish at whatever he does. We follow him in his relationship with Sandra, who becomes his wife early in the film, and in his relationship with Moraldo, who is both Sandra's brother and a *vitellone.* In the course of the movie, Fausto has four potential "learning experiences." Each involves a "conquest" or an "attempted conquest" on Fausto's part. Each causes a kind of unhappiness for Sandra, and three of the four force Moraldo to choose between his loyalty to his fellow *vitelloni* and some other standard behavior such as loyalty to family or obeisance to law. In all four situations, Fausto could learn the social lesson that his pursuit of self-gratification can cause pain and consternation to those close to him and that he needs to weigh these costs against any pleasure he is able to secure. He could gain, in short, an adult sense of responsibility.

The first potential "learning experience" is Sandra's pregnancy. Her condition comes to light after she faints at the beauty contest where she is named Miss Siren of 1953. Fausto sizes up the situation and attempts to slip away. At Fausto's home later, Moraldo announces the pregnancy, and Fausto, in response, proclaims his love for Moraldo's sister and states his need to go to Milan to find a job. Fausto may or may not believe what he tells Moraldo. He tells so many glib lies so earnestly in the course of the movie that it is quite possible he has learned to deceive even himself. More important, though, is the nature of the lie. Fausto's lies always have about them a childish quality. They are always designed to put off present unpleasantness to a future time and to win sympathy for himself. Fausto's attempt to leave town is finally blocked not by Moraldo but by Fausto's father, who forces his son to accept responsibility for the situation and to marry Sandra.

The second experience involves Fausto's pursuit of a seductive, older woman who sits next to him in a movie theater. Fausto had come to the theater with Sandra for a night out after a successful day at his new job. The older woman asks Fausto for a light for her cigarette, permits a certain amount of foot touching, and then departs. The temptation is too much for Fausto. He pursues the woman, kisses her, and wins the promise that she will meet him again in the future. When Fausto returns to the movie theater, he finds Sandra outside waiting for him forlornly. He tells her the lie that makes everything all right, "I'll always be beside you." Again, he may believe what he tells her at the time he says it. But he is contrite as a child is contrite: for the moment and after the cookie has been eaten.

The third potential learning experience for Fausto comes during his attempt to begin an affair with the wife of his boss. Shortly after Fausto's return from the honeymoon, Sandra's father arranged for Fausto to work as a clerk in a store where religious articles are sold. Fausto serves as an assistant to the store's owner and the owner's wife. Predictably, he is bored, and this boredom may well be a factor in his attempt to begin an affair with the wife. At the Carnival ball, he sees her in a strapless gown and becomes aware of her as a sexually desirable "object," perhaps for the first time. The next day, he approaches her again and kisses her on the neck. Fausto's attempt at further seduction, however, is interrupted by the owner's return. The owner takes in what has happened. He invites Fausto to the couple's apartment above the shop that evening to celebrate the couple's fifteenth anniversary, and there, after a brief speech, the owner fires Fausto. The speech, a kind of homily on married love, could provide an occasion for Fausto to learn something about a serious commitment between two adults. However, the homily, of course, passes over Fausto's head. Later, at the pool hall frequented by the *vitelloni,* he tells Moraldo the comfortable, self-serving lie: He has been fired because he resisted the wife's advances.

The fourth potential learning experience is his final fall. Fausto makes love to a showgirl in the traveling troupe that comes to town. On the way home that night, a dour Moraldo tells Fausto, "Wipe off your face. You're full of lipstick." Fausto does so and then repeats the wiping in front of the mirror of his bedroom. Sandra, who is lying in bed and still awake, sees what he does, and the next morning, without leaving any word, she takes her child and departs from the home. A worried Fausto and the *vitelloni* look for her throughout the day. In the course of the search, Fausto and Moraldo confront each other, and Fausto makes the romantic declaration, "If she doesn't come back, I'll kill myself." But Moraldo now has had enough of Fausto's declarations and responds, "You? You won't kill yourself. You're a coward."[52] The response could also serve as part of an education for Fausto. It is the kind of straight talk he received earlier from the shop owner, but now the straight talk comes from one inside his group. There is little to suggest, however, that Fausto benefits from the moment. As we learned in chapter 1, Fausto does find Sandra in the home of his father and does receive an appropriate spanking from his father for the grief he has brought Sandra. If he promises Sandra tearfully, "You make me feel so awful, Sandra. I'll never do it again," we have to remind ourselves he has told the pleasing lie several times earlier. The true solution, as we saw in chapter 1, lies in the fact that Sandra at last sees her husband clearly and is now prepared to play the role of the stern parent to Fausto's delayed adolescent.

In a similar fashion, Leopoldo and Alberto go through experiences in which their make-believe worlds are punctured, and they have to take a long, cold look at themselves. The experiences could provide the kind of shock that might allow each to grow, but as with Fausto, such does not prove to be the case.

Leopoldo is the group "artist." He dreams of being a famous playwright. This is his fantasy, and in the final analysis, it doesn't differ much from Titta's fantasy of being a race car driver in *Amarcord*. To give Leopoldo credit, however, he does seem to have actually finished a manuscript. It is a tragedy concerning the unhappy love of Roberto and Frida. The ridiculousness of the play and of Leopoldo's dream of being a great playwright is made clear in the sequence in which he asks for approval from the has-been actor Sergio Natali, who comes to town with the traveling show mentioned earlier. We get to see a portion of Natali's performance as Leopoldo and the *vitelloni* sit in his audience. The performance is shamelessly melodramatic and patriotic. Our reaction, very likely, is that the approval of one such as Natali will not count for a great deal in the world of serious dramatic production. But while we may see these things, Leopoldo is blind to everything except the notion that his moment of recognition is near. What follows is cruel. Fellini allows Leopoldo's expectations to mount. Natali promises to contact a great actress for the part of Frida in Leopoldo's drama and to summon Leopoldo to Milan in the near future. Leopoldo reads his play aloud to Natali in a restaurant, and then, because the *vitelloni* and the chorus girls are making too much noise, Natali and Leopoldo walk outside. Natali invites Leopoldo to come with him on the beach toward the deserted pier, and at last Leopoldo sees the real source of Natali's interest in him. Leopoldo's manuscript is no more to Natali than a means to a homosexual liaison. The sequence is cruel, because the punishment Leopoldo receives, the disappointment, seems much more severe than the crime of foolish pretentiousness he has committed. Unlike Fausto, Leopoldo doesn't really hurt anyone other than himself (if we discount the two aunts who support him but whom we never see). The shattering of his fantasy, however, could serve as a useful moment of development for him. As with Fausto, though, there is no evidence that Leopoldo grows up.

Alberto is the group clown. He is the most playful and the most inventive. He is also the most shameless in the way he exploits his sister for money. The sister, who works at a secretarial job, is the chief wage earner of the family and in this sense is the "man" of the house, not Alberto. One morning,

Alberto visits her at work and asks for money. He has a deal in the works, he tells her, and he promises to pay her back. The sister gives Alberto money, perhaps to get rid of him before he can jeopardize her job, and then listens resignedly as Riccardo calls to Alberto and tells him about a "sure winner" at the trotting races in Bologna. Moreover, Alberto is totally insensitive to his sister's feelings or rights. Later, after Alberto has discovered his sister on the beach with a married but separated man, he bleats at her, "I don't want to be made a fool of by my friends because of you." When she rejects his attempts as a brother to order her to stop seeing the man, he tries to force guilt on her: "If you make mama cry. . . ." But when the crisis point arrives and the mother is discovered crying in the bedroom with the sister, Alberto is too intent on putting together his costume as a woman for the Carnival ball to take much account of the situation. After the ball, the sister confronts Alberto and tells him she is leaving home. The moment is ripe for Alberto to rise to the challenge and become now the "man" of the house, despite the costume dress he is ironically wearing. After his sister drives off, Alberto climbs to his apartment and seeks to comfort his mother. "We don't need anybody," he declares, "I'll get a job." But Alberto delivers his lines draped over the arms of a soft chair, his costume dress still on, inert except for a dangling foot that twitches momentarily. When his mother asks if he has actually found a job, he moans, "No!"

Fausto, Leopoldo, and Alberto, then, are classic cases of delayed adolescence. Fausto lives for the sexual chase, a combination of sexual experimentation and risk taking. Leopoldo nurses his impossible fantasy. Alberto cannot give up play. Yet if we look at the adult world that awaits them, we can sympathize with their hesitancy to grow up. The shop owner works a tedious routine, and his marriage to his wife, with all its commitment on both sides, is more a relationship of security than of excitement. Alberto's sister works long hours and seems to find scant enjoyment. Even her departure with her lover is an occasion more for tears than for happiness. In short, the adult world in this movie is singularly without joy, and joy is the quality the *vitelloni* seem best qualified to nurture and most eager to hang on to.

The *vitelloni* have the gift of being able to invent situations that amuse each other. The return of Fausto from Rome after his honeymoon with Sandra is a good example. He knows he will be the center of attention, and he comes prepared with a portable record player and a mambo record. Probably, he has been practicing his steps, too, in advance. Yet there is also a quality of spontaneity to the dance in the street he performs for his friends, and when Alberto joins him, Fausto demonstrates the steps and then moves smoothly into a dance for two. In the sunshine of the street, with smiling friends around them, Fausto and Alberto create a moment of energy and joy. By the same token, when the *vitelloni* discover a tin can in the street, they convert it to a soccer ball and commence a spirited soccer game, much to the delight of everyone involved. And then, without the tin can, they link arms and dance as a kind of chorus line through the streets of the town late at night. The dance is obviously a ritual activity for them. We see them do it twice. More importantly, they dance five abreast with the kind of synchronization that can come only from constant repetition. It is their dance of camaraderie.

If Fausto is the "spiritual leader" in the sense he is the boldest and most successful with women, Alberto would have to be the master of revels. With his inexhaustible spirit of playfulness, he invents situations that amuse the group. One of his chief ploys is to single someone out to make fun of for the amusement of his audience. His victims, however, are almost always tough enough to absorb his mockeries and in some cases return them with interest. The sad-faced waiter Antonio, for example, is a favorite target for Alberto. In the opening sequence, we see Alberto down his drink on the veranda of the resort hotel and then dash off with the rest of the crowd in the midst of the sudden storm, eluding Antonio's presentation of the bill. Later, at the pool room, we see him summon Antonio to the table as if for an order and then chide Antonio for standing in the way of a pool shot. Antonio bears it all with an impassive face. He remains a challenge for one such as Alberto. Toward the end of the movie, as the group searches for Sandra, Alberto rises in the car and gives a dramatic arm gesture to a group of workers repairing the road. He is affecting the role of the young nobleman, perhaps. He pays for the gesture and for his other harassments in the film, however, when the car stalls and he is put to flight. To be sure, Alberto is more than a little old for such antics. But he does make his friends laugh. He is a natural clown who has to seek out the comic possibilities of almost any situation and inject liveliness into it.

Alberto's finest moment is the Carnival ball, before it ends so disastrously for him. Alberto's impersonation of a woman is his most extended piece of play. He is utterly immersed in his role and plays it faithfully throughout the ball. Alberto's preparations are elaborate. Before the ball, he applies his make-up and practices his feminine gestures before the mirror. He sends his dress back to the seamstress for more padding and models the hat he discovers in his mother's trunk in a number of different ways to find the most becoming angle. Alberto is a caricature of a flapper. His figure is too broad, and his legs too bandy. However, he knows what he looks like and overplays his part appropriately at the ball itself: He dances cheek-to-cheek with a giant papier-mâché clown's head. With this dance, Alberto raises the level of his performance one more notch toward circus performance. Alberto thus is the real artist of the group. There is more imagination and more theater in his performance than in anything we hear from Leopoldo's manuscript.

Another appeal of the *vitelloni* lies in the support the group gives to its members. When a member of the group needs help, the *vitelloni* will usually rally to his aid, and when a member has something to celebrate, the group will contribute to the festivities. Most dutiful, of course, is Moraldo. After the Carnival ball, Moraldo insists on seeing the drunken Alberto to his house, despite the protestations of the pretty girl who has decided to end the evening with Moraldo. "It's Alberto, he's a friend of mine," Moraldo says simply. When Sandra runs away, Riccardo gets his father's car and drives Fausto, Alberto, and Leopoldo to the wet nurse's house in search of her. Leopoldo gathers his friends around him when he goes to meet Natali, hopefully to share his good fortune but also perhaps to cheer him if Natali were to reject his manuscript. The group turns out in full force for Fausto's wedding. Riccardo sings. Alberto manages the picture taking in an overly zealous manner. All see the couple off on their train to Rome.

Of course, the group support has its limits. The group must, after all, amuse itself. Alberto is the most irreverent. He doubles over with laughter when he sees the chastened Fausto after the "spiritual leader" has been informed by his father that he must marry Sandra; he leads the mock excitement of the group over the religious figures in the window of the store where Fausto works; and he guffaws loudly with the *vitelloni* and the chorus girls when they overhear some of the lines Leopoldo reads to Natali. Furthermore, the interest span of the group is relatively brief. After paying a certain amount of attention to Leopoldo's reading of his play, the interest of the *vitelloni* shifts quickly to the chorus girls when they burst into the room. And although the *vitelloni* want to help Fausto find his runaway wife, they can't be expected not to inquire what the wet nurse is serving for lunch or debating whether a bird call they hear is that of a lark or a robin.

Nevertheless the bonds of the group are strong. Moraldo is the only one who is able to break them. He is the character most nearly modeled on Fellini—the one who broke away from life in the provinces. Moraldo is presented from the start as more detached than the others. When we first see him, he is sitting on a wall of the veranda, apart from the group, musing on the beauty of the approaching thunderstorm. During the mambo in the street, he is detached enough to ask Sandra whether she is happy while all the rest are absorbed in Fausto's performance. And when the *vitelloni* try to charm and amuse the chorus girls, he sits so quietly that one of the girls feels she must ruffle his hair and draw him into the conversation. There is, then, something of the observer about Moraldo. It is this detached quality that allows him to see things from a larger point of view than the group's; at the same time he enjoys the joyful play, the inventive imagination, and mutual support that the group offers.

In Fellini's depiction of the delayed adolescents, we rarely find them discussing or arguing over ideas of any substance. Argue they do, but they usually argue over matters such as the best place to honeymoon, Rome or Africa, and the best person to go off with, Esther Williams or the redhead from the beach the previous summer. If there is any example of the Konopka group's fourth attribute, the reevaluation of values, it comes only from Moraldo, and it comes quietly, without external debate. He holds back from Fausto's invitation to run away and tries to hang back from Fausto's scheme to steal a statue from the shop owner who fired Fausto. Finally, he reminds Fausto of his responsibilities to Sandra after his friend's fling with the chorus girl and then denounces him after Sandra runs off. We have to assume that a part of Moraldo's detachment stems from his mulling over the pros and cons of the values of the group. He holds off on his judgment for most of the length of the movie, but when it comes, it is a denunciation of Fausto's pursuit of immediate gratification with little regard to consequences.

Although Moraldo dares to break away from the group, he does not, however, join the adults. His solution is to take the train in search of another alternative, one that presumably would allow him to retain the best of his adolescent world and couple it with a more responsible, more disciplined adult attitude. In this, as we have seen in chapter 1, he is perhaps influenced by the young boy he meets and becomes friends with. The boy skips through the streets (not unlike the *vitelloni*) and looks at the skies and wonders about them (not unlike Moraldo), but he accepts his job at the railway station as a normal part of his life and is careful to show up on time at the station. The boy looks like a younger version of Moraldo. Paradoxically, he may signal to Moraldo a future role Moraldo may grow into.

Potentially, Moraldo's dream, "If I could just get out of town. . . ," could be no better than Leopoldo's dream of finding recognition through his manuscript. But Moraldo's dream does seem to be more firmly based in reality. He has outgrown the irresponsibility of the adolescent group, and the provincial town offers nothing that would enable him to achieve a life with the best qualities of the *vitelloni* preserved. He simply wishes to move on to the next stage. For those familiar with the Fellini legend, the next stage will, of course, involve an artistic career in Rome. Moraldo's artistic bent is, of course, not as well established as that of Alberto or Leopoldo. Yet there are indications of a fanciful nature in him when he muses on the thunderstorm, and there are a watchfulness and a discipline in him that the others simply don't have—enough to suggest, at least barely, the seeds of an artistic career. But Moraldo, like Fellini when he left Rimini, does not know his goal. He has simply every adolescent's aim: to grow and become. And he is willing to take a risk to do so.

It should come as no surprise to us that Fellini affords privileged status to childhood and adolescence in his autobiographical films. He finds in them qualities he wants to celebrate. In chapter 1, we saw that Fellini's style of excess seeks to convince us of a reality too vast and too mysterious to be contained within a frame or a closed narrative, and in chapter 2, we recognized that Jung's intellectual system gave Fellini a framework and some materials with which to play out this notion. Now we may add that his autobiographical sequences and autobiographical films give him specific situations to work with.

Fellini's method is to create a legend about himself and choose materials from the legend to film. The legend is, in the final analysis, a series of stories, generally well crafted through various tellings, that takes considerable liberties with the facts of Fellini's life but that is well designed to show us certain qualities. With childhood, as we have discovered, Fellini emphasizes the child's sense of wonder at a show, a performance, or a piece of magic and at the mysteriousness of sex, with its power, gentleness, and illicitness. Further, Fellini emphasizes the child's anguish over estrangement from his or her parents. All these situations are emotionally intense and mysterious beyond the child's comprehension. The child is usually passive, astounded before these moments. With adolescence, however, Fellini presents a more proactive hero. The Fellini adolescent still likes to witness a good show, but now he also tries to put one on himself, as Titta and his friends do on the hotel veranda and as the *vitelloni* do at the Carnival ball. The Fellini adolescent likes to play, but his sense of play is usually directed at putting on a performance either for himself or, more often, for his peer group. At the same time, the Fellini adolescent now attempts to enter the arena of sex rather than observe it from the outside. Woefully inexperienced, he is almost always a figure of fun whether he be Titta in the movie theater with Gradisca or Fausto in perhaps the same movie theater with the beautiful lady who signals her availability. If the result of the adolescent's forays is usually failure—ignominious failure, at that—the situation is no less strong. The adolescent is indeed engaged now in a mystery he cannot master. He is almost literally grappling with it. Additionally, the various revolts of the Fellini adolescent against parents and teachers are surely the stuff of comedy. Yet, in the context of earlier childhood estrangement, the struggles of the Fellini adolescent can be seen as a kind of fighting back, perhaps a prerequisite for some sort of parity between adolescent and adult and eventually a prerequisite for reconciliation.

Fellini's motives seem twofold. His re-creation of childhood and adolescence in his autobiographical films brings about a return to what Spengemann has called an "enlightened state in the past" in his definition of "philosophical self-exploration." Fellini recreates a state of high emotional intensity that his adult figures seem often to have lost in their personal lives. This is a touching of base with the "plasticity and spontaneity" of mind, as Hall put it, which may have a nourishing effect for the adult who remembers. But also the examination of childhood and adolescence may be seen as part of a forward drive to the "present enlightened state" of the filmmaker, as in Spengemann's mode of "self-recollection." Childhood and adolescence must end. *Amarcord* hints at this. *I Vitelloni* insists on it. However, Fellini will not accept an adult state that does not carry along with it some of the elements of play and wonder from childhood and adolescence.

4

AUTOBIOGRAPHY AND
FELLINI'S PORTRAIT OF THE ARTIST

When Federico Fellini moved to Rome in January 1938, he described the experience as a new beginning: "Rome became my home as soon as I saw it. I was born that moment. That was my *real* birthday. . . . When I had just arrived and didn't know people or how I would earn my way or what my life would be, I was not afraid or lonely. I wasn't afraid, not just because I was young, but because Rome was magic for me."[1] This view of the city, as Luchino Visconti has pointed out, is essentially that of the naive young man newly arrived from the provinces.[2] Fellini looked on Rome as Nick Carraway looked on New York City at the opening of *The Great Gatsby.* It was a place of many possibilities to choose among, a place of enormous, almost furious energy, and even, on occasions, a place of breathtaking sophistication. Vast dreams could be realized there. But there were risks as well. Without the support systems of the small town, the city was a place where one could fail badly and disappear from sight. In short, Rome was a testing ground where a young person could prove himself or herself. For Fellini's autobiographical protagonist, Rome is the place where he feels the exhilaration of choice, decides on a career as a creative artist, and, most important, finds the resolve to stay the course.

The first section of this chapter, then, will deal with Fellini's version of *la vie bohème*—the young man in Rome trying to choose his career. For Fellini, finding a career and becoming an adult are one and the same thing.

The second section will take up the career itself—Fellini's portrait of the artist as film director. The first section will involve the kind of autobiography we called "philosophical self-exploration" in chapter 3, where the author returns to an earlier stage of his career and revels in the energy of that stage. The second section will be "historical self-recollection," where the author demonstrates the teleological end toward which the series of autobiographical films has been moving, the justification for the whole of the autobiographical pattern discussed in the previous chapter.

La Vie Bohème

The biographical "legend" for Fellini's early days in Rome is presented in his essays "Via Veneto: Dolce Vita" (1962) and "Sweet Beginnings" (1962) and in interviews, especially with Charlotte Chandler, for whom he elaborates on material introduced in these two essays. In "Via Veneto: Dolce Vita," Fellini describes his situation in Rome in 1938 when he arrived. The portrait is that of the struggling young adult looking to find his way.

> Rome as I knew it then was a tiny casbah of furnished rooms around the main station, with a jumbled population of frightened immigrants, prostitutes, confidence tricksters, and Chinamen selling ties. The fact that it was close to the station gave me a feeling of home, made me feel less far from Rimini. If things go wrong, a voice inside me kept saying, the train's there. I was tall and thin, I wore white canvas shoes and wandered about the sleazy pizza-bars and neon restaurants, trying not to let the holes in my trousers show.[3]

Fellini captures here the mixture of excitement and fear he must have felt as a young man setting out in life. What he does not state is that, as biographer John Baxter discovered, Fellini was accompanied to Rome by his mother and younger sister.[4] The mother set up a home on Via Albalonga in the southeast part of Rome and looked after her son for about a year before returning to Rimini with the sister. At this point an aunt found Fellini a place in a boardinghouse, and he was, at last, the kind of young man on his own whom he describes in the passage above.

In "Via Veneto: Dolce Vita," Fellini describes a variety of activities he pursued during his early days in the city. He tells of working as a caricaturist with his friend Rinaldo Geleng and failing ignominiously at an attempt to paint an advertisement on a storefront window for money. He recounts landing a job that lasted about three years with the satiric magazine *Marc' Aurelio.* (Baxter notes that Fellini published some seven hundred pieces with the magazine.[5]) At the same time, we may add to the material in the essay, Fellini did some interviewing of stars and celebrities for the small fan magazine *Cinemagazzino* and, in 1940, made his first trip to Cinecittà, the gigantic film studios built by Mussolini in 1937, where Fellini interviewed the handsome leading man Osvaldo Valentini.[6] Fellini also interviewed, on another occasion, the vaudeville comedian Aldo Fabrizi and spent long evenings later discussing with this new friend the backstage stories of performing troupes, material Fellini put to good use in his first film *Variety Lights* (1950). A column Fellini wrote on a young married couple for *Marc' Aurelio* was converted to a radio show, *The Adventures of the Newlyweds Cico and Pallina,* in 1940, and the work he did for the radio, in turn, led to various jobs as a comic sketch writer in films. Looking back on this period, Fellini has told Chandler that he thought his career might lie in journalism: "Perhaps as a journalist I could uncover great stories, and I would have a byline. That was my highest aspiration, since I had no idea where my destiny was taking me, except that I felt very early it was to Rome."[7]

In retrospect, Fellini's movement into movies seems a gradual thing—from magazine work to radio writing to screenplay collaboration. But this is perhaps not dramatic enough for the legend. In "Sweet Beginnings," Fellini represents himself as having been "discovered" by the great Neorealist film director Roberto Rossellini. Fellini relates that Rossellini visited him when Fellini was drawing caricatures in a souvenir store called the Funny Face Shop shortly after the end of World War II. There is, of course, something about this story that echoes other discovery myths about stars being found in unlikely places. The director wanted to enlist Fellini's aid in signing Aldo Fabrizi to act in a short film about a priest who was executed by the Germans for his work in the underground. As negotiations went on later, with Fellini as a participant, the short film subject was combined with the idea of treating Roman children who defied the Germans also. As Fellini puts it, "And so in a week working in my kitchen because it was the only warm place in the house, we got up this script, which was *Rome, Open City.*"[8] One could hardly make a more auspicious beginning than this. Unfortunately, Fellini did not film this part of his legend, but he did film one almost as good in *Intervista,* with his portrait of the Fellini protagonist's first day at Cinecittà.

Fellini has told Chandler that when he arrived in Rome he was a virgin.[9] In the anonymity of the city, he sought out the houses of prostitution to gain sexual experience. As we discussed in the previous chapter, the element of sin made the pursuit of sex all the more intriguing for him. Yet as he recounts the legend version of his first night with a prostitute to Chandler, the experience is not Felliniesque in the sense of bigger than life, and it is certainly nonthreatening. It is, in fact, quite gentle.

> I was lucky, because just as I entered a house, there was only one girl free. She was young. Only a little older than me. She seemed to be a nice girl, just sitting there waiting for a friend. I was that friend.
>
> She was not wearing black lace or red satin, as worn by the other women I saw later. Such an obvious mode would probably have frightened me away. I think at that moment I was so nervous that almost anything could have frightened me away.[10]

What might interest us here, as we take up Fellini's portrait of the fledgling artist, is that Fellini was looking for sexual experience but not the kind of love that might lead to marriage or to an entanglement that might distract him from his goal, even though he did not know, prior to his involvement with *Rome, Open City,* exactly what that goal was. Fellini comments, "I was anxious to go beyond myself, but I wanted to do it without commitment."[11] The idea of keeping oneself open for the possibilities of the career is very much a part of Fellini's portrait of the young artist. He or she must be one who stays the course.

The film *Fellini's Roma* (1972) gives us Fellini's fictional version of the autobiographical protagonist's entry into the city. The movie is, in part, about coming of age, and the sequence dealing with the young man's arrival is one of the best sections in Fellini's rendering of autobiographical materials, for it captures well the mixture of hopeful anticipation, uncertainty, and, finally, relaxation that comes to the young person at the point of entry into adult life. Picking up from the ending of *I Vitelloni,* Fellini has his hero descend from the train Moraldo had boarded to leave Rimini. The young man wears the "white canvas shoes" of Fellini's legend and a white summer suit. Moreover, he is tall and thin, with a mop of bushy black hair, looking much like Fellini in photographs from his late teens and early twenties. The young man is the embodiment of hopefulness and curiosity as he looks at the new world around him. Fellini puts us in the character's place with a number of subjective tracking shots while the young man makes his way through the crowded station and while he rides the tram to his pensione on Via Albalonga. There are, of course, no mother and sister accompanying him. The fictional hero is very much on his own.

At the pensione, the young man's sense of being overcome with new elements intensifies. As the maid leads him through a labyrinth of rooms, the young man meets the other boarders. In chapter 1, we have discussed this section of *Fellini's Roma* as a "gallery of grotesques." Suffice it to say here that the hero must attempt to take in and deal with about a dozen new people, several of whom seem intent on telling the young man who wants to become a journalist something of his or her life story. Granted that the protagonist, if we see him as a continuation of Moraldo of *I Vitelloni,* has known his share of colorful characters back in Rimini; the point in this sequence is that the young man is propelled through a series of introductions to new "colorful characters" in the course of his first fifteen minutes in the pensione.

The young man's first day in Rome concludes with an evening meal at a sidewalk restaurant on the Via Albalonga. The scene is one of those spectacles for which Fellini is noted, as discussed in chapter 1. The spectacle is put on by the people of the neighborhood as they eat. The people are both the performers and the audience. There is a couple who dramatize their love relationship, with the "macho" male, who wears a dark shirt, gold chain, and hairnet, calling down his dramatically made-up and sulky girlfriend, the "countess," from her balcony to join him at the table. There is a little girl who stands on her chair and sings a rhyming off-color ditty, apparently taught her by her father, who feigns embarrassment. And finally there is the spectacle of the food itself, which is presented to the customers and to the camera with equal flourish. We see pasta, snails, and half a head of a lamb with the eye in the center of the serving. The young man, still dressed formally in his white summer suit, is seated by the hostess with a family from the neighborhood. He is polite and correct in his manners. The mother of the family complains of heartburn and advises the young man on choices for his dinner. At the end of the evening, the young man has taken his suitcoat off and put his elbows on the table. He is relaxed. He smiles. He is now at home in Rome.

The young man's sexual initiation is depicted also in *Fellini's Roma*. Fellini shows us three different brothels of the late 1930s, ranging from an inexpensive "meat market" to a luxurious house of prostitution. In each place, the voice-over narrator tells us, the customers can hear the sound of church bells, reminding them of the sinfulness of what they are doing and perhaps adding an element of risk. In two of the establishments, the women parade back and forth or circle before the male customers, challenging them to "be man enough" to go upstairs with the prostitutes. There is, then, much of the aspect of danger to the sexual event, as we have come to expect in chapters 2 and 3. But when the Fellini protagonist makes his selection of "the most beautiful girl" in the luxury brothel early in the morning, the sexual event seems to evolve gently, very much as Fellini described his own initiation to Chandler. To be sure, the prostitute is dressed as the Empress Messalina[12] and glares at the young man from beneath dark eyebrows and heavily made-up eyelids while they ride the elevator upstairs. But in the room, after sex, as the woman puts her costume back on and the young man rests in the bed, the two chat pleasantly together.[13] As on his first day in Rome, the young man ends the sequence happy and relaxed. A second threshold has been passed.

The discovery of the young man's avocation, however, comes in a later film, *Intervista* (1987). This later movie is a metafilm that takes place on several levels of reality, in two different time periods, with several narrative threads.[14] The section that concerns us here is Fellini's rendering of his initial visit to the studios of Cinecittà in 1940. For him, the studios have always been a place of magic and a place for creativity. In interview with Giovanni Grazzini, for example, he has described Theater 5, his soundstage within the Cinecittà compound, as "a space to fill up, a world to create" that he has always approached with "total emotion, trembling, ecstasy."[15] His purpose in this section of *Intervista* is to allow his autobiographical protagonist, now called Sergio Rubini,[16] to discover the magic of filmmaking and to find his goal to drive toward—that of filmmaking.

Rubini travels by tram to the studio as a young journalist to interview a movie star for a fan magazine but is soon dazzled by the activity he finds inside the walls of the studio. He discovers a wedding scene being shot.

Confetti flower petals are blown by a wind machine, the director up on a tower shouts directions to the actors, and, in the scene, a bride and a groom separated by a great distance run excitedly toward each other's arms. As a novice to a movie set, Rubini finds himself in the sightlines of the camera and must drop flat on the ground so that the action can go on around him. He is, however, so charmed by what he has seen that he wishes to participate in some manner. He shouts for the assistants to bring the director the pear that he requested, and Rubini compliments the actress on the job she has done. He is smitten by the excitement of moviemaking.

His enchantment deepens when he interviews the movie star Katia Denis in her trailer while she prepares for her role as a maharani in a romantic epic set in India. Fellini has changed his legend here, giving Rubini a female star rather than a male to interview.[17] Clearly, Fellini wishes to emphasize in a playful way the "seductiveness" of the protagonist's situation.[18] Rubini first sees Katia in nude silhouette through the frosted window of her shower. To make Rubini even more self-conscious than he would otherwise have been, Fellini gives the young man a pimple on the tip of his nose. When Katia emerges from the shower, she dons a robe, eats her lunch by dramatically sucking out the interior of a raw egg, and lies back in her make-up chair. Rubini's questions are feeble: "How can a person be so beautiful?" and "When did you first think of being an actress?" However, citing the need to "help a beginner," the diva, so childish and so difficult in many ways, comes to the young journalist's rescue with material he will be able to use. His seduction is complete.

The final scene of this section is, however, a debacle. We follow Rubini to the set of Katia Denis's movie, and everything that could go wrong does go wrong. From a position on a high crane, the *Intervista* director yells at Katia for being three hours late, and the producer lectures Rubini on the cost overruns of motion picture making. As the scene in the Indian epic proceeds, Katia climbs stairs, wiggling her hips as the director orders, to a pagoda on top of a huge artificial elephant, while her husband, the maharajah, sings. But after Katia settles on her perch, she announces she cannot continue, and she must be mollified by an assistant. As the action resumes, the mechanical trunk of one of the other, smaller constructed elephants on the set falls off. In a rage, the director descends from the crane, insults the producer for not getting him real elephants, and then knocks over a line of the artificial elephants.[19] Rubini, who has watched the events with growing consternation, tiptoes to the door of the soundstage and leaves. He acts somewhat like a child who does not want to be present when the adults are behaving badly. But Rubini does not run off in alarm or fear. He has, after all, had a fine show, and that is enough for his first day in the studios. He has seen how films are made, the high energy and the drama of the profession, the myriad problems to be solved, and the whole has been intermingled with a variety of pretty women who are kind to him. We know that he will return. The youthful protagonist has discovered the place where he wants to be.

The fullest depiction of Fellini's early days in Rome is *Moraldo in the City,* an unproduced screenplay written by Fellini and his collaborators Tullio Pinelli and Ennio Flaiano in 1954. The screenplay was intended as a sequel to *I Vitelloni,* but Fellini put it aside to make *Il Bidone.*[20] Fellini has stated in a letter to me, "I can tell you that the screenplay draws on my memories of my first years in Rome. Pinelli and Flaiano helped with the construction of the tale, but the episodes, the characters, and the situations were more or less those I experienced and encountered in those distant years."[21] The story constitutes then, Fellini's version of *la vie bohème.* It pictures the things the "struggling artist" must do to survive in the city before his career is launched, the various high jinks and cons he performs with his fellow aspiring artists, and the pitfalls or distractions he must avoid if he is to succeed. Above all, the story is about the need for the aspiring young artist to stay the course. This last point is perhaps an obvious one, but for Fellini it is nevertheless a crucial one. Fellini is, of course, not alone in emphasizing the need for the aspiring artist to have a high level of commitment to his or her quest. Virtually all writers on the subject of creativity make the same point. For example, Margaret A. Boden offers this argument about Mozart in her book *The Creative Mind:* "His motivational commitment was exceptional. . . . People who live a normal life, filled with diverse activities largely prompted by other people's priorities (employers, spouses, babies, parents, friends), cannot devote themselves wholeheartedly to the creative quest. One of the ways in which Mozart was special is that he chose to do so."[22] Fellini's Moraldo is not yet Boden's Mozart, but in the course of the screenplay, he does gain something of Mozart's resolve.

Moraldo comes to Rome to seek a literary career. Unlike Sergio Rubini of *Intervista,* this protagonist has not yet found his goal. At the outset of the story, Fellini tells us, "Three months ago he left his hometown and his gang of friends to come to Rome in search of decent work and above all in search of himself. He feels the need for a purpose in life different from that of others his age. But what purpose?"[23] A journalist named Blasi has offered to launch Moraldo as a reporter, but in the first scene of the story Moraldo goes to the paper's office and learns that his sample article has been rejected by the editor. This is the first in a series of rejections or failures Moraldo encounters. He will, for example, fail at an attempt to paint advertisements on storefront windows; he will also fail at selling memorandum books to store owners; he will be rebuffed by a buxom cashier he tries to date; and he will be evicted from his pensione. Moraldo's task in the story is to persevere in his search.

Aiding Moraldo are three roguish characters who live by their wits and teach Moraldo much about resilience. The first is the poet and travel writer Gattone.[24] Fallen on bad times, Gattone supports himself haphazardly by writing children's fables for the newspaper that has rejected Moraldo. Gattone moves in with Moraldo in his pensione and shows his young protégé how to use a suitcase key to open the landlady's cupboard to get food. The second rogue is the painter Lange, a crony of Gattone. It is Lange who suggests to Moraldo that they paint advertisements on storefronts.[25] Moraldo, however, botches his assignment, as did Fellini in his legend, when Moraldo gets the characters and lettering out of proportion and then smears the whole of the painted scene when he tries to rub the oil paint away without using turpentine. And the third rogue is Ricci, a man who sells goods on consignment out of the back seat of his car. Ricci takes an interest in Moraldo and tries to make a salesman of the young man, but Moraldo finds it nearly impossible to sell the memorandum books Ricci wants him to convince wary store owners to buy. Virtually all of the schemes of the three rogue friends fail. The rogues, however, refuse to be defeated. On the next day, they always promise, they will think of something better, and then all will be well. They are, thus, demonstrations to Moraldo of human resiliency, and they are embodiments of human good spirits. It is unlikely that Moraldo could have survived the challenges of the city without the emotional support of these resourceful men.

Two havens of security are offered to Moraldo. They, however, constitute dangers to Moraldo's quest for his career. The havens involve women who can provide clearly structured relationships, with implied sets of values, that could replace the family structure in Moraldo's previous life back in the provincial hometown. The problem with these relationships is that they would cut down or eliminate the kinds of free choice of career that Moraldo has come to Rome to discover.

The first danger is presented by Signora Contini, a wealthy lady in her thirties with literary pretensions.[26] She has begun a journal called *Life and Letters*, and she offers to publish an article by Moraldo in a future issue. What she really wants, however, is to take Moraldo for a lover. When Moraldo needs money to pay the bill at the Savoy, he asks for a loan from Signora Contini and then moves in with her. She can provide Moraldo with a firm financial base and a foothold in the literary world. In return, however, she requires that Moraldo remain completely dependent. In fact, at a literary cocktail party she throws, she acts more like an overbearing parent than a lover. The guests understand the situation perfectly. One guest refers to Moraldo as "Signora Contini's boy." Because the older woman's control becomes so oppressive at the party, it is relatively easy for Moraldo to break off the relationship and walk away with his friend Gattone after the party ends.

It is more difficult for him to free himself from the second woman with whom he has a relationship. This is a pretty young lady Moraldo first encounters during his unsuccessful attempt to paint the store window. Her name is Andreina.[27] Fellini describes her as "a beautiful, well-groomed girl." After Moraldo meets her again later by chance in a restaurant, a relationship begins between the two, and she and Moraldo become lovers. Unlike Signora Contini, Andreina makes a strong emotional commitment to Moraldo. The danger that Andreina poses is that the kind of middle-class life Moraldo would share with her would be severely limiting, consisting of Sunday dinners followed by a nap or a radio program, a home resembling those of her parents and his, and a job in a government bureaucracy with little for Moraldo to do but wait out the day. After a morning working in such a job, Moraldo breaks off his engagement to Andreina. He realizes that life with her would offer "serene, peaceful, and sweet things." It would not, however, offer the kinds of challenges he came to the city to test himself against, and it would divert him from his search for his calling.

Probably the severest blow Moraldo must overcome is the death of Gattone. Of Moraldo's three male friends, Gattone offers the most support, and his loss is therefore extremely painful for Moraldo. Gattone dies of acute alcoholism in the hospital for indigent people on Isola Tibertina. In particular, Moraldo is struck by the terrible loneliness of the situation, for Gattone dies without any family members around him. And, most important, the death reveals to Moraldo the vulnerability of even the most resourceful and resilient of men. At this moment of despair for Moraldo, his father comes for a visit and extends to Moraldo an invitation to return home. With great difficulty, Moraldo finds the strength not to accept, and then, on an early morning walk, surrounded by a variety of people—a girl who gives him a smile, a boy on a bicycle whistling a tune, a pair of young lovers—Moraldo feels his spirits begin to rise. He recognizes again the possibilities before him.[28]

Moraldo does not achieve a breakthrough in this screenplay. There is no deus ex machina named Roberto Rossellini who offers him the chance to collaborate on *Rome, Open City* as in the Fellini legend, and there is no trip to Cinecittà as in the legend and *Intervista*. We may, however, conclude that Moraldo's will has been thoroughly tested and that he has decided to continue his quest for a career. This may, in fact, be the main point of most versions of *la vie bohème*—to test the will of the struggling young artist.

A mirror opposite to Moraldo is the protagonist Marcello in *La Dolce Vita*. This movie was conceived by Fellini, Pinelli, and Flaiano as an updated revision of *Moraldo in the City* set in the Rome of twenty years later. Hollis Alpert describes the collaboration:

> [Fellini] met with Pinelli and Flaiano to consider a new approach to the Moraldo story: make him a man in his mid-thirties who was still in Rome after those intervening years . . . . He would have become a journalist, they decided, of the sort that went after gossip and sensation, the kind who would frequent the Via Veneto. They gave him a problem: the struggle between his instincts to be a serious writer and the necessities of his daily work.[29]

Although the hero's surname is changed to Marcello, his family name remains that of Moraldo and Sergio, Rubini. Moreover, the problem that Fellini and his collaborators give Marcello is not radically different from Moraldo's problem. At issue is whether Marcello can hold to his artistic goal to be a writer of serious books. The principal distraction from the goal, as life with Signora Contini and with Andreina were potential distractions in the earlier story, is his newspaper career, which leads him toward stressing the scandalous or the contrived event. Of course, things are a bit more complicated here. Marcello could write thoughtfully and honestly about some of the events he covers for the newspaper—events such as a false miracle staged by two children and the suicide of Marcello's friend, the intellectual Steiner. There is, in other words, a middle ground between "literature" and "tabloid press" that Marcello could follow if he chose. Indeed, Steiner points this out to Marcello when he praises an article written by Marcello as "clear" and "convincing." For Marcello, however, the goal is to finish the book that he has promised to write, and in trying to pursue this goal, whether it is a realistic goal or not, he fails to stay the course. He becomes, therefore, Fellini's version of the artist manqué.

The need to get back to writing his book becomes apparent to Marcello when he attends a cocktail party in Steiner's apartment.[30] Anna, one of the guests, greets him on his arrival with the question, "Have you finished your book, yes or no?" Marcello avoids answering and goes on to another subject. Later, Marcello tells a poet, Iris, that he admires her work, that he has thought of writing poems himself a few years earlier, and that he is now "doing work [he] dislikes." Caught up in the midst of a group of people who actually bring their works to fruition, Marcello confesses to Steiner,

> I should change my environment, I should change so many things. . . . You know, your home is a real sanctuary. Your children, your wife, your friends—they are all wonderful. Your books, too . . . I'm wasting my time. Will I ever accomplish anything? Once, I had ambition, but . . . perhaps I'm losing it, forgetting everything.[31]

The confession, of course, has a whining, self-pitying cast to it. It is the statement of someone accustomed to making excuses. There is ample evidence that Fellini was not at all like Marcello. Indeed, Fellini seems to have been someone who went from film project to film project with almost a compulsive haste. However, there must have been something in Fellini that allowed him or even forced him to see his opposite, a kind of shadow figure—someone who represented his worst fear, the would-be writer without drive. Within *La Dolce Vita*, however, Steiner takes Marcello's statement at face value and tries to help him.[32] He states,

Marcello, I can only be your friend, and it's almost impossible for me to advise you. But if you want me to help you change your circumstances, I can introduce you to people—an editor, for instance, who would give you a good job . . . and you would have enough spare time to do something that interests you.[33]

Steiner, in effect, calls Marcello's bluff.[34] If Marcello wants to rearrange his life so that he will have the opportunity to write, Steiner will help him do exactly that. Marcello's response is to hesitate and then murmur yes. He does not jump eagerly at the opportunity Steiner presents. The offer seems to cause him more than a little anxiety.[35]

Because Steiner commits suicide, we never get the chance to see whether Marcello would follow up on Steiner's offer. The next scene does, however, show us the difficulty Marcello has when the circumstances are "right," and he has free time in which to write. In a deserted outdoor restaurant in Fregene, where Marcello has gone to escape distractions, he sits at a typewriter and attempts to write. Crumpled pieces of paper lie on the floor around him. He asks the young waitress Paola to turn off the blaring jukebox so that he can concentrate, but as Paola sets the tables for lunch, she asks him politely about typing, and he responds by paying her a compliment. Virtually all critics of *La Dolce Vita* have seen Paola as an embodiment of freshness and innocence.[36] Like Marcello, she comes from a small provincial town. She represents the kind of life Marcello has put behind him, his past and his youthful hopefulness. This reading is a valid one. However, in the context we are pursuing here, Paola is also a distraction for Marcello from his writing, although a rather timid one. They talk briefly about where she comes from and where she hopes to go. He studies her profile and pronounces her an "Umbrian angel," as we saw in chapter 2. His attempt at writing is now over. Paola asks whether she may turn the jukebox back on, and Marcello assents. The portrait of Marcello in this scene is an unforgiving one. At the first distraction, he loses his concentration. His earlier posturings, then, must be seen for what they are—empty gestures. In a sense, then, Marcello's failure shows us what it is Fellini admires about Moraldo's steadfast drive in *Moraldo in the City.* And the hesitation and self-doubt of Marcello show us something of what Guido must overcome in *8 ½.*

The Creative Artist

"I'm not sleeping. I'm thinking," Guido, the hero of *8 ½*, tells the women in his harem fantasy after one of them accuses him of falling asleep when in bed with a woman.[37] In context, Guido's statement is a denial that he is an aging lover. On another, less literal level, however, the statement calls attention to Guido's mental activity when, as a creative artist, he is trying to envision and shape the materials of the movie he wants to make. Guido dreams, fantasizes, and plays mentally with his materials until his conception of his movie begins to seem right to him. It is precisely when he might appear to be sleeping that he is doing his kind of thinking best.[38]

We know that Fellini changed the profession of his protagonist in *8 ½* from writer to director-writer at least in part so that Fellini would have some external activities to photograph. He has remarked, "It's difficult to portray a writer on the screen, doing what he does in an interesting way. There isn't much action to show in writing. The world of the film director opened up limitless possibilities."[39] The director may be shown choosing, auditioning, and coaching his or her actors. The director may be shot discussing his project with his or her cowriter, production staff members, and producer, and the director may be shown selecting locales or constructing sets. All these activities provide, of course, ways of externalizing the director's ideas about the film being made, and they are more interesting than a person seated at a typewriter. Fellini uses all of these elements in *8 ½*. Indeed, many filmmakers, such as Stanley Donen with *Singin' in the Rain* (1952), François Truffaut with *Day for Night* (1973), and Karel Reisz with *The French Lieutenant's Woman* (1981), use such elements in their metafilms. But these movies tell us much more about the nature of the medium itself than about the creative mind behind the film dreaming it up. What makes *8 ½* unique is that Fellini takes us inside the mind of the creative artist when he is in the process of doing his mental work. The movie, then, shows us at least some things about the creative process at the same time it shows us much about a specific man, Guido Anselmi, age forty-three, going through what Jung termed the midlife crisis. It seems likely, however, that what the movie demonstrates about the creative process brings us closest to where *8 ½* is autobiographical in its most meaningful way.

Most of Fellini's adult life was devoted to making movies. He seems to have had little time for activities outside the realm of filmmaking and, in fact, little time for a personal life that was not in some way connected with his avocation. He told Tullio Kezich in interview, "My work coincides with my own life; I completely identify with whatever I'm doing."[40] The result is that we may safely conclude that Fellini's depiction of himself as an adult and his depiction of himself as a creative artist are one and the same thing.

The legend of Fellini as a creative artist comes in two parts. The first part concerns his general work methods, and the second concerns the specific details of his work on *8 ½*, some of which translates over into the film itself. Interestingly enough, many of Fellini's statements about his work methods have been published after he made *8 ½*, and it is not clear whether *8 ½* shaped the legend or the legend shaped *8 ½*. Nevertheless, the legend can shed light on some aspects of the creative process that the movie treats. The first legend, dealing with Fellini's general work methods, is always much the same.[41] An image or an idea captures Fellini's imagination. He has called it "a spark of light."[42] When Fellini plays mentally with this spark of light, he is usually able, metaphorically speaking, to discover the window, the house, and the town from which it comes. To help him fill out his idea, Fellini discusses his idea with cowriters he feels comfortable with, usually in a cafe, and they help him map out scenes. Each collaborator brings a different quality to the project. The two major collaborators during the first half of Fellini's career and during the making of *8 ½,* as we noted earlier, were Tullio Pinelli and Ennio Flaiano. Pinelli was a whimsical and imaginative man who would urge Fellini on, and Flaiano, called the "demolisher" by Pinelli, would point out problems that needed to be solved.[43] Faces were of supreme importance to Fellini. He maintained a file of photographs of the faces of potential actors for his films, and when he began a project, he sent out a casting call for nonactors to come to his office so that he could examine their faces and body types for his film. Additionally, Fellini liked to draw sketches of his characters and his sets as an aid to his costumers and his set designers. He has said, "I prefer to draw the characters and the sets. . . . I have liked drawing the ideas that come to me, and translating every idea into an image. There are even ideas that are born all at once in the form of an image. 'Reading' it all comes later.'"[44] Also, there is always the irksome problem of finding a producer who will pay for the filmmaking even though he may understand very little about the story Fellini wants to tell. (In Fellini's legend, producers are always obtuse.) And finally, when a script was ready, Fellini liked to begin shooting with the sense that he might vary, to a certain extent, from the script to take advantage of something serendipitous he discovered on the set. "Contrary to what some people think," Fellini remarked to Chandler, "I like to be totally prepared, and then to make changes."[45]

Ideally, these elements should conspire to keep a project alive and interesting to the creative artist making the movie. Each aspect should bring something for the filmmaker to play with in his or her mind. We might, however, ask what if the situation is not ideal and the director does not find a clear sense of direction for the project? Then the creative situation may become a nightmare, as each element presses in on the filmmaker, demanding answers and choices he cannot supply.

This, of course, is the basic situation of *8 ½*. The elements in the process of the filmmaking turn against the writer-director, and they do so with a vengeance. Pace, the producer, arrives at the spa where Guido is working, presents the director with a wristwatch (as producer Angelo Rizzoli had done at the end of work on *La Dolce Vita*), and begins asking questions about production costs and shooting schedules. Pace urges Guido to choose among the actresses who are viewed in screen tests in an auditorium at the spa, and he arranges an outdoor press conference with clamoring and attacking reporters, apparently in an effort to pressure Guido into action. In his room at the spa, Guido surrounds himself with photographs of actresses and actors. His assistant brings him three nonprofessionals to look over as candidates to play the role of his father in his proposed film, and Guido must deal with the high-strung French actress he has brought in and urged to put on weight, presumably to play the part of his mistress Carla. The photographs and the people do not, however, stimulate Guido. Instead, they bewilder him. In *8 ½,* Guido does not sketch costumes and settings—a departure from the Fellini legend—but he does visit the production rooms for his film and does look at photographs of a possible model for his farmhouse sequence. Again, he is not stimulated by what he sees.

Finally, Guido must contend with Daumier, modeled on Flaiano, whom Guido has invited to collaborate with him on his screenplay. This acerbic intellectual attacks the screenplay at every opportunity. What makes his attacks particularly stinging is that they have a measure of truth about them, at least in terms of the cold, hard logic of narrative construction. Near the beginning of *8 ½*, for example, Daumier challenges Guido's screenplay brutally: "A first reading makes plain the lack of a central idea that establishes the problematic of the film or, if you wish, of a philosophical premise, and therefore the film becomes a series of absolutely gratuitous episodes."[46] Guido, as did Fellini, feels the need to have a "demolisher" on the project as someone to point out the problems to be solved. However, here, there is no encouraging, perhaps a more intuitive collaborator such as Pinelli, to counterbalance such a figure. All the elements from the Fellini legend that could be helpful and stimulating are, in fact, in *8 ½* lined up against the creative artist.

The second legend, the one more closely connected with the making of *8 ½*, provides more material to complicate the artist's situation and then perhaps to solve the situation. Fellini has spoken several times about having a form of writer's block prior to making *8 ½*. He relates that he had a good notion about the autobiographical and fictional scenes he wanted in his film but that he did not have a clear idea of the core idea or "feeling" that would hold them all together. (This is essentially the criticism voiced by Daumier within the movie.) Fellini had a signed contract and a staff ready to begin work, but he felt stymied. Under the circumstances, he thought he must go to his office in Cinecittà and write to producer Angelo Rizzoli that he wished to give up the project. Then there occurred something that we will come to call the "'Eureka!' moment." Fellini relates the story to Chandler:

> Before I could send the letter one of the grips came to fetch me. . . . The grips and electricians were having a birthday party for one of them. I wasn't in the mood for anything, but I couldn't say no.
>
> They were serving spumante in paper cups, and I was given one. Then there was a toast, and everyone raised his paper cup. I thought they were going to toast the person having the birthday, but instead they toasted me and my "masterpiece." Of course they had no idea what I was going to do, but they had perfect faith in me. I left to return to my office, stunned.
>
> I was about to cost all of these people their jobs. They called me the Magician. Where was my "magic"?
>
> Now what do I do? I asked myself.

But myself didn't answer. I listened to a fountain and the sound of
the water, and tried to hear my inner voice. Then I heard the small voice
of creativity within me. I knew. The story I would tell was of a writer
who doesn't know what he wants to write.[47]

The story, which is perhaps a little too good to be true, does demonstrate
the position of Guido in *8 ½*. First of all, it illustrates his quandary. Like
Fellini, Guido has some sense of the episodes he wishes to use but has no
sense of the core idea that will hold them together. There are, however, as
we shall see, some ideas that he must get rid of before he can make progress.
Then, through a series of pressures and releases, he will come to his solution much as Fellini claims to have done. By showing us the inner work-
ings of this interior journey, Fellini gives us one of the fullest depictions of
the artistic process in the cinema that we have, and he gives us the final piece
of his autobiographical strand, the teleological end toward which the other
pieces in his other autobiographical films drive.

In the contemporary era, there has been much research and speculation
about the nature of the creative mind by psychologists, scholars in the field
of artificial intelligence, and creative people themselves. Most of the writers on this subject tend to treat the issue as a kind of original problem solving. This is an approach that applies well to Guido's situation in *8 ½*. The
scholars generally start with French mathematician Henri Poincaré's four
stages of creative thought. Margaret A. Boden, in *The Creative Mind,* outlines these stages.[48] The first is the *preparatory phase,* which involves "conscious attempts to solve the problem, by using or explicitly adapting familiar
methods." The second phase, an *incubation period,* may last for minutes or
for months or years. As Boden explains, "The conscious mind is focused
elsewhere, on other problems, other projects—perhaps even on a sightseeing
trip. But below the level of consciousness, . . . ideas are being continually
combined with a freedom denied to waking, rational thought." At this phase,
the notions of reverie, dreaming, and even moving about may be important.
The third phase is the "flash of insight," or the *"Eureka!" moment,* when the
thinker finds the solution. The fourth and final phase involves *verification,*
where as Boden puts it, "deliberate problem-solving takes over again, as the
new conceptual thoughts are itemized and tested." In Guido's case, this last
stage would be his making of his movie, which presumably takes place

immediately after the events of *8 ½,* unless we consider, in metaterms, that *8 ½* is the movie Guido goes on to make.

Of the four stages of the creative act outlined here, the second stage, incubation, is clearly the most important. Virtually all writers on the subject agree that the kind of thinking that goes on in this phase is different from the traditional or standard level of Aristotelian logical thought. That level of thinking takes place in the first phase. The second phase involves a freer, more wide-ranging kind of associative thinking. In *The Act of Creation,* essayist and playwright Arthur Koestler writes of the "bisociative pattern of the creative synthesis: the sudden interlocking of two previously unrelated skills, or matrices of thought."[49] For Jung, as we have seen in chapter 2, this kind of "thinking" would take place in the unconscious at the level of archetypes, and as we also saw in chapter 2, Fellini seems to allegorize this kind of creative journey in the final section of *The City of Women.* For the Freudian psychologist Silvano Arieti, in his *Creativity, The Magic Synthesis,* creative thinking takes place in the "primary process" of the unconscious and then merges with logical thinking of the conscious "secondary process" in a "magic synthesis."[50] And for the phenomenologist philosopher Gaston Bachelard, it takes place in a state of reverie that is somehow "put on track" or directed.[51]

Fellini discusses the creative act in almost precisely the same terms as these writers on the subject. "For me," he states, "inspiration means making direct contact between your unconscious and your rational mind. An artistic creation has its own needs, which present themselves to the author as indispensable. . . . As soon as I work on one idea, an outpouring of other ideas comes, often unrelated to the first, and all of the ideas compete."[52] As we know, he felt many of his best ideas came to him when he was dreaming or daydreaming, and in discussing this aspect of creative thinking, he introduces the important idea of visual thinking at the second phase of creative work. He has commented, "In my sleep I have some of my best thoughts, because they are images rather than words."[53] In this, Fellini sounds remarkably like Albert Einstein, as quoted by Koestler, on the subject of visual thinking:

> The words or the language, as they are written or spoken, do not seem to play any role in my mechanism of thought. The physical entities

which seem to serve as elements in thought are certain signs and more or less clear images which can be "voluntarily" reproduced and combined.[54]

We will need to do much more studying of how the brain works to learn more precisely how it functions in the kind of associative play that goes into creative activity, but visual thinking certainly provides a filmmaker with a valuable means for rendering the creative act. Visual thinking can be simulated on film.

We might add two more elements to our discussion. The first is the notion of chaos that is suggested by Boden. She finds "rampant disorder, a medley of elements drawn from widely diverse sources" to be extremely useful to the creative artist as a means for him or her to "stir things up" and break conventional thought patterns or attitudes.[55] This idea seems to carry over in *8 ½* when Guido invites his wife Luisa to join him at the spa. Since his mistress Carla is already present, Guido's invitation to Luisa seems the height of folly. But if Guido's motive, an unconscious one perhaps, is to create a chaotic situation that may lead him to a new way of viewing his midlife situation, he has, in fact, acted wisely.

The second element is the notion of a limit. This is suggested by Fellini himself in discussing a useful function of producers: "Their power over me," he says "is in limiting me, by not letting me have enough money to do everything I want to do."[56] In *8 ½*, the limit is time. Pace, the producer, urges Guido to begin shooting, for time is money, and the various agents for actors apply a pressure, too, when they suggest that their "talent" have other engagements they want to move on to. Guido, then, is free to dream and to think "artistically" but, at the same time, there is a pressure on him to solve his artistic impasse. Indeed, as I suggested earlier, the movie can be seen as a series of relaxed, freely associating reveries on Guido's part with a series of moments when he very much feels the pressure of the film entourage to find his solution. The rhythm of reverie and applied pressure may, indeed, help Guido. It is clear that he cannot dream forever.

The harem sequence of *8 ½* is a remarkable piece of filmmaking for the way it renders the artist's mind at work. Usually, the sequence is discussed as a kind of exposé of Guido's male wishes to assert his potency and to demonstrate control over the women in his life. The sequence is, to be sure, just such an exposé, yet it is also an illustration of the artist's mind in a state of reverie choosing elements, combining them with other elements, adding some new elements, and producing a small narrative. The harem sequence presents the kind of visual thinking we have been discussing, for many of the elements are visual images that may be translated into concepts. Furthermore, we have seen many of the elements Guido works with here earlier in the film, and therefore we can note precisely how he changes and recombines the elements to make things new.

The harem sequence is set in the farmhouse of Guido's grandmother, where as a boy he was bathed in the wine vat with his cousins, wrapped in sheets by two nannies, and tucked into bed in a room with the other children. As we noted in chapter 3, the wine vat flashback was a sequence of unqualified maternal love. Here what should interest us is, however, the way the earlier material is adapted into something different. In this fantasy, Guido enters as an adult. He wears an overlarge, western version of his black fedora and a pair of dark-rimmed glasses—part cowboy, part intellectual. He comes in from a snowstorm, very much the patron of the house, his arms filled with Christmas presents for all the ladies in his life. Yet they treat him at first like the little boy of the earlier wine vat scene.

Luisa, Guido's wife, has taken on the role of the grandmother. She wears a black peasant smock and has her hair wrapped in a kerchief. Walking in a comic, stiff-legged manner, perhaps to indicate age, she busies herself throughout the sequence with household tasks. Most important, she seems to take on something of the grandmother's doting amusement with the antics of little Guido. Luisa is not her usual judgmental self.

Also present is a black dancer, of whom Luisa says Guido has spoken often, although he cannot remember her now. The dancer wears a sheet wrapped around her like a tunic, recalling the costumes of the spa guests who went to the steam baths earlier, and as a gift from Luisa to Guido, she does a faster and more athletic version of the rumba Saraghina, the prostitute, did for Guido and his school chums on the beach in Guido's "initiation" scene. The dancer then introduces just a bit more sexuality into the sequence, nudging it slightly at this point beyond its previous mood of "maternal love." After Guido emerges from bathing in the wine vat in this fantasy, however, he is dried and bundled in sheets by the same nanny in a white blouse who cared for him earlier. She is still nurturing in her care of Guido, but she also has taken on some aspects of other more sexual women in Guido's life. She now wears on her right cheek the beauty mark that Carla, Guido's mistress, normally wears on her left cheek, and the nanny crinkles her nose at Guido in the same manner the French actress used when she wanted to charm Guido and learn more about her part. The characters thus slide into and interchange with other characters. In short, the sequence takes us inside the creative artist's mind during what we have called the incubation phase. We watch him play with his materials and try out new combinations.

In this sequence, Guido also fashions a small, comic narrative with a beginning, middle, and end. If the sequence begins with a certain harmony and with Guido effortlessly in control of his harem, conflict arises with the entry of the new character, Jacqueline Bonbon, the first "artiste" in Guido's life. Because of her advanced age, she has been banished to the upstairs of the farmhouse, but she wishes Guido to make an exception and allow her to remain below. When Guido refuses, the incident sets off a rebellion among the women that Guido will have to put down. The incident is, of course, an exercise in wish fulfillment on Guido's part. As a man of forty-three years, Guido is acutely aware that he is no longer young, and he wants very much to banish all reminders of age. And the incident provides Guido with an opportunity to demonstrate his machismo. He seems never to doubt he will subdue the rebellion. "He needs to act like this," Luisa explains, within the sequence. "He does it almost every night."[57] More important here, however, is that Guido as the creative dreamer of the scene extends the earlier materials of the wine vat flashback and puts the characters at his disposal through their paces in ways amusingly appropriate to each. Guido as the would-be master of the harem rises to his feet, creases back the brim of his cowboy hat, and in the alert crouch of an animal trainer faces the women ringed around him and snaps his bullwhip at them. Saraghina, the most physically imposing of the women, hisses at him like a lioness, "It's not fair!" The athletic black dancer swings on a furled, hanging sheet and, as she lands on a platform, calls out, "Down with the tyrant!"[58] The beautiful, unknown woman from the spa, chosen in part because she will forgive her lover anything, remonstrates gently, "Ah, Guido, Guido, they are certainly right," and tries to calm the angry, aroused male. The French actress, an insistent person outside the fantasy, is equally one within it. "Bastard! Liar!" she spits out at Guido. He responds by snapping the French combs, her snail-like antennae, from her hair with his whip and driving her back to a post, where she is enveloped in a sheet and bound with rope. And Gloria, the young girlfriend of Guido's middle-aged chum Mezzabotta, who tends to respond to events in dramatic and unconventional ways, croons, "Oh, delicious!" when the whip snaps her behind. As Guido gains the upper hand and subdues the rebellion, he receives the applause of the women ringed around him. Jacqueline is permitted to perform a final musical number, giving the sequence its vaudevillian "big finish." And finally, Guido delivers an epilogue on the happiness he had hoped all would find within the fantasy world of his reverie. The harmony that was established at the beginning is restored—at least from Guido's point of view, in his very male fantasy.

We do not know whether the harem fantasy will find its way into Guido's movie, but we have seen him in action as writer. Before our eyes he has put together a scene that he could use. The creation is not a tightly reasoned or planned composition. There is a tentative quality to it, as if Guido were wondering, "What would the nanny look like if I gave her Carla's beauty mark and the French actress's facial gesture?" or "What would the beautiful, unknown woman do, if she were present at a revolution?" The sequence, then, is a kind of experiment, a trying out of possibilities. Moreover, the reverie helps him move toward his moment of discovery, his "Eureka!" moment, for it offers him a vision of his hero in the center of a circle, albeit an imperfectly formed one here, of the other people in his life. This image eventually will give Guido the central, guiding principle for his movie, and it will give Fellini the image for the ending of *8 ½*. But before Guido gets to his moment of insight, he will have to modify and even destroy some misleading premises and images. That, too, is a part of the artistic process.

The lady in white is an element of his film that Guido must redefine, if not eliminate completely. She appears three times as a fantasy figure for Guido as he tries to think of ways he might use her as a central image in his movie.[59] The sound track is always silent when she appears, and she has the smooth, high cheekbones of the idealized Madonna we see in Guido's flashback to his punishment scene in his Jesuit boarding school. The lady in white, then, has something of the ideal about her, in terms of both classical beauty and religious mysticism. She appears first to Guido at the spa in the white uniform of an attendant and offers him a glass of mineral water. Then later at night she comes to Guido in his room, still in the uniform of an attendant, to turn down his covers. She leafs through his screenplay and laughs softly to herself. Then, wearing only her white slip, she lies under the covers of his bed and offers to make his problems vanish. "I want to make order. I want to cleanse," the lady in white promises. Finally, when Guido tries to explain the character to Claudia, the actress who will play her in Guido's movie, the fantasy figure comes to life again in his mind as a girl the hero meets at the springs, in Guido's words, "both young and ancient . . . a child yet already a woman . . . authentic . . . radiant," and she sets a table for two at night in a deserted square. This figure is, to be sure, a mysterious one. Early on, Guido asks, "What if you were the symbol of purity . . . of spontaneity?"[60] Then, however, he pulls back from this interpretation and quotes the critic Daumier on the need for Guido to move beyond such symbols. Is the lady in white a religious figure? A mistress? A young wife? Is she to be a source of inspiration, a muse, for the middle-aged filmmaker, who worries that his creative powers are failing him? Without answering any of these questions specifically, Guido finally tells Claudia that her character will be the hero's "salvation."

Guido's conversation with the actress Claudia provides a means for Guido to clarify the natures of his hero and of the lady in white for himself. As they drive out into the countryside, Guido explains his hero as someone who "wants to take hold of everything, to devour everything. He cannot give anything up. He changes direction every day for fear he might miss the right path."[61] The lady in white, then, will be the hero's salvation in the sense that she will be the one person in his life to whom he can dedicate himself and around whom he can organize a new life: the ideal Other. Guido puts this notion in the form of a question to Claudia: "Would you be able to give up everything, to start life all over again . . . to choose one thing, just one thing, and be faithful to it . . . to make it the one thing that gives meaning to your life?"[62] His film, Guido explains, will begin with the hero's discovery of just such a "one thing" in the form of the lady in white. Claudia, though, senses that he is improvising on the spot and asks if the part is written yet. It, of course, has not been written. Guido, is, in effect, "writing" it through his conversation. Once he has clarified the function of the lady in white for Claudia and himself, however, he can see that the character will not work.

The idea of the lady in white being the one element around which the hero could build a new life is a neat literary device, but choosing the one element is not, finally, something his hero could do, if the hero is to be Guido's autobiographical portrait. Guido rejects his conception of the lady in white and explains to Claudia, "I don't want to tell . . . another story that's filled with lies." Guido is quite simply someone with too many interests and desires, with too much curiosity, to be focused on one element or person. As Charles Affron has said in his introduction to 8 ½, "Claudia's unity is ultimately not Guido's. The director's demands are much greater than her symbolic and iconic presence can satisfy."[63] And yet the longing for some central, organizing element is, or has been, an important element in Guido's psychological make-up. Furthermore, Guido's process of clarifying and then rejecting his conception of the lady in white will prove immensely useful. If the answer is not the lady in white, then perhaps it is something nearly her opposite.

Another element that Guido must redefine or purge from his conception of the movie he wants to make is the spaceship launch tower he has built. Prior to shooting the film, Fellini told journalist Deena Boyer that a spaceship launch scene was to be the climax of Guido's movie within Fellini's movie. Guido's problems were to be considered "part of a much broader crisis that touches everyone." Under this circumstance, Fellini told Boyer, "There's nothing to do but abandon the earth and start over elsewhere. . . . So all humanity, thousands and thousands of men, women and children, the Catholic Church in the lead, piles into a gigantic spaceship."[64] Perhaps even a bit more grandly, in 8 ½, the producer Pace explains to the visitors he has brought at night to the expensive set of the launch tower: "The sequence begins with a view of the planet Earth completely destroyed by thermonuclear war. In this . . . appears a true Noah's Ark . . . the spaceship that tries to escape the atomic plague. The rest of humanity looks for a safe haven on another planet."[65] In both explanations, the notion of blasting off to a new planet implies the leaving behind of one's past life completely and the beginning of some kind of new existence. The launch tower is a strange and frightening construction. Fellini has claimed he modeled it on Breughel's painting "The Tower of Babel."[66] When Pace brings the visitors to see it, the tower is lit ominously with spotlights from below, and the music on the sound track is the quivering electronic music we associate with eerie moments in science fiction movies. More clearly, though, the tower is wrong as a dominant image for Guido's movie. Guido cannot and finally will not give up his past, those things that have marked him psychologically, to make the kind of utterly new start implied by the idea of blasting off from the launch tower in a spaceship. Guido is too much the sum of his previous experiences. When Guido orders the tower torn down, his act is a significant one. It is as significant as his act of renouncing the lady in white as the one value in his life. In both instances, Guido as a creative artist clears away false visual images and leaves the field of his mental activity open for the discovery of other images that will work.

The two new visual images that Guido finds to give his movie an organizational concept are the group of major characters in white, as opposed to the single character, and the circle, as opposed to the tower. The first image, that of the group, is easily arrived at, once Guido discards the lady in white as the single transcendent value in his life. If Guido is a person with a variety of needs and interests who cannot commit himself totally to anyone, then it seems a relatively simple next step to replace the one lady in white in his imagination with a throng of people in white, each representing a different need or interest. The second image, the circle, is a more complicated matter. The circle is, of course, in Jungian terms, a basic part of the mandala, and therefore we should not be surprised that it appears here as an image of the harmony Guido wishes to find for his final stage of his movie. However, in Freudian terms, the circle is a feminine symbol, and it comes as an alternative to the very masculine, very phallic tower. It might seem surprising that the apparently macho Guido and the generally considered macho Fellini should turn to such an image at the crucial point of *8 ½*. On reflection, though, we might note that Fellini habitually turns to the other side of his nature, the side brought out by anima figures, to understand himself. In this sense, the circle with its variety of possibilities, its ability to suggest complexity, seems more appropriate than the single, aggressive, phallic tower. Within *8 ½*, we might consider that the image of the circle entered Guido's creative thinking process with the memory of the wine vat. It then grew with the circle of women, albeit an imperfect circle, in the harem sequence when Guido, as an animal trainer, tries to organize the women inside a circus ring. The image becomes at the end the circus ring with characters, many now in white, moving around Guido in a joyful dance.

If we were to try to visualize the movie *8 ½* as a single image, we would probably want to do it as a circle with Guido at the center and the major characters of his imagination, most of them in white to demonstrate their importance, along the outer rim. A graphic rendering might look like that in figure 4.1.

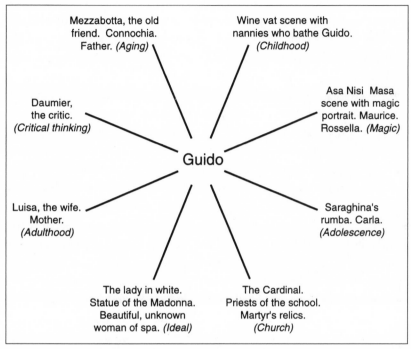

Fig. 4.1. The circle of *8 ½*

The diagram is stripped down. Many more characters and incidents could be added. The diagram does, however, hold many of the more important elements of Guido's life. The wine vat scene, as we have said, recalls a moment of uncritical, maternal love directed at Guido, a sensation from his childhood that he will not give up. Saraghina's rumba introduces him to the excitement of illicit sex, which he attempts to recreate in his adult life with his mistress Carla, who dresses in a somewhat more stylish version of Saraghina's costume and who, with Guido's direction, plays the role of prostitute in Guido's bedroom. And Luisa, his wife, offers him a more adult kind of relationship between two intellectually equal partners, a relationship Guido seems both to want and to fear. She also brings into his life a judgmental morality like that of his mother, which troubles him. The magic portrait scene, along with the magician Maurice and Luisa's friend Rossella, with her powers as a medium, demonstrates Guido's lifelong fascination with magic and the paranormal. The Cardinal, the priests, and the martyr's bones seem to show us Guido's antipathy for the Church, an antipathy, however, from which he cannot shake free. The lady in white, as we have said, is an ideal he would like to commit to fully, but cannot. The statue of the Madonna and the unknown, beautiful lady at the spa, both with features of classical beauty, are extensions and further reminders of her. The Madonna perhaps also represents a more attractive kind of religious appeal to be set against the images of frailty and age of the Cardinal, the priest, and the martyr. Daumier, the critic always on the attack, a kind of shadow figure as we saw in chapter 2, is someone Guido invites to collaborate and therefore seems to bring to Guido a capacity for critical thinking and self-criticism that Guido must feel he needs. Finally, Mezzabotta, the old friend now pursuing a younger women, Connochia, a former director now working as Guido's assistant, and the ghost of Guido's deceased father, who returns in his dreams, all remind Guido of the aging process and add to his sense of anxiety about creating a truly fine film before he loses his creative powers. All of the figures and the events on the diagram are important in the sense that they bring out sides of Guido's character. More important than any one of them, however, is the multiplicity of them.

Moreover, the characters and events bear on Guido almost simultaneously. He is never too far removed from any one of them at any time. Therefore, to get a grasp on his movie as he would like it to be, Guido needs to arrive at a mental construct somewhat like the diagram, that is, something like a gathering of "signs and more or less clear images" that Einstein spoke of or a grouping of images in the "primary process" described by Arieti. We should remember that Fellini himself complained he did not have a feeling of what *8 ½* was about until just before shooting, and we might add that he did not have his own image of the ending of the film until he chose between two possibilities, both of which he filmed, one set in the dining car of a train and the other in the circus ring. The image of the circle with many of the characters dressed in white along the outer rim, which Fellini finally selected, is, then, the solution to the problem of the film for both Guido and Fellini. The solution presumably gives Guido a place to begin. It gave Fellini his ending to *8 ½*.

The ending of the movie is Guido's "Eureka!" moment. As the workmen begin to tear down the tower and Daumier praises Guido for abandoning his project, the magician Maurice summons Guido from his car with the words "We're ready to begin." Figures in white walk onto the beach around Guido. The first, of course, is the lady in white, but then come the other major characters from Guido's imaginative life who have now also been raised to the stature of figures in white equal to the one played by Claudia. There appear in succession the nannies of Guido's childhood wine vat scene, Saraghina, Guido's mother and father, Carla, the Cardinal and his entourage, Guido's grandmother, the French vaudeville dancer, the beautiful, unknown woman, and finally Luisa and her friend Rossella. With a few exceptions, these are the characters of our diagram. Mezzabotta, for example, is not included in this group in white, and Daumier has been left behind, presumably still talking, in the car Guido abandoned. For the most part, however, the characters now present in white are those most important to Guido, and now they share the same level of importance as the lady in white.

At this point, Guido, in effect, verbalizes what he sees. He speaks the following lines ostensibly to his spirit wife Luisa but, perhaps more important, to himself and to us. The words constitute his solution, and they come with the rush of excitement artists often use to describe the "Eureka!" moment.

> What is this sudden joy that makes me tremble, gives me strength, life? . . . I don't understand. I don't know. How right it is to accept you, to love you! And how simple it is! Luisa, I feel as if I've been freed. Everything seems good. Everything is meaningful. . . . Oh, I wish I knew how to explain myself. . . . Everything is confused again. But all this confusion . . . it's me, myself. Myself as I am, not as I would like to be. And it doesn't frighten me anymore. To tell the truth, what I don't know, what I'm looking for, what I haven't yet found! Only this way do I feel alive, and can I look at your faithful eyes without shame. Life is a holiday! Let's live it together. . . . Accept me as I am, if you can. It's the only way we have to try to find each other.[67]

Guido's speech falls into two halves. The first deals with the exhilaration he feels, and the second consists of his verbal interpretation of what is coming to him from his vision of the characters in white around him. Guido accepts himself as a man pulled in many different directions, with a variety of wants and desires, and is now prepared to begin his movie anew, this time with a protagonist such as he now sees himself.[68]

What remains for Fellini is to find symbolic or visual means to show us Guido's internal state of well-being. As we have suggested, this will be done with the image of the circle. He has Guido seize a bullhorn and try to direct the figures. Sometimes they follow his lead, and sometimes they seem to follow ideas of their own. The figures in white are joined by characters in darker clothes from the production company and from the spa where Guido was taking his cure, perhaps giving us a sense of Guido's fantasy moving toward real life. Maurice invites all the characters, those in white and those in darker clothes, to join hands, and he leads them at last to form the circle we have been waiting for in a circus ring.[69] The last bit of visual imagery is in place.

Until now, most of the elements seem to have to do with Guido's solution to his creative problem and with the starting up of his film project again. However, at this point, Guido takes the hand of his fantasy wife and leads her into the circle with him. Some critics have objected that this part of the "solution" is too easy.[70] They have argued that the real Luisa, who has in fact left her husband, would not be as likely to take her husband's hand after the fantasy ends, nor would she have been as moved by his earlier entreaty to accept him as he is. The objection is well taken. Guido has not solved all of his problems. His marriage will still be in trouble. But he has come to a kind of self-knowledge, and more important for our purposes here, he has solved the problem of his artistic creation. He now has a clear image of what it is he wants to show in his movie. Of course, he will have to rewrite and film his new vision in what we have called the *verification* stage of the creative process. What *8 ½* wishes to celebrate, however, is the moment of breakthrough—the "Eureka!" moment.

8 ½ is not quite finished yet. The final image involves a dream version of Guido as a schoolboy leading a marching line of clown musicians. The clowns move away, leaving the boy to play his flute alone in a spotlight. In terms of showmanship, Fellini has reduced his crowded finale to a single figure small in the frame and his full orchestration of the circus march *La Passerella di Addio* to the simple, pure sound of a single flute. He has gently led his audience down from the excitement of Guido's illumination to a calmer state. He has, in a sense, prepared the viewers to leave the theater. Yet the image of the schoolboy in white lingers in the mind after it leaves the screen. Christian Metz has called the boy "the ultimate, and first, inspirer of the whole fantasy."[71] He is that and more. The little boy is not just the originator of *8 ½*. He is the originator of the whole autobiographical strain in Fellini's oeuvre. This boy takes us back to the child who responded, frightened and captivated, to the sight of a circus tent being raised outside his house in *The Clowns*—the beginning of a creative performance. To be sure, there are more elements in the autobiographical sections of Fellini's oeuvre than art and the creative process. But these two are the constants. The teleological end for Fellini's self-exploration is the excitement of the artist arriving at the "Eureka!" moment. This, for Fellini, is what it all moves toward.

5

THE PERSONAE OF GIULIETTA MASINA

During a four-minute scene in *The White Sheik* (1952), the prostitute Cabiria, played by Fellini's wife, Giulietta Masina, must comfort the main character Ivan Cavalli, played by Leopoldo Trieste. Cavalli has been abandoned by his new wife on their honeymoon, and as part of a nocturnal ramble, he meets Cabiria and her fellow prostitute in a deserted square. Learning of Ivan's situation, Cabiria tries to cheer him up. She offers him a cigarette and mops his brow. Then a sack of wedding-favor candy falls from Ivan's pocket. The candy provides Masina with the main piece of business she will use as an actress to externalize her feelings in the scene. She pops a candy into her mouth as Ivan produces some photographs of his wife. Masina chews energetically with her mouth open. Her interest is piqued. The first snapshot shows a very young girl. Scandalized, Masina stops chewing and, we could almost say, "chokes" on the candy. Ivan explains that the picture was taken years ago when his wife was at her first communion, and Masina resumes chewing the candy, this time with her mouth closed, more thoughtful perhaps, while Ivan shows additional photographs commemorating various stages of his wife's growing up. Then, as Ivan nears the end of his collection, Cabiria starts digging into her cheek with her tongue, searching for that last piece of the candy. Throughout the scene, Fellini's camera is generally placed to the left, Cabiria's side of the three-character grouping. We see Masina in a medium close-up by herself, in a medium-close-up two-shot with Ivan, and in a medium-close-up three-shot with Ivan and the other prostitute. Always she is nearest the camera, and we get a clear view of her facial expressions. Masina's lines of dialogue are minimal. For the most part, she merely listens and reacts, but with Fellini's connivance, Masina "steals" the scene with her pantomime of eating candy. The "stealing" is a nice stroke, however. By this point in the movie we have witnessed enough of Ivan's grief over his wife's departure. It is important that we recognize his grief is still acute, but we need not concentrate on his stricken face anymore. We need instead the relief of a digression—in this case to meet a character of energy.

In four minutes of screen time, we come to know Cabiria pretty well. She enters demonstrating a dance step to her companion, and she concludes the scene by asking a fire-eater, who wanders into the square, for a demonstration of his trick. In between, she shows keen interest in the plight of the hero, Cavalli. But her interest lasts, quite literally, as long as it takes her to eat a piece of candy and no longer. It is not that Cabiria dismisses Cavalli's grief. However, like a parent willing to give a child some time for his or her bruise, Cabiria will not linger on it overlong, and she puts Ivan's grief into a kind of comic perspective by treating the adult as something like a child. The scene is "pure Fellini." And yet it is also "pure Masina," as we will come to see. It is the result of an intriguing collaboration between director and actress.

Some of the most stirring and effective moments in Fellini's films are the result of his work with his wife. The collaboration, however, was not always a comfortable one, for Fellini was nothing if not a controlling director who attempted to keep his vision of his movies close to himself and play out slowly to his actors and actresses what they needed to know only shortly before shooting.[1] Masina was, on the other hand, a serious modern actress who wanted to know as early as possible, in actors' terms, the "through line" of her character and the final "superobjective" toward which her part would build. Yet, at the same time, Fellini was clearly fascinated with his wife's ability as an actress and her visual presence on the screen. In interview, he has stated, "Her mimicry, for example, and that little round face which can express happiness or sadness with such poignant simplicity. That little figure, with its tenderness, its delicacy, fascinates me no end. Her type is crystallized, even stylized for me."[2] This statement, which might at first seem derogatory with its emphasis on littleness, softness, and type, is something more. It is Fellini's declaration that Masina gives him yet another means to defamiliarize the material of his movies—to set the material off from the quotidian train of events we experience—and to have us see the material as something new or as something on the level of myth or fairy tale. Fellini is attracted to Masina's gifts as a mime, particularly if we define the mime as a performance artist who does not just simulate an action, but who, in the words of mime Angna Enters, "enlarges, emphasizes, particularizes, [and] comments on the character."[3] At the same time, as we will see, Masina was an actress who insisted on building her characters "from within," and she brings to the mix a certain grounding in internal motivation that gives her characters more resonance than we find in many of Fellini's other characters. Fellini's task, then, in collaborating with his wife was to balance external expressiveness and internal character building. For Masina, Fellini created essentially two personae: the clownlike "waif" in *The White Sheik, La Strada,* and *Nights of Cabiria* and the "deceived wife" in *Variety Lights, Il Bidone (The Swindle), Juliet of the Spirits,* and *Ginger and Fred.* The uses Fellini and Masina make of these two personae constitute a distinctive and interesting strand of Fellini's oeuvre.

Before we can proceed further, however, it will be useful to review Masina's beginnings as an actress and to consider the two traditions that seem to inform her work or at least can help us understand it—one generally called "representational" and the other "presentational."

Masina essentially learned to act by doing. Although born in San Giorgio di Piano near Bologna in 1921, Masina spent her school years in Rome with her wealthy Aunt Giulia, who supervised her education.[4] The aunt sent Masina to a school run by the Ursuline sisters. There, Masina took lessons in voice, piano, and dance but not acting. She did, however, perform on stage, and she notes that her last performance at the school was in Carlo Goldoni's farce *The Antiquarian's Family.* Masina moved on to the University of Rome in 1940 as a student of modern literature and immediately tried out for a place in a troupe of university players, Teatro-GUF, using a selection from *The Antiquarian's Family* as her audition piece.[5] One of her mentors appears to have been the director Gerardo Guerrieri. The group was an experimental repertory group, and it was here Masina developed her skills in plays by a wide variety of writers such as Thornton Wilder, Pirandello, Vitaliano Brancati, Ugo Betti, Plautus, and again Goldoni. On the basis of her work with the university players, playwright Gherardo Gherardi offered Masina a job in a prestigious professional group, and the critic and teacher Silvio D'Amico offered her a scholarship to the Academy of Dramatic Arts, but she turned down both opportunities to satisfy her aunt's wish that she complete her university degree.[6] She did, however, take a paying job in 1942 as the young wife in a radio comedy about the adventures of the couple Cico and Pallina, written by Federico Fellini. Her marriage to Fellini took place shortly after, in 1943, and her debut in films came in 1946 as a walk-on in Roberto Rossellini's *Paisan,* a project on which Fellini served as a writer and assistant director.

When biographer Tullio Kezich asked Masina in 1985 how she prepared a part, she gave two answers, the first describing her work with directors other than her husband, and the second, with Fellini. For the first situation, which seems her preferred one, she states,

> I read the script; I fondle it; I brood over the character. I never try intonations out loud or poses in front of the mirror. I do not try to invent the character from my point of view. Instead I try to get the character inside me. When it seems to me that I have found the character, all the other successive choices (clothes, hairstyles, gestures, and ways of speaking) come to light, and generally they are correct. I always ask for tryout footage of how I put it all together, how I dress. And then I never go to view the dailies in the projection room. That's something which blocks me.[7]

Her description is one that has become almost the traditional one for actors who work from the "inside out," who try in some sense to "be" the character. Masina is following here the dictates of a "representational" theory of acting of which the foremost spokesman is the Russian theorist Konstantin Stanislavsky. In her description, Masina is performing what Stanislavsky would call "the work of an actor" in building a character.

For the second situation, that with Fellini, Masina shows a certain resentment toward her director, perhaps because Fellini wishes to keep a large amount of the work to himself.

> At first he tells me nothing. Some sentences, some hints, but woe to the person who tries to learn more! Any intervention during the preparatory phase, by me or anyone else, disturbs him greatly. Only he may play

with the project. At a certain point, he gives me the script. I read it. He asks me what I think. I try to give him my thoughts. After a minute, he taps his foot, wrings his hands together nervously, pumping them up and down, and orders, "Synthesize!" After various unhappy attempts to communicate, I end up writing long letters, pages and pages, with observations, suggestions, and questions which have come to me. He never seems to gather them up to read them, but later on, I can tell that he values some of them which prove useful and forgets the rest.

From me, he demands that I understand everything without explaining anything to me. . . . Everything must happen through telepathy. . . . On the set, his continual instructions are, "Give more, do less."[8]

Clearly, this description reveals a director who does not want to share much of the creative side of filmmaking with the actor. The problem is perhaps particularly acute between a husband and wife when the husband simply expects that the wife, the person closest to him, will anticipate what he wants. More than this, there is perhaps a general impatience in Fellini with intellectual "work" on the part of the actor. With Masina, we see the traditional and professional desire of the actor to work up a character well in advance of the shooting, and with Fellini, we find more an emphasis on spontaneity at the moment of the take. In an interview with Charlotte Chandler, Fellini has more or less confessed that he "manipulates" his wife's performances to bring out more of her spontaneity.

I can manipulate her performance, for good or for bad. In the interest of what I, as director, determine is best for the film, I can overcome any resistance I feel in her toward the interpretation of the character. . . . She is a professional, but even more important, she has a wondrous innocent intuition. She can still allow her emotions to rule, and when the source deep within her is touched, she draws on a wellspring which touches all of us.[9]

Clearly, then, there is a tension between director and actor, with a certain amount of manipulation involved, but the struggle of wills has produced happy results—some film moments that are very powerful indeed.

The kind of representational acting that Masina describes is, as mentioned earlier, the kind most closely linked in modern theater and film with the "Method" of Konstantin Stanislavsky, the director of the Moscow Arts Theater from 1898 until 1938. His ideas were laid out in his two books *An Actor Prepares* (1936) and *Building a Character* (1949), and the ideas were most strongly promoted in the west by the Actors Studio founded in 1947 in New York City by Elia Kazan, Robert Lewis, and Cheryl Crawford.[10] The Method of Stanislavsky is a movement against a declamatory style of acting and toward a kind of realism on the stage. It emphasizes a "fourth wall" between the actor and the audience. The actor must act with other actors or with himself or herself as if alone, without awareness of the audience. Most important, Stanislavsky was concerned with the actor "living the part," or as he states, the actor "must fit his own human qualities to the life of this other person, and pour into it all of his own soul." The assumption is that if the actor can effect this empathy with the character, the other external aspects necessary for communicating with the audience will follow naturally.[11] In *An Actor Prepares,* Stanislavsky stresses the actor's need to "be" the character rather than "seem" the character. As a practical aid, Stanislavsky suggests the actor develop a rich "emotional memory" and use "recall" of memories to stimulate external reactions similar to those of a character in analogous situations. He also argues that the actor needs to develop a "through line" that leads to a clear statement of the basic essence of the character (the "superobject"). Without this through line, Stanislavsky argues, the performance would be a series of unrelated gestures as opposed to a dance. In *Building a Character,* he adds the idea of a "subtext," which is "the inwardly felt expression of a human being in a part, which flows uninterruptedly beneath the words of the text, giving them life and a basis for existing."[12] And he develops the ideas that characters have their own rhythms, both internal and external, at which they function. He was particularly interested in characters with different rhythms, as perhaps in the case of a quick-thinking person who moves slowly.

It must be stated immediately that the Stanislavsky Method came to Italy relatively late. *Il lavoro dell' attore,* a volume combining *An Actor Prepares* and *Building a Character,* was first translated into Italian in 1956. Giulietta Masina could not have studied the Method in the 1940s when she was a student actor in Teatro-GUF. However, it is reasonable to assume that Masina became generally familiar with the Method in the early 1950s. In the first place, the person who wrote the introduction to *Il lavoro dell' attore* in 1956 and stressed the importance of Stanislavsky's work was none other than her former mentor at Teatro-GUF, Gerardo Guerrieri. From this knowledge we may conclude that the topic of Stanislavsky was present in the conversation of Masina's circle of actor friends in Rome. Secondly, American actors who came to Italy to work in the 1950s would certainly have brought with them notions about the Actors Studio and the Method. Anthony Quinn is a prime example. He learned about Stanislavsky from Russian emigré teacher Max Pollack in 1936 as an acting student in Los Angeles and then joined Elia Kazan's Actors Studio in 1947 when he was preparing to follow Method actor Marlon Brando in the theater version of *A Streetcar Named Desire*.[13] In 1953 Quinn came to Italy, where he acted with Masina in Giuseppe Amato's *Donne proibate* in 1953, and in 1954 he joined her in Fellini's *La Strada*. Most important, whatever the route taken, the attitude expressed by Masina in her remarks on acting to Tullio Kezich, quoted earlier, follows the general thrust of the Stanislavskian approach.

Perhaps, however, the qualities for which Masina is best known are the externally expressive ones of her "live face" and her body movement—qualities most associated with the art of mime. In his 1985 interview with Masina, Kezich asked the actress how she felt about the American dictum for screen actors that "less is more." Her response shows a good deal of self-awareness: "I would agree [with the dictum], but how can I with a face like mine? I can hide nothing. I exalt feelings. I make them explode."[14] Although, for certain roles, Fellini seems to have asked Masina to hold herself in ("Give more; do less"), he certainly encouraged her to use fully her gifts as mime in the roles of Gelsomina and Cabiria. By cutting her hair short or pulling it back, he emphasizes the circle of her face. He uses heavy base make-up to flatten her face like a mask or mime's face. He draws on artificial, dark eyebrows and makes up the eyes with eyeliner. Finally, he emphasizes Masina's lips with a heavy use of lipstick. Masina's face becomes a clownish one that seems drawn by a child with a crayon. The challenge for her is, then, to see what she can do on the large exaggerated scale of the mime with the few materials at her disposal—eyebrows, eyes, and mouth—and, of course, with the aid of the close-up camera to magnify each expression on the large screen. Important, too, is Masina's use of her body. She has described herself, at least as a young actress, as "androgynous." It might be more accurate to say that she has a dancer's body. (Her training as a dancer when young is relevant here.) As we will see, she was quite good at portraying character by reproducing the heaviness or lightness, the creeping slowness or jaunty swagger of the character. Masina is often compared to Chaplin in terms of the waiflike character she plays or because of the Chaplin-like derby she wears in *La Strada,* but the best comparison might be the sudden explosions of lightness and agility both actors produce in characters who have previously seemed burdened and slow. Stanislavsky, of course, would have appreciated Masina's ability to work out internal and external rhythms for her characters, but the exaggeratedness of the results would have made the performances something other than the kind of realistic theater he wanted to produce.

The mime qualities of actors like Masina are usually considered part of a tradition of "presentational" acting by which the actor works against the idea of a "fourth wall" and communicates more directly to the audience.[15] "Do you get what I am trying to mime?" the performer seems to ask the audience over and over again. Moreover, the emphasis is on artifice, self-proclaimed and self-acknowledged, rather than realism. The pantomime tradition seems to have had three sources. First, mime is associated with the Roman satirist Livius Andronicus in the first century BC; second, with troupes of the commedia dell'arte from Italy who were prohibited from speaking French in their performances in France at the end of the seventeenth century; and third, with the English actor John Rich in the early eighteenth century, who chose to perform the part of Harlequin silently because he had a weak speaking voice.[16] In all these instances, pantomime depends on the idea of replacing speech and many physical objects and activities with silent expression and the use of body movement and gestures, and it very much involves the spectators in the performance in terms of figuring out the missing elements.

Although scholars differ about where and when mime began, they seem to agree that the man who attempted to systematize the art was the Frenchman François Delsarte (1811–71). He was a teacher who set out to explain expressions and gestures and their meanings for his students.[17] Most interesting was Delsarte's idea that gestures and stances can be classified as "eccentric," "concentric," and "normal." As mime Tony Montanaro explains in *Mime Spoken Here,* eccentric poses are "open, extended, outward, extroverted, big, loud"; concentric poses are "closed, contracted, inward, introverted, small, quiet"; and normal poses are "neutral, a point between eccentric and concentric."[18] Consequently, according to Montanaro, we can easily "read" characters for their mood at a given moment or perhaps their basic natures, as least in the Jungian terms of extrovert and introvert. Montanaro cites the example of a comic drill sergeant with legs spread and feet planted apart, elbows flared out, chest puffed up, and eyes bulging. These are all eccentric poses, and they show an aggressive character. At the same time, however, the drill sergeant may have his hands on his hips, his hands folded into fists, his chin tucked in, and the corners of his mouth pulled down. These are concentric poses. Montanaro argues, following Delsarte, that the eyes, mouth, and hands are elements of the body where soft gestures may be made. Such gestures are suppressed here. He concludes, "This drill sergeant *flaunts* brute strength and *conceals* any potential for tenderness."[19] The larger point, though, is that mimes use Delsarte's ideal of eccentric and concentric body language to build characters, whether the mimes acknowledge their source or not. Certainly, the strategy is a part of the arsenal used by Masina.

The collaboration of Fellini and Masina, then, involves the play of a representational approach and a presentational one. In her remarks on acting, Masina seems more interested in the representational one, associated with Stanislavsky, and Fellini appears to be more interested in the presentational one, the one associated with mime. Clearly, with the persona of the waif, Fellini is the winner. Perhaps, with the persona of the deceived wife, it is Masina. But in both cases, the tension exists.

The Waif

The waif is an underdog figure (fig. 5.1). Despite having a counselor or a friend, the waif is essentially alone, cut off from family and a love relationship such as she envisions in an ideal marriage. The waif is both emotionally vulnerable and resilient.[20] With Gelsomina, Fellini will finally choose to emphasize the first quality, and with Cabiria, the second quality.[21] There is a childish aspect to the waif in her simple outlook on life. But above all else, the waif seeks to draw from the viewers of *La Strada* and *Nights of Cabiria* a full and unabashed emotion—sympathy. In this sense, then, the waif is a cathartic figure. The action of the movies and the structures of works are designed to further this affective goal, and the emotional tug between character and audience is of supreme importance.

Fig. 5.1. Fellini's sketch of Gelsomina as the waif figure of *La Strada.*
Federico Fellini Copyright © 1982
Diogenes Verlag AG Zürich.

Biographer Angelo Solmi gives the following anecdote about how Fellini discovered the relationship that was to become the basis for *La Strada,* the relationship between Gelsomina and Zampano:

> One evening [Fellini] had gone out into the country and had seen two nomads camping in the open. While the woman was stirring soup in a pot over a fire, the man waited apart from her. They never exchanged a word all the time Fellini watched them. For the first time the director understood directly the inability to communicate between two people destined to live together.[22]

The anecdote may be apocryphal. Fellini backed away from the account later in his career.[23] However, it provides a useful symbolic scene, for it illustrates well the central situation of the movie: two people locked together in a relationship without communication or love. We might consider that this loneliness is worse than the loneliness when one is by oneself, since the loneliness between two people is opportunity wasted. In any case, this is exactly the situation in which Fellini places his waif in *La Strada*.

Further, Fellini is clear about his initial conception for the character of Gelsomina: "It became real when I drew the circle on paper that was Gelsomina's head."[24] He elaborates: "Gelsomina personified innocence betrayed, so Giulietta was the perfect actress to be Gelsomina. As a person, she was still that sheltered girl who looked with awe at the mysteries of life."

As we have seen in chapter 1, Fellini likes to pair a smaller character against a larger one. Giulietta Masina, whose height may be placed approximately at five feet, two inches, is paired with Anthony Quinn, who is at least a foot taller.[25] Quinn portrays Zampano, the itinerant strongman who buys Gelsomina away from her mother to help him with his traveling strongman act. He is, as Donald P. Costello has pointed out, "brute power. He breaks things—furniture, doors, people. Power is even his profession."[26] Quinn's height differential is enhanced by the bulky, leather flight jacket he wears to make him seem much more powerful than Gelsomina, as well as taller. He is dark-skinned, whereas she is extremely light, and his darkness is increased by his unshaven stubble of facial hair and his bushy eyebrows. Moreover, the knit stocking cap that he often pulls down over his head gives him a Neanderthal appearance: He seems to have no forehead. On the other hand, Gelsomina is short, soft, and fair. She wears a simple jersey, a tattered striped vest, a dark skirt, and tennis shoes. Over these clothes, she wears either a cloak or a long military coat. The cloak makes her look like an Italian schoolchild, and the coat, which hangs almost to her ankles, makes her seem a small person lost in a big garment. For the part, Masina had her hair cut short and bleached. A mixture of shaving cream and talcum powder was added to her hair to make it bristly.[27] Finally, Fellini asked her to smile with her lips closed tightly, as he had observed in Masina's childhood photographs, to capture a little-girl look.[28] The result of the pairing is a couple that resembles two fairy-tale figures. Fellini has even spoken of a "cruel fairy-tale atmosphere" in the movie,[29] and the specific tale most often mentioned by critics is "Beauty and the Beast."

Gelsomina is retarded, or "slow." She seems to lack the fifth and final stage of child development according to psychologist Jean Piaget—the acquisition of critical-thinking ability and the capacity for abstract thought. Neither Fellini nor Masina was willing to discuss this aspect head-on. Fellini speaks about Gelsomina in quasi-literary terms, calling her a "bambina-vecchina [child-woman] who is both a little crazy and a little saintly,"[30] and Masina describes Gelsomina as a "humble fisherman's daughter" who is socially deprived.[31] However, it is clear from the way Masina plays the part that she sees Gelsomina as someone who does not always understand what is happening around her. As Masina puts it, Gelsomina "is always like someone in a trance."[32] The character cannot solve problems, but she can ask the child's question "Why?" and sometimes can accept a solution when it is given to her.

Analyzing her character in relationship to Zampano, Masina tells us,

> I always tried by means of a sometimes exaggerated acting style to express the difficulty of communicating with others, which often becomes transformed into an artificial vivacity or into the feeling of not being in the proper place but, rather, being trapped inside a deep sense of embarrassment. Therefore, I often "perform" for Zampano, even when we are not putting on a show.[33]

The notion of a performance within the performance of the movie for a particular audience within the movie is an important element we will need to return to, for it is a major device Fellini uses in his films with Masina. Here, however, it is part of Masina's conception of the waif's character. Gelsomina communicates by acting out, rather than speaking, her feelings.

Body language is, of course, very important in Masina's portrayal of Gelsomina. The actress has stated that her character walks "with her shoulders down as if she were carrying an invisible cross."[34] This burdened movement is one of the character's external rhythms. Biographer John Baxter has stated correctly, however, that there is a second rhythm, that of lightness and energy, which comes also from the way Gelsomina walks. Baxter writes, "Since she had little dialogue, none of it profound, Masina worked extensively on Gelsomina's movement. 'She has a very unusual walk. All the agility is in the feet.'"[35] We may add that Gelsomina also has a rocking motion to her body whenever she is either particularly sad or happy. She shifts from left to right and right to left perhaps to soothe herself—rocking herself like a baby—when things are not as she wishes, and she uses the same motion, but more briskly—perhaps letting off excess energy—when things go her way. And further we may add that her hands have something of the agility and quickness of her feet. Sometimes they seem to have almost a life of their own.

A sequence early in the film shows us Gelsomina's character quite clearly and demonstrates much of the nature of her relationship with Zampano. The sequence involves a dinner that Zampano and Gelsomina treat themselves to in a trattoria after they have taken in a large sum of money by their performance earlier in the day. The situation is a new one for Gelsomina. It may be that Gelsomina has never eaten in a restaurant before, for she orders both entrees, not realizing she is supposed to choose between them. It is even more likely that she has never seen Zampano so flushed with success before. Clearly, Gelsomina wants to share the glorious moment with her partner. As is typical in many of her scenes, Masina does not so much act as she does react.

Gelsomina responds to the situation in two ways, and they are to some extent contradictory. First, she tries to imitate Zampano's actions. This seems her way of affirming her closeness to him. When he enters, Zampano greets two men at the counter and pulls down the hat of a friend at a table. Certainly he wishes to be noticed. Gelsomina follows quietly behind, looking around and basking in the attention, too, but finding no one to greet. At the table, she sprawls her elbows out "eccentrically" as he does, chooses a toothpick from the jar on the table, as Zampano has done, and experiments with picking her teeth in further imitation. After the meal, she drains her wine glass with a gulp that exceeds the swig Zampano has just taken. Then Gelsomina goes too far in trying to affirm her relationship with Zampano: She tries to start a conversation. "Where do you come from?" she asks pleasantly enough. Zampano, of course, rebuffs Gelsomina. He orders more wine and calls over a redheaded prostitute. The new arrival gives Gelsomina, who does not realize the woman may become a rival, a chance to begin again building her relationship with Zampano. Gelsomina will be "one of the fellows" with him. When Zampano slaps the woman on the butt as she sits down or smacks her hand when she reaches for some of his money, Gelsomina smiles and rolls her shoulders like a male in hearty laughter. All of this, of course, has to do with fitting in, becoming a part of Zampano's way of life.

At the same time, Gelsomina acts more circumspectly than Zampano. In fact, Gelsomina acts like a polite guest who has been invited into someone's home. Perhaps, this has to do with her unfamiliarity with restaurants, but more likely it has to do with the manners she has learned at home. She is on her good behavior. This strand of behavior, contradicting the first strand, gives the scene its depth and shading. After Zampano makes his entrance by flinging open the restaurant door, she carefully and quietly shuts the door behind them. Gelsomina rises and bows slightly to the red-headed prostitute when she comes to the table and offers her own wine glass to the newcomer. Furthermore, when Gelsomina smiles and rolls her shoulders at Zampano's pranks with the prostitute, there is also a shy, modest cast to the acts. Gelsomina looks downward "concentrically," qualifying the robustness of the other gestures. Finally, when Zampano knocks over a chair in his haste to leave with the prostitute, Gelsomina pauses to pick up the chair and put it back in place, and she bows slightly to the owner from the door as if to say, "Thank you for having me in your house." This level of behavior, especially in juxtaposition with Zampano's loutishness, must draw the audience to Gelsomina's side and position audience members to root against what they know will happen eventually—Zampano's abandonment of Gelsomina for the night.

When Zampano orders Gelsomina to stay behind as he rumbles off in his motorcycle-driven van with the prostitute, Gelsomina sits down on the curb to wait. With the camera above to look down on her, she contracts into a near ball. Then Fellini adds a piece of action that deepens the loneliness. We hear the clopping sound of a horse approaching offscreen. Gelsomina looks up. The horse is, of course, one of those surreal apparitions that, as we saw in chapter 1, appear out of nowhere in Fellini movies, with no explanation.[36] Here the effect is somewhat different than elsewhere, however. We anticipate, as does Gelsomina, that the horse will bring some new element into play that will interrupt the loneliness. Such is not the case, though. The horse clops past without even acknowledging Gelsomina's presence. Expectations have been raised, only to be dashed.

Gelsomina's more positive moments come in her scenes played with the Fool, portrayed by Richard Basehart. The Fool is an agent introduced into the narrative to intensify the situation. Modeled somewhat on Harlequin of the commedia dell'arte, the Fool has a double nature. Like a guardian angel, he teases Gelsomina and encourages her, and like a devil, he mocks and angers Zampano. One of Gelsomina's most pleasant moments comes when the Fool invites Gelsomina to perform with him in a comic bit. He will play the tune "Tranquillo" on his tiny violin, and she must interrupt him on cue with comic blasts on a huge trombone. The tune, known also as "Gelsomina's Theme," is one she has heard before and one that haunts her with its sadness and beauty. When Gelsomina, spellbound by the Fool's music, does not come in on cue, he berates her (as Zampano has done in an earlier rehearsal scene); however, when she gets her part right on her second try, the Fool praises her. Overjoyed at being appreciated and at being in an act with her favorite piece of music, Gelsomina responds with pure joy. She follows the Fool around the ring, embellishing her part and still blaring on cue. Masina accomplishes her aim of portraying Gelsomina's joy by the lightness of her moves. Gelsomina follows the Fool with quick, sprightly movements on the balls of her feet, and then she pivots once and performs a jeté with her toes pointed down in the manner of a ballerina. The point is made that here is a character capable of performing with gracefulness if given a chance.

A sequence that seems designed to show off Masina's ability to use her "live" face in close-up occurs when the Fool delivers his famous parable of the meaning of a pebble. The Fool's monologue essentially presents Gelsomina with the idea that "everything that exists in the world has some purpose," even a pebble that the Fool picks off the ground. Her purpose, the Fool instructs, may be to teach Zampano to care for someone beyond himself. Critic Frank Burke has dismissed the parable as "bleak instrumentalism."[37] He is probably correct in this, but for our purposes here, the parable gives Gelsomina a function in life that she accepts. Since she began the sequence in despair, asking, "What am I doing in this world?" (a version of the child's question "Why?"), we can understand that the parable gives her a direction she very much wants, be the direction right or wrong from our point of view. As the Fool speaks and moves around, Gelsomina remains still, taking in carefully everything he tells her. The scene takes place at night, and Gelsomina has wrapped herself in a dark blanket. The camera is placed slightly above and directly in front of her. Her face is lit with diffused key light. Most visual elements other than her face are eliminated. In the first part of the sequence, her eyes are down, her chin is often tucked in, her mouth downturned, and her hands are folded piously across her abdomen. She is a textbook model of what Delsarte means by "concentric," turned in on herself. At one point, she even hides her face in her handkerchief, and at another, she buries her face in her blanket. Then slowly she begins to unfold outward into "eccentric" expressions as the Fool talks. This begins when the Fool invites her to stay with him to learn his high-wire act. Her posture now becomes more erect; she smiles her child's closed-lipped smile; she thrusts her chin out, and her eyes become wide open, with the camera creeping in to magnify them. When the parable is finished, Gelsomina rises to her feet and walks back and forth, waving her arms in large declamatory gestures. She vows that she will stand up to Zampano in the future and make him acknowledge her importance in his life. In a sense, she is preparing a scene or a "performance" she envisions in the future, and she and the Fool share a laugh at her staginess. We may feel, however, that a character who was asleep has come awake.[38]

Another important scene in which Masina's ability to use her facial expressions in close-up comes at the moment when Gelsomina hovers over the body of the Fool, whom Zampano has killed in a fight that went too far. For this crucial moment, Masina needed an expression of grief and a gesture not yet seen in the film in order that this scene have a strong impact.[39] Using something like "emotional memory," she reached back to expressions seen previously in photographs. She tells us, "I remember at that moment there flashed through my mind the remembrance of certain photographs I had seen in a sensationalistic weekly magazine that was published then, *Crimen*. There had been a cave-in in Sicily in a sulfur mine, and in the photographs the women were bent over the bodies of their men, in rigid attitudes, their faces deformed with grief."[40] Masina renders her version of the images of the Sicilian women by putting her two hands to her face with her fingers apart. The hands seem to want to constrain or hide the mouth, but since the fingers are spread, the mouth remains visible. The mouth is open in a little circle, and Gelsomina makes a small, sad, birdlike peeping sound. Gelsomina also denies that the Fool is dead by saying over and over, "He is hurt," not "He is dead." But on another level of awareness, she knows the Fool is dead and shows this by the noises she emits between her spread fingers. The scene is one of the most striking in the movie.

The character of Cabiria in *Nights of Cabiria* is made of sterner stuff. She will go through a series of disappointments of varying degrees of serious-

ness but always will bounce back. Cabiria has the vulnerability and innocence of Gelsomina but also a tough resilience that Gelsomina lacks. It is
perhaps for this reason that Masina considers Cabiria the character who
resembles her the most.[41] Certainly, Masina respects the character's ability
to "bounce back."

Cabiria is a prostitute on the outskirts of Rome. She maintains the hope
that her condition will change and has something of a confident swagger
that she puts on almost continually to hide her vulnerability. The job of
Masina, the actress, is first to show Cabiria's bravado as an ongoing performance that fools even Cabiria when it is in progress, then to show a few
moments when the bravado falls aside, and finally to show resilience.

The bravado is displayed well in the scene where the famous movie star,
played by Amedeo Nazzari, picks up Cabiria and takes her out on a "night
to remember." Again Masina's physical presence and body language are
extremely important. Her hair is pulled back into a ponytail, making her
round face stand out once again. This time, however, her eyebrows are
drawn on as two dark slash marks rising from the center of her face so that
she seems frequently on the verge of being furious. Her body language is
usually eccentric. Her elbows are bent outward, and as she walks her legs
are spread apart in a masculine manner. Her habitual gesture is to pull down
her cinch belt, which seems always to "ride up" on her. Masina speaks with
a Roman accent. This leads her to push out her lips, especially her lower
one, when she speaks emphatically. As she talks, she frequently shoves out
her right hand in a Roman gesture, palm up, hand shoulder-high, fingers
pointed down, as if to say, "Here is what I have for you, served up and presented on the palm of my hand." Moreover, the prop she carries, a collapsible umbrella, serves her in good stead. Masina can use it to extend her gestures when she wants to point or poke at another character. Further, Masina
has the ability to smile with one side of her mouth while turning the other
side down in a sneer. (A difficult facial contortion, indeed!) The move seems
designed to show a smile she does not really believe in, a cynical smile.

One of Cabiria's finest moments comes in the movie's nightclub scene.
It begins when the actor's girlfriend deserts him, and the star picks up
Cabiria on the street as a replacement. He whisks her away to the nightclub. Fellini has admitted that this scene owes a debt to Chaplin's *City Lights*
(1931). Fellini states, "Her exaggerated dance in the nightclub is reminiscent

of Chaplin, and her encounter with the movie star is similar to that of the tramp's encounter with the millionaire, who recognizes Charlie only when he is drunk."[42] The comparison is not exact, but it is an extended one. Both waifs are lifted above their normal spheres, and both enjoy the experience thoroughly as long as it lasts. Chaplin's situation, though, is tinged with desperation. His tramp is drunk, thanks to the numerous pourings of the millionaire friend, and the dance floor of the nightclub is highly polished. As the tramp whirls faster and faster on the floor, his dance becomes a violent struggle to stay upright. Cabiria's dance is different. When she enters the nightclub wearing her tacky uniform of the street, Cabiria is clearly a fish out of water (much more so than Chaplin's tramp in *City Lights*, who is too drunk to know he is out of place). Cabiria becomes entangled in the curtains at the entryway, and after the maître d' helps her through, she can only smile her one-side-up and one-side-down smile and point boldly at the actor at the bar to prove her right to be present. Fortunately, the actor, wishing to escape an agent and a starlet who want to monopolize his time, invites Cabiria to dance. The music is a mambo, and we have seen Cabiria improvise steps to a mambo twice earlier in the street. She cannot stop herself now, it seems. She breaks away from the actor and does her crossover kicks to the dance as he looks on and the other dancers pull back to watch also. Unlike Chaplin, who makes an embarrassing spectacle of himself in the nightclub, Cabiria becomes the star of the dance floor. She injects energy into the previously staid and dull situation. When the music stops and the actor leaves the club, Cabiria gets to make a triumphant walk to the bar for her purse—almost like a curtain call—before she tugs down her belt for emphasis and follows the actor out. Moreover, outside, in the convertible, she rises to her feet to crow to the two tall prostitutes who had disdained her earlier, "Hey, look who I've got!" This is the waif winning a competition beyond her wildest dreams and having the high spirits to savor the moment. In this, of course, she resembles Chaplin's tramp, too, for he knows how to enjoy his triumphs, fleeting as they may be.

The inevitable letdown occurs in the actor's villa after he has taken Cabiria there for a late-night supper. The girlfriend of the star returns, and Cabiria must hide in the bathroom for the night so that the two lovers may reconcile. The letdown, however, does not occur until after Cabiria has the chance to revel in the sumptuousness of the actor's marvelous quarters.

Three situations work particularly well, for they allow Masina to react to the various "treasures" in the villa. In one, Fellini shoots Masina through a glass aviary as she stares wide-eyed at the actor's exotic birds, taps the glass wall, and smiles (with both corners of her mouth) in glee at the reaction she gets from the birds. In another, Fellini photographs Masina in medium close-up as she turns 360 degrees to locate the source of music that plays as the actor opens the serial mirrored doors of his clothes closet. She is as surprised and delighted and disoriented as a child in a toy store! And, finally, Masina reacts in medium long shot with a mixture of curiosity and apprehension as she lifts with two fingers a shellfish from the containers of food the actor's servant has wheeled into the room. The reactions, mixed with a variety of other ones, come in rapid succession. The "treasures" allow Masina to show her repertoire of reactions. All of them seem childlike, and they show us something of the gentler aspects of the character beneath the bravado Cabiria has put on earlier in the nightclub. Moreover, Cabiria has the good sense to get the star to autograph a photograph for her so that she can prove her experience to her fellow prostitutes after the evening ends. For once, Cabiria sees her situation for what it is, a glorious exception to the rule that cannot go on forever. The autographed photograph, in a sense, cushions the blow of the girlfriend's return that ends Cabiria's evening. Indeed, we may suspect that Cabiria relishes the idea of telling her tale later almost as much as she enjoys the events as they unfold.

Important to the depiction of the waif is the idea of a performance within a performance. We have already seen that Gelsomina, as a traveling performer with her strongman partner in *La Strada,* is often practicing a routine or actually performing one for an audience within the film and that Cabiria does her impromptu mambo for the people in the nightclub. The idea of a performance for an audience within the film is, of course, a time-honored device for allowing gifted performers to do their expected turn. The motivation for the action need only be the need to entertain a group of people within the diegesis, but of course, it is we, the audience outside the film, who get what we have bought our tickets to see. Certainly, Fellini wishes to use the device to showcase Masina's talents as a mime as much as possible. In fact, in *Variety Lights,* Masina's first performance in a film written by Fellini, he creates the opportunity for her to do a stage act of imitating various historical figures such as Napoleon, Verdi, and Garibaldi. But, of course, the staged performance can do more than provide a showcase. It can draw the audience outside the diegesis into the movie, since the audience outside, in effect, becomes equal to characters in the diegesis, and thus the device can strengthen the ties between the performer and us. The "fourth wall" is removed. And the staged moment can, of course, be used, as Hamlet has suggested, to comment upon the action in the unstaged portion of the work. The performance within the performance is, then, a highly concentrated opportunity—one that Fellini likes to use particularly with the waif.

The most important performance within the performance in *Nights of Cabiria* comes when the vaudeville magician calls Cabiria out of the audience to help him with his act. As she stands on the side of the stage watching the magician hypnotize a group of men and have them act out a shipwreck scene, Cabiria goes through reactions similar to those she displayed in the actor's villa. She leans forward, hands on her knees, staring wide-eyed in amazement at the performance. Then a bit later when the audience taunts her about where she lives and how she lacks a husband, she marches forward on the stage to stare them down, hands on hips and chin jutted out at them, like Montanaro's example of the sergeant major. But when the magician puts her under hypnosis and introduces her to an imaginary suitor, Oscar, a transformation takes place. Cabiria becomes an innocent young woman again, discovering love. The transformation is achieved primarily through Masina's skills as a mime. She relaxes her facial muscles for the first time in the movie. Her eyebrows level off. There is a faint smile on her mouth. And she plays the scene with her eyes gently closed. The magician gives Cabiria directions about strolling with Oscar in the park, but Cabiria soon takes over the part and improvises her own movements and lines. She kneels slowly to pick imaginary flowers, and then, as the magician calls for the orchestra to play, Cabiria begins to waltz gracefully with the imaginary suitor. She wears a raincoat and has a shoulder bag strapped on her shoulder. The costume should be absurd, but it is not. The raincoat is white, and it becomes a neutral garment. We are aware not so much of it but of a figure in white who is moving. Masina holds her hands out in front of her, not quite as one would hold a partner and not quite in the stereotypical sleepwalker's pose. She then stops and, looking down at Oscar's imaginary hand in hers, asks whether his feelings for her are sincere. The transformation is complete, and the magician, in his concern for what is taking place beyond his control, brings the performance to an end. The transformation on stage has worked primarily because Masina has changed the rhythm of the character. What was brusque and assertive, or energetic and high-spirited, before has now become graceful and delicate. If we said Gelsomina comes awake in her scene about the parable of the pebble in *La Strada,* then here it is as if a rambunctious child matures into a woman. The scene is a tour de force. More important, though, in this key moment, when she has our full attention, Masina shows us what we need finally to know about Cabiria—what we have perhaps known but have not seen so definitively—that Cabiria wants the ideal of a romantic love that can change her life from what it is into something finer. This is, of course, not a movie in which such wishes will be granted. The con man in the audience who adopts the name Oscar will use what he has learned about her on stage to dupe her one last time in the film. Yet, under hypnosis on the stage, she does have her wish for a moment.

It is appropriate that *Nights of Cabiria* ends with a close-up of Cabiria's face. After the con man has taken all of Cabiria's money and deserted her in the countryside, she begins to walk back to town and is overtaken by a group of celebrating young people who start to revive her good spirits. As we saw in chapter 1, this is a dance of life that often seems to energize Fellini characters. Here it allows Masina to give a final image of Cabiria's resilience. With one teardrop of mascara, like the painted teardrop on a clown's face, Cabiria begins to show the first traces of a smile. The victories of the waif are muted. Gelsomina's victory comes only after she dies, and we can see the effect her loss has on the anguished Zampano. Cabiria's victory lies only in the ability to begin to smile after her betrayal by her ruthless suitor. Such triumphs are indeed small, and they are tinged with a sad, even melodramatic sense of injustice. The waifs have deserved better. The final shot of *Nights of Cabiria* seems the appropriate last shot for such figures. Cabiria looks toward the camera just off to the right, then off to the left, and back to the left again, as she begins to smile.[43] For a fleeting moment, she looks directly into the camera as her eyes travel, and Masina breaks the fourth wall to establish direct contact with the viewers. Her link with us is the presentational one of performance art.

The Deceived Wife

The figure of the "deceived wife," as played by Giulietta Masina, runs through Fellini's oeuvre from the start almost until the end (fig. 5.2).[44] Four films are involved: *Variety Lights* (1950), *Il Bidone* (1955), *Juliet of the Spirits* (1965), and *Ginger and Fred* (1986). The figure resembles the waif in that the wife is something of an underdog. She seeks to preserve a relationship with an incorrigibly unreliable husband and is thereby doomed to failure. A major difference between the deceived wife and the waif is the scale on which Masina acts. In the role of the deceived wife, Masina acts, relatively speaking, on a realistic plane. Her performances have less of the tour de force quality of the mime that we have become accustomed to in *La Strada* and *Nights of Cabiria*, but these "realistic" performances are, in their own way, equally interesting. If we look at the chronological development of the figure of the deceived wife from its beginning in *Variety Lights* to its culmination in *Ginger and Fred*, we find that the figure develops from something of a Mediterranean stereotype of wife as victim, a figure of fun, perhaps, to a rather sympathetic and vibrant character who stands on her own two feet and makes tough decisions. The development of the deceived wife over the course of the four films reveals a kind of growing sympathy in Fellini for the situation of the woman in marriage, particularly in Italian marriages, that viewers may find surprising. In any case, this is the place to look if viewers wish to gauge Fellini's reaction to the changing status of women. The place not to look is in the films like *Amarcord, 8 ½, Fellini Satyricon,* and *City of Women,* which present women primarily as archetypal figures of the anima for the male psyche. The growth and change of the figure of the deceived wife may very well be the result of the forcefulness Masina brought to the role that finally had to have its day.

Despite the fact that Fellini remained married to Masina for fifty years, his public pronouncements about marriage have often been negative. He tends to describe marriage as a limitation on the partner's, particularly a husband's, means of developing potential aspects of character. For example, in response to an interviewer's questions in 1966, after the release of *Juliet of the Spirits,* he claimed, "Marriage is tyranny, a violation and mortification of natural instincts."[45] The general thrust of Fellini's remark seems to echo some of Jung's ideas in his essay "Marriage as a Psychological Relationship."

Fig. 5.2. Fellini's sketch of Juliet as the deceived wife figure of *Juliet of the Spirits*. Federico Fellini Copyright © 1982 Diogenes Verlag AG Zürich.

Jung describes marriage as often being a relationship between someone who has a complex and powerful personality and someone who has a simpler, more dependent personality. The first, Jung calls a "container," and the second, the "contained." Writing about the European culture of the first quarter of the twentieth century, Jung tended to think, as did Fellini, of the container as usually male and the contained as usually female, although this did not necessarily have to be the case. If the container were male, however, he would attempt to project his anima or his various feelings for women on the contained wife and would find the wife not suitably complex for the role. Then an adjustment of some sort would be required of the husband. He might seek the anima within himself, or he might pursue other women. For the contained female whose life is defined by her husband's world, Jung speculates that a crisis in the marriage might prove a good thing, if it brings her to expand her world or to look more deeply within herself: "Her acceptance of failure may do her a real good by forcing her to recognize that the security she was so desperately seeking in the other is to be found in herself."[46]

Jung, then, seems to find inevitable, or at least useful, a crisis in the marriage. Ironically, given the strong male biases of Jung and Fellini, the crisis might prove especially beneficial to the woman. This is a central truth for Fellini's depiction of marriage in the four films that starred Masina as the deceived wife. The discovery of deception can be the beginning of growth for this figure.

Masina seems to have taken on the role of the deceived wife with a certain amount of anger directed toward the characters she had to play. Fellini's own pursuits of other women, particularly actresses—whether real or invented—were frequently discussed in the tabloids, and the gossip items never failed to nettle her.[47] But her anger seems to go deeper than this. It is directed at the passivity of the types she was asked to play. For example, she told Kezich about the main character of *Juliet of the Spirits,*

> The Juliet on the screen is timid, oppressed, and full of complexes. I will tell you that I have always been antithetical to her. I could never swallow her. I don't like this type of Mediterranean woman who is first submissive to her parents and then a parasite in her relationship with her husband. I have never been submissive to anyone.[48]

Masina adds that she played the part of Juliet as a kind of "unconscious defense" against what she might have become if she had not been as independent-minded as she was. The anger against the characters she plays shows up not so much in the characters themselves as perhaps it does as a force behind the chronological development of the deceived wife toward becoming a stronger woman.

The major attributes of the figure of the deceived wife fall into three categories. First, she has a good heart, loves her partner, and dreams of an ideal relationship to be attained sometime in the future. Second, she has a strong motherly streak. She enjoys taking care of her "little man." And third, the character is a good manager of practical affairs. The assumption often is that if the husband can appeal to her skills in the last two categories, he will be able to touch her heart in the first category and be forgiven almost anything. This is certainly the case with Masina's character, Melina Amour, in *Variety Lights* in her behavior with her vaudeville partner Checco Dalmonte. She nurses her "little man" when he seems to have a fever and makes sure he has food to eat when the theater troupe is on short rations. Moreover, she keeps track of their savings so that they will have sufficient capital to settle down, marry properly, and open a shop when their vaudeville days are over. She is, then, a mother and a manager for Checco. When he wishes to raise money for a show to feature Liliana, the new young woman in his life, he goes to Melina for help with the appeals that as a "doting mother" she must do whatever it takes to make her unhappy "little man" happy again and that as a good manager of money she must provide the funds he cannot possibly find on his own.

The first interesting crisis situation, as Jung has described it, comes, however, in *Il Bidone*. Masina plays the part of Iris, the young wife of a fledgling con man nicknamed Picasso, portrayed by Richard Basehart. The husband claims to be a salesman, and Iris would like to believe this fiction. (His real career is the deception here. There is no "other woman.") Moreover, Picasso does seem to have at least a modest amount of talent as a painter— a situation that allows Iris to dream of a romantic future as the wife and helpmate of a famous artist. Further, when Picasso presents Iris with one hundred thousand lire he acquired on his last swindle, she tells him she will be a good manager and help promote their dream: "You'll see. I'll make it last a month. That way you can do some painting." However, the illusion on which Iris's marriage is founded is destroyed for her when Picasso takes her to a New Year's Eve party given by a wealthy drug dealer, and Iris has to take a good look at Augusto and Roberto, the two so-called salesmen Picasso works with, and at the milieu the con men aspire to. The party provides the crisis for the marriage of Iris and Picasso.

The sequence is set up as a series of events to which Masina reacts, using in particular her "live" face. As the sequence progresses, she reacts increasingly more somberly to what she learns about her husband, or to put it another way, she finds it increasingly harder to retrieve her polite, smiling party face each time she loses it. At first, Iris is slightly ill at ease when she enters the party. She wears a black cocktail dress with a high collar behind the neck, a small waist, and full bouffant skirt. She is, in fact, quite fashionable by 1950s standards,[49] but she has misjudged the formality of the occasion. The other women are dressed in strapless evening gowns. Iris holds her champagne glass a little too high and watches it a little too carefully. When Picasso introduces Iris to the host and hostess, they each greet her politely but hurry on to other people. Masina looks down at her hands each time this happens, yet recovers her party face quickly, smiling bravely at her husband. Then three events happen that trouble her more deeply. First, Roberto explains to Picasso that the host has made his money by trafficking in drugs. He explains this, however, by putting a finger beneath his nose and sniffing. Iris smiles as if she understands the gesture, but when Roberto finishes, she looks at her husband, puzzled, for an explanation he does not give. Next, Picasso tries to interest the host in buying a painting that he has brought with him. "This is a De Pisis," Picasso says proudly. The host, who is not to be conned, suggests, however, that Picasso himself is the painter and touches the work to see if the paint is dry. At the start of the conversation, Iris stands at full height with a hopeful smile on her face. Apparently, she had thought her husband would attempt to sell the work as his own. While the interchange goes on and as she understands what is taking place, Iris looks down again, embarrassed, but ends by slipping her hand loyally under Picasso's arm to console him. However, the final event of the night is one from which Iris cannot recover. The host confronts Roberto for having stolen a gold cigarette case from one of the guests and demands its return. Standing in the background of the confrontation, Masina's eyes go from the host to Roberto to her husband. Iris has to recognize that her husband is a partner to a thief. She turns and leaves the party ahead of Picasso. As she comes outside the building, Masina walks directly toward the camera, allowing us to see her crying, stricken face. Fellini gives Masina her one extended speech in the sequence as she addresses Picasso outside: "I knew very well what kind of people they were. And how many times did I tell you . . . and you nothing, ever . . . always lies. . . . You come, you go, I don't know where your money comes from, you're in trouble all over the place, and every time somebody knocks on the door my heart skips a beat. I can't take it anymore."[50] The crisis at the party, then, forces Iris to look at the fears she had previously been unwilling to acknowledge. Once her fears are spoken to Picasso, she cannot take them back.

The party sequence is Iris's final appearance on screen in the released version of *Il Bidone*. Fellini brings her to the point of the crisis and stops. We do not know what will become of her. There is another scene involving Picasso in which he joins Augusto and Roberto for a new scam, but drunk and afraid of losing Iris, Picasso pulls out of the scheme and vows to return home. Whether he will hold to his resolve is not clear, however. His decision does not necessarily assure a happy resolution for the marriage, either, since we do not know how Iris will receive Picasso. Further, an additional scene involving Iris was cut from the movie to shorten it. Fellini has called the scene one of Masina's best. He describes it as a scene "in which Iris, who has left Picasso, confronts Augusto, blaming him for her husband's life of crime."[51] This additional scene would have made Iris a more forceful character who has taken much more control over her life. With the movie as it stands, we have only the deceived wife who has seen through the deception of her marriage and has named the deception for what it is.

Juliet of the Spirits takes us a step further. In this film we see the deceived wife survive the crisis experience. Fellini has called attention to an intense contention between Masina and him on the film: "She had many criticisms pertaining to the character of Juliet, and I think they made me stubborn in defense of my creation. I wanted to protect *my* concept of character. She wanted to protect *her* character."[52] Out of this battle of wills, however, came the advancement of the figure of the deceived wife.

The scene in which Juliet learns the full truth about her deceiving husband, Giorgio, is another of those strong scenes, like the end of the party sequence in *Il Bidone,* in which Masina must show her pain at what she has discovered. In this scene, as we have come to expect, she speaks little. She reacts silently. The detective shows her a film of Giorgio cavorting with a model named Gabriella on a trip to the country along the Appian Way and entering a house with her, and the detective plays for Juliet a recording of Giorgio talking as a lover with Gabriella. We get a series of six close-ups of Juliet as she watches and listens. In the first, we see her head and shoulders while she sits bolt upright in her chair. She smokes a cigarette and blinks as she gets used to the semidark of the room. She wears a white tunic dress, a fashionable version of a black Chinese coolie hat, and a pair of long black gloves. Clearly she has dressed formally for what she suspects will be an important event. In the second shot, the camera dollies in for a tighter shot of her face. She lowers her eyelids and shakes her head slowly from side to side as if to say, "It can't be so." The next three shots are extreme close-ups. The light in the room is such that we can make out clearly only Masina's eyes and forehead. We see tears emerge in her eyes. The sixth close-up is a slightly fuller shot in which Masina wipes away one of the tears with her gloved hand. According to Masina, Fellini got these reaction shots in one take. He narrated the events of the detective's film to her, and Masina responded to what he said. The experience, she said, was both torturing and easy.[53] We may speculate that the situation was torturing for her in that she could well imagine such a situation in her own life and easy in that once she did imagine it, as a sort of emotion recall, the tears came readily. Important, then, to the dynamics of the acting situation was that Masina's own husband was narrating to her the activities of a deceiving husband. We are dealing here with a trick, perhaps even a sadistic one, but the kind that directors use with actors to get strong results. Masina seems to have borne no resentment, however, other than to call the scene "torturing." As an actress, certainly she was willing to pay a price to get the desired results. The most startling shot of the scene, however, is the last one when Juliet rises to leave. The camera is behind Masina. The shot is a medium one showing her head and torso. Because of the lighting in the room, she appears as a silhouette on the lit movie screen in front of her. The peculiar shape of Juliet's coolie hat, which seems almost like a lamp shade, makes her an odd, surreal figure such as we discussed in chapter 1. There is a touch of comedy to the shot. Yet because the situation is so serious for the character, audiences rarely laugh. The shot that involves Fellini's setup of the silhouette effect and Masina's rigid, almost mechanical rising from her seat is, quite simply, powerful.[54]

A similar kind of scene occurs when Giorgio leaves Juliet at the end of the movie. This time, however, she loses her composure after he leaves and breaks down in sobs. In interview with Kezich, Fellini describes this scene interestingly, even if a bit inaccurately.

> For example, the scene I am now shooting, Giorgio's departure from Juliet's home. Excellent dialogue, really very well written, just right. But I ended up shooting the scene so that neither of the characters said a word. She finds him while he is packing his suitcase, she gives him something to eat, and they stand together in silence. At the end he says,

"Ciao," and he leaves her in an unadorned, empty room, from which I had all the furniture removed.[55]

Fellini should have said that he has reduced Masina's dialogue to very little. Giorgio actually speaks a great deal. As he eats, he talks to Juliet while she sits primly in the living room, pretending to watch the TV. At first, he tells Juliet that he must go to Milan on a business trip for two days. Then he adds that he might stay away longer at his doctor's suggestion, to escape the pressures of his work. And finally, he admits to a "friendship" with a certain person, "nothing definite or irreparable." He wants to be alone to deal with his "confusion." Juliet knows that in fact he is going on a trip with Gabriella, for she has just come from Gabriella's apartment and has learned of the trip from Gabriella's maid. Yet she says nothing, allowing Giorgio's explanations to stand unchallenged. Her silence is puzzling. She may be too proud to enter into a messy scene with Giorgio, or too inhibited.[56] Another explanation, however, is possible. Earlier, the American psychotherapist Dr. Miller has suggested to Juliet, "You long for your husband to go away. . . . Without Giorgio, you would begin to breathe, to live." Juliet may, then, be waiting quietly for Giorgio to play out his scene so that she can get on with a new era of her life. Before that will happen, however, she must lose her composure, held since the beginning of the film, when Giorgio forgot their anniversary. In dramatic terms, it could be said that Juliet's need to finally give up her iron self-restraint is the "through line" of the film and her tears, the "superobject." Once she gives way to the mixture of emotions in her, she is well on her way to battling the hallucinatory elements—the apparition of her overbearing mother, the images from the church in her life emphasizing martyrdom, and various male objects of her sexual desire—which Fellini brings forward into the house that he has indeed stripped of its furniture as he claimed.

The ending of the film itself is a series of long takes of Juliet leaving her beautiful white house in the country and walking along the high white picket fence toward the forest of lovely plane trees nearby. Like Nora in Ibsen's *A Doll's House,* she leaves the psychological confinement of her marriage.[57] The terms Fellini uses to describe her final state, however, sound more like those of Jung than of Ibsen. Fellini describes the condition of one who has been contained becoming free: "Juliet alone, at the end of the film, should mean the discovery of individuality. The thing she feared the most, the departure of her husband, is revealed as a gift of providence."[58] Masina, however, finds Fellini's statement too optimistic and too masculine a reading of the situation. "What could Juliet do at that point in her life?" Masina asked Fellini. "It's too late. It's different for women than it is for men."[59] Masina's point is well taken. In 1965, the date when the film was completed, Juliet would not have been able to get a divorce from Giorgio and therefore would not have been able to start a new and perhaps better marriage.[60] She has not trained for a career. Juliet is, then, a classic case of the wife deceived not just by her husband but also by the social norms in which she grew up. Like Ibsen's Nora, perhaps, there are few places for Juliet to go once she walks out of her house. The movie, then, seems incomplete. A further statement is necessary.

This further statement comes in *Ginger and Fred,* Masina's last film with her husband, made when she was sixty-four. The story of Ginger, a former music-hall performer who is called out of retirement for a TV Christmas special, was originally to have been written and directed by Fellini as an episode for a TV series.[61] Producer Alberto Grimaldi, however, persuaded Fellini to develop his episode into a feature film. This Fellini did by adding an ongoing satire of commercial television in Italy, with its many advertisement breaks and its quick run-throughs of human-interest events and bizarre people.[62] At base, though, Fellini has always maintained that the movie "was intended to be a love story,"[63] and it is this strand of the movie we will take up here.

Important to the movie is the idea of the *couple.* Giulietta Masina is paired with Marcello Mastroianni. She plays Amelia Bonetti, and he, Pippo Botticella, two music-hall dancers of the 1940s who did imitations of the movie dance routines of Ginger Rogers and Fred Astaire. The premise of Fellini's movie is that the two old-timers are to be reunited on the TV show "We Are Proud to Present" after more than thirty years of retirement and separation.[64] Although never married, Amelia and Pippo had been together as a couple for fifteen years. They were both dance partners and lovers. Interestingly enough, Masina has insisted that she and Fellini should be considered a *couple* rather than a *family,* since they did not have children.[65] She has argued that Fellini and she remained together not because they had to for the sake of family, but because they chose to as people well suited for each other, despite their occasional spats. There is something highly romantic in her assertion, and that romantic element carries over into *Ginger and Fred.*

The through line of the movie is based on the romantic dance routine Amelia and Pippo are famous for doing on stage. In this routine, Amelia as Ginger stands by an ocean liner ready to depart. The whistle of the ship sounds. Ginger strikes a balletic pose of farewell, her right arm raised in a kind of salute to all she is leaving behind, and she murmurs, "Addio." Then Fred appears on the other side of the stage, casually smoking a cigarette that he throws down and grinds out with his foot. Perhaps he has swallowed his pride and has come to ask her not to leave but cannot quite bring himself to begin. "Fred," she calls out and runs to him, unfolding her arms toward him. Then they dance a duet to a medley of "The Continental," "Dancing Cheek to Cheek," "Let's Face the Music and Dance," and "Putting on My Top Hat," with various ballroom passes and glides and with inserted tap dance solos—all designed to show Fred courting and winning Ginger back. Visually and rhythmically, the two performers demonstrate they are a couple who belong together. This romantic fable of two lovers reuniting informs the situation of the movie as a whole. Amelia practices or demonstrates parts of the routine by herself, and she and Pippo rehearse parts of the routine together. What we wait for, indeed expect, in the movie itself is a final complete performance of the routine that will, in some way, reunite the couple who have been apart.

Pippo is the irresponsible male partner we have come to expect. He drinks far too much; he criticizes Amelia's facial expressions and her steps; he insults or teases most of the people he meets; and he coins bawdy aphorisms that are all essentially the same. Amelia broke up the team thirty years in the past at least in part because of what they refer to as his behavior as a "sexual nomad." At the time of the breakup, Amelia now learns, Pippo had a breakdown and was hospitalized. In the present, he sells encyclopedias from door to door. Fellini wished to show Mastroianni as a character who is down-and-out but still retains some charm and appeal. The director had Mastroianni's hair thinned and a bald spot created with wax. He left some wisps of hair, however, "to symbolize [a] man clinging to his failing potency."[66] Further, Mastroianni seems to have deadened the left side of his face, as if his character has had nerve damage, a characteristic that becomes obvious when Pippo smiles. And Mastroianni has his character gasp for breath after virtually every exertion. Yet Pippo can still dance with gracefulness and even energy. He is thus the perfect partner for the Masina heroine. While he can still offer a certain charm, he needs Amelia's skills as a mothering caretaker and as a financial manager. In short, he is like the relatively helpless little boys we have seen before.

Amelia is the deceived partner, if not the deceived wife. Pippo's deceptions with other women are well in the past now, however. The issues are whether she will respond to his obvious needs for her as a mother and a manager and whether she will give in to the romantic dream of Amelia and Pippo as an enduring and perfect couple like Ginger and Fred. To prepare for her part in the film, Masina worked out with a dance instructor for a month and a half before shooting began,[67] and indeed, she does very well with that aspect of performance that has always been one of her strengths. Her face, however, has changed. As she herself put it, "I no longer have a round face."[68] Her famous childlike face has now become almost gaunt in comparison to the fullness it had. Fellini's strategy in *Ginger and Fred* was to photograph her, despite her objections, without softening focus on her face.[69] The change in her face, shot relatively honestly, provides an equivalent to Mastroianni's thinned hair. Like Fred, she is physically past her prime. Unlike him, however, she is not down-and-out financially. After her breakup with Fred, Ginger married a man named Enrico, had a daughter, Anna, and now has two grandchildren. With the death of Enrico, Ginger has become the manager of the family's company. Ginger is a woman of substance who carries herself as such. However, she still harbors a certain amount of romantic longing for the dream of being once again with Pippo and for being once again the Ginger of the legendary couple "Ginger and Fred." This we learn not only from her behavior when she produces her mirror from her purse with the lightning skill of a sleight-of-hand artist and primps for the moments when she thinks she is about to meet Pippo once again but also from her crestfallen reaction when she does meet him as the scruffy man snoring loudly in the room next door who tells her that he did not recognize her when he first saw her. As opposed to the other women in the series we have been considering, Amelia has a substantial life outside her relationship with her deceptive, unreliable partner. Yet the pull of the romantic relationship is nonetheless strong.

Amelia and Pippo seem made for one another. In the first place, they look like a team. Amelia wears a plaid coat and cape with a red hat modeled on a man's fedora. Pippo wears a checked coat and hat with a red scarf. Both wear brown-and-white two-toned shoes. Of course, the "retro" costumes identify both characters as figures from the 1940s existing in the world of the less stylish 1980s around them, but more important, both characters seem together as a pair in their difference from the others. In this sense, they are more like an "old married couple" than a glamorous dance team. Pippo knows, or remembers, well how to hurt Amelia and how to woo her. He will, on the one hand, call her "shorty" and compare her to one of the midgets in the troupe "Las Lilliputs" performing on the TV show. On the other hand, he will tap out with his hands "I love you" to Amelia as part of an interview with a reporter about tap dancing as a kind of secret language. This act will make her look down at her lap, embarrassed but pleased. For her part, Amelia will try to come to his rescue when she sees he needs help. For instance, when he loses the sense of his sentence during his interview, she finishes his sentence for him. Thus saved, Pippo is able to conclude the interview in a charming manner. That Amelia and Pippo seem the well-matched pair both visually and in terms of their knowledge about each other encourages us to think that they may indeed reunite.

They perform their act on the TV stage toward the end of the film. The dance routine, however, is interrupted by a power failure just as Ginger begins her run toward Fred. The performers are told to hold their places on stage until the power is restored. The interruption, of course, prolongs suspense. It also provides a quiet, intimate moment for the two characters. In the half-light from a backup system, they speak honestly with each other for the first time in the film. This begins the "crisis" situation of this movie, but it is a crisis of reunion, not separation. Pippo admits his breakdown after Amelia left him. She tells him she would have come back to him if she had known of his situation. She then confesses that she agreed to do the TV special to see him again, not to please her family nor to satisfy a general nostalgia for performing. He responds gallantly, if less ardently, that he too has returned to see her, although it seems clear that the money for the performance is important to him also. At this point, as they prepare to steal away together from the stage, the power returns and they must finish their routine, the dance performance we have been waiting for since the beginning of the film. At first they perform, as we might expect, in character. Pippo blanks out on the routine, and Amelia must coach him *sottovoce* and lead him through the steps. Then Pippo gets a cramp in his foot and falls. After regaining his feet, however, he dances better than before. Indeed, the couple performs brilliantly. The movements of the two are perfectly synchronized, and the movements become faster, more challenging. Neither performer is perfect. Amelia stumbles backward slightly on one of her kicks, and Pippo wheezes and loses control of his smile during his tap solo. But the two are clearly once again a successful team on the stage.

The ending of the movie is less romantic. Pippo walks Amelia through the train station. Since they have not yet been paid, he is short of cash, and Amelia, ever the caretaker and manager, must give him a loan. She will catch a train home to Liguria, and he will stay on in Rome. They embrace, and she walks away. Then Fred calls to her and makes the sound of the boat whistle. Their routine dictates that she is to call his name and run to him. The "crisis" has come to its peak. This moment in the "real" situation in the train station in the diegesis is the moment of truth the movie has been pointing toward, not the moment on the stage when the outcome was choreographed. Important to the scene is the fact that Pippo, like Checco in *Variety Lights,* knows very well how to play on Amelia's emotions. He must show his need to be nurtured and to be managed, and he must offer a romantic myth of the two together in the future. When he borrows money, he shows his need for someone to look after him, and when he blows the whistle, he calls up all the magic of their routine as the perfect couple, Ginger and Fred. This time the Masina figure refuses to fall for the trick. Amelia throws up her arm and calls "Fred," but her arm gesture turns into a good-natured shrug. She smiles, shakes her head, and walks to her train.[70] To be sure, she pauses at the first step onto the train to look back and see if he has followed, to see if the "crisis" is indeed over. And then she leaves.

The Masina "wife" here is tougher than the earlier women. Amelia is older, and she has survived a previous parting. Maybe just as important, however, is that, unlike Juliet, she does have something to go on to beyond her relationship with Pippo. She manages her own company, and she has a daughter and two grandchildren to care about. She does not need to stay within the kind of romantic myth she and Pippo perform on the stage. She has a more functional role she can play—that of head of a household and, apparently, chief provider. This is by no means to argue that Fellini has become a feminist. There is too much evidence in too many other movies to the contrary. But Amelia's final statement—that of shrugging good-naturedly and walking away—does demonstrate a willingness on Fellini's part to give Masina a chance to play her character in the way she seems to have wanted to all along. Fittingly, the statement comes as an act of mime, but one with a considerable amount of subtext.

6

THE COMEDY OF TYPES:
EARLY AND LATE

One of the real strengths of Federico Fellini was his skill as a comedy writer. It is a strength that runs through virtually all of his films. In looking at the early days of Fellini's career, we would do well to remember Fellini's work included screenwriting for variety-hall and movie comics Erminio Macario and Aldo Fabrizi during the years 1939–1943.[1] Furthermore, Fellini's subjective documentary *The Clowns* (1970) clearly establishes both his childhood interest in the antics of circus clowns and his adult willingness to theorize about the nature of this kind of comedy. His interest in comedy, then, was a long-standing one, and it was a thoughtful one.

Fellini's forte as a comedy writer lies in his handling of type characters. He knows how to set up his types quickly and deftly. He then propels them into an escalating series of situations that they must "solve" while remaining in type. Because of the escalation in the degree of difficulty of the situations, a certain tension or level of frustration is built up. During this buildup we, of course, may laugh at the characters as they struggle to solve their situations while at the same time fulfilling our expectations of how characters of their type must perform. (We are superior to them at all times, unless they find clever ways to solve their situations that we do not anticipate, and then we are delighted *with* them.) What the movies press for and what we desire is comic release from the tension and frustration produced either by the characters themselves or by the author who manages the situations. At the point of release, however reached, we may identify with the characters, laugh *with* them, and savor their release, if it is a joyous one, or we may sorrow with them, if the release is a bittersweet one. There is nothing particularly new about this formula. It is the formula of many silent comedies that turn on the buildup and release of frustration, and it is the formula of many TV situation comedies that seek solutions to vexing problems or misunderstandings before their half hour is up. The point to be made here is that the formula works.

Fellini's type characters act in type most of the time but not all of the time. There are generally moments when the characters go beyond type and either "deepen" themselves by displaying more complicated thoughts and emotions than we would have thought them capable of or, more often, present other kinds of type characteristics that might allow us to say they "widen" their characters. In a somewhat different sort of discussion of Fellini's early works, Peter Bondanella has introduced the term "unmasking."[2] He follows Luigi Pirandello's distinction between "mask" (socially defined role) and "face" (the more intimate personality underneath). Unmasking, then, for Bondanella is a kind of stripping away of a social role played by a character to reveal the more complex and psychologically interesting personality beneath the facade. The idea is an intriguing one, especially if we shift the definition of "mask" to refer to comic type. In this sense, most of Fellini's characters do unmask when they go beyond their types. It is as if Fellini wished to argue that human personality is too various ever to be reduced simply to a predictable type.

The most extended statement Fellini made on comedy is his essay "Why Clowns?" which serves as an introduction to his published screenplay of *The Clowns*. Here he outlines the classical distinction between the white clown and the Auguste: "The white clown stands for elegance, grace, harmony, intelligence, lucidity, which are posited in a moral way as ideal, unique, indisputable divinities. Then comes the negative aspect, because in this way the white clown becomes Mother and Father, Schoolmaster, Artist, the Beautiful, in other words *what should be done*. Then the Auguste, who would feel drawn to all these perfect attributes if only they were not so priggishly displayed, turns on them. The Auguste is the child who dirties his pants, rebels against this perfection, gets drunk, rolls about on the floor and puts up endless resistance."[3] What is most interesting about this distinction is that Fellini demonstrates by it the importance of *pairing*. In his early comedies, Fellini paired romantic couples. The men tend to be white clowns in that they long to be adult figures who can impose an order, *their* order, on the world around them. The women they are paired with, however, are not Augustes, that is, naughty children; rather they are projections, psychological *others* who embody attitudes or sexual stances that the men desire or fear. The result, though, is the same as it would be if the women were Augustes. They destroy the attempts of the men to attain or maintain adult control, and they reduce the men to children. The men, however, deserve to be reduced to the role of children, for they are all adult poseurs in the first place, and as we have seen in our discussion of *I Vitelloni, contrapposto,* or poetic justice, is important in Fellini comedies. The men must be punished to just the right degree. If they are punished too much or too little, the work may seem either too harsh or too cynical, but if the degree of punishment is just right, the movie will seem to have comic equilibrium, and we will very likely applaud the author's cleverness.

Pairing of Men and Women in the Early Comedies

Variety Lights (1950) was Fellini's first movie. It was based on a story treatment by Fellini, which in turn was based on conversations with the variety-hall performer Aldo Fabrizi.[4] The screenplay is a collaboration among Ennio Flaiano, Tullio Pinelli, Alberto Lattuada, and Fellini, and the film itself is codirected by Fellini and the veteran moviemaker Lattuada. Yet despite the well-acknowledged contributions of these other men, the film seems very much Fellini's in that it sets the pattern for the comedies to follow. *Variety Lights* is a backstage drama dealing with familiar type characters and situations: the clown who loves the beautiful woman, the young starlet on her way to the top, and the discarding of the mentor figure by the star once success is achieved. The movie echoes works such as *Pagliaccio, Footlight Parade, All about Eve, A Star Is Born,* and numerous other backstage dramas. If *Variety Lights* is not a highly distinguished addition to the list, it is at least a competent one, and it shows Fellini and his collaborators in control of the formulas.

Checco, the protagonist, is a second-rate comedian who would be a grand impresario, or to put it another way, he is an awkward child who would be a sophisticated adult. Where he becomes comic instead of pathetic are those moments when he pretends to be what he is not. At one point, in a nightclub when Checco is dressed in evening wear, a performer costumed as a parrot calls Checco a penguin. The label is apt. Checco is a funny, scurrying little creature trying to affect white-tie-and-black-tails dignity. His type is established early on, when in the first sequence after finishing a turn on the stage, he complains, "They should have let me do another encore. . . . The audience was begging for me,"[5] and after learning that the troupe's money has been sequestered by a hotel owner, he sputters, "They can't sequester my pay! . . . I'm a nationwide star." Checco has convinced himself that he is more than he is—a barely adequate comedian playing the variety stages of the provinces.

There are two women in Checco's life. Melina Amour is Checco's fiancée, and she is something of a mother to him, as we noted in chapter 5. She handles their joint bank account prudently and generally bolsters his ego when he needs it. In short, Melina is the managerial and maternal woman with whom the childish Checco should stay for his own practical well-being. Checco, however, longs for more. He longs for the woman who can make him an impresario and an adult.

The woman who seems capable of fulfilling this longing is Liliana, the beginner on the way up. Her type character gives Fellini and his collaborators a chance to have some fun with the formula of the "big break" in the young performer's career. Instead of profiting from the traditional injury or illness of the veteran star, Liliana succeeds when she splits open the seams of her too-tight slacks while dancing in the chorus and earns the applause of the largely male audience because of the shapeliness of her legs and the aplomb with which she continues to dance after the accident. Given this opportunity, Liliana, like the plucky heroines of innumerable backstage dramas, begins her ascent. For Checco, however, she is a promising newcomer he can guide as a protégé and team with in her rise. She is at once his ticket to the big time and a lover-daughter figure who could make him appear a sophisticated adult as the result of their relationship.

The movie consists of two challenges for Checco. In each, he plays the covetous father–lover trying to keep up with the youthful Liliana and to fend off the attempts of other men who would take over his role. In the first instance, a country lawyer named Renzo invites Liliana and the troupe to his home for dinner. The walk to Renzo's villa is a kind of chase. Checco must literally struggle to keep the lawyer and Liliana in view. Then at the villa, he must watch the lawyer dine with Liliana at the far end of the table, dance with her, and offer her the gift of a pearl necklace. Checco's role as a father figure is clearly established in this section. At the outset when Renzo comes backstage to meet Liliana, he inquires of Checco politely, "Excuse me, are you the young lady's father?" Then when Liliana asks Checco at the party if he is angry with her, he responds indignantly, "You're not my daughter. . . . I judge you on the stage, that's all."[6] Clearly, Checco is sexually attracted to the young girl. She first gains his attention when she shows him photographs of herself in scanty costumes and raises her skirt to reveal her legs to him. As sexually alluring as the poses are, however, they are also the conventionally fetishized poses of the stage,[7] and I would argue that the latter may be more important to Checco than the former. He can recognize in her someone who would be sexually alluring on the stage, and thus he has discovered someone he can instruct at the outset and then pair with to achieve great success on the big city stages of the north. Checco does manage to "solve" the situation at Renzo's villa by acting up to type. He plays the indignant father when he catches Renzo preparing to slip into Liliana's bed and chastises him, "She's just a child; you should be ashamed."

In the second challenge, Checco is less successful. This takes place in Rome as Checco tries to line up a show for Liliana and him. At first, Checco wants to find backers, and he takes Liliana to a nightclub where important people like the producers Parmisani and Conti gather. While Checco talks to Parmisani, Conti dances with Liliana and starts his seduction of her. Then begins a second chase, which is a more frustrating version of the walk to Renzo's villa. The producers and their friends take Liliana away to another nightclub, leaving Checco to pursue on foot, since he has no money for cab fare. This chase ends eventually at Liliana's pensione where a confrontation takes place. Here an equal balance of power is established. Checco demands sex; Liliana indicates a willingness to pay her "debt"; he slaps her for her willingness; and she comforts him with the dream of success: "We two have so far to go." As I have suggested earlier, what Checco really wants from Liliana is not sex (indeed, he turns that down when it is offered). What he wants is loyalty to his hopes for them as a successful team. Liliana acknowledges the validity of his claim. But, on the other hand, she has discovered an alternative mentor-father-lover, and this frees her from dependency on Checco. From this point on, the balance of power tips more and more to her.

The unmasking scene according to Bondanella is the confrontation scene at Liliana's pensione where Checco slaps her. He "catches a brief glimpse of her true face beneath the mask of innocence she normally wears," and with his slap "reject[s] her lack of morals and commitment to genuine human feelings."[8] Checco, in turn, reveals "his basic honesty and goodness." The scene is, indeed, one of unmasking, and the characters do broaden their types. We see the ruthlessness of Liliana clearly. But Bondanella overstates the case for Checco and grants him too much moral superiority. He is, after all, just as ruthless as Liliana when a few scenes later he plays on Melina's sympathy to get hold of their savings in order to finance a show for Liliana. The slap seems less an indication of moral superiority than a sign of frustration over the potential loss of his future claim on Liliana. (If she did pay her "debt," he would have no further claim on her.) Moreover, the slap seems perfectly in character for Checco. It is in type for him to make grand gestures whenever the occasion presents itself.

More interesting than the slap, however, is Liliana's ability to recover from it and to win control of the situation by fanning the flames of Checco's dream of success on the stage. "What success lies ahead! . . . In every theater we'll play in. With huge colored posters . . . and my name this high . . . and yours, too, in lights up on the marquee . . . flashing on and off."[9] While we might view the obvious narcissism of Liliana's speech with alarm, Checco does not. Liliana's dream matches his perfectly. In effect, he takes over the scenario she presents him with and vows to start his own company to make it come true. She is, then, a kind of ultimate temptress in that she leads him to put into focus his dream of being an impresario and seems to offer him the means, her sexual appeal to audiences, which will allow him to realize the dream. But, of course, he deserves such a temptress because of his own attempts to use Liliana. Comic justice will be served in Fellini's comedies!

As in virtually all of the comedies, however, a partial fulfillment of the dream is granted. In front of the performers of his old troupe, Checco receives a gift from his star. She gives him a fedora to replace his old beret and even arranges it on his head like a crown. The fedora, along with glasses and an umbrella, is usually in Fellini films a badge of middle-class dignity.[10]

Here it is a sign of adulthood and sophistication, as opposed to the beret, which was so clearly out of place in Rome when Checco wore it with his evening garb. The moment, then, is a proud one for Checco. So, too, is a later one when Checco makes the traditional presentation of his star to the new company he has assembled to showcase her. Danger signals abound: His former friends laugh at him; Liliana would prefer her name before his on the posters; and the new troupe seems woefully inept in rehearsal. Yet, for these two moments, completely oblivious to the danger signals, Checco is permitted to have his dream come partially true. He seems, in his own eyes at least, an impresario.[11]

The White Sheik (1952) is a minor comic masterpiece. It is based on the story idea proposed by Michelangelo Antonioni that a feature-length film be made about the addiction of female fans to Italian photo-romances.[12] (These romances are stories told in panels like comic strips, but with each frame consisting of actors photographed in poses.) In the film, a honeymoon couple comes to Rome for two days. Wanda, the wife, wishes to see the White Sheik, her hero of the photo-romances, and the husband, Ivan, plans a visit with his relatives to see the Pope. Like *Variety Lights, The White Sheik* turns on the device of pairing. The romantic pair in this movie, however, is an "odd couple," that is, two opposites teamed to give each other fits in the manner of the neat Felix and the messy Oscar, the gruff, bossy Ollie and the gentle, silly Stanley, and, of course, the white clown and Auguste. Wanda is the moony romantic, with a dippy, glazed-over expression and a country-mouse timidity, the kind who would idolize a White Sheik, and Ivan is too fussy, too rigid, too dignified, a man with a buttoned-up rain-coat and a hat planted squarely on his head, the kind who would feel it important to attend a ceremonial audience with the Pope if only to let the folks back home know what he had done. Ivan and Wanda do not stay together, however, as most comic pairs do. They follow their separate adventures. Nevertheless, we can use the one as a measuring stick for the extremes of the other, and more important, we can see that according to the laws of comic balance, the two characters deserve each other.

The conventional reading of the film tends to be moralistic.[13] The argument goes as follows. Ivan and Wanda have a chance to learn about themselves on their separate adventures, to move toward some sort of reasonable middle ground between their two extremes, and to escape their types. A key moment is their reconciliation scene in the Roman hospital near the movie's end. Here, they have every reason to talk about their separate activities and, in effect, unmask for each other. They do not. Instead, reverting to type, Ivan becomes more prim than ever and orders his wife to dress for their visit to the Pope. As they approach St. Peter's, Wanda, too, reverts to type by speaking her romantic clichés again and adopting her "enraptured" look. Thus, as the conventional reading has it, they fall short of their human potential.

Correct as this reading undoubtedly is, it does little to explain the delightfulness of the movie. Delightfulness in Fellini movies often lies in a subtext beneath the moralistic surface. For Ivan, the movie constitutes an anxiety dream in which all his worst fears of losing adult control of his life torment him; but, for Wanda, the movie is a wish-fulfillment dream, where for one glorious day she is the beloved slave girl of the White Sheik. This is a source of joy tucked into the middle of the movie, a "guilty pleasure" we can indulge in with Wanda, for we know her married life with Ivan will be dreary enough to serve as payment for it later. The joyfulness of the "stolen moments" Wanda has with the White Sheik make this movie much richer and more satisfying than *Variety Lights*. In this comedy, anxiety is matched with joyfulness.

Ivan's prim character is set up quickly. A *piccolo borghese,* he likes to be in charge and he likes things to be neat and orderly. What better opportunity for him than a trip to Rome, where he can show his young wife the sights of the city with the help of his important uncle? Literally and figuratively, Ivan is concerned with appearance. Riding to the hotel in a carriage, he sits erect, eyes straight ahead, as if posing for a photograph as the head of the family firmly in control. In the hotel room, while talking to Wanda about his plans for their stay, he catches sight of himself in the mirror and automatically straightens his necktie. Furthermore, Ivan is full of instructions. At the train station, he hands a suitcase to the porter and tells him, "Careful, the contents are fragile. Stay close to me," and he directs his wife down the train steps, "Come, dear. We're here."[14] Above all, however, Ivan is proud of his ability to schedule his day. "The whole day is well planned," he informs Wanda, consulting his notebook. "I have each minute of the day planned. 7:00 AM: arrival in Rome. Rest in the room until 10:00. From 10:00 to 11:00, meet the family and get to know each other. At 11:00, see the Pope followed by lunch with Aunt and Uncle. From 1:00 PM to midnight, we won't have a single free moment. We'll be seeing the sights with Aunt and Uncle the whole time. . . . Then, of course, we'll have an intimate supper, followed by a restful night." Since Ivan approaches his bride gently during the last part of his speech, it is clear he is not without romantic interest in Wanda, but we must note that he has postponed the marital coupling to its decorous place after all other duties, familial and public, have been observed. That Ivan will not be able to maintain the order and control he seeks is also established in the opening scenes. The porter at the station ignores his instructions; a disembarking passenger knocks off Ivan's hat, as ever a metonym for middle-class dignity; and, at the hotel, Ivan reaches mistakenly for the key the desk clerk intends for the bellboy and stumbles into a priest waiting in line behind him to register. But Ivan's chief antagonist, as we have said, will be his wife, who will create many problems for him to solve if he is to keep his dignity before his relatives and maintain his own sense of adulthood.

Wanda is a romantic, and she has a childlike curiosity. While Ivan stares ahead in the carriage, Wanda looks around wide-eyed at the new sights of the city, and as Ivan phones his uncle, she explores the hotel lobby and follows the bellboy to the room when he tells her to come with him. We know from the start, then, that Wanda is bound to exasperate Ivan, for she will never stay in place; she is a type character destined always to wander off. Her romantic nature best reveals itself when she steals away to deliver her drawing of the White Sheik to Fernando Rivoli, the actor who plays the part, at the offices of the magazine. She introduces herself by the name she puts on her letters to the Sheik, "Bambina Appassionata," and confides to the lady story editor, "I am always dreaming." When the story editor asks Wanda to supply a line for Fatima, the slave girl, to speak when she is alone in the desert without her White Sheik, Wanda can easily enter the part and supply the sentimental banality, "My word but I am distraught." Given Wanda's desire to enter the dream world of the photo-romances, she easily gives in to the invitation to travel to the beach outside Rome where the day's shooting will take place, and her separation from Ivan, of course, creates, in turn, the series of problems he must try to solve while remaining in type.

Ivan's task of maintaining his dignity is made difficult in a variety of ways. While trying to track Wanda down in the street, Ivan is swept up in a quick-stepping parade of elite *bersaglieri* troops celebrating a holiday, and then while explaining his wife's absence to his relations from Rome ("She's got a headache."), he finds he must spring up the stairs to head off his aunt, who has taken the elevator and seeks to comfort the stricken bride. By afternoon, Ivan's anxiety to recapture his bride is so great that he goes to the police station to get aid, despite his fears that the police will make public his disgrace. He gives bits of information to the commissioner but withholds other pieces. The result is a jumble, and the commissioner thinks Ivan insane. To us, however, he is a would-be adult reduced to the state of embarrassed schoolboy before an authority figure. In his nervousness, Ivan simply cannot control his hands. He plays with the official rubber stamps on the investigator's desk until the man moves the stamp rack away, and he toys with the commissioner's inkwell, again like a schoolboy, and inadvertently smears the ink on his own face with further nervous gestures. Unmasked, Ivan has regressed to the state of child, a state he has been trying desperately to hide beneath his pose of competent adult.

Counterbalancing Ivan's experience, Wanda has a day that far exceeds her fondest wishes. She sets out simply to give the White Sheik her drawing and has a romantic adventure worthy of the magazines she reads so avidly. The dreamlike segment of wish fulfillment is introduced by tinkling chimes played on a xylophone whose hypnotic repetitions may well suggest sleep. Disembarking from the truck at the site for the photo session, Wanda wanders in the pine woods and suddenly looks up to see the White Sheik swinging on his trapeze and singing (see fig. 1.6). He drops lightly to his feet before her. From her point of view, there is a magic to his sudden appearance from the sky. Moreover, he remembers her letters, and he praises her drawing. Already she has fulfilled her modest wishes to meet Fernando Rivoli and present her sketch. But the dreamlike adventure gets better. The White Sheik romances Wanda. He suggests they go to a snack bar, "a little oasis," for something to eat and drink. The sunlight falls perfectly dappled through the latticework. Then a man drives up with his car radio playing a dance tune, and the Sheik glides Wanda into a smooth dance, replete with tango steps and improvised moves. Of course, to us, Fernando, as played by Alberto Sordi, is simply a Latin lover with a baby face and a pudgy waist who cannot resist trying to seduce a woman who is already seduced, a bird perched on the tip of his blunderbuss. But to Wanda, none of this is apparent. She is in a dream come true: dancing with her favorite actor before the admiring and approving eyes of the others at the snack bar, the envy of all the women. And still the adventure gets better. Fernando arranges for Wanda to play the part of the slave girl Fatima in the scene where she is to say the line she composed earlier for the story editor. Now she is actually in the photo-romances that she has dreamed about in the past, and more than that, she will have a permanent record of her day with the White Sheik. It is not too much for us to imagine Wanda sneaking out at the crack of dawn to buy a copy of the photo-romance when it first goes on sale in her town, smuggling it into her house, and hiding it away from Ivan as her own secret treasure.

The Cinderella-like dream, of course, must come to an end. Rivoli takes Wanda for a sailboat ride to complete his seduction. However, he is hit on the head twice by the boom of the sailboat, saving Wanda from seduction.[15] The two of them must then return to shore and face the real anger of Rivoli's real wife. Fleeing to the woods, Wanda, in effect, wakes up in a spot near where the dreamlike segment began, to the sound again of the same tinkling chimes.

As the moralistic reading of the film implies, neither Wanda nor Ivan is sufficiently grown up to be ready for marriage. Ivan is a lonely, frightened child pretending to be an adult in control of the world around him. Wanda is an adolescent, dreaming of a fantasy lover who will make the world magic and ever exciting, a place where emotions will always be at the extreme. Ivan and Wanda are equal in their immaturity. But from another point of view, they are comic opposites. Because he is so overbearing, Ivan deserves to be exposed to us, if not his Roman relatives, as the child he is. We can chortle at his discomfort. On the other hand, Wanda, the romantic adolescent married to this rigid, dull fellow, is granted one glorious day of wish fulfillment. Her joy, short-lived as it is, balances Ivan's anxiety and gives the movie an almost perfect comic equilibrium.

The final early comedy to be considered here is *The Temptation of Dr. Antonio* (1962). This film is a fifty-minute episode in the anthology film *Boccaccio '70* produced by Carlo Ponti from a suggestion by Cesare Zavattini that a group of modern filmmakers put together a variety of tales in the witty, earthy style of Giovanni Boccaccio's *Decameron* (1353).[16] To some extent, the Fellini episode is a response to calls for censorship made against *La Dolce Vita,* Fellini's previous movie.[17] *The Temptation of Dr. Antonio,* then, constitutes Fellini's comic revenge on critics who found *La Dolce Vita* immoral or indecent. We have discussed the film briefly in chapter 2 as a kind of Jungian confrontation with a figure from the unconscious. Here, we will look at the film in terms of its comic formulas.

The protagonist of the movie is Antonio Mazzuolo, a middle-aged man of some means. (He is portrayed by the actor Peppino De Filippo, who played Checco in *Variety Lights.*) Initially, his type is that of the zealous prude who wishes to suppress all public displays of the female body and all expressions of sexual involvement between men and women. Moreover, he displays all the external badges of the respectable adult: the fedora, glasses, and an umbrella. At the point of his unmasking, however, Antonio becomes a parody of a Freudian case history of the repressed man who never developed beyond the oedipal stage and therefore could not endure the discoveries of puberty.[18] *The Temptation of Dr. Antonio* thus is a film in which one kind of type character gives way to a different but related one. It is useful, though, to recognize that two different types are involved, for each provides his own source of comedy. The zealous prude is a public nuisance. His crusade is an impossible one: opposing the god of love, Eros, in one of the god's favorite cities, Rome. Antonio must have a comeuppance so that normal, spontaneous social life can run its course. The repressed mama's boy, on the other hand, gets another chance at puberty and fails a second time. Here the comedy turns once more on the more personal situation of the would-be adult who is reduced to the state of child. To defeat Antonio on both the public and private levels, Fellini pairs him with Anita Ekberg, sex goddess and star in *La Dolce Vita.* She is a giant, reclining figure on a billboard, urging consumers to "Drink more milk," who comes to life one night and confronts Antonio with her sexuality or, in Jungian terms, with feelings from his unconscious.

There is a mock-heroic element in the movie. The title of the film invites us to compare Antonio's trials with the temptations of St. Anthony, the first-century ascetic who is generally considered the father of Christian monasticism and is famed for resisting a series of temptations by the devil. The particular myth Fellini seems to have had in mind concerns an attempt by the devil in the guise of a beautiful queen to lure St. Anthony into a city of sin and there seduce him. In the Fellini movie, of course, Dr. Antonio Mazzuolo already lives in the city of sin to begin with, but the sinfulness of Rome seems to become epitomized for our saintly protagonist by the nightly gatherings of prostitutes below the billboard of Anita, an area he labels "Babylon." Furthermore, near the movie's end, as Anita prepares for her final temptation of Antonio, she tells him, "I can confess to you now. Yes, I am the Devil!"[19] Antonio is also compared with St. George, the warrior saint who slew a dragon in defense of a princess or womanhood in general. A reproduction of Raphael's St. George on horseback spearing the dragon (c. 1506) hangs on Antonio's living room wall, and a primitive version of a dragon with female features appears on the wall of the office of the government official Antonio visits in his quest to have the billboard covered over. Additionally, at the movie's end, as Antonio resists Anita's temptation, he becomes miraculously transformed and appears in St. George's armor, with a spear fashioned from a cafe-table umbrella and with the hooves of a noble steed intruding into the frame, presumably from a statue in the street. Furthermore, toward the end of the movie, we find Antonio cast in the role of a hero in a Japanese science-fiction movie trying to protect the city from the invasion of a terrifying creature. We hear "unearthly" electronic sounds. Blinding spotlights search the darkness. A gigantic shadow moves across a skyscraper. Antonio calls out, "Stop! Who'll be able to stop that monster! Two million souls will be corrupted if she goes into town!"[20] All these comparisons emphasize Antonio's ineffectualness.

The temptation of the hero begins on the day Antonio gives out awards for courage to the Boy Scouts in the park. In his address to the assembled scouts (who are, of course, another gallery of grotesques), Antonio recounts a story of his own youth when he was able to resist temptation. He tells the scouts that when he was fifteen he spent a vacation at the home of a friend's aunt, who, as we noted in chapter 2, disrobed in his presence, thinking him asleep. "A demon appeared before my eyes," he relates, and then he adds fervently, "I closed my eyes!" The homily of Antonio's adolescent rejection of the sight of a naked woman is, of course, utterly inappropriate for the awards ceremony. Only someone as obsessed with a desire to reject female sexuality as Antonio could fail to grasp this fact. But in terms of the movie's narrative, the homily is absolutely appropriate, for as Antonio tells it, he is interrupted and occasionally drowned out by workmen putting up the billboard that displays Anita Ekberg in a low-cut, clinging gown. Frank Burke has said "the billboard of Anita . . . is virtually born out of Antonio's words."[21] I would go farther and say that the story of Anita and the homily of the aunt mirror each other. Anita will go on to present Antonio with another "demon" of feminine sexuality when she too undresses before him. Given that Antonio has done all he could in the past to halt public displays of sexuality, we would have to say that such a "demonic" spectacle is his worst fear. Yet, in another sense, we will see that it is also his fondest wish.

The putting up of the billboard takes the form of a festival, which, to the consternation of Antonio, becomes almost Dionysian. Black American musicians, passing by on a bus, stop and play along with the recorded song from the billboard's loudspeaker. A crowd quickly gathers. Recognizing the star from *La Dolce Vita,* the Boy Scouts jump up and down and cheer, "Hurrah for Anita Ekberg!" While this happens, Antonio, in turn, displays an alarming array of psychogenic tics. The corner of his mouth twitches, his chin rotates to the right and up, his shoulders hunch, and most obvious, his right hand flies up sometimes to his necktie, sometimes just to shoulder height, with his fingers fluttering out of control.[22] In a basic text, *The Psychoanalytic Theory of Neurosis,* popular at the time Fellini made his movie, Otto Fenichel has said, "The symptom of psychogenic tic owes its origin to the mechanism of conversion. Just as in the case of cramp, paralysis, contracture or major attacks in hysteria, here, too, the voluntary musculature of the body refuses to serve the ego and functions independently of the will."[23] As Antonio watches the billboard go up, his longings make themselves known through the tics. Indeed, it may not be too much to suggest, given the bust size of Anita Ekberg and the prop glass of milk she holds, that the pattern of Antonio's tics suggests a child groping for his mother's breast.

The final unmasking of Antonio comes when Antonio faces Anita coming to life. The sequence is a dream. It takes place at night and begins with a weary Antonio ready for bed after his victory celebration party. During the night, a thunderstorm washes off the paper strips that cover Anita. Each time Antonio looks at the billboard from his window, Anita seems to change position and make mocking gestures. At last, Antonio goes forth, an unlikely hero in bathrobe, glasses, and fedora, carrying the requisite umbrella. Now Anita steps out of the billboard and challenges him: "Why are you so scared of me, Mr. Mazzuolo?" She is the giant woman, and Antonio, the small, boylike man. All the devices of special effects movies like *King Kong* and the Japanese science-fiction films are used. Anita is photographed in a scaled-down model of the city so that she appears to tower over it; Antonio is photographed in a real section of the EUR district of Rome. Anita is shot from a low angle or else in such tight close-up that she seems too big to be captured in the wide-screen frame; Antonio is shot from above and at a distance so that he seems just another part of the landscape. Anita's voice is magnified through an echo chamber, and her sentences are punctuated by rumbles of thunder; Antonio's voice is diminished on the soundtrack despite the fact we can see he is trying to shout. The dream, however, is not entirely a nightmare, for Anita is playful and sometimes quite gentle with Antonio as a mother might be with an engaging, if naughty child. When she picks him up and places him on her breast,[24] in fact, his fears of falling give way to utter delight, and the dream becomes one of wish fulfillment. (See Fellini's drawing of the scene [fig. 6.1].) Anita sings a lullaby. Then Antonio presses his face to her enormous breast and strokes it with his right hand. At last Antonio is unmasked, and the Freudian joke is completed. Antonio has not progressed beyond the oedipal stage, and he can neither admit the sexual nature of his love for a mother figure (except in his dream) nor transfer his sexual longings to another, more suitable recipient. As a citizen who has tried to censor public displays, he has in effect conferred his private problem onto the public.

Antonio, however, gets one more chance to grow up and to accept female sexuality. Anita does a striptease for him, duplicating the experience he had as a fifteen-year-old. Again Antonio becomes a public nuisance: he tries to cover the camera so *we* cannot see; and he fails his personal test a second time: he covers his own eyes. All that remains is for him to throw his spear as a mock-heroic St. George and to be taken from the site of the billboard in the morning (where the dreamer has apparently sleepwalked) by medics who will treat him for his final catatonic state. A crowd watches the ambulance speed off. The public nature of his offenses, after all, requires a certain amount of public humiliation.

In each of these early comedies, then, a kind of white clown is set up, a would-be adult who wants to exhibit self-importance and control of himself or the

Fig. 6.1. Fellini's sketch of the giant, Jungian anima mediatrix figure of Anita with the tiny protagonist Antonio in her cleavage for *The Temptation of Dr. Antonio.* Federico Fellini Copyright © 1982 Diogenes Verlag AG Zürich.

world around him. He is paired with a woman who is, in some sense, exactly what he deserves and who destroys his pose as an adult. The point here is not that Fellini supposed adult behavior impossible. A part of his definition of the artist, after all, is that adult sensibility needs to be brought to bear on childish and adolescent wishes and fears. Rather what we encounter in these early comedies is another form of Fellini's antirationalist bent. The white clown would be *too much in control,* and this Fellini will not allow.

The Later Comedies: Documentaries in the World of Art

The later comedies of Fellini considered here involve group protagonists rather than pairs. It is as if the minor characters have taken over.[25] In an early work such as *The White Sheik,* the minor characters are very much a part of the fun of the movie: an unctuous desk clerk who never misses a chance to sell postcards; the female story editor who loves flattery and adoring fans; an undershirted sunbather who gets in the way of the photo sessions in his eagerness to see what is taking place; and, of course, Cabiria, the small, outgoing prostitute who wants to put a smile on Ivan's face. In later works such as *The Clowns, Orchestra Rehearsal* (1979), and *And the Ship Sails On* (1983), the "little people" assume control and give us portraits of the worlds of clowns, orchestra members, and operatic performers. These movies have about them the teeming quality of Brueghel that we discussed in chapter 1. Fellini's success in these films depends as never before on pacing and balancing. He must give each type character time enough to establish himself or herself and then go on to perform in type in interesting situations or to move beyond type, and he must contrive to make statements about the group as a whole, all while not repeating himself, but instead being consistently surprising. Needless to say, Fellini did not always succeed in juggling these various priorities, but *Orchestra Rehearsal* and *And the Ship Sails On,* in particular, are often striking precisely because of the way Fellini managed to handle his groups of diverse type characters.

The form in all three films is that of the documentary. Fellini's first documentary was *Fellini: A Director's Notebook,* made in 1969 for NBC-TV. This brief movie detailed Fellini's thoughts, preoccupations, and work methods as he moved from a failed project, *The Voyage of G. Mastorna* (1965–67), to a future venture, *Fellini Satyricon* (1969). Despite his misgivings about filming for television, Fellini enjoyed the project and, after finishing *Fellini Satyricon,* proposed the idea of a documentary on clowns to RAI-TV in Italy. *The Clowns* is a bona fide documentary and was aired as such on television. *Orchestra Rehearsal* and *And the Ship Sails On,* however, are fictional documentaries that imitate the form. In all three cases, Fellini or a surrogate interviews the characters, and in all, a camera is present to record a final cataclysmic event. The comedies all take the form of investigations, then, and in each case, what is investigated is a world of performers in an art form that is either in crisis or in decline. Perhaps it would be enough to say Fellini chose art forms in decline to balance his comedy with a certain amount of pathos. In addition, however, there seems also to be present the true documentary impulse to record an art form that has once been magnificent before it vanishes.

The issues of these later comedies are somewhat different. Fellini, of course, continued to deflate the posturings of his type characters who would appear grander and more in control of things than they have a right to be. But, also, he was concerned with finding those aspects of the little worlds he investigates that are worth holding onto, and further, in *Orchestra Rehearsal* and *And the Ship Sails On,* he was interested in teasing out the various possibilities these worlds have when their demises are used as parables.

The Clowns establishes the pattern of the later comedies. Crucial to this pattern is the figure of the investigator. Within the film, Fellini as on-camera narrator states his purpose to be akin to that of a cultural anthropologist: "The clowns of my childhood, where are they today? That terrifying, comic violence, . . . that noisy exhilaration? Can the circus still entertain? Certainly, the world to which it belonged no longer exists. The theaters transformed into circus rings, the glowing, ingenious sets, the childish naiveté of the public . . . they no longer exist. What remains of the old circuses? Subtle, worn traces. And that's what we'll seek out."[26] In the essay "Why Clowns?" Fellini is a little more emphatic about whether the circus can still entertain: "I think that the circus in spite of some obvious discrepancies between it and the contemporary world, should be rescued." His defense is based on his notion that the circus "has gathered together within itself, in an exemplary way, certain lasting myths: adventure, travel, risk, danger, speed, [and] stepping into the limelight."[27] The narrator's purpose, then, we may assume, is not innocent. As he pokes among the "subtle, worn traces," he will be looking for those aspects of the circus or, more specifically, of clowns that would justify their rescue.

Fellini undercuts his role as narrator by making himself and his staff something of a group of bumblers. In "Why Clowns?" he describes his trip to Paris to interview former clowns and circus managers as a "parody of an inquiry." Fellini asks questions that his subjects often evade or even refuse to answer. He takes us to see a movie of the three Fratellinis, and the film burns on the projector. Then he takes us to see an archive print of Rhum, the famous Auguste clown, but this film is too brief and fails to capture the point of the gag it seeks to record, let alone the essence of the clown himself. Fellini's secretary, Maya, drops her notes all over the floor in one instance and reads from the wrong place in them in another. And when Fellini begins to explain the purpose of his own film to a critic, an empty bucket falls over Fellini's head. Thus, any whiff of pretentiousness the narrator might aspire to in his inquiry is dispelled. Yet, as we shall see, the narrator does accomplish his purpose.

With the opening sequence of *The Clowns,* Fellini insists we recognize the personal nature of his documentary. The movie begins with Fellini's reconstruction of his first visit to the circus. The boy watches the performance as if spellbound and then bursts into tears. The narrator says of the clowns, "They frightened me. Those chalky faces, those enigmatic expressions, those twisted, drunken masks, the shouts, the crazy laughter, the absurd atrocious jokes . . . they all reminded me of other strange and troubled characters who roam around every country village." Clearly, the clown's stylized presentations of the antic, irrational, and even cruel side of life has marked Fellini the boy in an important way. However, if this tells us something about Fellini, it also tells us much about clowns and encourages us to pay attention to the rest of the documentary. The subjective opening, then, is a kind of "hook."

The old clowns, circus people, and others interviewed by Fellini may in fact give us relatively little hard information. The interviews, however, serve as useful springboards for Fellini to recreate the comic routines connected with the people he is interviewing. These reconstructions are the real meat of the documentary, for it is what the clowns achieved in the ring that is important—the performances more than the performers. Two examples may suffice to illustrate Fellini's method.

In the first example, one of the Orfei brothers tells us that the Auguste clown was originally modeled on the idea of a servant who is so clumsy he makes everyone laugh, and later, clown historian Tristan Rémy tells us that the white clown as played by the famous Antonet was an authoritarian who bossed and yelled at Auguste. This basic dichotomy established, albeit sketchily, Fellini recreates a routine performed by Antonet and Beby, his partner, which brings the dichotomy to life. The routine is the classic one still performed today—the cake in the hat. As with many of the routines, this one involves a few simple props and an everyday action that the white clown executes supremely well and the Auguste imitates extremely badly. In this case, Antonet seeks to demonstrate his skill as a chef. He borrows a hat from a gentleman in the audience and puts into it eggs, flour, and a little water. Then he stirs the mixture over a candle. Finally, Antonet pulls a perfect cake from the hat and returns the hat undamaged to the owner. Now Beby must try the same experiment. He, too, borrows the hat. He selects an egg. Here, however, he adds a flourish. (Hubris is ever a problem for the

Auguste clown.) He tosses the egg into the air and attempts to catch it in the hat. The egg lands squarely on the bald pate of Beby. The gentleman from the audience chases Beby off stage to get back his hat from an obvious incompetent. And Antonet bows gracefully.

The second example takes place after Fellini's unsuccessful attempt to see the old film of the three Fratellinis. He talks to their descendants, leafs through a scrapbook, and then recreates some of their performances as "The Musicians." The Fratellini troupe consisted of an Auguste, a white clown, and a third clown in top hat and tails who usually joined the white clown against the Auguste, making him more the underdog than ever. In their first routine, the trio plays their instruments for the patients of a hospital. Suddenly, the tuba of the Auguste explodes with a burst of powder. The other two clowns apologize for him as he investigates the interior of his horn. From within, he pulls out an alarm clock, a basket of flowers, a seemingly endless string of silks, and finally, as the "topper," a live goose. Here, the Auguste is defeated not by the other clowns, although they are vexed with him, but rather by some implacable force that has sabotaged him. In the final routine, however, the mysterious force seems to come over to the side of the Auguste and to grant him a surprising power. The three clowns play now in an insane asylum. The Auguste is dressed as a buxom woman with pigtails, and this time he plays a clarinet. As we listen to his playing, we see the other two clowns slowly rise into the air (on visible wires) as if his music had caused them to fly. Some of the inmates of the asylum are charmed by the spectacle, but others pay little attention. Perhaps the inversion of nature's laws brought on by the piping of the Auguste seems perfectly normal to them.

By now it should be clear that Fellini has fastened on the dichotomy of the two types of clowns as the basic wisdom clowns embody for us. It is this dichotomy we should add to the list of "certain lasting myths" the circus "has gathered together with itself." In "Why Clowns?" Fellini elaborates: "This is the struggle between the proud cult of reason (which comes to be a bullying form of aestheticism) and the freedom of instinct. The white clown and the Auguste are teacher and child, mother and small son, even the angel with the flaming sword and the sinner. In other words, they are the two psychological aspects of man: one which aims upwards, the other which aims downwards."[28]

There are, in essence, two endings to *The Clowns*. Both state the death of the clown and then invoke his return. The first ending is a funeral routine that Fellini has devised out of hundreds of pieces of clown business. An Auguste clown is announced to have died. At the wake, one clown fills a bucket with his tears, and then another gratefully soaks his feet in it. The grieving widow preens as she admires how well she looks in black, but her seamstress bursts the balloon that makes up one of her buttocks. An impossibly long will is produced. The white clown, of course, delivers an uncomplimentary eulogy. The horses, played by clowns, refuse to pull the funeral hearse despite the commands given them by the authoritarian driver. The most rebellious of the horses farts and squirts water at him. In keeping with the rebelliousness and irreverence of the sequence, the Auguste clown himself refuses to stay dead. The top and sides of his hearse fall away, a giant champagne bottle pops its cork, and the Auguste suddenly soars in the air above the madness. Thus, the sequence gives us an abundance of comic material as the clowns refuse to take death seriously, and it gives us Fellini's wish for the dead clown's return.

The second ending, however, is perhaps even better. It comes from a routine told to Fellini by the clown Bario.[29] This sequence shows the sentimental or pathetic side of the clowns, balancing all the earlier high jinks. More important, it reduces the clowns to their basic myth: a white clown and an Auguste in a single spotlight. In this routine, the Auguste learns of the death of his partner. From a position in the empty stands, he plays the unabashedly sentimental "Ebb Tide" on his trumpet as if in farewell. From another part of the stands, however, a second trumpet calls back. We discover the white clown answering the solo. Gradually, the two types come together in the center of the ring, playing the song now in duet, as the movie draws to a close. This ending, too, involves a return from death, but in addition it places emphasis on the relationship of the white clown and Auguste as the aspect most worth holding on to.

It is a short jump from the bona fide documentary of *The Clowns* to the fictional one of *Orchestra Rehearsal*.[30] Fellini has said in interview that the notion of doing a film about a symphony orchestra in rehearsal had come to him from his observation of the ways in which musicians function during the recording sessions for his movies: "I was always struck with surprise and incredulity each time to see a miracle unfold. Very different individuals would arrive at the recording studios with their various instruments and also their personal problems, their bad humor, their illnesses, and even portable radios on which to hear the sports results. I was astonished to discover that, after repeated attempts, the unique, abstract form of a piece of music could be produced by this unruly group of people like schoolchildren. The operation of order being made from disorder moved me very much. It seemed to me that this situation contained in some emblematic way the image of a society where the self-expression of the group and the self-expression of each individual were compatible."[31] In this interview, Fellini states the ideal that his movie flirts with. It might be more accurate, however, for us to say that the movie demonstrates how difficult it is for the ideal to be attained and how fragile a thing to be preserved.

Virtually all critics who have discussed *Orchestra Rehearsal* regard it as a political parable of one sort or another.[32] Since the movie was made shortly after the abduction and murder of former Prime Minister Aldo Moro by the Red Brigades in 1978, Italian critics and viewers have seen the film as an overtly political work commenting on the destructiveness of terrorism by the Left in contemporary Italy and warning of the possibility of a dictator of the Right rising to power out of the confusion. American critics, of course, have been less interested in seeing the film as a specific commentary on the state of affairs in Italy, but even they have contended that it is a fable about social power in general and a conflict of principles between egalitarians and elitists.

Orchestra Rehearsal is, at bottom, a dystopia.[33] An ideal world such as Fellini discusses in his interview is hinted at but essentially ruined by the continual power struggle between the two sides. Fellini presents the case for each side and demonstrates the excesses. His lament is that the "miracle" he speaks of in his interview occurs only briefly and then is lost in the power struggle. His unspoken assumption, something of a startling discovery for him at this late point in his career, is that the world of art is not at all exempt from the politics of power and indeed is a microcosm of the outside social world, not an escape from it. As always the comedy depends on type characters. They are amusing and interesting in their own right, but perhaps more important, they shade the portrait of one side of the political spectrum or the other.

The idea of the interview is crucial in *Orchestra Rehearsal*. In fact, the movie consists primarily of individual interviews and group action sequences. The film begins with Fellini as an off-screen interviewer arriving at a thirteenth-century church oratory to do a TV documentary of the symphony orchestra that rehearses there. To prepare for the movie, Fellini claims to have interviewed about one hundred musicians and to have learned that getting them to talk about their instruments was a good way for him to find out about the musicians themselves.[34] Fellini carries this interview strategy over into his fictionalized movie and uses it to introduce us to the type characters in the orchestra. Much of the wit of the movie, indeed, comes from Fellini's ability to demonstrate so many different types through essentially one device—that of asking the musicians to tell him about their instruments.

Our overall impression of the orchestra members is that they are an extremely diverse group of types in the tradition of the commedia dell'arte and that if they were to come together for a unified effort, Fellini's term "miracle" would be the correct one to supply. The characters share a love for music and for their instruments—with a few exceptions—but most plump for the importance of their individual instruments within the framework of the orchestra. Moreover, we are encouraged early on to think of the characters in terms of "territoriality" when two violinists quarrel about the placement of a chair. A few examples of some of the type characters should be enough to demonstrate Fellini's range of diversity.

Mirella, the pianist, is the group beauty, its Gradisca. Her hair is shoulder length and sprayed to stay in place without losing its "bounce" when she tosses her head or inclines it gracefully. Her smile is perfect, and it is constant. When she enters, the first violinist helps her remove the "heavy" cover from her piano, and when it is her turn to speak on camera about her piano, she tells us that one of the male members of the orchestra helped her prepare a written statement. (There is, of course, no reason for the group beauty to exert herself physically or mentally when there are men around to help her!) She describes the piano as a king. It dominates any room in which it stands, and it must be approached subserviently. The implication is that Mirella, by virtue of her relationship with her king, is herself a queen. But to do her justice, she wears her majesty lightly.

The elder statesman of the group is the cellist. His heavily hooded eyes are his most prominent feature. He seems a man who conceals his thoughts and knows how to keep his emotions hidden behind his heavy lids, and yet when there is cause, as when he feels the orchestra should be paid for giving interviews, he can rise to his feet and argue the case with all the energy of a candidate for office. He wears a dark suit, vest, and tie, the uniform of the diplomat. In interview, he calls the cello an "ideal friend." It is, according to him, discreet and faithful.[35] These are qualities, we may assume, he would like attributed to himself. He listens to the others, sometimes agreeing with their ideas and sometimes disagreeing but always managing to give the impression that he weighs their words carefully and takes their ideas seriously. He is, in short, a politician.

The group zany is the female flautist. Her hair is stringy; her eyebrows are bushy; her nose large; and her lipstick runs over the edges of her lips. She wears a tunic dress and boots. The flute, for her, has supernatural qualities: "It's the instrument of magic spells, both solar and lunar." A slightly off-center flower child, she has, of course, studied in California. The flautist admits that all her puffing may have had the effect of making her slightly "batty," and to illustrate the point, she turns a somersault. Her major physical attribute, however, is her high-pitched giggle, with which she responds to virtually all situations.

The trombonist is the ironic observer of the group, with a flare for pranks and with a certain amount of Leftist awareness of class distinctions. Visually, he suggests the young radical. He is tall and gangly and has tousled, dark hair and the scraggly beginnings of a beard. He wears a checkered shirt with an open vest. "The trombone," he says, "is a unique instrument with a grave voice that admonishes with kindness. And it is also very comical, accompanying clowns as they squirt water and take falls." This young man savors and may well have perpetrated the gag of a prophylactic attached within the trumpet bell of the musician in front of him: As the trumpeter warms up, the prophylactic expands like a balloon and bursts. At the rehearsal intermission, the trombonist describes his fellow musicians to Fellini as if they were factory workers: "I wanted to say that many of us are from the provinces. . . . The actual truth though is that we are limited culturally. We've no real interests in anything! We spend our lives with a piece of wood or tin, blowing away or plucking."

Pitted against the orchestra with its diverse types is the conductor. He is clearly the authoritarian prima donna. We first see him at his podium with his head bowed, waiting for the orchestra members to cease their child-like games with a mouse discovered in the back of the oratory and to di-rect their attention where it properly belongs—to him in the front. He is like a teacher suffering through the wait until a raucous class settles down. The conductor is a slim, handsome man, with receding, light hair. He wears a dark sweater with sunglasses tucked into its neck. Intense and high-strung, he wastes no words but makes his points directly and stingingly, and he speaks with a German accent.

Fellini's method of presenting the character of the conductor is the re-verse of his method with the others. We see the conductor in action first as he leads the rehearsal, and then during the break later, we get to listen to him describe himself in interview. While conducting, he is humorless and overbearing. He seems incapable of understanding the point made by mem-bers of the clarinet section that a line they play is light and whimsical. During one piece, he roars at the strings, "With finesse! We're not in an amusement park. Sentiment, but with eloquence. You're violins, not trum-pets!" Elsewhere, he yells, "Where are we? On a soccer field? Take me for an umpire? Too strong! Too penetrating!" Through all this, the orchestra members respond in type: The pianist smiles; the trombonist glowers; the cellist takes off his coat and does what he can to work at the conductor's furious pace; and the flautist giggles and throws up the skirt of her dress. Finally the conductor blows up completely and shows his buttocks to the orchestra in anger.

During the interview in his private dressing room, the conductor sips champagne and tells us more about himself. We learn what we may well have already guessed: that he loves music but detests the musicians who produce it. The interview is his moment of unmasking. He explains that he should be a sergeant who goes around "kicking everybody in the ass" but is "forbidden" to do so by "absurd laws" of the union. He would like to put up screens so that he would not have to look at the unbearable faces of some of the musicians. "The time of greatness is *kaput,*" he tells Fellini. The interview, however, does not put the conductor in a totally unfavorable light. As with most of the unmasking in Fellini comedies, the character earns a certain sympathy by showing his vulnerable areas. In this instance, the conductor shows his love for the music he conducts and his sadness that his power to lead effectively, as he sees it, has been contested now by union rules.

After the break comes the revolt by the musicians. Graffiti is spray-painted on the walls. Portraits of Mozart and Vivaldi are splattered with mud or excrement. Musicians beat the kettle drums loudly. Oversized shadows flicker on the walls. The rebellious musicians chant, "Orchestra, terror! Conductor, death!" They decide to replace the conductor's podium with a giant metronome, and then some decide not to accept even that kind of symbolic leader and topple the metronome. As was the case earlier, however, they are not completely united. Fellini again shows us the differing responses of the various types. The trombonist makes a fiery speech: "We've had enough of their music. It's degrading. We play it; we'll create it; we'll manage it." Mirella, the pianist, allows herself to be drawn underneath the piano for a passionate embrace by a drummer, all the while bringing with her a cushion and a sandwich as if going on a picnic in the midst of the revolution. The madcap flautist seems to be everywhere at once: she scrambles up and down a ladder with a spray-paint can, shouts slogans, attacks the trombonist in the battle of the metronome, and then after receiving a kick in the abdomen, hurls her spray can at the trombonist. The cellist, too, decides to support the revolution. He tears up his music and makes a speech advocating a return to primitive existence. The debacle is at last brought to an end when a giant wrecking ball breaks down the wall of the oratory from outside and hangs in view of the musicians like a dark cipher. The power struggle between orchestra and leader seems to have returned to point zero.

At this moment, we get Fellini's approximation of the miracle he described in his interview. The conductor asks softly for help in setting up his podium. Again he is like a teacher who will restore the classroom to order after a disruption, but this time, he proceeds more patiently than before. He tells the musicians, "Everyone must give undivided attention to his instrument. That is all we can do now. . . . The notes are saving us. The music saves us." Ashamed by the consequences of their acts, the musicians return slowly to their places, and the conductor, appearing to take them more seriously, begins to lead. In the dust from the cave-in, they play their first piece again. This time, the brass and the strings balance each other. The tempo is right, and the sound is compact. The conductor does not stop the orchestra. The musicians and the conductor have come as close to a moment of harmony as we get in the film. However, as the conductor realizes he has regained power, he grows more and more assertive. The film ends with a darkened screen and the conductor screeching hysterically at the orchestra in German. The power struggle has resumed after the all too brief, nearly perfect moment. The utopia again has become a dystopia.

If *The White Sheik* is Fellini's early comic masterpiece, *And the Ship Sails On* is his late one. "The theme of the film," Fellini has told the journalist Ornella Volta, "is a sea voyage to carry out the ritual of expressing a profound nostalgia for something that no longer exists."[36] The movie marks the end of the art-for-art's-sake world of nineteenth-century grand opera and of *La Belle Époque* of Western Europe that the elite opera group epitomizes. Literally, a collection of singers, conductors, impresarios, entertainers, and wealthy people have hired the ocean liner *Gloria N.* to fulfill the last wish of the greatest of the sopranos, Edmea Tetua, that her ashes be scattered on the sea near the Greek isle of Erimo where she was born.[37] The funeral voyage takes place in July 1914, after the assassination of the Archduke Ferdinand in Sarajevo and ahead of the outbreak of World War I in August. Before the journey can be completed, the harsh realities of the social and political world in the form of Serbian refugees and an Austro-Hungarian battleship shatter the closed world of the opera group. In the course of the movie, however, we find justifications for the art-for-art's-sake group. These justifications consist of moments of performance that are startlingly good—perhaps even better than the clown acts in *The Clowns* and the final playing of the musicians in *Orchestra Rehearsal.* They are the "miracles" of this film, and they make the demise of the group a touchingly sad, if necessary, event.

It has been reported that Fellini, who had resisted opera most of his life, was finally persuaded by composer and collaborator Nino Rota shortly before Rota's death to attend a Verdi opera and was won over to opera by Verdi's music.[38] Be that as it may, the opera world presented Fellini with material for another parable like that of *Orchestra Rehearsal* but with richer possibilities. He and writer Tonino Guerra completed the screenplay rapidly, in a matter of some three weeks.[39] Because of Rota's death, Fellini had to seek out a new music director. He chose the young composer-pianist Gianfranco Plenizio to weave together themes by Verdi, Rossini, Strauss, Tchaikovsky, Schubert, Saint-Saëns, and Debussy. For the beginning and ending, Fellini asked the Venetian poet Andrea Zanzotto to compose lyrics in the manner of the librettists of Verdi and Rossini so that these sections could be done as a choral drama.[40] The overall effect of the music, coupled with the mannered gestures and controlled voices of the actors, is the creation of an aura of a very polite society. Against this aura, Fellini plays off the eccentricities, petty jealousies, and childish silliness of the characters according to the basic formula of high comedy.

Like the other two late comedies considered here, *And the Ship Sails On* is a documentary of sorts. "The film is presented as an old documentary," Fellini has said, "like a document from an epoch miraculously rediscovered, or perhaps even like a false document."[41] The movie begins in a grainy sepia tone like an old black-and-white movie or an old photograph that has faded. It is silent except for the clicking sound of a motion-picture camera at work. People pose and mug for the camera. Gradually, color and sound fade into the film, and eventually we find ourselves looking at intimate scenes in staterooms where no documentary camera could reasonably be. Yet at the outset, we are given the sense that our movie is a documentary filmed in the year 1914 and now brought forward for us to see in the present.

Fellini has a surrogate narrator in the character of Orlando, who is a journalist assigned to cover the journey along with the motion-picture cameraman and a still photographer. Again, as in *The Clowns,* Fellini pokes fun at the figure of the interviewer. Orlando gets names wrong and fails to recognize important people. Perhaps he drinks a little too much, and certainly he loves to pass on a juicy bit of gossip. He is not treated with much deference. The maître d', for example, asks Orlando to move to the side, out of the way of the waiters, when he begins to introduce to us the various characters seated in the ship's dining room, and people in the opera group frequently cut him short when he tries to obtain interviews with them. The most extended piece of fun with Orlando, however, comes in a sequence in which he tries to interview the Grand Duke of Herzog, an enormously chubby boy with blond hair and a blank expression, about the political situation in Europe. Orlando speaks in Italian, and the Grand Duke in German. The interview must pass through an interpreter, and it is subject to various "clarifications" by other members of the grand duke's staff. The result is that genial, smiling Orlando, hoping for important insights, is puzzled by the Grand Duke's reply, "We are on the edge of a volcano," when the sentence is passed on to Orlando as "We are on the mouth of a mountain." A final absurdity about Orlando is that he is there at all, for he is an interviewer in a documentary that purports to be silent.

Orlando, however, is more than an interviewer. He is a narrator in the sense of storyteller. He offers background information about the characters, speculates on their relationships, poses questions about what they will do, and even supplies a variety of hypothetical answers. At one point, Orlando reads from a sheaf of his own notes and speaks the typical lament of the postmodern storyteller: "'I write. . . . I tell. . . . But what do I want to tell? A sea voyage? A voyage through life? But it is not told. It is made.' Trivial, isn't it? Has this been said already? And better? But everything has already been said and done!"[42] Orlando thus shares with us some of his sense of frustration and challenge as a storyteller wishing to speak to an audience who has seen and heard much, if not everything. Toward the end of the movie, as the *Gloria N.* is under siege from the Austro-Hungarian battleship, Orlando begins speaking in the past tense about the action he is participating in at the moment and about events that will take place in the near future. In other words, he speaks as if he were an author telling the event from his study long after it occurred: the author within the text has become the author outside the text. And at this point, the camera pulls back to reveal Fellini in the process of filming the final scene on the constructed set of the *Gloria N.*'s deck. Thus we are made very much aware of our situation as audience to a story fabricated by an author rather than as unguided onlookers to a slice of reality. The situation is, of course, the standard one for postmodern fiction, and as we have observed in chapter 1, self-conscious artifice has grown steadily to be a major aspect of Fellini's style.

The self-conscious artifice is, of course, not limited to Fellini's treatment of the narrator. It is present everywhere. There are, for example, homages to silent films. Orlando changes hats before the camera as if it were a mirror, in imitation of Buster Keaton in *Steamboat Bill.* Hildebranda Cuffari, the soprano on board the *Gloria N.,* dresses like Theda Bara. And the Austro-Hungarian battleship resembles the poster depiction of the *Battleship Potemkin.* Furthermore, the gradual changes from silence to sound and from black-and-white to color call attention to the movie's artifice. We again have Fellini's plastic waves. The backdrops are obviously artificial. The choral pieces at the beginning and end performed by all members of the cast bring the artifice of the opera stage to the movie screen. And finally, of course, there is the pullback shot of the *Gloria N.* in the middle of the soundstage, with Fellini behind another camera. These things, however, do not raise epistemological questions about our ability to separate illusion from reality as in, say, the dramas of Pirandello or Brecht. Rather they simply allow Fellini to have fun with the form of the documentary and to "make opera" out of it, rather than vice versa.

The type characters are presented to us by Orlando in the dining room. The place is well chosen. It is the sanctum sanctorum of the ship. The passengers wear formal attire, and they eat politely in rhythm with Tchaikovsky's "Dance of the Flowers." We meet Hildebranda Cuffari, the proud soprano, and her entourage. She is the heir apparent to the crown of Edmea Tetua and a little bit uncertain of how to act in that role. Beneath her regal appearance, she has her fears, as we see when a seagull flying into the room through an open window drops a feather that falls delicately on Cuffari's neck and nearly sends her into hysterics. Aureliano Fuciletto is the hammy tenor. A large, round man with black whiskers and a big smile, he looks remarkably like a caricature of Luciano Pavarotti. Fuciletto displays his hamminess by whooping loudly about the gull and joking when he flies away, "Captain, the seagull has left, sending regards. It didn't like the menu!" On board is his nemesis, Sabatino Lepori, another tenor, but with the dashing good looks of a matinee idol, and Fuciletto will never miss an opportunity to feud with this rival. Sir Reginald Dongby, impresario of Covent Garden, and his wife, Violet, who has a passion for working-class men form a sexually kinky team.[43] Also present are two old singing teachers, the Rubetti brothers. Their cottonlike hair askew and their formal attire rumpled, they seem slightly dotty pedants. A tall, dark, somber Russian named U. O. Ziloev is introduced to us as precisely what he appears to be— a basso profundo. And the rotund Grand Duke makes an entrance to a trumpet fanfare. A toy soldier, he is resplendent in his blue-green uniform with gold braid and medals.

Where *And the Ship Sails On* seems superior to the other two late comedies is in its middle section. Longer than either *The Clowns* or *Orchestra Rehearsal,* the film provides Fellini opportunities to put all of his various type characters through situations or scenes that will test their prowess, let them demonstrate type, permit them to show a more serious side to their natures, or allow them to unmask. We might ask ourselves, for example, what would two old, somewhat batty music teachers do on board an ocean liner? The answer in this film is that they go to the kitchen, lay out the crystal on a table, and by filling the containers with water to different levels, make musical instruments from the crystal. By rubbing the rims of the goblets, tapping the sides, and blowing into decanters, the old teachers are able to produce a haunting version of Schubert's "Moment Musical," op. 94, no. 3, in F minor.[44] Or we might ask what would a basso profundo do on the ship? Here he calls for a chicken from the cook, and by sustaining a very low note, he hypnotizes the chicken so that it stands on one leg in a trance. A similarly delightful piece of business involving the tenors and the sopranos occurs when all the singers visit the engine room. The workers ask Signora Cuffari, the proud diva, to sing for them. When she declines, Fuciletto, the hammy tenor, bursts forth with a selection from an aria. The other tenor follows him with a piece of his own, and then a mezzo-soprano joins the competition. The diva must now defend her position, and so Hildebranda Cuffari sings a snatch of an aria. Fuciletto tries to win the contest by singing the last line of "La donna è mobile" from *Rigoletto*. All the others attempt the line, and then Hildebranda wins the competition with her final version, which no one dares challenge. In all three of these sequences, the characters perform in type, but they are so surprisingly skillful within their types that they astonish their audience in the film, the kitchen staff and the furnace workers, and charm us, the audience outside the film.

Another grouping of scenes, staged in staterooms rather than in work spaces, serves to unmask or deepen certain of the type characters. In her cabin at teatime, Hildebranda Cuffari listens to the two professors praise the voice of Edmea Tetua. They claim that she could range easily over three octaves and get as high as F natural above high C. The stunned Cuffari asks them humbly to tell her the secret of how a singer attains such range, and they respond that Edmea imagined the spirals inside a seashell and willed her voice up the spirals. "She was different from anyone else. Unique. There'll never be another like her," one of the professors states flatly. The clear implication is that Hildebranda could never match the inner strength of Edmea. When Hildebranda's lover returns to the cabin after the professors have left and pays her a routine compliment, she slaps him angrily. The slap reveals her frustration. The old professors seem to have touched on Hildebranda's worst fear, that even at her best she will always be second to the legendary Edmea. Similarly, the precise nature of the sexual game Sir Reginald and Violet play is revealed in their stateroom. On the prowl for his wife, Sir Reginald returns to their cabin and finds the steward and the maid leaving. He enters the cabin, sniffs the air, and accuses his wife of having had sex with the steward. She denies and then agrees with his accusation. In this instance, she may well be innocent of the charges, but if so, she is willing to give her masochistic husband the kind of humiliation he so obviously craves.

As in the other late comedies, the last section of *And the Ship Sails On* is an extended group action. Our final portrait is that of the group rather than of individuals, and Fellini's final statement is directed at the social frivolousness of the opera people as a whole. The last scenes take place on the ship's deck, which is not unlike an opera stage. At issue are questions of how the elite group will react to Serbian refugees picked up at night from the sea by the ship's captain, how they will respond to the demand from the Austro-Hungarian battleship that the refugees be turned over, and how they will grieve for Edmea Tetua, the best and brightest of them, now gone. The answer in each case, as we might predict, is that the group turns the situation into opera. Except for the funeral rites, which are after all a ceremonial farewell with music, the group's response may be considered irresponsible and even silly, but we must finally admit that they do it magnificently. The comedy Fellini produces at the end is that inherent in opera: outlandish situations are often matched with glorious music. Fellini merely tilts the balance a little more in the direction of outlandishness.

Individually, our characters continue in type. When the Serbians are discovered on board, one of the dotty old professors strokes the hair of a little girl with more fondness than her mother will tolerate. After the Serbians gather around the dining room to watch the opera people eat and threaten to intrude as the seagull did earlier, Violet Dongby carries out a silver tray of cakes to them and enjoys exchanging glances with the Serbian males. Hildebranda Cuffari, on the other hand, descends to her cabin at the first opportunity to lock away her jewels in a strongbox. And later that night at a dance on deck to the music of the Serbians, Aureliano Fuciletto announces he has much to learn from a certain brunette and plunges into the group of Serbian dancers with his usual gusto.

The dance on the deck is the first of three operatic scenes that conclude the movie. The Serbian folk music breaks down the reserve of the elite opera group. The music historians can explain the origins of the music. Fuciletto and Violet can enjoy dancing with members of the opposite sex. A beautiful girl from the elitist group can fall in love with a handsome boy among the Serbians. The soprano voices of the Serbians can seem as excellent in their way as the soprano voices of the opera group we have heard earlier. (The same off-screen singers perform for each group.) But this "perfect" rapprochement between the two social groups is based only on music and therefore lasts only as long as the music does.

The funeral rites for Edmea Tetua constitute the second operatic scene. As the Austro-Hungarian battleship waits, the opera group plays a recording of Edmea's voice singing the aria "Cieli azzurri" from *Aida*[45] and scatters her ashes to the sea. This scene also is "perfect." It is one of the "miracles" the opera group is able to produce. But the moment can have no final bearing on the historical forces at work. When the services end, the Austro-Hungarians want the refugees as prisoners. The rites seem almost a tribute to a lost deity who no longer holds the power to affect the real world.

The third operatic scene involves the relinquishing of the refugees and the sinking of the *Gloria N.* It is the most preposterous of the three and certainly owes a debt to the famous historical situation of the *Titanic* sinking as the band played "Nearer My God to Thee." Here, to Verdi themes from *Aida, Nabucco, La Forza del Destino,* and *La Traviata,* the opera group sings of a glorious, heroic refusal to give up the refugees to the tyrants on the battleship: "No, no, no, we will not give them to you! / Death, death to overbearing might!"[46] Unfortunately, as the group sings its bold defiance, we watch the refugees being herded into lifeboats by the crew to be turned over to the Austro-Hungarians, an action undercutting completely the stance of the singers. In a final flourish of romanticism, the pretty girl of the opera people joins the handsome Serbian boy, but this lover's sacrifice, like the singing, does nothing to alter the situation that one aristocratic group is surrendering the refugees to the navy of another aristocratic group. Fellini, however, will not let the opera group off with such hypocrisy. The laws of comic justice demand their punishment. The Serbian boy throws a grenade onto the battleship, and the Austro-Hungarians fire on the *Gloria N.* in return. As their ocean liner goes down, the opera people enter lifeboats and continue to do what they do best and what is their only saving grace—they sing the music of Verdi. Their time has passed, but they know how to take their final bows elaborately and well.

In these late comedies, Fellini grew more ambitious than he was in his earlier ones. He attempted statements about the art world his type characters populate. In each case, the world of the performers is threatened with a kind of extinction. Fellini or his surrogate narrator investigates the world in its last stages, tries to preserve on film what is excellent about it, and to some extent weighs the validity of each art world's claim to continue. *The Clowns* is Fellini's defense of clown art worked out primarily in terms of the mythic importance of the white clown–Auguste duality. With *Orchestra Rehearsal* and *And the Ship Sails On,* Fellini deals with the relationships between the art worlds and the social-political ones in which they reside. He demonstrates that the divisive power struggle in the symphony orchestra at rehearsal is the same as that in the battles between the Left and the Right in contemporary Western Europe, and he pinpoints a shocking disengagement from the real social-political world by the elitist opera people on the eve of World War I. But in these two films, as in *The Clowns,* are the "miracles" of performance that, if they do not exonerate the performers, do give them value.

7

THE ADAPTATIONS: FELLINI'S VALEDICTORY

In the second half of his career, Fellini did four adaptations from literary sources: *Toby Dammit* (1968), *Fellini Satyricon* (1969), *Fellini's Casanova* (1976), and his last film, *The Voice of the Moon* (1990). All of these mark occasions in Fellini's life when he paused and turned away from his usual autobiographical works, his films built on the personae of Giulietta Masina, and his comedies of types. We might suspect that the first three of the projects, at least, would allow Fellini to "recharge his batteries" before returning to the more demanding task of beginning original story treatments again. After all, the kind of energy involved in the making over of material from another medium, while hard work of its kind, we might argue, does not require the same amount of emotional self-commitment. Yet, all of the works, the last one included, seem connected with issues raised in other Fellini films, most notably *La Dolce Vita* and *Fellini's Roma*. These are issues concerned with a society that has reached a decadent final stage of overripeness and needs to die in order to begin anew. And if the adapted works seem tired, they do so in a special way. Fellini has filled or even overloaded these four films with imagery of excess, grown conventional. Excess in these films does not liberate or force its way through boundaries; rather it weighs down and in itself constitutes boundaries for the human spirit of the characters. The adaptations, then, constitute a kind of valedictory from the mature Fellini on the inevitability and necessity of change.

As virtually all the critics have remarked, there is a coldness and a clinical detachment about the literary adaptations that set them off from the other Fellini films.[1] To be sure, some of this coldness and detachment in the first three might be attributed to Fellini's collaborator, Bernardino Zapponi, whose own short stories exhibit these traits. But we must recognize that Fellini considered Zapponi the right collaborator for these projects and did not seek to balance Zapponi with a more genial cowriter, as he had done earlier in balancing the acerbic Ennio Flaiano with the gentler, more playful Tullio Pinelli. Moreover, Fellini did return to his old friend, the whimsical Pinelli, as his principal cowriter for *The Voice of the Moon,* and the tone of this work does not differ noticeably from the first three adaptations. The coldness and detachment, therefore, should be considered "intended," in some sense of that word, whether on a conscious or unconscious level of Fellini's mind.

Whether Fellini's informing metaphor of death and change comes from Oswald Spengler's theory of historical cycles or the Marxist-Leninist theory of dialectical materialism in which the young and strong supplant the old and tired,[2] Fellini clearly believes he is living at the end of an era and seems hopeful sometimes that this era will be followed by another with interesting possibilities we cannot yet imagine. If Fellini's emphasis is on the decadent end, it is because that stage of the process seems clearly before him in the present. A Marxist would say that Western Europe is in the final, decadent stage of late capitalism; Fellini would say simply that the traditional Italian society of his parents seems to have reached its end. The earlier film *La Dolce Vita* (1960) could be read as a forerunner of this position. The protagonist travels through a civilization that seems on the verge of yielding to a different kind of society. We are interested both in the protagonist and in the various institutions of the contemporary society he guides us through. We discover that the institutions of church, family, and marriage are no longer the stabilizing factors they were in the Italy of the past. Neither the aristocrats nor the intellectuals provide leadership. The protagonist finds that he lives in a world whose chief characteristic is destabilization and whose chief form of activity is the divertissement of endless parties.[3]

The themes of decadent ends and new beginnings are ones we often associate with creative artists in the later stages of their lives. There is, of course, a certain consolation in these themes for those who have started to feel the weight of their years, since the themes suggest a larger, continuing cycle that absorbs and makes sense of individual deaths. And there is also a certain glorification of the self involved in the equation of personal situations with those of societies. Both of these elements seem present in at least the last three of Fellini's adaptations, *Fellini Satyricon, Fellini's Casanova,* and *The Voice of the Moon.* More and more as Fellini matured, he brought into his work the notion of death. In the late, documentary-style comedies discussed in the previous chapter, the defense against death was the act of putting significant moments on film and thereby preserving them. Here the defense seems to be for Fellini to incorporate the phenomenon into a historical cycle. *Toby Dammit* is a brief tuning up; *Fellini Satyricon* and *Fellini's Casanova* are full-length treatments of the need to return to a zero point; and *The Voice of the Moon* seems Fellini's farewell address on the subject. In retrospect, the basic requirement Fellini seems to have sought in the literary works he adapted was that they provide him with a strong sense of an ending.

Toby Dammit: *The Tuning Up of a Theme*

Toby Dammit is a loose adaptation of Edgar Allan Poe's minor comic tale "Never Bet the Devil Your Head" (1841). In the hands of Fellini and his cowriter Zapponi, the tale becomes an extended study of a man in the last twenty-four hours of his life, that is, a rendering of the decadent end of an individual. There are comic elements in the movie. Some of Fellini's favorite targets for mockery—church officials, fashion models, traffic jams, celebrity interviews, and awards ceremonies—are exploited for their absurd effect. These things do not, however, comprise the central issue of the film. They provide instead a background of fragmentation and garishness against which the hero's last stages of disintegration are shown. The focus is on the man, Toby Dammit, and the movie seeks to sustain the mood of his despair as he tries both to ward off and to hasten his own end.

The project of adapting a Poe story was suggested to Fellini by a French production team headed by Roger Eger.[4] The proposal came at an opportune time for Fellini. He had just broken off work on the film *The Voyage of G. Mastorna* and was recovering from a difficult case of pleurisy. Furthermore, Fellini had just severed relations with his cowriters of long standing, Flaiano and Pinelli, and the Poe story provided the opportunity for him to begin to assemble a new team. The project was to be an episode of forty minutes. It would appear along with episodes by two other directors in a Poe anthology called *Spirits of the Dead*. For the screenplay, as we noted earlier, Fellini enlisted the aid of Bernardino Zapponi. He had discovered by chance Zapponi's volume of short stories *Gobal* and had found the stories detached and macabre in a way that suggested Zapponi would be an ideal collaborator on Poe.[5] Fellini's assistant, Liliana Betti, maintains that Fellini never read the Poe tale until after the filming was completed.[6] He worked instead from a summary of the story furnished by her. Certainly very little of the Poe story was used by Fellini and Zapponi: only the protagonist's name and the tale's grisly ending.

In the Poe tale, Toby, a child-man, has the annoying habit of backing up most of his assertions with offers to wager. His favorite phrase is, "I'll bet the Devil my head." One day while making his way through a dark covered bridge, Toby brags that he can leap over the stile at the bridge's end and offers "to bet the Devil his head" if he doesn't cut a splendid pigeonwing in midair as he does so. From the shadows of the bridge, the devil, a "little lame old gentleman of venerable aspect," wearing a black apron, accepts the wager. Toby leaps, only to fall back, his head severed by a flat iron crossbar fixed some five feet above the stile. The decapitation gave Fellini and Zapponi the conclusion for their movie version. Their lead-up to it, however, constitutes an utterly different kind of story.

Zapponi's contributions to the movie were major. In his essay "Edgar Poe e il cinema," he puts forward two ideas that were incorporated into the film and that seem important organizing principles. His first idea is that Poe is generally present in his tales as the informing psyche. The second is his notion that Poe's short stories are not as much suspense tales as they are works of sustained pitch. Zapponi states about Poe's stories, "Suspense, which could be attractive to filmmakers, is, however, more apparent than real. The march toward death does not build to a crescendo, but is a single sustained note which disturbs us deeply through its persistence."[7]

The presence of Poe, or at least that of the tortured artist, is insisted upon by the physical presentation of Terence Stamp in the leading role. Toby Dammit in the diegesis is an English actor whose performance of *Hamlet* has won praise but who now has a drinking problem and comes to Italy to act in a spaghetti western in order to make money and to receive a Ferrari. In this role of the tortured artist, Stamp is made up to resemble Poe. Stamp's hair is tousled and stringy. He has a trace of a beginning mustache. He wears a black jacket and a black foulard. His forehead is broad, and his cheeks appear gaunt. During the awards ceremony as Toby, sleepy with drink, sits at his table waiting to go on, he strikes a series of poses in close-up that suggest a haunted or brooding presence such as we may attribute to Poe in his persona as the Romantic poet. Yet, while Toby resembles Poe physically, he may differ from him psychologically. We do not know the root causes of Toby's malaise. We do know he now despises his audience and drinks so much he can no longer find employment in England. We also know that Toby has effectively cut himself off from the belief that his career as an artist can be the organizing principle for his life, a principle that has served as the stabilizing factor for the Fellini autobiographical hero. Toby, then, is a brooding artist figure not so much because he suffers for his art, as we may want to assume Poe did, but because he suffers from his estrangement from it.

Toby is also cut off from any ideal love that could serve as an ordering force in his life. In this, he is, of course, like many of Fellini's heroes who "seek, but do not find" such an ideal love. Toby encounters two feminine ideals, which are typical Fellini types: the housewife and the love goddess. The first is a model who seems to be rehearsing a commercial at the TV studio where Toby is being interviewed. Her hair neatly in place, wearing a black dress and a crisp white apron, the model dances merrily around a beautifully set dining room table. She is the perfect wife and hostess. Attracted to her and the idealized scene, Toby murmurs, "Will you marry me?" only to look again and discover the flesh-and-blood model now a plastic mannequin who cannot respond to his proposal. The second ideal, the beautiful romantic love goddess, is not unlike the lady in white of *8 ½*. She appears to Toby as he dozes in his alcoholic stupor prior to the awards ceremony. This dream figure strokes Toby's hair and promises to be his perfect, everlasting love and his solace against loneliness: "Don't be afraid anymore. I'll take care of you. Always. Yes, always. I understand you. I know you. I've always known you. You will never be alone anymore because I'll be with you always."[8] Significantly enough, Toby rejects this love goddess during his drunken speech at the ceremony. It is as if the deception of the mannequin earlier in the day has been the last time Toby will allow himself to be taken in by the notion of an idealized love. With this hope or illusion gone, Toby is ready to pursue only the attractive promise of a pleasant, easy death.

Toby's disturbed mental state is externalized by a variety of means. Almost immediately in the movie, we encounter a fragmented, discontinuous external world. At the airport and during the limousine ride into Rome, for example, Fellini alternates between shots done through a red filter and shots done in natural color. Furthermore, the nationalities and garb of the people we see are diverse: nuns in black carrying musical instruments; Hassidic Jews; a surprised, well-dressed black woman; praying Muslims; bearded, Cuban revolutionary soldiers; stewardesses; construction workers repairing the road to Rome; glamorous models posing on the flatbed of a truck; and a band of gypsies.[9] Moreover, we must take in two languages almost simultaneously as the producer, Father Spagna, explains Toby's role in the proposed movie in Italian and a lady translator gives Toby a running account in English. These kinds of juxtapositions are especially disturbing because they seem to be the norm of the world Toby has entered, not the exceptions.

Counter to this disturbing atmosphere is the calm, implacable sense the movie gives us that Toby is approaching his end. A certain mood of fatality is present in the work from first to last. At the outset, Toby tells us, "I had the odd feeling that this trip, put off for so long, was to be very significant in my life. For a moment, I had the absurd hope that the plane wouldn't land but would take me far from Rome. It was not to be. The airport's invisible nets had already snared the plane and were dragging it helplessly toward earth." From this point on, Toby himself will seem caught in "invisible nets" pulling him "helplessly" to his death. On the ride into the city, when the limousine is stopped, Toby shows his palm to a gypsy fortuneteller to read. She glances at it and pushes it away ominously with the murmur, "I don't want to." Most strongly, though, we get a sense of fatality when Toby sets out in his Ferrari after the awards ceremony for what will prove to be his death drive. He seems to be making his way through a maze with only one outlet. Frequently, he comes to dead ends, courtyards, or blocked routes, forcing him back to find the one passageway that will let him through. Marking his way are five ghostly white figures—four wooden figures in cook's uniforms as signs before restaurants and one department store mannequin in a white tuxedo jacket. They indicate that he is on the appointed route.

The devil appears four times in the movie, each time in the guise of a little girl playing with a white ball that makes no sound when it bounces.

Toby tells his interviewers, "For me, the Devil is friendly and joyful." The promise the devil holds out to him is that of joining the pleasant game of a child far away from the trials and disappointments of the everyday world. The child appears to Toby, but not to us, at the airport. Then in a flashback from Toby's memory as he rides to Rome, we get a reenactment of the earlier scene and can now see the child bounce her ball to Toby. He comments, "She seemed convinced that eventually I'd join her game." Again she appears, smiling, during the TV interview, visible to Toby and to us but not to the interviewers, and finally the child comes into view for Toby and us as an apparition on the far side of a collapsed bridge under repair. Joining her game thus becomes the appointed goal of Toby's drive in the Ferrari and indeed of his trip to Rome from the point where the "invisible nets" pulled his plane "helplessly toward earth." There is, of course, a final grotesque trick, the legacy of Poe. As Toby races his sports car off the end of the collapsed bridge in a vain attempt to reach the other side, he decapitates himself on a steel safety cable stretched across the bridge's end a few feet above the roadway surface. One of the last shots of the film shows the child picking up Toby's severed head. The game, then, has been played more for her grisly amusement than for his pleasant release.

In the final analysis, *Toby Dammit* may seem little more than an exercise. Fellini and Zapponi duplicate Poe's ability to hold a "single sustained note which disturbs us deeply through its persistence." That note is Toby's tortured yearning for the release of death. Yet, if *Toby Dammit* is an exercise, it is also a preparation. Toby has lost the belief in values that might sustain him, the two traditional Fellini values of art and love. He has reached a point of decadence or overripeness where, to put it bluntly, it is time for him to die. This is surely a harsh statement to make about a human being. It may be, however, a less harsh statement when it is made about a society. Fellini's next step is to do precisely that. In his next three, more ambitious adaptations, he will choose societies in their decadent final stages, when it is time for them to die and then, as history has suggested, to be replaced by something other.

Fellini Satyricon: *The End of an Empire and a New Start*

Fellini Satyricon is about the need to begin again. The movie is an adaptation of the *Satyricon* of Petronius Arbiter, and it deals with aspects and institutions of the Roman Empire in the first century after Christ, during the reign of Nero. In an interview with Alberto Moravia, Fellini has described the film as a "documentary of a dream."[10] If so, what the dream embodies is the profound wish that a social structure crumble so that new adventures may begin and new structures with a variety of possibilities may start to form. But it is not the new possibilities that the movie documents. It is the decadence of the old society and the gradual readying of the protagonist to go beyond it.

Petronius's *Satyricon* is an unusual work.[11] The title can be translated as "a satirical work" or "a work about satyrs," and the *Satyricon* appears to be something of each, and more. It is considered a Menippean satire, that is, a potpourri of materials in poetry and prose ranging from parody to philosophic statement. It draws on and plays with sentimental Greek romances of separated lovers, the epic journey of a hero as in the *Odyssey* or the *Aeneid,* the oral tradition of rhetorical declamation before an audience, and Milesian tales (forerunners to the modern short story) that may be set into the narrative. Moreover, the *Satyricon* exists only in fragments from a much longer work.[12] These fragments concern the adventures of Encolpius, the narrator and protagonist. He is hopelessly smitten with love for the fickle and opportunistic boy Giton and competes with his fellow student and rival Ascyltus for the boy's affection. In a mock-heroic vein, Encolpius incurs the wrath of the god Priapus by observing the secret rites of a priestess and by killing a sacred goose, and toward the end of the fragments, Encolpius must seek to overcome the god's curse on him that comes in the form of impotency. There are two mentors for Encolpius—Agamemnon, a professor of rhetoric, and Eumolpus, a poet. Both inveigh against the present age and compare it unfavorably to a golden past. With Agamemnon as his sponsor, Encolpius attends a dinner given by the wealthy freedman Trimalchio in the longest and most celebrated of the fragments, where the outlandishly showy behavior of the host seems a means for Petronius to mock Trimalchio as a parvenu and perhaps also Nero and his court as not sufficiently different from the ostentatious freedman and his circle of friends. With Eumolpus as leader, the pair of Encolpius and Giton journey on the ship of the fierce, one-eyed Lichas and his licentious female passenger, Tryphaena. Because of betrayals in the past, Encolpius and Giton must try to conceal their presence from the masters of the ship, and they must try to survive a storm at sea. The fragments end with the journey of Encolpius, Giton, and Eumolpus to the town of Croton, where the citizens aspire to live their lives on inherited wealth. As an indictment of the citizens, Eumolpus reads a will in which he promises a bogus fortune to the citizens if, and only if, they will devour his corpse. Taken together, these fragments of the *Satyricon* show a decadent world without ideals beyond expediency, without a sense of beauty, and without opportunity for heroic action. Yet, as Erich Segal has pointed out in his comparison of Petronius's work with Fellini's movie, the *Satyricon* shows also a world where mirth, laughter, and physical enjoyments are celebrated in a life-affirming way, coming as they do before the end that Petronius intuits.[13] Fellini clearly chooses to emphasize and even extend the decadence of Petronius's version of the Roman world. The more life-affirming aspect he defers to the final section, where the hope of a new start begins to take shape.

The Process of Adaptation

Fellini has said that he first read the *Satyricon* in his adolescence "with all the energy and greedy curiosity a schoolboy can muster."[14] He seems then to have reread it in 1939 while working for the comic magazine *Marc'Aurelio* and to have considered adapting it as an anti-Fascist parody.[15] Finally, he took it up again during his convalescence from pleurisy in 1967 and found it fascinating as a text he could work over imaginatively. He liked especially the mysterious, open quality of the fragments.[16] On the basis of his rereading of Petronius and after completing *Toby Dammit,* Fellini proposed the adaptation of the *Satyricon* to producer Alberto Grimaldi in 1968 and set to work at once on the project with cowriter Bernardino Zapponi.

For the undertaking, Fellini hired Professor Luca Canali of the University of Pisa as his consultant on the Roman era, visited the sites of Pompei and Herculaneum, and assigned assistants Liliana Betti and Norma Giacchero extensive reading on the history of the period.[17] The Italian journalist Dario Zanelli has listed the many scholarly books he observed heaped on Fellini's desk,[18] and the director himself has named several classical texts he wanted to incorporate into his version of the *Satyricon*.[19] However, the works that are the most demonstrably important to the movie in its final form are relatively few. They are Jerome Carcopino's *Daily Life in Rome,* Domenico Comparetti's *Vergil in the Middle Ages,* Apuleius's *The Golden Ass,*

Suetonius's *The Lives of the Twelve Caesars,* and Tacitus's *Annals.*[20] These books, we might add, are not used particularly to "authenticate" Fellini's recreation of the world of the *Satyricon,* rather they are used as additional source material for Fellini to create his own vision of the late Roman era.

Fellini's adaptation moved through three distinct stages: a short, forty-two-page story treatment; a full-length screenplay; and the movie itself.[21] Some of Fellini's initial decisions at the first stage, that of the story treatment, were obvious ones that helped condense or unify the narrative. He combined the two mentors into one, Eumolpus, the poet. He deleted two long poems Eumolpus recites in the original work and cut all the Milesian tales except the most famous one concerning the widow of Ephesus. The role of Ascyltus, on the other hand, Fellini expanded. In Petronius's *Satyricon,* Ascyltus disappears from the narrative just before the journey on Lichas's ship and does not return. Fellini, however, makes him a fellow voyager and keeps him in the narrative until nearly the end. The change tends both to bind the work together a little bit more tightly and to draw attention to Encolpius's love-hate relationship with his rival, who becomes in the Fellini version a Jungian shadow figure. In addition, Fellini retained from his source Encolpius's pursuit of Giton, the episode of Trimalchio's feast, the voyage on Lichas's ship in somewhat altered form, and the situation of Encolpius's impotency.

To this skeleton form Fellini and Zapponi added five blocks of new material at the treatment stage. Four of the blocks have scholarly or classical sources; the other appears to have been invented by Fellini and Zapponi. Four contribute to the atmosphere of decadence or apocalyptic ending in the work, and one sets up the positive movement of readying the protagonist to move on.

The first block could be called the Roman section. Whereas the fragments of Petronius seem to begin somewhere in the area of the Bay of Naples, Fellini starts his work in the capital of the empire and then works his way to the more "primitive" south. The Fellini story treatment opens with a robbery during a spectacle at the Circus Maximus. Then come scenes at a mime theater, a Roman brothel, and the huge multistory apartment building known as the Insula Felicles. Much of this material was derived from Jerome Carcopino's *Daily Life in Ancient Rome.*[22] The apartment scene ends with the collapse of the huge structure, providing Fellini with a strong apocalyptic image for the opening portion of his film.

Fellini and Zapponi also inserted two death scenes. One involves a young, albino Caesar who is set upon by his soldiers and beaten to death at sea, and the other treats the suicide of a dignified patrician couple who cut their wrists after learning that the new Caesar will confiscate their villa and exile them. The albino Caesar is a composite of three emperors: Elagabalus, who became ruler at fourteen and died at the hands of his soldiers at eighteen; Caligula, who was pale and weak in appearance and also was slain by his soldiers; and Nero, who, aided by his secretary, took his own life before the centurions could get to him. The suicide of the patrician couple, one of the few serene sections of the work, is almost surely a tribute to Petronius by Fellini, for it follows Tacitus's account of Petronius's own suicide when he learned that Nero had ordered his arrest.[23] Although quite different in tone, both of these death scenes add a more funereal aspect to the work.

The most striking of Fellini and Zapponi's borrowings is the tale of how the witch Oenothea acquires the power to restore potency. For this sequence, the writers adapted a medieval story concerning Vergil, who was regarded in his old age as something of a magician by storytellers in the Middle Ages. The tale is contained in Domenico Comparetti's *Vergil in the Middle Ages*.[24] In this story, the elderly Vergil falls in love with the daughter of a Roman emperor. She promises him entry to her room at night by means of a hoist, but when Vergil attempts the entry, she leaves him suspended in the hoist below her window to face the ridicule of the citizens in the morning. For revenge, Vergil banishes fire from the city and advises the citizens they may light their torches from a source between the legs of the emperor's daughter. This story Fellini and Zapponi simply transfer to Oenothea, a character already in the *Satyricon*. The episode establishes her as a much stronger figure. For Fellini, she becomes the Jungian archetype of the Great Mother and plays a major role in readying Encolpius to leave the world that is dying around him.

The block of material invented by Fellini and Zapponi is a sequence about the demigod Hermaphrodite. This sequence is vintage Fellini. It concerns the pilgrimage of people of the Roman Empire to the cavern of a curious, half-male and half-female being. Like the murdered emperor, the so-called demigod is a sickly albino. If there is any borrowing here, it involves Fellini borrowing from himself. As modern Italians in *Nights of*

Cabiria and *La Dolce Vita* go to religious sites looking for miracles that do not occur, so here the people of the Roman Empire come to the hermaphrodite hoping for answers and cures that the frail, pathetic creature cannot provide. The segment constitutes another of Fellini's relentless attacks on those who are gullible enough to go to staged miracles.

At the next stage, that of the screenplay, Fellini and Zapponi revised their opening and conclusion and added five sequences. These revisions and expansions bring the work very close to its final form. For the opening and the conclusion, Fellini introduced the idea of characters seen against a blank wall as if they were figures on a fresco. At the outset, Fellini and Zapponi deleted the scene in the Circus Maximus and began instead with shots of a light marble wall before which Encolpius soon appears to lament the loss of Giton and the betrayal by Ascyltus. The new ending of the work now involves the death of Eumolpus, the poet, and the recitation of his will by a young sea captain. We are told that Encolpius laughs and that the story "breaks up, goes off into a series of discontinuous images." Then the characters are gradually transformed into figures on "antique fresco; a discolored fresco in Pompeiian colors. . . where Encolpius is only one of many faces."[25] The characters, then, are to be seen as forms on a fresco who have come to life for the length of the movie and finally return to their source.

Two brief scenes were added to introduce the characters of Eumolpus and the new emperor. The first takes place in a picture gallery. The scene comes directly from Petronius without change other than its position in the work. Fellini moves it earlier to introduce Eumolpus sooner and to establish his character clearly before he conducts Encolpius to the feast of Trimalchio. In this scene, the poet Eumolpus uses the paintings from the past as a text for a diatribe against the lack of concern with beauty in the present. The second scene depicts the march of the new emperor toward Rome. The scene is probably taken from Suetonius's description of the march of Galba to Rome to replace Nero.[26] In the eventual movie version, however, the march will be more somber than Suetonius's rendering of it. It will depict an apprehensive young Caesar and his weary soldiers bringing back booty, animals, and slaves from a campaign. With its heavy, martial drumbeats, the march seems almost a funeral procession. As such, it is, of course, appropriate to Fellini's general intention of showing a world ready to die.

The other sequences added at this stage deal primarily with sexual malaise. The theme is, of course, central to Petronius. He depicts it most obviously in the unstable love triangle of Encolpius, Ascyltus, and Giton, which, as we will see, constitutes a parody of romantic love, and he demonstrates it in the various debauches Encolpius has with goddesses and mortal women. Fellini, however, seems intent on bringing into his version of *Fellini Satyricon* a depiction of Eros that is less robust and more troubled. He and Zapponi invented two of the additions. One concerns an insatiable woman who is transported across a desert in a covered wagon by her husband, and the other takes place in a Garden of Delights, where Encolpius attempts unsuccessfully to cure his impotency.[27] In both, Fellini emphasizes aspects of humiliation and sadomasochism.

The most important and most interesting of the added sequences dealing with sexual malaise is, however, one adapted from Apuleius's *The Golden Ass.*[28] This sequence involves Encolpius's battle with the Minotaur and his discovery in public of his impotency. In Apuleius's tale, the hero serves as the butt of laughter in a mock trial held in a town's theater. He is the victim of a ritual humiliation that the townspeople perpetrate on a stranger each year. The hero believes he has killed three men when, in fact, he has only run his sword through three inflated wineskins. Fellini and Zapponi extended the mock-heroic aspect of the episode. They have the townspeople cast the frightened Encolpius in the role of Theseus and force him to do battle with a muscular foe cast as the Minotaur. The episode, as we will see, becomes one of utter humiliation for Encolpius.

At the final stage of adaptation, that of the movie itself, Fellini alters primarily the sequence on board Lichas's ship. This sequence had proved a troublesome one for Fellini and Zapponi. They had tinkered with it at each stage and, in each of the successive revisions, had made Lichas a more prominent character. Petronius's version of the episode was largely comic, involving as it did the attempts at disguise by Encolpius and Giton, who wished to avoid discovery. For his story treatment, Fellini transposed material concerning Encolpius's orgy with a priestess of Priapus early in Petronius's fragments to the ship episode. For the screenplay, Fellini added the material that Lichas decides to stage a homosexual marriage between Encolpius and himself. Here Fellini seems to have drawn on accounts by both Suetonius and Tacitus of Nero's scandalous public marriages with men.[29] Finally, at the movie stage, Fellini added a scene in which Lichas wrestles with Encolpius, defeats him, and kisses him.[30] Clearly, one of the results of the successive changes is that Lichas grows more and more to be a tyrant of the world he governs, imposing his will and his whims on the people of his ship.

The Vanity of Human Wishes

The theme of the vanity of human wishes is inherent in the material Fellini took over. Petronius's fragments are full of people who would like to be more than they are. There is, of course, something poignant about such a theme when it is illustrated by characters at the end of a historical era, for the result that their wishes come to less than they had hoped may reflect a similar outcome for the era. Fellini has seized the theme of the vanity of human wishes and perhaps even extended it in his film.

A case in point is Trimalchio. The feast he gives is the most celebrated section of Petronius's work. Fellini has said that he did not dare change it, for the section is too well known and revered.[31] In fact, however, he did condense the section. To some extent, Petronius's episode is a symposium in which the guests offer set-piece declamations against such things as old age, inflation, incompetent doctors, the lack of religion, and the softness of the youth of the day. With the exception of crusty old Homer's long-winded attack on Encolpius as a typical, ungrateful member of the younger generation, Fellini cuts back the declamations of guests to a few lines here and there. Similarly, Fellini reduces Petronius's descriptions of the food that is consumed and the "artful" manner in which it is served. One major visual example suffices—that of the gutting open of a hog to reveal various delicacies inside. The result of Fellini's editing is to place full emphasis on the character of Trimalchio. He is a man who has accomplished much, for he has risen from slave to wealthy landowner and merchant, but he pretends to more. As Lichas does on his ship, Trimalchio pretends to the role of a petty emperor in his home, and in this, he appears the fool.

Fellini has declared he wanted his Trimalchio to be "a sort of gloomy, stolid Onassis, with a glazed look in his eye: a mummy."[32] The role is played by a seventy-year-old restaurant owner, Mario Romagnoli, who does, in fact, bring the desired stolidness to the part. He has bushy eyebrows, bags under his eyes, jowls, and a blockish physique. His movements are made with a heavy solemnity. For his introduction to his guests, Trimalchio is borne in on a litter by his slaves with trumpet fanfare. He wears a crown of oak leaves. The guests chant, "Hail, Gaius Trimalchio!" He boasts that all the food served has been grown on his land and defines the vastness of his holdings. In the background, a mosaic of Trimalchio is being constructed by artisans so that the story of his life will live on after him. As Nero aspired to the role of singer, Trimalchio aspires to that of poet. He has invited Eumolpus to the feast in order to pretend, as Eumolpus explains, that the two are colleagues. When Trimalchio recites some lines of Lucretius as his own, Eumolpus, pushed beyond endurance, turns on his host and exposes him. The situation, however, only underscores Trimalchio's power and willfulness. He orders Eumolpus to be taken to the kitchen and beaten.

Trimalchio's major project is that of erecting his own tomb, and at the conclusion of the feast, he marches the guests to the site. "Only an emperor or two," he boasts, "will have a mausoleum equal to mine." Trimalchio lies down in the excavation and asks the guests to mourn his passing. A eulogy is delivered. Then after Trimalchio gives a piece of gold to one grieving black slave, he is mobbed by other slaves and guests asking for similar "bequests." This outcome might be humbling, if Trimalchio had wit enough to perceive the irony of the situation. This man who has laid claim to "greatness" because of his accumulated wealth has the opportunity to see that the wealth is, in fact, his only value to those he will leave behind, that and nothing more.

The Journey of the Hero

Encolpius, the hero of *Fellini Satyricon,* undergoes a process of regeneration. He returns to a zero point so that he can grow again and become a young man with a new range of potentials. In this sense, his journey recapitulates the fall and return to zero of his era. As in the fragments of Petronius, the Encolpius of Fellini plays a mock-heroic role. He is like the intoxicated lovers of the early Greek romances and like the warrior heroes of the Greek-Roman myths and stories, but he is almost always unsuccessful in his endeavors. For Fellini, the aim here is not literary parody, as it surely was for Petronius. Fellini's goal seems to be to set up a hero with several layers of cultural myth superimposed on him in order to strip off those layers and return him to a pristine state. For this process, as we might expect, Fellini draws on his versions of the Jungian archetypes of the shadow and the anima.

The role of romantic lover is one that Encolpius burns to play. At the outset of the movie, Encolpius tells us in soliloquy how much he laments the loss of Giton, the boy he loves, who has been stolen away by Encolpius's friend and rival, Ascyltus: "Shame on him! He is a disgrace! And now holding each other in their arms, they spend entire nights together and laugh at me. . . . I loved you, Giton, and I still do. I can't share you with others because you are part of me. You are me. You're my soul. . . . You're the sun; you're the sea; you're the gods."[33] Similarly, at the art gallery, Encolpius looks at depictions of the pretty youths Ganymede and Narcissus and of the lovers Apollo and Hyacinth, and he complains, "The old myths tell us of loves that are unequaled. Only I have a cruel love." Clearly, Encolpius would like to be a character in the old Greek romances, such as Xenophon's *Ephesiaca*, in which lovers are separated by chance, subjected to various trials and temptations, but remain faithful to each other and thus may reunite happily at the end. Such a reunion is not the case for Encolpius. Moreover, the love between Encolpius and Giton may seem slightly off center in that it is homosexual,[34] but as the paintings at the gallery demonstrate, Encolpius has ample precedent among the gods for his love for a boy. Encolpius's problem is not homosexuality; it is Giton's utter faithlessness. In Encolpius's room, Giton is seductive and loving with Encolpius, but when challenged later by Ascyltus to choose between Encolpius and him, Giton speaks his one line of the movie and chooses Ascyltus. In Petronius's fragments, Giton will later explain that he chose for pragmatic reasons the stronger of the two men contending for him, but in Fellini's movie, Encolpius must simply confront the fact of Giton's betrayal without explanation. Given his romantic stance at this point in the narrative, Encolpius's thoughts go to his knife and presumably to suicide, with only the chance event of an earthquake and the collapse of his building saving him from a tragic lover's death.

The dark side of Encolpius's nature is represented by the shadow figure Ascyltus. This alter-ego character is visually opposite to Encolpius. Whereas Encolpius is blond and tends to carry himself with relaxed body movements, Ascyltus is dark and seems always to hold himself tense, flexed, and on guard. Clearly, Ascyltus is more physically violent and more sexually rapacious than Encolpius. Frequently, Ascyltus must come to the aid of Encolpius in battles, and he generally takes the lead or outperforms Encolpius in sexual encounters. In their rivalry for Giton, Ascyltus opposes Encolpius's romantic notions of love with a more pragmatic doctrine of might. The stronger lover will "take" Giton and do with him what he pleases. The purpose of Ascyltus in the narrative, then, as we have said earlier, is to lead Encolpius away from his too romantic outlook. It is not that Ascyltus's view is the right one; it is that his view can counterbalance Encolpius's and, in that sense, educate him.

Two-thirds of the way through *Fellini Satyricon,* there is a moment of rapprochement between Encolpius and Ascyltus. It involves a second love triangle, this time without Giton. Encolpius and Ascyltus discover a female slave in the otherwise abandoned villa of the Roman couple who have committed suicide. Ascyltus leads her to the impluvium, where he and Encolpius make love to her, and then the two males embrace each other. The situation is quite different from the earlier one involving Giton. No longer present is the romantic notion of the perfect soul mate. Encolpius has moved in the direction of Ascyltus. He has not gone to the extreme of Ascyltus's rapaciousness but has put aside his exaggerated romantic ideals and enjoyed physical pleasure in a simple, straightforward way. The educative function of the shadow figure has achieved its purpose, if only for the moment.

The role of warrior hero, one more suited to Ascyltus, is forced on Encolpius against his will by the organizers of the Festival of Laughter. The result of Encolpius's trial, though, is his realization of how far he is from the mythical role of hero he is forced to play. Cast as Theseus and armed with a torch and a spiked glove, Encolpius must prowl a labyrinth in search of the Minotaur, played by a giant of a man wearing the mask of a bull's head and carrying a large club. We are put in Encolpius's place as he makes his way. Many of the shots are subjective tracking shots, and we hear only Encolpius's breathing, the roar of the wind, and the odd chanting music of the onlookers. In short, we are encouraged to share Encolpius's fear. When he confronts the Minotaur, Encolpius falls to his knees and pleads to his conqueror, "Why aren't you fighting a gladiator instead of me? I'm a student. Don't take your anger out on me. Spare me. I don't know why they are playing this joke on me. . . . I am not a Theseus." At this point in the festival, it is clear to all that he is no warrior hero. Indeed, the events seem to suggest that in comparison with the tall, powerful male with the large, phallic club he has competed against, Encolpius is a mere boy. This implication is further developed in what follows, when Encolpius fails sexually in his coupling with the voluptuous Ariadne, to whom he is sent as his reward. The situation recalls Guido with Saraghina in *8 ½* and Titta with the tobacconist in *Amarcord* in terms of matching a boy with a powerful, experienced woman. Moreover, like Titta if not Guido, Encolpius is strikingly unsuccessful. The process of his humbling is almost complete. It needs only Encolpius's visit to the Garden of Delights. There, utterly reduced to an unsure adolescent unable to have an erection, he can begin again the journey toward adulthood.

The new journey involves Encolpius's encounter with the anima mediatrix figure of Oenothea. We have seen that Fellini has increased her importance by adding the story of how she gained the power of fire within her vagina. Now we should add that Fellini increases her mysteriousness by putting her through a series of transformations before Encolpius's eyes. She is at first a spidery-thin young black woman, crouched behind a fire. Next she is a charred effigy seemingly within the fire and perhaps also a stork who walks across the room as Encolpius cringes from the vision of the effigy. Finally, Oenothea is a large, sturdy, bare-breasted, middle-aged black woman. Encolpius falls on his knees before this powerful woman and pleads his abject humiliation: "Oh Great Mother, can you see my disgrace? The culprit facing you is guilty of treachery and murder and profaning a temple and is now a soldier without weapons." Oenothea is now the Jungian archetype of female sexuality. She is fearful and mysterious but also tender and nurturing. As she lies back on her bed by the fire, she twists her muscular arms above the fire, but when Encolpius falls on her, she gently strokes his head against her breasts. The moment is one of revitalization for Encolpius in the sense that he undergoes a new rite of passage from inexperienced adolescent to a second beginning toward adulthood.

As Encolpius undergoes this revitalization, we see the ferryman wound Ascyltus outside Oenothea's hut, presumably in an attempt to rob the young man. This act, not in Petronius's fragments, is thematically appropriate to Fellini's version of Encolpius's development. He has moved beyond the need for the kind of shadow figure Ascyltus served for him. Encolpius runs across the marshes, shouting back at Ascyltus, "I want to make up for lost time. The flower of youth withers so soon. Run!" But Ascyltus cannot run. He falters and dies. The implication of the last part of the film is that Encolpius, in contrast to Ascyltus, will go forward afresh toward the fulfillment of new dreams. The era of the Roman Empire may be in its final decadent stages, but Fellini gives us in this movie a hero who knows that a return to zero involves the possibility of a new beginning as well as the sorrow of an ending.

Fellini's Casanova: *The End of the Courtly World*

In *Fellini's Casanova,* Fellini holds his character at arm's length and treats him with irony. His distaste for Casanova's *History of My Life* is well known. In interview, Fellini has explained that he read the memoirs only after he had signed the contract to do the film and that he discovered a deep-seated antipathy for the project.[35] As a result, the film has a coldness to it that goes far beyond that of *Fellini Satyricon.* There is no young man who will survive the end of his era as Encolpius did; Casanova grows old with his epoch and indeed is left behind by the new age as an absurd remnant. More than this, however, there is very little to like about Casanova. He will lead us through the various eighteenth-century courts of Europe—Venice, Paris, Parma, London, Roma, Dresden, Württemberg, and Dux in Bohemia— all vestiges of old feudal societies in their last stages of overripeness, ready to fall with the French Revolution and the spirit of social reform of the approaching nineteenth century.[36] Like other Fellini heroes we have discussed, Casanova will try to define himself through his love relationships with women. But he will learn nothing about the end of an era from his travels or about himself from his loves. This unwillingness to learn or dig beneath the surface of things is finally his most maddening limitation, for Casanova does witness a great deal and he does set himself up as a writer when he undertakes his memoirs. However, Casanova as a protagonist is a very useful figure for Fellini to employ in summarizing an epoch that has become obsessed with surface and form.

The Process of Adaptation

The project of adapting Giacomo Casanova's *History of My Life* was suggested to Fellini by producer Dino De Laurentiis in the spring of 1974 after Fellini had completed work on *Amarcord.* At once Fellini enlisted the aid of Zapponi to help with the screenplay and Danilo Donati with the set designs. There was, however, a falling out between Fellini and his producer by midsummer, largely over the choice of the actor to play Casanova. By the end of the year, a new producer, Alberto Grimaldi, took over the project. He and Fellini were able to agree on Donald Sutherland for the leading role, and Grimaldi was able to secure funds from Universal Studios for a coproduction.[37]

The extreme length of Casanova's memoirs provided Fellini with much more material than he could ever hope to use in a movie. The twelve-volume English edition edited by Willard R. Trask, for example, runs to 3,639 pages of text.[38] The primary material consists of Casanova's accounts of his love affairs and of his traveler's reports on his visits to the major centers of European culture. The memoirs, however, are also sprinkled with short tales that involve witchcraft, earthy sexual comedy, swindles, duels, and risk taking, all worthy of a place in Boccaccio's *Decameron* on the basis of their robustness. For the most part, these tales have been cut away. The only real taste of these kinds of materials in the movie comes in Casanova's contest with a Roman coachman over which of the two can have the more orgasms in an hour and in Casanova's swindle of Mme. D'Urfé, the French aristocratic lady who wishes to be reborn as a male. Furthermore, Casanova's lengthy description of his escape from the Piombi prison in Venice, a masterpiece of suspense, is reduced in the movie to a few brief shots of Casanova clambering along the prison rooftop, and his account of how he organized the Paris lottery in 1757, a clear example of Casanova performing shrewdly in the world of politics and finance, is not presented at all. What we see in Fellini's movie, then, is a somewhat defanged Casanova, rendered more passive and indeed more pathetic than Casanova's version of himself.[39]

Where Fellini has taken the most latitude with his source materials, however, is in his visual depictions of the European cultural centers Casanova travels through. Here, with the aid of Donati and a considerable amount of historical research,[40] Fellini has made his own versions of these places. In the memoirs, Casanova gives almost verbatim recountings of the major conversations of his life, but he offers scant detail about the visual space he moves through. This absence of visual detail in the memoirs, of course, meant that Fellini was free, within certain historical limits, to give his own renderings. The result is that the movie is one of his most visually interesting. The color selection is usually limited to a small number of hues in each sequence, with Casanova in white, rust, or black set against more vibrant colors in the rooms he passes through. More important, the scenes are full of visually intriguing objects. A list of such objects might include the giant head of Rèitia that is hoisted from the Grand Canal of Venice;

Casanova's mechanical bird, which raises its head and flaps its wings when Casanova performs his sexual feats; the painted, wooden clothes mannequins in one of Casanova's bedrooms; the turning, tiered serving dishes of cantaloupes at a dinner; the chandeliers of candles at the Dresden theater; the organs mounted at various heights on the wall in the palace of Württemberg; and, of course, the life-sized mechanical doll who is Casanova's last love. The cumulative effect of all these objects added by Fellini, however, is eventually that of surfeit. Where Casanova gave too little visual detail, Fellini gives too much, and the result for us is the sense once again that we are in an era that has become overripe, this time with too many bright objects and toys.

As was the case with *Fellini Satyricon,* the adaptation of *Fellini's Casanova* passed through stages. The process, however, is more difficult to chart, for the quantum leap between the original screenplay and the movie cannot be broken down into gradations. The starting point, of course, is Casanova's *History of My Life.* All of the episodes in the movie have some basis, however slight or great, in the memoirs, except the final sequence, in which Casanova is an old man, writing and living in the castle at Dux.[41] The original screenplay for the film was written by Fellini and Zapponi for Dino De Laurentiis in 1974.[42] This screenplay is, with a few exceptions, a faithful rendering of a variety of episodes from the memoirs. Clearly, the main interest of Fellini and Zapponi at this stage was to select material from their source and to get it on paper in dramatic form without much concern about revising the material. The screenplay contains blocks of material set in Venice, Paris, Parma, a monastery in the Swiss Alps, London, Turkey, Amsterdam, Vienna, Rome, Voltaire's villa in Switzerland, Dresden, Naples, Württemberg, and Dux. In 1975 Fellini commissioned the American writer Gore Vidal to revise the screenplay.[43] It seems to have been commissioned mainly to appease the executives at Universal, and Fellini seems not to have drawn on it at all.[44] The original screenplay of Fellini and Zapponi, however, did undergo a great deal of change. It was much too long, and for the movie, Fellini and Zapponi deleted the episodes in the Swiss Alps, Turkey, Amsterdam, Vienna, and Naples. Furthermore, they changed the episode in Voltaire's villa to one in the laboratory of a fictional entomologist, Dr. Moebius, in Bern. And they revised in some way all of the other episodes they retained. Then as the film was being shot in the fall and winter of 1975,

Zapponi wrote his own novel version, *Casanova: In un romanzo la storia del film di Fellini,* which parallels the movie.[45]

The episodes that appear in the movie fall into two categories. The first consists of scenes and sequences where Fellini and Zapponi stick fairly close to their source material but compress, shift, or add material and, in some cases, change the emphasis. The episodes set in Venice, Paris, Parma, and Rome are in this category. The second type consists of scenes and sequences where the writers use a germ from the memoirs and build a series of new events of their own. Such episodes are those which take place in London, Bern, Dresden, and Württemberg.

The opening sequence, set in Venice, is a particularly interesting example of the first type, because Fellini and Zapponi manage to change the emphasis of the source material merely by altering a few elements. In this initial sequence, we witness first the giant head of Rèitia, goddess of healing of the Veneti people of three thousand years ago, being hoisted from the depths of the Grand Canal as costumed revelers look on.[46] Casanova is among the crowd, dressed as Pierrot, the sensitive clown of the commedia dell'arte. To his surprise, he receives a note sent by a nun who invites him to a romantic tryst on the island of San Bartolo. Once Casanova has arrived, the nun, M. M. in Casanova's memoirs, asks him to wait until her wealthy lover, the French ambassador, Abbé De Bernis, is in position to watch them through a peephole in the wall of their chamber. When all is ready, Casanova activates the mechanism of the artificial bird he carries with him, and as the bird raises his head and flaps his wings, Casanova goes through a series of intricate and stylized sexual maneuvers with the nun, based on some of the positions described by Pietro Aretino in his *Sonetti lussuriosi.*[47]

Up to this point, Fellini has altered his material mainly by compressing it. In the memoirs, Casanova receives the note on All Saints' Day, not during Carnival. There are several meetings instead of one. M. M. does not wear her nun's garb until the third such meeting, and it is also at this time that Casanova learns of De Bernis' presence as a voyeur. Later still, now during Carnival, Casanova dresses as Pierrot and goes to M. M.'s convent and then to her private house of love. By compressing all these elements into one night for the movie, Fellini and Zapponi, of course, achieve a gain in dramatic intensity, but perhaps more important, they make it possible to begin with a rendering of a masquerade in which Casanova plays the appropriately symbolic part of a clown. The masquerade furthermore initiates a series of highly theatrical moments that continues throughout the work and influences how we come to understand the character of Casanova.

There are also two additions not mentioned in the memoirs or original screenplay. These are the giant head of Rèitia and the mechanical bird. The first makes a symbolic statement and establishes a funereal tone as it rises, has a moment of splendor, and then sinks back to nothingness. It seems an embodiment of the general theme of cycles that informs both *Fellini Satyricon* and *Fellini's Casanova*. The second addition begins a motif of visual references to mechanicalness and artificiality that will eventually condemn the social worlds Casanova visits.[48]

As the sequence comes to its conclusion, Fellini and Zapponi alter the source material to achieve a different emphasis. In the film, De Bernis speaks to Casanova from the other side of the wall in an aloof and condescending manner. He critiques Casanova's sexual performance. Then Casanova offers himself as one eager to undertake commissions for the French ambassador. He gets no response. Apparently, De Bernis has departed. This ending is sheer invention. No such interchange takes place in the memoirs. In fact, De Bernis shows friendship for Casanova. He arranges to dine with Casanova, M. M., and a novice nun who had formerly been Casanova's lover, and later on, in Paris, De Bernis even finds a commission for Casanova to undertake. Thus Fellini and Zapponi have completely changed the way De Bernis behaves, with the result that Casanova in the movie version is made to appear a far less powerful figure.

The episodes in the second category, wherein Fellini and Zapponi build on material from the memoirs to create essentially new situations, resemble those sequences in *Fellini Satyricon* in which the writers brought in material from other sources, classical or modern, to further certain themes. A case in point is the London sequence of *Fellini's Casanova,* which serves a purpose much like the sequence of the witch Oenothea in *Fellini Satyricon,* but with a sadly different result.

The point of departure for the London sequence is Casanova's thought to commit suicide over his unhappy affair with the adventuress La Charpillon. In the *History of My Life,* La Charpillon vows to conquer Casanova and indeed carries out her boast. She extracts sizable amounts of money from him on the promise of future sexual rewards for her benefactor, which she always manages to withhold by one ploy or another. When Casanova discovers her with another lover, he threatens her and smashes her furniture. The next day, he is told that she is having convulsions and lies near death. In remorse and despair, Casanova decides on suicide: "I go out, fairly intending to drown myself in the Thames." As he walks the streets, however, he meets a friend, Sir Wellbore Agar, who eventually leads him to a dance, and there Casanova discovers a perfectly healthy La Charpillon dancing with yet another lover. For the movie, Fellini and Zapponi condense the conflict between Casanova and La Charpillon to an angry shouting match among Casanova, the adventuress, and her mother as they ride over a bridge in a carriage. La Charpillon accuses Casanova of impotency, and the mother forces him at gunpoint to give up his claim to the jewelry he had previously given her daughter. Abandoned near the Thames in his sad plight, Casanova considers suicide. What saves him in the movie is not his British friend but the sudden mysterious appearance of a giantess and her two dwarf assistants. This mysterious apparition piques Casanova's curiosity and offers him another woman to pursue. The giantess is a Fellini invention—one we are not unfamiliar with, the Oenothea of this work, the archetypal Earth Mother.

Perhaps the true inspiration for the London sequence lies not so much in the *History of My Life* as in the engravings and drawings of William Hogarth, Thomas Rowlandson, and Gustave Doré. Zapponi implies as much when, in his novel version, he refers to Casanova's London as "twisted, deformed as in the caricatures of Hogarth and Rowlandson,"[49] and Fellini has added in interview that the London evening scenes are done "in the milieu of Hogarth, according to the taste of Gustave Doré."[50] What the three artists have in common is that their depictions are teeming with grotesques—a Fellini trait in itself—and that their situations exist just outside the bounds of polite society but contiguous to it and reflecting a darker or less constrained side of it. If Fellini had specific art works in mind as models, they would have to be Hogarth's *Southwark Fair* (1733–34) and *A Midnight Modern Conversation* (1733–34) and Rowlandson's *The Prize Fight* (1787).

Southwark Fair may well have been the imaginative point of departure for Fellini's rendering of his London fair. In the first place, a show cloth in Hogarth's engraving depicts a giant and two dwarfs, and this depiction could have nudged Fellini and Zapponi toward their creation of their giantess and her two little assistants. The hurly-burly of Hogarth's depiction may also have had an impact. The figures of *Southwark Fair* are arranged spatially in a circle around which the viewer's eyes travel continuously. They include actors falling from a collapsed platform, a dwarf blowing a bagpipe, a performing dog, an actress beating a drum, a bailiff arresting an actor, a fire swallower, a pickpocket in action, a customer at a peep-show box, and a swordsman on horseback—in short, a kind of gallery of Fellini grotesques. In the movie, Fellini's version of the hurly-burly is done sequentially rather than spatially, that is, with tracking shots identified with Casanova's point of view as he makes his way through the fair. This, of course, constitutes Fellini's accustomed way for rendering a gallery of unusual people, as we noted in chapter 1. His group is no less diverse than Hogarth's. Fellini's Casanova passes show cloths, a contortionist on a small stage, a large, rubbery man with a woman's face painted on his stomach, people on a merry-go-round driven by horses, a pipe player, a musician with a drum on his back, and a female mime who makes birdlike moves with her head. More important still, a show cloth representation of customers leaving the belly of a Trojan horse in the upper center of Hogarth's engraving may well have given Fellini and Zapponi the idea for the final piece of action of Casanova's walk through the fair: his descent into the belly of an embalmed whale. In the hands of Fellini and Zapponi, the descent becomes archetypal. The barker tells us it is a descent into the womb. From a Jungian viewpoint, it is a descent into the underworld, where the worst fears of the male unconscious assault Casanova. Clearly, the whale brings Casanova to a confrontation with a part of the mystery of sexuality and provides, at least potentially, an initial step toward the kind of education and renewal Encolpius achieves in the Oenothea section of *Fellini Satyricon.*

After the journey into the belly of the whale, Casanova meets his friend Egard in the confines of a smoky tavern. The setting seems to be derived from Hogarth's *A Midnight Modern Conversation,* and the character, from the friend Sir Wellbore Agar of *History of My Life.* The added scene gives us Fellini's version of a London den of strong drink and opium, and perhaps beyond this, its purpose may be to call our attention to the inwardness of Casanova's journey at this point in the narrative, for Egard draws a parallel between his own haunted, imagined voyages on opium and Casanova's so-called "real" journeys in the external world.

In the last portion of the London sequence, Casanova meets the giantess in the tavern and envisions her in flashback outfighting eight male opponents earlier that evening in a tentlike fight area. This arena seems more confined and therefore more terrifying than the one depicted by Rowlandson in the open air in broad daylight, but the arena probably owes its genesis to such an eighteenth-century depiction of prize fighting. And finally, Casanova spies the giantess in her bath. Here she is no longer a terrifying figure. Rather, like Oenothea in *Fellini Satyricon* when she caresses Encolpius's head, the giantess is a nurturing, gentle figure. The two extremes of fearful power and nurturing tenderness are, of course, the elements that make her an archetype of feminine sexuality and, beyond that, an embodiment of life's ineffability. Like Encolpius, Casanova has at this point returned to a basic starting point and is in a position to begin again with a renewed sense of life's mixture of possibilities. However, unlike Encolpius, Casanova is no longer a young man. He remains caught in the old world. In short, he fails the opportunity for renewal afforded him at the fair in the London sequence.

Casanova and Women

Casanova's character is defined through the women in his life. As is the case with Marcello in *La Dolce Vita,* Guido in *8 ½,* and Snaporaz in *The City of Women,* Casanova often projects his wishes and fears onto the women he encounters, and they, in turn, often bring out certain qualities, positive or negative, in him. With the nun who performs sexually with him before the eyes of her lover, Casanova can, for example, defy a religious taboo and do so exhibitionistically. In a sexual initiation of a young seamstress in Venice, Casanova claims to be Pygmalion, the sculptor, molding his Galatea from marble and bringing her to life, but we may be more inclined to detect a strain of necromancy in his desire for the pale girl who becomes most attractive to him when she swoons. Along similar lines, the aristocratic lady who has a rendezvous with Casanova in the seamstress shop and invites him to whip her buttocks gives him the opportunity to explore the role of sadist, a role that does not, however, seem to appeal strongly to him. And Casanova's sexual escapades with a hunchbacked stage performer in the cabinet-bed of the inn in Dresden allow him to revel in his curiosity about the physically abnormal. In all these examples, Casanova goes beyond a norm of some kind. This could make him an ultimate Fellini hero, someone whose curiosity about the mysteriousness of life leads him to explore its outer limits. Yet this is not the case. He does not set out to break through barriers in any programmatic way, and worse, once his encounters with women have taken place, he does not reflect critically on them and hence learns nothing from them.

Two women, in particular, intrigue Casanova. Both are figures from a love myth that has captivated the Western mind since the Middle Ages: They are "unattainable ladies."[51] Casanova can place these women on pedestals high above him and then attempt to climb to them to share in the godlike status he has attributed to them. Their unattainableness is a necessary part of their appeal, for if Casanova were to "attain" them for any length of time, he would have to deal with them as real people, and they could no longer function as ideal figures.

The essence of the first woman, Henriette, lies in her mysteriousness, her air of gentility, and her artistic sensitivity. Casanova discovers her at Forli disguised as a young soldier, in the care of a Hungarian captain. She will not explain who she is, why she has been in disguise, nor why she wishes to go to Parma. She is a woman of mystery.[52] When Casanova buys her the clothes of a lady, she becomes, in his words, "transformed." He kneels before her and kisses her hand. It is significant that the beautiful lady emerges from a disguise as a male soldier, for she is, in a sense, a dream figure created by the male. At a dinner given by the cynical hunchback DuBois, Henriette is the silent, enigmatic recipient of Casanova's romantic pronouncements about women and about love: "[Women] are gentler, more reasonable, more human beings than we are. These qualities which should give them superiority have instead put them at our mercy."[53] Ostensibly, Casanova makes his assertion in response to DuBois' mocking aphorisms that women are lighter than air and that a kiss is an attempt to devour one's lover, but in fact, Casanova looks to Henriette for approval after each of his pronouncements, and she smiles understandingly at him in return. At the conclusion of the meal, Henriette becomes an embodiment of the ideal Casanova espouses. She plays a slow and strikingly beautiful composition on the cello. Her playing seems a refutation of DuBois' operetta staged just prior to her performance, in which he depicts love in terms of a female praying mantis devouring her mate to the same musical composition played at a faster tempo. Henriette's delicacy and artistic sensitivity seem all the more striking in contrast to the grotesque show of the hunchback. The next morning, of course, a mysterious envoy, D'Antoine, must arrive to take the lady away, and Casanova, in turn, must play out his courtly pose to its conclusion; that is, he must weep and briefly contemplate the monastery or suicide. Yet, on another level, her disappearance must gratify him, because the disappearance insures she will remain an ideal.

Isabella, the second woman, is also a mysterious and unattainable lady, for she will never make clear her motives or the depth of her feelings in her relationship with Casanova. This allows Casanova to "read into" her character virtually anything he wishes, and he chooses to think of her as someone with an almost divine power to make him a new and more noble person. Casanova encounters Isabella and her sister in Bern at the home and laboratory of Dr. Moebius, their entomologist father.[54] In the close, heavy air of the laboratory, watching the two women impale insects on a display board, Casanova faints. The two women nurse him back to consciousness and a kind of rejuvenation through the use of a technique resembling acupuncture. On waking, Casanova professes his love for the more beautiful of his two nurses, Isabella: "You are enchantingly beautiful. Your laugh is like the laughter on the face of a figure on an Etruscan tomb, full of grace, yet reserved, at once radiant and sepulchral. . . . I want to annihilate myself in you, my wise Minerva." In addition to her beauty, Isabella has an intelligence and a learnedness that Casanova must respect. With her medical knowledge, she seems to have been able to affect a marvelous change in him. Yet Isabella could be a wise instructress, an anima mediatrix, in another sense. She invites Casanova to engage in introspection. "What a strange man you are, Giacomo," she tells him. "You can't talk about love without using funereal images. . . . Perhaps what you really want is not to love, but to die." The suggestion that Casanova has an interest in death and annihilation of the self is an intriguing one, but more important here is the fact Isabella makes such suggestions at all. By doing so, she invites Casanova to speculate on the nature of his obsession with women and love. Sadly, he avoids such speculation and proposes instead a romantic rendezvous in Dresden that Isabella does not keep. Again there may be a certain satisfaction for Casanova in Isabella's unattainableness, for he can keep her a goddess of wisdom and skill in his mind, but it seems also true that Casanova has failed a test with Isabella and has been rejected for his shallowness.

Two Worlds: One Old, One New

Most of the courts and salons that Casanova visits illustrate the final stage of the old feudal society of eighteenth-century Europe, which is about to collapse and give rise to the precapitalist society that will follow it. The behavior of the aristocrats is exaggerated. The social forms are carried too far, or else they are broken altogether. A measure of the decadence of such courts and salons is that Casanova is usually highly regarded in them. He can master the forms and then push them a step farther, which seems to be precisely what the aristocrats want for their amusement.

The most artificial of the eighteenth-century social worlds presented in the movie is the Parisian coterie of the Marquise D'Urfé at her dinner table. The music, the color strategy for the scene, and the formal arrangement of the dinner table create a sense of an overly elaborate preciousness. The music consists of an ostinato, a short musical phrase repeated over and over at the same pitch. It is played softly on a harp, a recorder, and a droning string instrument, all electronically modified to make the music seem strange and unfamiliar. The repetitiousness of the music is hypnotic. The colors used in the set and costumes are the three primaries, red, blue, and yellow, but they are rendered in light intensity. The dress of the Marquise and the drapes on the wall are light blue; Casanova wears a rose-colored costume; sweets on the table are light blue, rose, and light yellow; and the lady seated next to Casanova has blond strands in her wig. The single exception to this color scheme is a garish gentleman who wears a bright red-orange scarf of dark intensity. As the lone exception, however, his garishness points us toward an awareness of the subdued intensity of the rest of the colors. All these elements combine to give us a little social world that seems fragile in its decorousness.

The group of people gathered at Mme. D'Urfé's table seem final, recondite bearers of a medieval mentality interested primarily in the spiritual, be it religious or occult. The gross material world is of little or no interest to them. To fill out the conversation, Fellini and Zapponi insert into the dinner scene the character of Hedwig, a precocious young girl much interested in theological disputation, whom Casanova, in his memoirs, writes of meeting in Geneva in the home of a pastor.[55] She delivers a comically pedantic refutation of St. Augustine's theory that the Virgin Mary conceived Jesus through her ears. Then an abbot lectures at one moment on the theory that women have only two souls, whereas men have three, and at another moment he pretends to be in spiritual communication with the Queen of Sheba. One form of mumbo jumbo, Fellini seems to be saying, is as good as another for members of this circle. What seems to count for these people is theoretical self-consistency and a good rhetorical style. This is, of course, the kind of world Casanova can excel in, and he quickly dupes the Marquise with a scam about the Philosopher's Stone.

Quite different is the episode in the court at Württemberg. For this section, Fellini and Zapponi use only one sentence from their source material, an introductory remark: "Finally, I arrived in Württemberg, which at that time, boasted the most brilliant court in Europe." From this sentence, they construct their own version of the German court that is almost diametrically opposed to the French circle just discussed and that seems to look forward to a new age. The sequence takes place in the Duke's dining hall on the occasion of his birthday, when various gifts arrive for his inspection and a raucous celebration is going on. The music is again an ostinato, but it is done in a fast, martial tempo, with various instruments joining in to create a cacophony. The source of the music within the diegesis is six organs mounted at various heights on the walls, with musicians flailing away at their keyboards. The ostinato gives way to pseudo-German folk music, "The Dreamer of Swabia," performed by a solo tenor voice. Then this piece is overwhelmed by a chorus repeating the ostinato. The effect of all this is one of an almost unceasing din. The colors are mainly dark oranges, rusts, browns and blacks. Officers wear orange and rust, and Casanova, a blue-black courtier's suit. The Duke inspects a long skein of orange fabric. There is a roaring fire behind the Duke and a flaming brazier at an end of the hall. The tables show their bare planks, and they are littered with discarded tankards and scraps of food. The German court is thus vulgar and primitive in comparison with the French dining room, but it is also charged with an energy that presages a new era.

There are three emphases in the court at Württemberg: militarism, a curiosity about natural science, and a burlesquing of chivalrous activities. All seem a part of a heartier new attitude in which physicality has again become important. A cannon and suits of armor serve as the main decorations of the hall. One of the guests demonstrates the power of a crossbow. At the same time, however, the Duke listens, fascinated, to a large conch shell and inspects a giant tortoise brought to him as a birthday gift. Throughout the scene in the dining hall, two clowns offer each other mock challenges and fight a mock duel. Finally they attack the life-sized female doll that they have brought with them and provoke Casanova, who does not realize at first she is a doll, to draw his sword chivalrously in her defense.

It is a measure of the court's break with the forms of aristocratic feudal society that Casanova cannot perform well in it. Throughout the scene, Casanova tries in vain to win the favor of the Duke. The scene is one of frustration for Casanova. When he offers himself as a possible ambassador to another court, the Duke turns to inspect a skein of material. When Casanova offers plans for fortification based on the principles of Democritus and Lucius, the tenor and chorus drown him out. When Casanova offers the Duke some Spanish seeds with youth-prolonging powers, a drunken guest blows the seeds from his hands.

Fittingly, the only way Casanova captures the Duke's attention is as a source of merriment when he draws his sword to defend the female doll against the attack of the two clowns. The chivalry Casanova displays, which has worked so well in the past with the Marquise D'Urfé, has become for the Duke of Württemberg merely the final piece of comic business in the performance of his clowns. Certainly the age in which Casanova felt at home is over.

Fellini's Sad Farewell

Fellini's fourth adaptation, *The Voice of the Moon* (1990), his final movie, seems a fitting conclusion to the series of adaptations. Like the other three, this film depicts a world or culture that is falling apart and changing into something other. Millicent Marcus calls it a postmodern "culture that lowers all experience to the common denominator of mass communicability."[56] The emphasis this time, however, is not on what will come next in terms of social evolution. That optimistic thrust is now no longer present. The hero, Ivo Salvini, recently turned out of the asylum and wandering through the countryside and his town, wants nothing less than to find a "hole" or a "way through" the world around him to something more real "behind it all." His quest is, perhaps for the first time with Fellini, the metaphysical one of asking first questions—where do we come from and who or what is behind our world? Ivo hears voices. He would probably be diagnosed as mildly schizophrenic. He feels, however, that if he could just understand what the voices are trying to tell him, he would have the answers to his metaphysical questions.

The movie is a loose adaptation of the novel *The Voice of the Moon* by a Bolognese academic, Ermanno Cavazzoni.[57] The novel is a playful and thoughtful rendering of the possibilities of divergent thinking by mad people. The subject of madness is one that had interested Fellini for a long time. He has said that as a child, especially when visiting his grandmother's farm in Gambettola, he became aware of people who were different in a special sense: "Mental institutions weren't common, and it was not unusual to see the mentally retarded or the mentally ill wandering about or hidden in houses. I felt a fascination for these isolated persons who inhabit separate worlds."[58] The characters Uncle Teo, who is taken from the asylum for an outing in the country by his family in *Amarcord,* and Giudizio, the harmless madman who prowls the streets of Rimini playing games of make-believe in *I Vitelloni* and *The Clowns,* are examples of such people. In 1955 Fellini wrote a story treatment of a book, *The Free Women of Magliano,* by Mario Tobino, a doctor, about Tobino's experiences with patients in a mental hospital.[59] As part of his work on the project, Fellini visited an asylum, found the experience a grim one, and as a result, abandoned the work. He commented, "I saw people who had no happiness in their madness, but were endlessly trapped in their own nightmares. It was not as I had imagined it. These were prisoners of the torment of their own minds, an even more terrifying prison than that of the walls which confined them."[60] Part of the appeal of Cavazzoni's *The Voice of the Moon,* as opposed to Tobino's work, then, was the playful tone. The emphasis is not on imprisonment; it is on liberation and alternate ways of seeing things. Cavazzoni's hero, called Savani in the novel, has simply wandered away from his place of confinement, and he encounters a series of characters who egg him on in his own divergent thinking or who present him with bizarre examples of their own ways of seeing the world or who reinterpret major moments of history in highly unusual ways.

For the project, Fellini enlisted the help of his old friend and former cowriter Tullio Pinelli. (Cavazzoni, too, worked on the adaptation as an advisor.) Fellini and Pinelli kept the central situation of the novel—that of the hero, perhaps released from an asylum, wandering through the country-side and the town investigating voices he hears from wells that he suspects are initiated in some way by the moon. Fellini and Pinelli's Ivo meets two of the bizarre characters retained from the novel. The first is Nestor, who, in both novel and film, fears the highly charged sexuality of his wife, whom he likens to a train engine, and prefers, paradoxically enough, the gentle femininity of his household electrical appliances. Fellini and Pinelli play down Nestor's attraction to his appliances more than is the case in the novel and develop the character of the wife a bit more fully by giving her certain resemblances to Fellini's Gradisca from *Amarcord*. The second bizarre character the authors retain is Prefect Gonnella. He is a classic paranoid schizophrenic, with both delusions of grandeur and fears of phantoms out to get him. Gonnella has, in fact, been put on pension, but he thinks he has been assigned a high-level position to see through the facades and performances that fool other people. The two secondary characters, in both the novel and the film, recognize a kindred spirit in Ivo, reinforce his delusions, and urge him on with his researches. What Fellini and Pinelli do not retain from the novel are its various reinterpretations of historical events, arguably the high points of the novel. An example of such a reinterpretation of history is told to Savini and Gonnella by a student who is having fun with them. The story concerns the viceroy of the Two Sicilies, who wishes to defend his kingdom from invasion by the troops of the liberator Garibaldi. The viceroy, an intellectual, tries to devise strategy from his study, but because his Bourbon generals do not want to venture forth in battle, they report to the viceroy made-up reports. His strategies based on misinformation fail, and the viceroy feels himself matched with an uncanny adversary he cannot defeat. This story and the others like them might seem an endorsement of the need for accurate or "scientific" information, but generally the stories are, in fact, testimonies to the inventive quality of the human mind in devising strategies or theories or explanations for virtually any set of observations, randomly taken or made up. At bottom, the novel is a kind of comic reveling in postmodern uncertainty. In place of the missing historical stories of the novel, Fellini and Pinelli chose to stay closer to the issue of the hero's investigation of the voices he hears and the moon as the source of the mystery of the voices, and in doing this, Fellini and Pinelli moved the work toward a certain pathos when Ivo cannot solve his mystery.

The world of the town in which Ivo wanders is one in transition. Fellini has stated that he wanted to construct the typical town of north-central Italy with all the variety of architectural styles that might be present.[61] Gianfranco Angelucci, who worked with Fellini on several previous projects, has commented in an essay on *The Voice of the Moon,* "The village . . . represents a monster, a creature of Doctor Frankenstein, for which there is no successive sedimentation of styles, but, rather, havoc, destruction, and neoformation. The town represents a village of assimilated, postmodern Italy, unrecognizable because of its urban housing, and street speculation, because of the tumultuous and uncontrolled growth."[62] Angelucci's point is well taken. Here, however, we might consider the town as something of a reworking of Fellini's court of Württemberg in *Fellini's Casanova.* The physical layout simply has too much going on, architecturally speaking, at the same time. We see the massive stone structure of an Umbertine palazzo that Ivo enters in order to gaze on the sleeping Aldina, his beloved; we see also traditional Tuscan townhouses with their ochre, plastered walls, their long lines of green shuttered windows, and their tiled roofs; and we see the porticoed walkways associated with the area of Bologna. But at the same time, we discover poured concrete apartment blocks going up, some covered with plastic sheets as works in progress; an art deco barbershop; and, most striking, a postmodern church with a glass facade in the town square. A giant crane, run by the Micheluzzi brothers who represent the workmen of the town, occupies a prominent space in the main square. The tiled roofs are covered with TV antennae. And, in the climactic scene of the movie, two huge TV screens are erected so that the townspeople can participate in a new sort of town meeting designed for an electronic village. Clearly, the town is no longer the traditional one we were accustomed to in Fellini's Rimini of *I Vitelloni, The Clowns,* and *Amarcord.* However, what the town will become is not yet certain, either. The town is caught, photographed, in its period of transformation to something new, and this state is unsettling—for Fellini and Pinelli, for viewers, and especially for Ivo Salvini, who has been away and come back.

Ivo is a romantic who becomes disillusioned in his love for Aldina, a blond woman who dresses in white. Ivo puts her on a pedestal. He talks his way into her palazzo and gazes at her when she sleeps with the moonlight falling on her face. "She is like the moon. She is the moon," he states, and then he begins to recite verses from the poet Leopardi. When Aldina awakens, she hurls a shoe at Ivo, but he only catches the shoe and escapes with it as a fetish for his loved one. Ivo's disillusionment begins at the festival for gnocchi, the pasta for which the area is known. Aldina wins the title of "Miss Wheat" at the beauty contest, and then, to Ivo's horror, she dances with and allows herself to be kissed on the neck and shoulders by Dr. Brambilla, one of the town's leading citizens. Ivo's disillusionment deepens at the discotheque when like Prince Charming, Ivo tries Aldina's slipper on several of the young women at the dance and finds that the slipper fits the feet of all of the young ladies he tries. This scene is, of course, similar to the situation in *8 ½* when Guido renounces the one "lady in white" for the many women in his life and the situation at the end of *City of Women* in which the balloon figure of the ideal woman is shot down by a terrorist. In both of the previous instances, the events may be seen as a positive for the hero. However, such seems not to be the case here. Fellini comments, "It is very sad for me when Ivo finds that [Aldina's] shoe fits more than one woman—indeed, many women. It is the message of old age, at any age. It is the birth of cynicism. Romanticism has died within Ivo. He will never be able to hope totally again."[63] But if Fellini is right to assert that Ivo will never be again the hopeful romantic he was earlier, the movie demonstrates that he never loses all of his hopefulness, either, despite evidence that would shake a lesser, or a saner, man.

Cristina Degli-Esposti has argued that Ivo listens "to the voices that silence can produce" and that these voices are "from the unconscious."[64] Given Fellini's interest in Jungian psychology, Degli-Esposti is almost certainly right, but Ivo himself would not like to think so. He would like to think the voices are from a source beyond the world we live in. He tries frequently to break through to the source either by climbing or by descending. Early in the movie, when Ivo is visiting a mausoleum, he asks for a hole to climb through to a reality beyond life and discovers an opening in the roof that he climbs to and peers out from. Certainly, one of the aspects about his friend Nestor that appeals to Ivo is Nestor's fondness for sitting on rooftops, and one of the aspects about the workman Terzio Micheluzzi that Ivo finds fascinating is Terzio's love for riding up in the air on the platform of his crane. Also, however, Ivo thinks of breaking out by climbing down into the drainage pipe beneath the town where Giovannino Micheluzzi works and, toward the end of the movie, by descending into one of the country wells, seeking the source of the voices. Ivo never does succeed in breaking through to the source of the voices. However, in an ambiguous way, the source of the voices, the moon, comes to him.

In the final sequence, the Micheluzzi brothers capture the moon by means of their crane and a little flattery, and they drag it to earth in a network of ropes. After the intellectuals, the politicians, and a cardinal discuss the event and after Onelio, the barber, fires a pistol at a TV image of the moon, the celestial body escapes back to the sky and speaks to Ivo. The voice of the moon is Aldina's, a fact that should forewarn Ivo he will be disappointed. The message is that Ivo should be content that he hears the voices and should not try to understand what they say. It is enough that the voices speak to him. One possible interpretation of the message is that something is indeed out there and is letting Ivo know of its existence but that he should not press further to try to understand the mystery more deeply. This interpretation fits nicely with an original premise in this book—that Fellini finds life, at bottom, ineffable.[65] The message is one that we might expect. The moon immediately discredits itself by breaking for a commercial as if it were part of a TV show, and this complicates the movie's ending, but I would argue that the message is nonetheless a valid one. However, it is not the message Ivo wants to hear. He wants the mystery solved. Sadly, he ignores the point of the message and says in soliloquy, "But I think if there were a little more silence, if we were all a little more silent . . . perhaps we could understand something."[66] The wish is one that most viewers will sympathize with. In the midst of the breakups and the changes we see in the four adaptations, who would not want something solid to hang on to? Ivo's wish is a very human one. It is not, however, one that will be solved in a Fellini film. We may have a sense that something other is out there behind the cycles of change, the endings, and the new starts, but for Fellini, showing the mystery has to be enough, and indeed, as the moon points out, that may be a great deal.

FILMOGRAPHY AND AWARDS

NOTES

INDEX

FILMOGRAPHY AND AWARDS

Films Directed by Federico Fellini
Luci del varietà (Variety Lights), 1950

Codirector: Alberto Lattuada
Screenplay: Alberto Lattuada, Federico Fellini, Ennio Flaiano, Tullio Pinelli
(from story by Fellini)
Photography: Otello Martelli
Set design: Aldo Buzzi
Editing: Mario Bonotti
Music: Felice Lattuada
Production: Capitolium Film
Running time: 93 minutes
DVD: Criterion Collection, 2002
Cast: Peppino De Filippo (Checco), Carla del Poggio (Liliana), Giulietta
Masina (Melina Amour), Folco Lulli (Conti), Carlo Romano (Renzo), John
Kitzmiller (Johnny, the trumpet player), Gina Mascetti (Valeria Del Sole)

Lo sceicco bianco (The White Sheik), 1952

Screenplay: Federico Fellini, Tullio Pinelli, Ennio Flaiano (from a story by
Michelangelo Antonioni, Fellini, Pinelli)
Photography: Arturo Gallea
Set design: Raffaelo Tolfo
Editing: Rolando Benedetti
Music: Nino Rota
Production: Luigi Rovere, PDC-OFI
Running time: 86 minutes
DVD: Criterion Collection, 2003

Cast: Alberto Sordi (Fernando Rivoli, the White Sheik), Brunella Bovo (Wanda), Leopoldo Trieste (Ivan), Giulietta Masina (Cabiria), Fanny Marchiò (Marilena), Lilia Landi (Felga), Ernesto Almirante (director), Gina Mascetti (the Sheik's wife), Ettore Margadonna (Ivan's uncle)

I vitelloni (I Vitelloni / The Young and the Passionate), 1953

Screenplay: Federico Fellini, Tullio Pinelli, Ennio Flaiano
Photography: Otello Martelli, Luciano Trasatti, Carlo Carlini
Set design: Mario Chiari
Editing: Rolando Benedetti
Music: Nino Rota
Production: Lorenzo Pegoraro, Peg Films–Cité Films
Running time: 104 minutes
DVD: Criterion Collection, 2004
Cast: Franco Interlenghi (Moraldo), Franco Fabrizi (Fausto), Alberto Sordi (Alberto), Leopoldo Trieste (Leopoldo), Riccardo Fellini (Riccardo), Eleonora Ruffo (Sandra), Jean Brochard (Fausto's father), Claude Farrell (Alberto's sister), Carlo Romano (Michele), Lida Baarova (Giulia, Michele's wife), Arlette Sauvage (woman in movie theater), Enrico Viarisio (Sandra's father)

Un'agenzia matrimoniale (A Matrimonial Agency), an episode in Amore in città (Love in the City), 1953

Screenplay: Federico Fellini, Tullio Pinelli
Photography: Gianni di Venanzo
Set design: Gianni Polidori
Editing: Eraldo da Roma
Music: Mario Nascimbene
Production: Cesare Zavattini, Renato Ghione, Marco Ferreri, Faro Films
Running time: 18 minutes
Cast: Antonio Cifariello (reporter), Livia Venurini (Rossana)

La strada (La Strada / The Road), 1954

Screenplay: Federico Fellini, Tullio Pinelli, Ennio Flaiano
Photography: Otello Martelli
Set design: Mario Ravasco
Editing: Leo Catozzo
Music: Nino Rota
Production: Carlo Ponti, Dino De Laurentiis
Running time: 107 minutes
DVD: Criterion Collection, 2003
Cast: Giulietta Masina (Gelsomina), Anthony Quinn (Zampano), Richard

Basehart (the Fool), Aldo Silvani (circus owner), Marcella Rovere (the widow), Livia Venturini (the nun)

Il bidone (Il Bidone / The Swindle), 1955

Screenplay: Federico Fellini, Tullio Pinelli, Ennio Flaiano
Photography: Otello Martelli
Set design: Dario Cecchi
Editing: Mario Serandrei, Giuseppe Vari
Music: Nino Rota
Production: Titanus–S.G.C.
Running time: 92 minutes
DVD: Image Entertainment, 2000
Cast: Broderick Crawford (Augusto), Richard Basehart (Picasso), Franco Fabrizi (Roberto), Giulietta Masina (Iris), Lorella De Luca (Patrizia), Giacomo Gabrielli (Vargas), Sue Ellen Blake (Anna), Irene Cefaro (Marisa), Xenia Valderi (Luciana), Maria Zanoli (Stella Fiorina)

Le notti di Cabiria (Nights of Cabiria), 1957

Screenplay: Federico Fellini, Tullio Pinelli, Ennio Flaiano (with collaboration of Pier Paolo Pasolini on dialogue)
Photography: Aldo Tonti, Otello Martelli
Set design: Piero Gherardi
Editing: Leo Catozzo
Music: Nino Rota
Production: Dino De Laurentiis
Running time: 110 minutes
DVD: Criterion Collection, 1999
Cast: Giulietta Masina (Cabiria), Amedeo Nazzari (the actor), François Périer (Oscar), Aldo Silvani (the magician), Franca Marzi (Wanda), Dorian Gray (Jessy), Franco Fabrizi (Giorgio), Mario Passange (the crippled uncle), Pina Gualandri (Matilda)

La dolce vita (La Dolce Vita), 1960

Screenplay: Federico Fellini, Tullio Pinelli, Ennio Flaiano, Brunello Rondi (from a story by Fellini, Pinelli, Flaiano)
Photography: Otello Martelli
Set design: Piero Gherardi
Editing: Leo Catozzo
Music: Nino Rota
Production: Giuseppe Amato, Riama–Pathé Consortium
Running time: 180 minutes
DVD: Koch Lorber Collector's Edition, 2004

Cast: Marcello Mastroianni (Marcello Rubini), Anouk Aimée (Maddalena), Anita Ekberg (Sylvia), Walter Santesso (Paparazzo), Lex Barker (Robert), Yvonne Fourneaux (Emma), Alain Cuny (Steiner), Annibale Ninchi (Marcello's father), Polidor (the clown), Nadia Gray (Nadia), Valeria Ciangottini (Paola), Magali Noël (Fanny), Alan Dijon (Frankie), Adriana Moneta (prostitute), Harriet White (Edna, Sylvia's secretary)

Le tentazioni del dottor Antonio (The Temptation of Dr. Antonio),
an episode of *Boccaccio '70,* 1962

Screenplay: Federico Fellini, Tullio Pinelli, Ennio Flaiano
Photography: Otello Martelli
Set design: Piero Zuffi
Editing: Leo Catozzo
Music: Nino Rota
Production: Carlo Ponti, Antonio Cerevi, Cineriz
Running time: 53 minutes
DVD: NoShame Films, 2004
Cast: Peppino De Filippo (Dr. Antonio Mazzuolo), Anita Ekberg (Anita), Antonio Acqua (government official), Donatella Della Nora (Antonio's sister), Eleanora Maggi (Cupid)

8 ½, 1963

Screenplay: Federico Fellini, Tullio Pinelli, Ennio Flaiano, Brunello Rondi (from a story by Fellini, Flaiano)
Photography: Gianni di Venanzo
Set design: Piero Gherardi
Editing: Leo Catozzo
Music: Nino Rota
Production: Angelo Rizzoli, Cineriz
Running time: 135 minutes
DVD: Criterion Collection, 2001
Cast: Marcello Mastroianni (Guido Anselmi), Anouk Aimée (Luisa), Sandra Milo (Carla), Claudia Cardinale (Claudia), Jean Rougeul (Daumier), Edra Gale (Saraghina), Caterina Boratto (beautiful woman in lobby), Madeleine Lebeau (French actress), Mario Pisu (Mezzabotta), Barbara Steele (Gloria), Ian Dallas (Maurice the magician), Guido Alberti (Pace, the producer), Mary Indovino (Maya), Rossella Falk (Rossella), Annibale Ninchi (Guido's father), Giuditta Rissone (Guido's mother), Tito Masini (the Cardinal), Yvonne Casadei (Jacqueline Bonbon)

Giulietta degli spiriti (Juliet of the Spirits), 1965

Screenplay: Federico Fellini, Tullio Pinelli, Ennio Flaiano, Brunello Rondi (from a story by Fellini and Pinelli)

Photography: Gianni di Venanzo
Set design: Piero Gherardi
Editing: Ruggero Mastroianni
Music: Nino Rota
Production: Angelo Rizzoli, Federiz–Francoriz
Running time: 137 minutes
DVD: Criterion Collection, 2002
Cast: Giulietta Masina (Giulietta), Mario Pisu (Giorgio), Sandra Milo (Suzy-Iris-Fanny), Lou Gilbert (grandfather), Caterina Boratto (mother), Luisa Della Noce (Adele, Juliet's sister), Sylva Koscina (Sylva, Juliet's other sister), Valentina Cortese (Val), Valeska Gert (Bhisma, the medium), Alberto Plebani (Lynx-Eyes, the detective), José de Villalonga (Spanish gentleman), Silvana Jachino (Delores), Elena Fondra (Elena), Milena Vucotich and Elisabetta Gray (Juliet's maids)

Toby Dammit, an episode in *Tre passi nel delirio (Spirits of the Dead),* 1968
Screenplay: Federico Fellini, Bernardino Zapponi (from Edgar Allan Poe's short story "Never Bet the Devil Your Head")
Photography: Giuseppe Rotunno
Set design: Piero Tosi
Editing: Ruggero Mastroianni
Music: Nino Rota
Production: Alberto Grimaldi, P.E.A., Les Films Marceau, Cocinor
Running time: 40 minutes
DVD: Home Vision, 2003
Cast: Terence Stamp (Toby Dammit), Salvo Randone (priest), Antonia Pietrosi (actress), Marina Yaru (the girl/devil), Polidor (clown)

Block-notes di un regista (Fellini: A Director's Notebook) 1969
Screenplay: Federico Fellini
Photography: Pasquale De Santis
Set design: Federico Fellini
Editing: Ruggero Mastroianni
Music: Nino Rota
Production: Peter Goldfarb, NBC-TV
Running time: 54 minutes
Cast: Federico Fellini, Giulietta Masina, Marcello Mastroianni, Marina Boratto, Pasquali De Santis, and Genius the medium as themselves

Fellini Satyricon, 1969
Screenplay: Federico Fellini, Bernardino Zapponi (from Petronius's *The Satyricon*)
Photography: Giuseppe Rotunno

Set design: Danilo Donati
Editing: Ruggero Mastroianni
Music: Nino Rota
Production: Alberto Grimaldi, P.E.A., Les Productions Artistes Associés
Running time: 127 minutes
DVD: MGM Home Entertainment, 2001
Cast: Martin Potter (Encolpius), Hiram Keller (Ascyltus), Max Born (Giton),
    Fanfulla (Vernacchio), Salvo Randone (Eumolpus, the poet), Mario
    Romagnoli (Trimalchio), Magali Noël (Fortunata), Danica La Loggia
    (Scintilla), Giuseppe San Vitale (Habinas), Alain Cuny (Lichas), Capucine
    (Tryphaena), Joseph Wheeler (the suicide), Lucia Bosè (the suicide's wife),
    Hylette Adolphe (slave girl), Tonya Lopert (the emperor), Luigi Montefiori
    (the minotaur), Elisa Mainardi (Ariadne), Donyale Luna (Oenothea), Gordon
    Mitchell (the thief), Elio Gigante (master of the Garden of Delights)

I clowns (The Clowns), 1970

Screenplay: Federico Fellini, Bernardino Zapponi
Photography: Dario di Palma
Set design: Danilo Donati
Editing: Ruggero Mastroianni
Music: Nino Rota
Production: Elio Scardamaglia, Ugo Guerra, RAI TV, O.R.T.F., Bavaria Film,
    Compagnia Leone Cinematografica
Running time: 92 minutes
VHS: Xenon Studios, 1996
Cast: Federico Fellini, Maya Morin, Lina Alberti, Alvaro Vitali, Gasparino,
    Anita Ekberg, Victoria Chaplin, Pierre Etaix, Victor Fratellini, Annie
    Fratellini, Batiste, Tristan Rémy, Liana Orfei, Rinaldo Orfei, Nando
    Orfei, Franco Migliorini, various Italian clowns, various French clowns
    as themselves

Roma (Fellini's Roma), 1972

Screenplay: Federico Fellini, Bernardino Zapponi
Photography: Giuseppe Rotunno
Set design: Danilo Donati
Editing: Ruggero Mastroianni
Music: Nino Rota
Production: Turi Vasile, Ultra Film, S.P.A., Les Productions Artistes Associés
Running time: 113 minutes
DVD: MGM/UA Studios, 2004
Cast: Peter Gonzales (Fellini as a young man), Fiona Florence (beautiful
    prostitute), Pia De Doses (aristocrat), Renato Giovanoli (the cardinal),
    Alvaro Vitali (vaudeville dancer), Libero Frissi, Mario Del Vago, Gallianno

Sbarra, Alfredo Adami (vaudeville performers), Marcello Mastroianni, Gore Vidal, Anna Magnani, Alberto Sordi as themselves

Amarcord, 1974

Screenplay: Federico Fellini, Tonino Guerra
Photography: Giuseppe Rotunno
Set design: Danilo Donati
Editing: Ruggero Mastroianni
Music: Nino Rota
Production: Franco Cristaldi, F. C. Productions, P.E.C.F.
Running time: 127 minutes
DVD: Criterion Collection, 1998
Cast: Bruno Zanin (Titta), Armando Brancia (Aurelio, Titta's father), Pupella Maggio (Miranda, Titta's mother), Nando Orfei (Lallo, Titta's uncle), Peppino Ianigro (Titta's grandfather), Stefano Proietti (Oliva, Titta's brother), Ciccio Ingrassia (Uncle Teo), Carla Mora (the maid), Magali Noël (Gradisca), Maria Antonietta Beluzzi (Lucia, the tobacconist), Josiane Tanzilli (Volpina), Luigi Rossi (lawyer), Aristide Caporale (Giudizio), Gennaro Ombra (Biscien, the tall tale teller), Mario Liberati (movie theater owner), Domenico Pertica (blind man), Alvaro Vitali (Naso), Bruno Scagnetti (Ovo), Bruno Lenzi (Gigliozzi), Fernando de Felice (Ciccio), Donatella Gambiani (Aldina), Franco Magno (Zeus, the principal), Dina Adorni (the math teacher), Mauro Misul (the philosophy teacher), Mario Silvestri (the language teacher), Fides Stagni (the art history teacher)

Il Casanova di Fellini (Fellini's Casanova), 1976

Screenplay: Federico Fellini, Bernardino Zapponi (with Venetian verse by Andrea Zanzotto and contributions from Tonino Guerra, Antonio Amurri, and Carl Walken; from Giacomo Casanova's *History of My Life*)
Photography: Giuseppe Rotunno
Set design: Danilo Donati
Editing: Ruggero Mastroianni
Music: Nino Rota
Production: Alberto Grimaldi, Universal-Fox-Gaumont-Titanus
Running time: 165 minutes
Cast: Donald Sutherland (Casanova), Margareth Clementi (Maddalena), Cicely Browne (Marquise D'Urfé), Tina Aumont (Henriette), Olimpia Carlisi (Isabella), Daniel Emilfork (DuBois), Sandy Allen (giantess), Clara Algranti (Marcolina), Clarissa Roll (Annamaria), Adele Angela Lojodice (mechanical doll), John Karlsen (Lord Talou), Veronica Nava (Romana), Mario Gagliardo (Righetto), Angelica Hansen (hunchbacked woman), Dudley Sutton (Duke of Württenberg), Reggie Nalder (Faulkircher)

Prova d'orchestra (Orchestra Rehearsal), 1979

Screenplay: Federico Fellini, Brunello Rondi
Photography: Giuseppe Rotunno
Set design: Dante Ferretti
Editing: Ruggero Mastroianni
Production: Lamberto Pippia, RAI TV, Daime Cinematografica, S.P.A.,
    Albatros Produktions
Running time: 72 minutes
DVD: Fox Lorber, 1997
Cast: Federico Fellini (interviewer), Baldwin Bass (conductor), David Mauhsell
    (first violinist), Francesco Aluigi (second violinist), Elisabeth Labi (pianist),
    Sibyl Mostert (flautist), Daniel Pegani (trombone player), Franco Mazzieri
    (trumpet player), Ferdinando Villella (cellist), Andy Miller (oboe player),
    Giovani Javarrone (tuba player), Clara Colosimo (harpist), Umberto
    Zuanelli (copyist), Claudio Ciocca (union leader)

La città delle donne (City of Women), 1980

Screenplay: Federico Fellini, Bernardino Zapponi, Brunello Rondi
Photography: Giuseppe Rotunno
Set design: Dante Ferretti
Editing: Ruggero Mastroianni
Music: Luis Bacalov
Production: Renzo Rossellini, Opera Film Productions, Gaumon
Running time: 140 minutes
DVD: New Yorker Film Collector's Edition, 2001
Cast: Marcello Mastroianni (Snaporaz), Bernice Stegers (lady on train), Anna
    Prucnal (Snaporaz's wife), Ettore Manni (Cazzone), Iole Silvani (motorcy-
    clist), Donatella Damiani (Donatella), Rosaria Tafuri (young lady), Hélène
    Calzarelli, Dominique Labourier, Sylvie Mayer, Maïté Hahyr, Loredana
    Solfizi (feminists)

E la nave va (And the Ship Sails On), 1983

Screenplay: Federico Fellini, Tonino Guerra (with opera lyrics by Andrea
    Zanzotto)
Photography: Giuseppe Rotunno
Set design: Dante Ferretti
Editing: Ruggero Mastroianni
Music: Gianfranco Plenizio
Production: Franco Cristaldi, RAI TV, Vides Produzione, Gaumont
Running time: 132 minutes
DVD: Criterion Collection, 1999
Cast: Freddy Jones (Orlando), Barbara Jefford (Hildebranda Cuffari), Janet

Suzman (Edmea Tetua), Vittorio Poletti (Aureliano Fuciletto), Peter Cellier (Sir Reginald Dongby), Norma West (Lady Violet Dongby), Pina Bausch (Princess), Fiorenzo Serra (Grand Duke), Philip Locke (Prime Minister)

Ginger e Fred (Ginger and Fred), 1986

Screenplay: Federico Fellini, Tullio Pinelli, Tonino Guerra
Photography: Tonino delli Colli
Set design: Dante Ferretti
Editing: Nino Baragli, Ugo de Rossi, Ruggero Mastroianni
Music: Nicola Piovani
Production: Alberto Grimaldi, Stella Film and Bibo TV, Anthea, P.E.A., Revcom
Running time: 126 minutes
DVD: Warner Studios, 1991
Cast: Giulietta Masina (Amelia/"Ginger"), Marcello Mastroianni (Pippo/ "Fred"), Franco Fabrizi (master of ceremonies), Frederick Ledenburg (admiral), Augusto Poderosi (transvestite), Francesco Casale (mafioso), Jacques Henri Lartigue (priest), Toto Mignone (Toto), Luciano Lombardo (defrocked priest), Isabelle La Porte (TV hostess)

Intervista (Interview), 1987

Screenplay: Federico Fellini, Gianfranco Angelucci
Photography: Tonino delli Colli
Set design: Danilo Donati
Editing: Nino Baragli
Music: Nicola Piovani
Production: Ibrahim Moussa, RAI TV, Aljosha Produktion Company, Femnlyn
Running time: 105 minutes
DVD: Koch Lorber, 2005
Cast: Federico Fellini (himself), Sergio Rubini (young journalist), Paola Liquori (movie star), Maurizio Mein (assistant director), Nadia Ottaviani (archivist), and Marcello Mastroianni and Anita Ekberg as themselves

La voce della luna (The Voice of the Moon), 1990

Screenplay: Federico Fellini, Tullio Pinelli, Ermanno Cavazzoni (from Cavazzoni's novel The Voice of the Moon)
Photography: Tonino delli Colli
Set design: Dante Ferretti
Editing: Nino Baragli
Music: Nicola Piovani
Production: Mario Cecchi Gori, Vittorio Cecchi Gori, C. G. Group Tiger Cinematografica–Cinemax, RAI Uno

Running time: 120 minutes

Cast: Roberto Benigni (Ivo), Paolo Villaggio (Gonnella), Marisa Tomasi (Marisa), Nadia Ottaviani (Aldina), Angelo Orlando (Nestor), Uta Schmidt (Ivo's grandmother), George Taylor (Marisa's lover), Susy Blady (Susy), Chevalier (first Micheluzzi brother), Nigel Harris (second Micheluzzi brother), Vito (third Micheluzzi brother), Dario Ghirardi (journalist)

Screenwriting by Federico Fellini for Other Directors

1939   *Imputato, alzatevi!* (Defendant, Stand Up!), dir. Mario Mattoli; *Lo vedi come sei?* (Do You Know What You Look Like?), dir. Mattoli

1940   *Non me lo dire!* (Don't Tell Me!), dir. Mario Mattoli; *Il pirato sono io* (I Am the Pirate), dir. Mattoli

1942   *Documento Z3* (Document Z3), dir. Alfredo Guarini; *Avanti, c'è posto* (Come On, There's Room), dir. Mario Bonnard

1943   *Camp de' fiori* (*The Peddler and the Lady*), dir. Mario Bonnard; *L'ultima carrozzella* (The Last Carriage), dir. Bonnard; *Quarta pagina* (The Fourth Page), dir. Nicola Manzari; *Chi l'ha visto?* (Who Saw Him?), dir. Goffredo Allessandrini; *Gli ultimi Tuareg* (The Last Tuaregs), dir. Gino Talamo, never released

1944   *Apparizione* (Apparition), dir. Jean de Limur

1945   *Tutta la città canta* (The Whole City Is Singing), dir. Riccardo Freda; *Roma, città aperta* (*Open City*), dir. Roberto Rossellini; Fellini was also an assistant director.

1946   *Paisà* (*Paisan*), dir. Roberto Rossellini; Fellini was also an assistant director.

1947   *Il delito di Giovanni Espiscopo* (*Flesh Will Surrender*), dir. Alberto Lattuada; *Il passatore* (*A Bullet for Stefano*), dir. Duilio Coletti

1948   *Senza pietà* (*Without Pity*), dir. Alberto Lattuada; *Il miracolo* (*The Miracle*), an episode in *L'amore* (*The Ways of Love*), dir. Roberto Rossellini; Fellini also served as assistant director and acted in the film.

1949   *Il mulino del Po* (*The Mill on the Po*), dir. Alberto Lattuada; *In nome della legge* (*In the Name of the Law*), dir. Pietro Germi

1950   *Francesco, giullare di dio* (*The Flowers of Saint Francis*), dir. Roberto Rossellini; Fellini also served as assistant director; *Il cammino della speranza* (*The Path of Hope*), dir. Pietro Germi

1951   *Persiane chiuse* (*Behind Closed Shutters*), dir. Luigi Comencini: *La città si difende* (*Four Ways Out*), dir. Pietro Germi; *Cameriera bella presenza offresi* (*Attractive Maid Available*), dir. Giorgio Pastina

1952   *Europa '51* (*The Greatest Love*), dir. Roberto Rossellini; *Il brigante di Tacca del Lupo* (The Bandit of Tacca del Lupo), dir. Pietro Germi

1958   *Fortunella,* dir. Eduardo De Filippo

TV Commercials Written and Directed by Federico Fellini

1984 "Oh, che bel paesaggio! (Oh, What a Beautiful Landscape!), for Compari aperitifs

1986 "Alta società" (High Society), for Barilla pasta

1992 "Che brutte notti!" (Scary Nights), three commericals for Banca di Roma

Awards Won by Federico Fellini

1953 Venice Film Festival: Silver Lion for *I Vitelloni*

1956 Academy Awards: Best Foreign Language Film for *La Strada;* New York Film Critics Circle: Best Foreign Language Film; Venice Film Festival: Silver Lion

1957 Academy Awards: Best Foreign Language Film for *Nights of Cabiria*

1960 Cannes Film Festival: Golden Palm for *La Dolce Vita*

1961 New York Film Critics Circle: Best Foreign Language Film for *La Dolce Vita*

1963 Academy Awards: Best Foreign Language Film for *8 ½,* also Best Costumes (Piero Gharardi); New York Film Critics Circle: Best Foreign Language Film; Moscow Film Festival: Grand Prize

1964 Berlin Film Festival: Special Award for *8 ½*

1965 New York Film Critics Circle: Best Foreign Language Film for *Juliet of the Spirits*

1974 Academy Awards: Best Foreign Language Film for *Amarcord;* New York Film Critics Circle: Best Foreign Language Film

1976 Academy Awards: Best Costumes for *Fellini's Casanova* (Danilo Donati)

1985 Venice Film Festival: Golden Lion for life achievement

1993 Academy Awards: Honorary Award for life achievement

NOTES

Preface

1. I am not the first, however, to approach Fellini's films by means of grouping movies with similar aspects or issues out of chronological order. Peter Bondanella does this as well in *The Cinema of Federico Fellini* (Princeton, NJ: Princeton University Press, 1992). He is particularly good at researching primary materials of the profilmic work—drawings, scripts, notebooks—to comment on the films within the groupings. I have drawn on his work in several areas, although I think my applications are quite different.

2. John Caughie, *Theories of Authorship: A Reader,* British Film Institute Readers in Film Studies (London: Routledge and Kegan Paul, 1981).

3. Pam Cook and Mieke Bernink, *The Cinema Book,* 2nd ed. (London: BFI, 1999); Virginia Wright Wexman, *Film and Authorship* (New Brunswick, NJ: Rutgers University Press, 2003); and David A. Gerstner and Janet Staiger, *Authorship and Film* (New York: Routledge, 2003).

4. David Bordwell, *Making Meaning: Inference and Rhetoric in the Interpreting of Cinema* (Cambridge, MA: Harvard University Press, 1989).

5. See, e.g., Geoffrey Nowell-Smith, *Visconti* (London: Secker and Warburg, 1967 and 1973); and Peter Wollen, *Signs and Meaning in the Cinema* (London: Secker and Warburg, 1969 and 1972).

6. Pauline Kael, "Circles and Squares," *Film Quarterly* 16, no. 3 (Spring 1963): 12–26.

7. Pauline Kael, *The Citizen Kane Book* (Boston: Little, Brown, 1971); Peter Bogdanovich, "The Kane Mutiny," *Esquire* 78 (October 1972): 99–105, 180–90; and Robert L. Carringer, *The Making of Citizen Kane* (Berkeley: University of California Press, 1985).

8. Roland Barthes, "Death of the Author," in Caughie, *Theories of Authorship,* 213.

9. Caughie, *Theories of Authorship,* 208.

10. Again I am not alone. Most "playful" of other Fellini critics today is Sam Rohdie in *Fellini Lexicon* (London: BFI, 2002). Much like Barthes, he plays with possibilities and avoids definitive statements.

11. In Caughie, *Theories of Authorship,* 282–91. First published 1969 in Paris. Also relevant here is Michel Foucault's *The Archaeology of Knowledge,* trans. A. M. Sheridan Smith (New York: Pantheon, 1972). First published 1969 in Paris.

12. The groundwork for such criticism is generally thought to have been laid by the *Cahiers* critics' collective essay on John Ford's *Young Mr. Lincoln* in *Cahiers du cinema,* no. 223 (August 1970): 29–47. For a revisionist view of this essay, see Bordwell, *Making Meaning,* 85–86,

13. Gerstner and Staiger, *Authorship and Film,* 46. See also Cook and Bernink, "Authorship as 'Discursive Activity,'" in *Cinema Book,* 301.

1. Fellini's Manner: The Open Form and the Style of Excess

1. I draw here on two seminal works: Seymour Chatman, *Story and Discourse: Narrative Structure in Fiction and Film* (Ithaca, NY: Cornell University Press, 1978) and David Bordwell, *Narration in the Fiction Film* (Madison: University of Wisconsin Press, 1985). Following French structuralists, Chatman distinguishes between story and discourse in a manner similar to, if not precisely the same as, Bordwell's distinction, taken from the Russian formalists, between *fabula* and *syuzhet.*

2. My distinction between the discourse of resolution and the discourse of revelation comes from Chatman, *Story and Discourse,* 48. Chatman writes, "In the traditional narrative of resolution, there is a sense of problem solving, of things being worked out in some way, of a kind of ratiocinative or emotional teleology. . . . 'What will happen?' is the basic question. In the modern plot of revelation, however, the emphasis is elsewhere. . . . Early on we gather that things will stay pretty much the same. It is not that events are resolved (happily or tragically), but rather that a state of affairs is revealed." Bordwell, in *Narration in the Fiction Film,* 157–62, 206–13, finds the classical Hollywood film to be defined in part by a narrative structure similar to the discourse of *resolution,* and he argues that Italian Neorealist films and those of the European art cinema of the 1950s and 1960s are defined, again in part, by a structure similar to the discourse of *revelation.* He does not, however, use the terms *resolution* and *revelation.*

3. My ideas about visual style are informed by discussions of the subject in two widely read film texts: Louis D. Giannetti, *Understanding Movies,* 7th ed. (Englewood Cliffs, NJ: Prentice Hall, 1996); and David Bordwell and Kristin Thompson, *Film Art: An Introduction,* 3rd ed. (New York: McGraw-Hill, 1990). I have tried to hew close to the standard notions about style so that Fellini's deviations from the standard elements (and his adherences to them) will be all the more clear.

4. His early team could be said to consist of Tullio Pinelli and Ennio Flaiano as cowriters, Otello Martelli or Gianni di Venanzo as cinematographer, Piero Gherardi as art director, Leo Catozzo as editor, and Nino Rota as musical composer.

Then, for a variety of reasons including death and retirement as well as a conscious desire on Fellini's part to change his team, a new group of collaborators evolved into being, starting in the mid-1960s. The later group included Bernardino Zapponi and Gianfranco Angelucci as cowriters, Giuseppe Rotunno as cinematographer, Danilo Donati or Dante Ferretti as art director, Ruggero Mastroianni as editor, and Nino Rota or Gianfranco Plenizio as musical composer. Although the distinction is not precise, the early team is generally associated with Fellini's black-and-white films, and the later team with his color ones.

5. The most interesting treatment of how the ineffable is rendered in literature is Bruce Kawin, *The Mind of the Novel: Reflexive Fiction and the Ineffable* (Princeton, NJ: Princeton University Press, 1982). Kawin makes the point that the ineffable can be presented only obliquely, say, through a secondary character-narrator who perceives the ineffable quality of the life of a major character, or through the author's demonstration of the failure of literary form to capture all that there is to a given life situation. Fellini's method seems close to the second of these two approaches.

6. Quoted in Silvia Bizio and Sergio Di Cori, "Dream and Delirium: On the Set with Federico Fellini," *Los Angeles Weekly,* 9–15 December 1983, 43.

7. Victor Shklovsky, "Art as Technique," in *Russian Formalist Criticism,* ed. and trans. Lee T. Lemon and Marion J. Reis (Lincoln: University of Nebraska Press, 1965), 12.

8. My capsule summary of the narrative and visual conventions of classical Hollywood studio films is taken from David Bordwell, *The Films of Carl-Theodor Dreyer* (Berkeley: University of California Press, 1981), 25–26, 37–38. Bordwell's intent is to show the ways in which Dreyer plays off the Hollywood norms, as I hope to demonstrate Fellini does. See also David Bordwell, Janet Staiger, and Kristin Thompson, *Classical Hollywood Cinema* (New York: Columbia University Press, 1985), 1–84, for a fuller discussion of the stylistic norms of the Hollywood studio films.

9. Fellini is, of course, not alone in moving against the dominant form of the classical Hollywood film. Indeed, virtually all of the filmmakers in what has now become known as the European art cinema of the 1950s and 1960s could be said to have done the same thing. This group of filmmakers would include Luis Buñuel, François Truffaut, Alain Resnais, Ingmar Bergman, and Michelangelo Antonioni, along with Fellini. David Bordwell has outlined three major areas in which these filmmakers have moved away from classical Hollywood filmmaking: experimenting with "objective reality"; placing "subjective reality" on equal footing with objective reality; and rendering the narration in a self-consciously overt manner. "Art-Cinema Narration," in *Narration in the Fiction Film,* 205–33. Depending on the films considered, Fellini could easily be shown to have participated in each of these three activities with other members of the European art-cinema group. Approaching the issue of Fellini's rearrangement of traditional narrative units from a somewhat

different angle, Peter Bondanella likens the moviemaker to Picasso in his modernist rearrangements for his cubist canvases. *The Films of Federico Fellini* (New York: Cambridge University Press, 2002), 71–72. What I am most concerned with in this chapter, however, is the particular "mix" of elements that defines Fellini's manner.

10. Umberto Eco, *The Open Work,* trans. Anna Cancogni (Cambridge: Harvard University Press, 1989), 1–12. The work was first published as *Opera aperta: forma e indeterminazione nelle poetiche contemporanee* (Milan: Mandatori, 1962). Peter Bondanella, in *Umberto Eco and the Open Text* (New York: Cambridge University Press, 1997), 23–32, 172–73, outlines Eco's main ideas and traces their publication history.

11. Leo Braudy, *The World in a Frame* (Garden City, NY: Anchor Press– Doubleday, 1976), 44–47. For a more generalized discussion of the open form in music, painting, and literature, see Umberto Eco, "The Poetics of the Open Work," in *The Role of the Reader,* 47–66 (Bloomington: Indiana University Press, 1979). Eco is more concerned than Braudy with the role of the performer-viewer-reader to participate in the making of the text.

12. *Amarcord,* DVD (1974; Criterion Collection, 1998).

13. Valerio Riva, "La balia in camicia nera," *L'espresso* 19, no. 40 (7 October 1973): 12–13.

14. See, e.g., Vincent Canby, *"Amarcord,"* *New York Times* 20 September 1974, 32; Pascal Bonitzer, "Memoire de l'oeil," *Cahiers du Cinema* 251-252 (July-August 1974): 75–76; and James Hay, *Popular Film Culture in Fascist Italy: The Passing of the Rex* (Bloomington: Indiana University Press, 1987), 246–48.

15. This diagram and the one that follows it are simplified versions of those employed by Seymour Chatman in his general discussion of how narratives are organized. *Story and Discourse,* 53–56.

16. *La Dolce Vita* (1960) seems to be the first film in the Fellini canon that could be called "double." We are concerned with the protagonist Marcello—his pursuit of his career, his love relationships with various women in the film, and his relationship with his father. At the same time, Marcello is a guide who leads us on a tour of various aspects of 1950s Italian society and stands back, sometimes self-effacingly, to let us look at what is before us.

17. *The White Sheik* (1952) seems an obvious example, for the husband and wife, separated in the body of the movie, find each other at the end of the film. The ending answers the plot question of whether they will reunite. Another example might be *The Temptation of Dr. Antonio* (1962), in which the battle of wills between the prudish Mazzuolo and Anita, the woman on the billboard, is resolved in Anita's favor. Both of these endings, however, also involve "revelation" in that they show the final states of the characters involved, and both endings perhaps also involve comic twists.

18. *I Vitelloni,* in *Three Screenplays: "I Vitelloni," "Il Bidone," "The Temptations of Doctor Antonio,"* trans. Judith Green (New York: Orion, 1970), 129.

19. The ending seems also designed to set up the possibility for a sequel. The story treatment for such a sequel was, in fact, written but not filmed. Its title is *Moraldo in the City.* The treatment will be discussed in chapter 4.

20. Stephane Lévy-Klein and Denis Taranto, "Entretien avec Fellini sur *Roma,*" *Positif* 140 (July-August 1972): 10–11.

21. Geneviève Agel was the first to stress the "baroque" qualities of Fellini's films in *Les Chemins de Fellini* (Paris: Editions du Cerf, 1956).

22. Wolfgang Kayser, *The Grotesque in Art and Literature,* trans. Ulrich Weisstein (New York: Columbia University Press, 1981): 32–37.

23. William J. Free, "Fellini's *I Clowns* and the Grotesque," *Journal of Modern Literature* 3, no. 2 (April 1973): 214–27. So well does Free cover the subject of Fellini's use of grotesques that I have attempted here only to draw his ideas into my general argument about style and to add my own notion about Fellini's galleries. I might add that Mikhail Bakhtin's notion of the "carnivalesque" is often invoked in reference to Fellini's work. Indeed, the medieval and renaissance folk festivals, as described by Bakhtin, did privilege grotesques—"the clowns and fools, giants, dwarfs, and jugglers"—in a way that invites comparison with Fellini's world, but because my emphasis is on visual style here, I have chosen to concentrate on the art history tradition emphasized by Kayser rather than to deal with Bakhtin's more literary one. See Bakhtin, *Rabelais and His World,* trans. Helene Iswolsky (Bloomington: Indiana University Press, 1984).

24. Peter Bondanella has shown the boardinghouse of grotesques was suggested by the drawings of Attalo, a cartoonist for *Marc'Aurelio,* the satiric journal for which Fellini worked briefly in 1939–40. *The Cinema of Federico Fellini* (Princeton, NJ: Princeton University Press, 1992), 196.

25. Jacqueline Risset has called the apparition of the Sheik an embodiment of the romantic Orient based on exotic moviehouse images, Fellini's first view of the circus, Italian photo-romances, and ultimately Jean-Honoré Fragonard's painting *The Swing* (1765), all to evoke a world of childlike wonder and youthful romance. My emphasis here, however, is on the shock of the disparity between Wanda in her 1950s tailored suit and straw hat and the fantastic costume of the sheik, in a sense, Fellini's disruption of Fragonard's eighteenth-century rococo painting. *Le Chiek blanc: L'Announce faite à Federico* (Paris: Biro, 1990): 7–13, 19–25; sections translated by Kathleen Micham in *Perspectives on Federico Fellini,* ed. Peter Bondanella and Cristina Degli-Esposti (New York: G. K. Hall, 1993), 63–69.

2. Fellini, Jung, and Dreams

1. Fellini, *Federico Fellini: Comments on Film,* ed. Giovanni Grazzini, trans. Joseph Henry (Fresno: California State University Press, 1988), 87.

2. *Comments on Film,* 87–88.

3. *Comments on Film,* 10–12, 201–2; Hollis Alpert, *Fellini, a Life* (New York: Atheneum, 1986) 179–80, 245–46, 261–62.

4. Peter Bondanella has argued that "Jung provided Fellini not with a philosophical system or a tightly constructed psychology of the unconscious but, instead, with the intellectual justification the director needed to expand his own initially reluctant reliance upon his private resources of fantasy and imagination." I believe that Bondanella does not recognize how extensive or how profound Jung's influence was on Fellini. In this chapter, I argue that Jung provided Fellini with a kind of equivalent belief system that could supplant more traditional religious belief: in short, an ordering vision, if not a philosophy. See *The Cinema of Federico Fellini* (Princeton, NJ: Princeton University Press, 1992), 153.

5. C. G. Jung, *Memories, Dreams, Reflections,* ed. Aniela Jaffe (New York: Vintage Books, 1989), 302.

6. Fellini, *Comments on Film,* 165–66.

7. Fellini has remarked in interview, perhaps whimsically, "I have one great limitation, I feel—of not having general ideas about anything. Reading Jung has freed me from the sense of guilt and the inferiority complex this limitation gave me." Alpert, *Fellini, a Life,* 177.

8. *Comments on Film,* 162.

9. John Baxter, *Fellini* (New York: St. Martin's, 1993), 171–72.

10. Alpert, *Fellini, a Life,* 169.

11. Alpert, *Fellini, a Life,* 170.

12. The concept of the "self" has been neatly defined by Jungian analyst Marie-Louise von Franz: "The organizing center from which the regulatory effect stems seems to be a sort of 'nuclear atom' in our psychic system. One could also call it the inventor, organizer, and source of dream images. . . . Throughout the ages men have been intuitively aware of the existence of such an inner center. The Greeks called it man's inner *daimon;* in Egypt it was expressed by the concept of the *Ba-soul;* and the Romans worshipped it as the 'genius' native to each individual." "The Process of Individuation," in *Man and His Symbols,* ed. Carl G. Jung (New York: Dell, 1968), 161–62.

13. Jung, *The Structure and Dynamics of the Psyche,* in *Collected Works of C. G. Jung,* trans. R. F. C. Hull, Bollinger series 20 (Princeton: Princeton University Press, 1953–79), 8:141.

14. See Jolande Jacobi, *The Psychology of C. G. Jung* (New Haven, CT: Yale University Press, 1968), 10–18. Jacobi's discussion of the "function" is the clearest and the best I have found.

15. Jung, *Psychological Types,* in *Collected Works,* 6:330.

16. Jung, *Two Essays on Analytical Psychology,* in *Collected Works,* 7:155–56.

17. Quoted in Jacobi, *Psychology of C. G. Jung,* 30–31.

18. Jung, *The Archetypes and the Collective Unconscious,* in *Collected Works,* 9(1):42.

19. Jung, *The Spirit in Man, Art, and Literature,* in *Collected Works,* 15:81.

20. Jung discusses individuation extensively in *The Archetypes and the Collective*

Unconscious, in *Collected Works,* 9(1):275–354. Also, the concept is well discussed in von Franz, "Process of Individuation," in *Man and His Symbols,* 159–254.

21. Jung was amazed to find intricate mandalas in cultures as diverse as those of Pueblo Indians of North America and Buddhists of Tibet. He was surprised also to find mandalas among the drawings of dream images by his patients in Zurich. See Jung, *Archetypes,* in *Collected Works* 9(1):355–84.

22. There are at least two very fine Jungian readings of *8 ½* and one of *Juliet of the Spirits.* All three, however, seem to me to try to reduce Fellini too narrowly to the Jungian pattern of "individuation." My hope in this chapter is to show how Fellini can take Jungian ideas and images and play with them in his own configurations. Yet I must admit that the journey toward a fuller "self-realization" by a protagonist is usually Fellini's aim. See Albert Benderson, *Critical Approaches to Federico Fellini's "8 ½"* (New York: Arno, 1974); Isabella Conti, "Fellini *8 ½*: A Jungian Analysis," *Ikon: Revue internationale de filmologie* 23, nos. 82–83 (July-December 1972): 123–70; and Carolyn Geduld, "*Juliet of the Spirits:* Guido's Anima," in *Federico Fellini: Essays in Criticism,* ed. Peter Bondanella, 137–51 (New York: Oxford University Press, 1978).

23. Ornella Volta, ed., "Le journal des rêves de Federico Fellini," *Positif* 158 (April 1974): 2–9; and Lietta Tornabuoni, ed., "Fellini oniricon," *Dolce vita* 1, no. 3 (1987): 29–44. See also Pier Marco De Santi, *I disegni di Fellini* (Rome: La terza, 1982).

24. See, e.g., Jacobi, *Psychology of Jung,* 112, plate 4. Jacobi deals with the image of a mountain emerging from the sea of the collective unconscious.

25. Federico Fellini, *Fellini on Fellini,* ed. Christian Strich, trans. Isabel Quigley (New York: Delacorte–Seymour Lawrence, 1976), 5.

26. The dream aspects of *The Temptation of Dr. Antonio* have been discussed by Robert T. Eberwein in *Film and the Dream Screen: A Sleep and a Forgetting* (Princeton, NJ: Princeton University Press, 1984), 112–20. Eberwein describes the billboard on which Anita Ekberg appears as a "dream screen." Both Eberwein and I agree that Antonio is a man "who has never matured." I would stress, however, the Jungian aspect of Antonio's dreams, which offer him a final call to grow up.

27. Two obvious examples appear in *The White Sheik* and *8 ½.* Fernando Rivoli, in his costume of the White Sheik, appears to his admirer Wanda soaring on a swing among the treetops, and Guido escapes the traffic jam in his initial dream in *8 ½* by soaring up and out over a beach as if he were a kite. Both dreams have about them the feel of liberation.

28. Jung, *Alchemical Studies,* in *Collected Works,* 13:116–22.

29. Jung, *Archetypes and the Collective Unconscious,* in *Collected Works,* 9(1):216.

30. Robert Moore and Douglas Gillette, *The Magician Within* (New York: William Morrow, 1993), 63.

31. Moore and Gillette, *Magician Within,* 71, 76.

32. Interestingly, the magician in *Nights of Cabiria,* who calls Cabiria to the vaudeville stage to reveal her emotions about first love, wears a pair of devil's horns beneath his top hat. For all his kindliness to Cabiria, he does in fact put her in jeopardy with the con man in the theater audience.

33. Moore and Gillette, *Magician Within,* 133.

34. "Asa Nisi Masa" is a phrase derived from the word *anima* according to the rules of a child's game, not unlike pig latin, where after each vowel of the word to be translated an *s* is added, plus a repetition of the vowel. See Deena Boyer, *The Two Hundred Days of "8 ½"* (New York: Macmillan, 1964), 24.

35. Fellini, *8 ½,* ed. Charles Affron (New Brunswick, NJ: Rutgers University Press, 1987), 81.

36. See Jung, *Aion, Collected Works* 9(2): 11.

37. We find this motif in a number of scenes in *8 ½,* including the hanging sheets in Guido's nursery during his childhood vacation at the farmhouse, the veil or scarf used by the woman in white when she appears in Guido's hotel room, the veil Saraghina trails over her shoulder as she sings to the sea at the end of Guido's memory of his encounter with her, the scarf Luisa puts over the light in her bedroom scene with Guido, the sheet used to shield the Cardinal in Guido's fantasy of the mud bath, sheets in the farmhouse again and veils fluttered in front of the camera from unknown sources in the harem fantasy, and finally the gauzelike streamers in the movie's final scene.

38. In his Jungian reading of *8 ½,* Benderson notes the appropriateness of Maurice's appearance at this point in the film: "Significantly, in this regard, Maurice, the magician, also initiates the reconciliation fantasy which concludes the film. Standing beside Guido's car, he signals the fantasy to begin with a wave of his hand. Then he orders the lights around the circus ring to be turned on. He greets people as they enter the circle and shows them to their places on the rim. Finally, he leads the chain dance around the perimeter. . . . Certainly he embodies the magical power of the imagination." *Critical Approaches,* 105.

39. The idea of having a medium provide impromptu entertainment at a party seems characteristic of the well-to-do in Fellini films of the 1960s. The same kind of event is staged by the aristocrats in the castle in *La Dolce Vita.*

40. Geduld points out the seemingly endless pairings of opposites in *Juliet of the Spirits* and includes in her list the duality contained by Bishma. "*Juliet of the Spirits:* Guido's Anima," 145–47.

41. Jacobi, *Psychology of C. G. Jung,* 108.

42. Jung, *Aion,* in *Collected Works,* 9(2):8.

43. Jacobi, *Psychology of C. G. Jung,* 113.

44. Geduld considers Iris-Fanny-Suzy as an anima figure, which she would be if the hero were masculine or if she were a figure in *8 ½.* Here, however, Iris-Fanny-Suzy seems best treated as a same-gender shadow to the heroine Juliet, for she is,

as Geduld herself demonstrates, a nearly perfect mirror opposite of Juliet. See "*Juliet of the Spirits:* Guido's Anima," 141.

45. Conti has also discussed Daumier as a shadow figure in *8 ½*. Essentially, I wish to extend her argument here by considering Daumier a "test" that Guido seeks out. See "Fellini *8 ½*: A Jungian Analysis," 128–29.

46. von Franz, "Process of Individuation," 182. See also Conti, "Fellini *8 ½*: A Jungian Analysis," 128.

47. Fellini, *8 ½*, trans. Charles Affron, 114.

48. Jung, "Marriage as a Psychological Relationship," in *Collected Works*, 17:198.

49. von Franz, "Process of Individuation," 186.

50. Fellini, "Playboy Interview," *Playboy* 12, no. 2 (February 1966): 62.

51. James Hillman has studied the variety of different conceptions of the anima in *Anima: An Anatomy of a Personified Notion* (Dallas: Spring, 1985). I am indebted to his work, although I do not use all of the many versions of the anima he discusses, only those that pertain to Fellini.

52. von Franz, "Process of Individuation," 186.

53. Jacobi, *Psychology of Jung*, 121–22.

54. *Psychology of the Transference*, in *Collected Works*, 16:174. Conti, in her "*8 ½*: A Jungian Analysis," treats Fellini's use of these anima figures in an interesting manner. She goes wrong, I feel, in trying to force the fourth figure, Sophia, into the movie. It simply is not there. Yet her discussion of the first three figures is helpful.

55. Fellini, "Playboy Interview," 62.

56. Fellini, *La Dolce Vita*, trans. Oscar De Liso and Bernard Shir-Cliff (New York: Ballantine, 1961), 134.

57. Fellini, *La Dolce Vita*, 218.

58. Fellini, *La Dolce Vita*, 53.

59. In the sense that Fellini surrounds his protagonist with a variety of erotic possibilities, the parties of *La Dolce Vita* prefigure the harem sequence of *8 ½*, which we consider in some detail in chapter 4.

60. Qtd. in Hillman, *Anima*, 130.

61. Jung, *Collected Works*, 10:378.

62. Hillman, *Anima*, 131–33. The quotation within the quotation comes from Jung, *Archetypes and the Collective Unconscious*, in *Collected Works* 9(1):28.

63. Baxter, *Fellini*, 298.

64. *Fellini's Casanova*, 16 mm (Universal, 1977), English language version.

65. *Fellini on Fellini*, 12. Later, Fellini told feminist Germaine Greer that the woman he had his sexual "initiation" with was a maid named Marcella. The story may have been a bawdy tale largely made up to shock Greer. She treats it with amusement. In any case, the film version may be a combination of the hugs of the lay sister and the situation of the maid in the Fellini household. "Fellinissimo,"

in *Perspectives on Federico Fellini,* ed. Peter Bondanella and Cristina Degli-Esposti (New York: G. K. Hall, 1993), 231–32.

66. Baxter discusses the possibility that Fellini himself had had a certain leaning toward gays, despite the fact "there's no evidence of physical affairs." In particular, Baxter comments on Fellini's friendship with the young French critic Dominique Delouche: "The friendship between Fellini and Delouche was the first of a series of 'white marriages' the director contracted with attractive, sensitive, younger men, often—though not always—homosexuals." *Fellini,* 122. What Baxter presents as curiosity in Fellini's life would seem to be in Snaporaz's case fear of latent homosexuality.

67. Many critics have commented on Snaporaz's fear of castration in this scene and in *City of Women* in general. See, for example, Gaetana Marrone, "Memory in Fellini's *City of Women,*" in *Perspectives on Fellini,* 244–45; Bondanella, *Cinema of Federico Fellini,* 319–20; and Baxter, *Fellini,* 329.

68. Volta, "Le journal des reves," 20.

69. It might be argued that Fellini's film project *The Voyage of G. Mastorna* was intended to show, if not the "mystery within," at least the "mystery of death." The movie was to show Mastorna on a plane flight that he learns is in fact his journey after he has died. Fellini never finished this project, however, and his inability to do so is perhaps an indication that he was not comfortable with explaining away mysteries. Good accounts of the Mastorna project are to be found in Alpert, *Fellini: A Life,* 190–95, and Baxter, *Fellini,* 211–29.

3. Autobiography, Childhood, and Adolescence

1. Federico Fellini, *Fellini on Fellini,* ed. Christian Strich, trans. Isabel Quigley (New York: Delacorte–Seymour Lawrence, 1976), 51.

2. Boris Tomashevsky, "Literature and Biography," *Readings in Russian Poetics,* ed. Lasilav Matejka and Krystyna Pomorska (Cambridge, MA: MIT Press, 1971), 47–55; Roland Barthes, *Roland Barthes by Roland Barthes,* trans. Richard Howard (New York: Hill and Wang, 1977); James Olney, *Metaphors of Self: The Meaning of Autobiography* (Princeton, NJ: Princeton University Press, 1972); Elizabeth Bruss, *Autobiographical Acts: The Changing Situation of a Literary Genre* (Baltimore: Johns Hopkins University Press, 1976); and William C. Spengemann, *The Forms of Autobiography: Episodes in the History of a Literary Oeuvre* (New Haven, CT: Yale University Press, 1980).

3. Spengemann, *Forms of Autobiography,* 1–44, 62–91.

4. Tomashevsky, "Literature and Biography," 55. Tomashevsky's concept of the "legend" is discussed in a useful way for film scholars by David Bordwell in *The Films of Carl-Theodor Dreyer* (Berkeley: University Press of California, 1981), 9–10.

5. Camilla Cederna, "Confesso Fellini," *L'espresso-mese* 1, no. 3 (July 1960): 54–63, 108–9.

6. Jacques Delcorde, ed., *Entretiens avec Federico Fellini: texte extrait des emissions*

televisees "La Double Vue" (Belgium: Radiodiffusion television belge, 1962). Portions of this interview are translated into English by Rosalie Siegal in Gilbert Salachas, *Federico Fellini: An Investigation into His Films and Philosophy,* trans. Rosalie Siegal (New York: Crown, 1969), 93–97, 109–10, and by Susan Bennett in Suzanne Budgen, *Fellini* (London: BFI, 1966), 85–95.

7. Fellini, "Il mio Paese," in *La mia Rimini,* ed. Renzo Renzi, 23–43 (Bologna: Cappelli, 1967). Fellini's essay, translated into English by Isabel Quigley as "Rimini, My Home Town," appears in *Fellini on Fellini,* 1–40.

8. Angelo Solmi, *Storia di Federico Fellini* (Milan: Rizzoli, 1962). The first English language version was *Fellini,* trans. Elizabeth Greenwood (London: Merlin, 1967).

9. John Baxter, *Fellini* (New York: St. Martin's, 1993). Baxter has commented, "Most great film-makers have had their myth, and many, like Hitchcock, have actively maintained and lived up to it, but it is rare for anyone to acknowledge its existence so openly. Fellini, however, has always felt that he needs his more than most artists. . . . Without the myth, he feels, he is nothing more than the sum of some less than impressive parts" (9).

10. Fellini, "Rimini, My Home Town," 8.

11. Fellini, "Rimini, My Home Town," 8.

12. Fellini, "Whom Do You Most Admire?: Reply to Renato Barneschi," in *Fellini on Fellini,* 144–45.

13. See, e.g., Delcorde, *Entretiens avec Federico Fellini,* 6–7.

14. Solmi, *Fellini,* 64.

15. Fellini, "Rimini, My Home Town," 20.

16. Quoted in Baxter, *Fellini,* 15.

17. Quoted in Baxter, *Fellini,* 15. See also Eugene Walter, "Federico Fellini: Wizard of Film," *Atlantic* 216, no. 6 (December 1965): 65.

18. Delcorde, *Entretiens avec Federico Fellini,* 6–7. Fellini concludes the anecdote of the stained forehead by relating that he was discovered by an uncle who was not fooled and ordered him to get up at once and wash the ink from his forehead.

19. Delcorde, *Entretiens avec Federico Fellini,* 8. See also Budgen, *Fellini,* 85–86.

20. Baxter, *Fellini,* 26–27.

21. "Rimini, My Home Town," 13.

22. Solmi, *Fellini,* 64.

23. Fellini, "Rimini, My Home Town," 29.

24. Fellini, "Rimini, My Home Town," 10.

25. Fellini, "Rimini, My Home Town," 11.

26. Cederna, "Confesso Fellini," 59. Translation mine.

27. Fellini, "Rimini, My Home Town," 27.

28. Baxter, *Fellini,* 20.

29. Fellini, "Rimini, My Home Town," 9.

30. Quoted in Solmi, *Fellini,* 65.

31. Fellini, unpublished interview with John C. Stubbs, Rome, 31 May 1984, 1–2. Fellini has said similar things elsewhere. See, e.g., *Federico Fellini: Comments on Film,* ed. Giovanni Grazzini, trans. Joseph Henry (Fresno: California State University Press, 1988), 29–31.

32. Fellini, *8 ½,* ed. Charles Affron (New Brunswick, NJ: Rutgers University Press, 1987), 86.

33. Fellini, unpublished interview, 1.

34. *8 ½,* 57–58.

35. Fellini, *La Dolce Vita,* trans. Oscar De Liso and Bernard Shir-Cliff (New York: Ballantine, 1961), 161–62.

36. Fellini, *"Moraldo in the City" and "A Journey with Anita,"* ed. and trans. John C. Stubbs (Urbana: University of Illinois Press, 1983), 155–56.

37. Fellini, *"Moraldo in the City" and "A Journey with Anita,"* 144.

38. Fellini, *"Moraldo in the City" and "A Journey with Anita,"* 153.

39. Fellini, *"Moraldo in the City" and "A Journey with Anita,"* 151.

40. Fellini, *"Moraldo in the City" and "A Journey with Anita,"* 150.

41. Quoted in Patricia Meyer Spacks, *The Adolescent Idea: Myths of Youth and the Adult Imagination* (New York: Basic Books, 1981), 234.

42. Erik Erikson, *Identity: Youth and Crisis* (New York: Norton, 1968), 157–58.

43. Spacks, *Adolescent Idea,* 3.

44. Fellini, unpublished interview, 2.

45. Fellini, *"Amarcord:* The Fascism Within Us—An Interview with Valerio Riva," in *Federico Fellini: Essays in Criticism,* ed. Peter Bondanella (New York: Oxford University Press, 1978), 20–21.

46. Gisela Konopka, "Requirements for Healthy Development of Adolescent Youth," in *Readings in Adolescent Psychology: Contemporary Perspectives,* ed. Thomas J. Cottle (New York: Harper and Row, 1977), 33–51. I argue, of course, not for a direct influence but for a time proximity.

47. Baxter, *Fellini,* 20. Benzi was a more robust and perhaps more daring boy than Fellini. He went on to become a successful lawyer in Rimini and in the Emilia-Romagna region. At Fellini's request, Benzi wrote down and eventually published a series of remembrances. Although most of these memoirs deal with Benzi's adult life as a lawyer, some do treat escapades from his youthful friendship with Fellini, and these sections show an exuberant lifestyle much in the manner of the escapades of *Amarcord.* Benzi, *Patachedi: Gli amarcord di una vita all'insegna della grande amicizia con Federico Fellini* (Rimini, Italy: Guaraldi, 1995).

48. *Amarcord,* DVD (1974; Criterion Collection, 1998).

49. Fellini, unpublished interview, 7.

50. Benzi's memoirs contain a delightful episode in which Titta's father displays a comic frustration in trying to back his new car out of his garage for the first time. In this remembrance, the father is a "dead ringer" for Aurelio. *Patachedi,* 123–26.

51. Budgen, *Fellini,* 28.

52. Fellini, *Three Screenplays: "I Vitelloni," "Il Bidone," "The Temptations of Doctor Antonio,"* trans. Judith Green (New York: Orion, 1970), 123.

4. Autobiography and Fellini's Portrait of the Artist

1. Fellini, *I, Fellini*, ed. Charlotte Chandler (New York: Random, 1995), 37–38.

2. John Baxter, *Fellini* (New York: St. Martin's, 1993), 58.

3. Fellini, "Via Veneto: Dolce Vita," in *Fellini on Fellini*, ed. Christian Strich, trans. Isabel Quigley (New York: Delacorte–Seymour Laurence, 1974), 69.

4. Baxter, *Fellini*, 44.

5. Baxter, *Fellini*, 49.

6. Baxter, *Fellini*, 56–57.

7. Fellini, *I, Fellini*, 94.

8. Fellini, "Sweet Beginnings," in *Fellini on Fellini*, 43.

9. Fellini, *I, Fellini*, 29.

10. Fellini, *I, Fellini*, 30.

11. Fellini, *I, Fellini*, 29. It might, of course, be argued that Fellini did, in fact, marry his wife, Giulietta Masina, at a relatively young age. He was twenty-three, and she, twenty-two. The marriage may seem, then, to be a case in which love overcame a reasoned position. As an actress, however, Masina was not a distraction from Fellini's goal to make movies but rather someone who could help him obtain his goal.

12. We can make the identification because earlier in *Fellini's Roma* we saw a silent-film version of Messalina in Fellini's re-creation of the movie *Maciste all' inferno* (1926).

13. The naïveté of the protagonist's questions to the prostitute helps us realize the event is a first time for him.

14. The metalevels are at least three: (1) The Japanese interviewers are making a documentary about Fellini. (2) Fellini, in turn, is making a documentary about the early days of the Cinecittà studio. (3) The events involving the young protagonist's visit in 1940 come "alive" and thus provide another level of "reality" in the film. There is perhaps another strand still. Fellini is also casting for a film adaptation of Franz Kafka's *Amerika*. This activity, however, seems to me parallel to his activity as documentary filmmaker. It does not introduce a different level of activity in the movie.

15. Fellini, *Federico Fellini: Comments on Film*, ed. Giovanni Grazzini, trans. Joseph Henry (Fresno: California State University Press, 1988), 102.

16. Sergio Rubini is, in fact, the name of the actor who plays the young Fellini. The actor keeps his own name in his part. The actor's last name is, by odd coincidence, the same as Moraldo's in *I Vitelloni*. (Given what we know of Fellini's inside jokes and exaggerations, the coincidence may seem too good to be true.)

17. Fellini reports he was actually sent to interview a handsome leading man, Osvaldo Valenti, for *Cinemagazzino*. Baxter, *Fellini*, 57.

18. Carlo Testa has stressed the "coming of age" aspect of *Intervista* and has drawn interesting parallels between Rubini's experience at Cinecittà and the experiences

of Karl Rossman in Franz Kafka's *bildungsroman, Amerika,* which Fellini as the mature director in *Intervista* is attempting to film in another strand of the movie. I would argue, however, that coming of age has more to do with the young hero finding his avocation than it does with sexual initiation. The latter underlines the seductiveness of the former. See "Cinecittà and America: Fellini Interviews Kafka," in *Federico Fellini: Contemporary Perspectives,* ed. Frank Burke and Marguerite R. Waller, 188–208 (Toronto: University Press of Toronto, 2002).

19. The producer yells back that the circus is in Sicily and the elephants are not available. However, we have seen live elephants earlier being herded into Cinecittà ahead of Rubini, and we must wonder who is conning whom.

20. I have argued in my introduction to the screenplay that Fellini was not ready in 1954 to treat himself as the major subject of a film. The breakthrough film, I suggested, was *8 ½* in 1963, which came after he had considerable success as a film-maker and had made modest beginnings at autobiography in *I Vitelloni* and *La Dolce Vita.* Fellini, *"Moraldo in the City" and "A Journey with Anita,"* ed. and trans. John C. Stubbs (Urbana: University of Illinois Press, 1983), 4.

21. Fellini to John C. Stubbs, March 7, 1979.

22. Margaret A. Boden, *The Creative Mind: Myths and Mechanisms* (New York: Basic Books, 1992), 258.

23. Fellini, *"Moraldo in the City" and "A Journey with Anita,"* 31.

24. Fellini has indicated that Gattone was modeled on a poet and writer of children's tales who was named Garrone. Fellini to Stubbs, March 7, 1979. Tullio Pinelli has added, in another letter, that Garrone did, indeed, die in the manner depicted in the screenplay. Pinelli to Stubbs, May 20, 1979.

25. From the episode of the shop window described in Fellini's "Via Veneto: Dolce Vita," we may identify the artist Lange of the screenplay as Rinaldo Geleng, later a well-known illustrator who executed the frescoes for Fellini's "Subway Sequence" in *Fellini's Roma.* Fellini reconfirms this identification in his letter of March 7, 1979.

26. Signora Contini was identified by Fellini as a certain Signora Lenticchi, also in his letter of March 7, 1979.

27. Pinelli indicates that such a young lady did exist in Fellini's early days in Rome. As best Pinelli could remember, she was the daughter of a custodian of the Museum of Valle Giulia. Pinelli to Stubbs, May 20, 1979. (Fellini himself is dis-creetly silent on the subject of Andreina. He does, however, envision a role for the character Claudia in *8 ½* as a lovely daughter of a museum curator who provides the hero with inspiration.)

28. The ending seems an early version of the one Fellini will use for *Nights of Cabiria,* in which the heroine is cheered by what we have called a "dance of life."

29. Hollis Alpert, *Fellini, a Life* (New York: Atheneum, 1986), 122.

30. The scene seems to be a reworking of the literary cocktail party given by Signora Contini in *Moraldo in the City.* In both cases, the Fellini protagonist feels inferior to the other guests.

31. Fellini, *La Dolce Vita,* trans. Oscar De Liso and Bernard Shir-Cliff (New York: Ballantine, 1961), 134.

32. Steiner is generally considered by critics as a false intellectual whose fear of the future drives him to kill his two children before taking his own life. Frank Burke, for example, denounces him in the strongest terms: "Steiner who as an intellectual should be a vital force for the development of consciousness, contributes instead to its destruction. Suffering from characteristic intellectual paranoia in the face of reality, he dreams of eternal escape." *Federico Fellini: "Variety Lights" to "La Dolce Vita"* (London: Columbus Books, 1987), 89. However, from another point of view, Steiner is someone who likes Marcello, wishes him well, and tries to help him. Of course, Steiner's suicide will greatly disturb Marcello, but it is not clear to me that the suicide convinces Marcello to "give up" his attempt at writing a book. That decision, it seems to me, is made in the scene at the restaurant in Fregene, to be discussed in this section.

33. Fellini, *La Dolce Vita,* 135.

34. A similar kind of episode was written and then cut from the screenplay of *La Dolce Vita.* It involves Marcello's attempt to reopen a relationship with an established writer named Dolores. She offers him harsher words than does Steiner. Dolores tells him his writing is too often, like him, soft and unfocused. There are, however, some moments in his writing that are "authentic." He needs to begin again, pursuing the authentic elements more deeply. Fellini may well have cut the sequence because he felt it went over, perhaps somewhat more didactically, the same ground as the Steiner material. See Fellini, *Quattro Film* (Torino: Einaudi, 1974), 197–210.

35. This is, of course, my reading of Marcello's face on the screen, his slight frown. Not all viewers would agree. Some might well argue that Marcello realizes the moment is not right to press Steiner for names and addresses. This being the case, the next scene, showing Marcello at his typewriter, is especially important, for it reveals why he might actually fear free time in which to write.

36. An eloquent spokesman for this point of view is Stuart Rosenthal in *The Cinema of Federico Fellini* (New York: A. S. Barnes, 1976), 46–47.

37. Fellini, *8 ½,* ed. Charles Affron (New Brunswick, NJ: Rutgers University Press, 1987), 149.

38. Sam Rohdie has described this activity as an entry into the world "where images live. This world because it is filled with memories of what has passed, and desires of what is projected, is a world of the not yet living." It is the job of the artist to bring the world alive. *Fellini Lexicon* (London: BFI, 2002), 120.

39. Fellini, *I, Fellini,* 149.

40. Fellini, "The Long Interview," in *Juliet of the Spirits,* ed. Tullio Kezich, trans. Howard Greenfield (New York: Orion, 1965), 12. Fellini does add later that as he has grown older he has been able to think of himself "apart from my work" a bit more. The evidence suggests the opposite, however, in the sense that he moved to a new project almost as soon as he completed the previous one.

41. Versions of this legend given out by Fellini may be found, for example, in "How I Create" (interview with G. Mazzocchi), *Atlas* 9, no. 3 (March 1965): 182–85; "The Birth of a Film" (interview with Enzo Siciliano), in *Fellini on Fellini,* 159–66; and "And His Ship Sails On" (interview with Gideon Bachmann), *Film Comment* 21, no. 3 (May-June 1985): 25–30.

42. Fellini, "And His Ship Sails On," 26.

43. Baxter, *Fellini,* 78.

44. Fellini, *Fellini on Fellini,* 100–101.

45. Fellini, *I, Fellini,* 102.

46. Fellini, *8 ½,* 45.

47. Fellini, *I, Fellini,* 148. Another version of this story appears in Fellini, *Comments on Film,* 160–62. Peter Bondanella also offers an excellent summary of the prehistory of *8 ½* in *The Cinema of Federico Fellini* (Princeton, NJ: Princeton University Press, 1992), 163–65.

48. Boden, *The Creative Mind,* 19–20.

49. Arthur Koestler, *The Act of Creation* (London: Hutchinson, 1976), 121.

50. Silvano Arieti, *Creativity, The Magic Synthesis* (New York: Basic Books, 1976), 12.

51. Gaston Bachelard, *The Poetics of Reverie,* trans. Daniel Russell (Boston: Beacon, 1969), 6.

52. Fellini, *I, Fellini,* 319.

53. Fellini, *I, Fellini,* 86.

54. Einstein quoted in Koestler, *Act of Creation,* 171.

55. Boden, *The Creative Mind,* 222.

56. Fellini, *I, Fellini,* 89.

57. Fellini, *8 ½,* 151.

58. Not all viewers will find the sequence comic. It is certainly politically incorrect. Some viewers will object that the general situation wherein the male hero subdues women with a whip is inherently unfunny. Others will object to specific pieces of business. The situation of the black dancer swinging as if on a vine may well be racist. While we might argue that the racism is Guido's, not Fellini's, the business is nevertheless troubling, for Fellini never calls Guido to account for it.

59. I exclude here her brief fourth appearance in the movie's ending because I want to concentrate on the three appearances wherein Guido is wrestling with the problem of how he can use her in his film.

60. In this aspect, the lady in white recalls the character of Paola, the young girl from the outdoor restaurant in *La Dolce Vita.*

61. Fellini, *8 ½,* 173.

62. Fellini, *8 ½,* 173.

63. Fellini, *8 ½,* 16.

64. Deena Boyer, *The Two Hundred Days of "8 ½"* (New York: Macmillan, 1964), 11.

65. Fellini, *8 ½*, 130.

66. Angelo Solmi, *Fellini*, trans. Elizabeth Greenwood (London: Merlin, 1967), 165.

67. Fellini, *8 ½*, 186–87.

68. Frank Burke tackles this issue on a more "meta" level, citing it as the moment when Fellini stops seeing characters as "centered" individuals and moves to a more postmodern view of them as "fragmented" selves: "His evolution from fixed identity to decentered spirit is complete." *Fellini's Films: From Postwar to Postmodern* (New York: Twayne, 1996), 137.

69. Too much has been made of the fact that the lady in white is not a part of the group in this circle. Donald Costello, for example, writes, "The ideal may have inspired Guido, but that is an evasion. It is the real people of his life whom he needs, and now accepts. Claudia knew that she had no part in the film, as she had no part in the harem, and will have no part in the final circle." *Fellini's Road* (Notre Dame: University Press of Notre Dame, 1983), 140.

The explanation seems simpler. The actress Claudia Cardinale officially left the filming of *8 ½* at the end of July 1962 to begin work in Sicily on *The Leopard*, directed by Luchino Visconti. She did come back, however, on various occasions for additional shootings and retakes. On October 9, she returned for the shots of her walking on the beach, which were apparently intended for Guido's suicide fantasy before Fellini decided to use them for the movie's ending. She does not seem to have been available two days later, however, when the circus ring dance was shot. My assumption is that Fellini used the shots of Claudia walking on the beach to make viewers think of Claudia as present in the movie's ending even though she is not in the ring of people dancing on the circus set. See Boyer, *Two Hundred Days of "8 ½,"* 123–27, 134–36, and 196–98.

70. Perhaps the first to make this point was Dwight McDonald in "*8 ½*: Fellini's Obvious Masterpiece," in *On Movies* (Englewood, NJ: Prentice-Hall, 1969), 22. The argument has been extended by Albert Benderson in *Critical Approaches to Federico Fellini's "8 ½"* (New York: Arno, 1974), 136–37.

71. Christian Metz, "Mirror Construction in Fellini's *8 ½*," in *Federico Fellini: Essays in Criticism,* ed. Peter Bondanella (New York: Oxford, 1978), 136.

5. The Personae of Giulietta Masina

1. Fellini often cited Marcello Mastroianni as the actor with whom he was most comfortable, since Mastroianni rarely pressed the director for too much information in advance. Fellini has quoted with approbation the following statement by Mastroianni to a reporter: "Yes, I know what Federico is going to do. In a general way, I know the story. But I prefer not to know too much, because I have to try to maintain the same curiosity as to what will happen tomorrow, the day after tomorrow, all during the story, throughout the shooting, the same curiosity that the leading character has to have." Fellini, *I, Fellini,* ed. Charlotte Chandler (New York: Random, 1995), 119.

2. Fellini, "Playboy Interview," *Playboy* 13, no. 2 (February 1966): 64.

3. Angna Enters, *On Mime* (Middletown, CT: Wesleyan University Press, 1965), 3.

4. The only reliable account of Masina's career is Tullio Kezich, *Giulietta Masina* (Bologna: Editrice Cappelli, 1991).

5. Teatro-GUF was an acronym standing for University Fascist Group. Masina maintained, however, that the group was apolitical—simply a theater group with no political agenda. Kezich, *Giulietta Masina*, 24.

6. It is not clear in Kezich's biography whether, in fact, Masina did eventually complete her degree.

7. Kezich, *Giulietta Masina*, 21. Translation mine.

8. Kezich, *Giulietta Masina*, 21.

9. Fellini, *I, Fellini*, 159.

10. James Naremore offers a good short version of the "Method" in *Acting in the Cinema* (Berkeley: University Press of California, 1988), 197–203.

11. "Naturally" is, of course, a vexed term. Naremore charges Stanislavsky with being, at bottom, a romantic much enamored with an organic self from which actions grow naturally. The position of the romantic is contrasted with that of the modernist as represented by Bertolt Brecht, for whom performance is always artificial and contrived. *Acting in the Cinema*, 2–3.

12. Konstantin Stanislavsky, *Building a Character,* trans. Elizabeth Reynolds Hapgood (New York: Theatre Arts Books, 1967), 108.

13. Anthony Quinn, *The Original Sin, a Self-Portrait* (Boston: Little, Brown, 1972), 198, and *One Man Tango* (New York: Harper Collins, 1995), 192–97.

14. Kezich, *Giulietta Masina*, 21.

15. The dialectic between representational acting and presentational acting is a generally acknowledged aspect of most discussions of acting in the twentieth century. For example, Naremore uses the dialectic as a starting point for his book *Acting in the Cinema.* The theoretician for presentational art is usually taken to be Bertolt Brecht, especially in his various attempts to define an "epic theater" and the "alienation effect." Here, however, the pole of presentational acting seems best represented by the tradition of mime.

16. A brief history of mime is given in Tony Montanaro, *Mime Spoken Here* (Gardiner, ME: Tilbury House, 1995), 16–18.

17. Naremore reproduces some amusing drawings of expressions and gestures done by Charles Aubert, a follower of Delsarte who, however, never mentions Delsarte in his book *The Art of Pantomime* (1927). See *Acting in the Cinema*, 56–60.

18. Montanaro, *Mime Spoken Here*, 129.

19. Montanaro, *Mime Spoken Here*, 130.

20. It is generally argued that Fellini's conception of the waif is indebted to Charlie Chaplin's tramp. However, Peter Bondanella argues convincingly that

Fellini also drew heavily on American cartoonist Frederick Burr Opper's character of Happy Hooligan (know in Italy as Fortunello). *The Films of Federico Fellini* (New York: Cambridge University Press, 2002), 10, 12, 54.

21. It is, of course, tempting to look to Fellini's famous distinction between the Auguste clown and the white clown in the film *The Clowns*. Clearly, the waif is like the Auguste in that she is an underdog and sometimes a feisty one at that. But the waif has also occasionally the gracefulness and softness of some white clowns. The distinction, then, only demonstrates the two sides of the waif.

22. Angelo Solmi, *Fellini,* trans. Elizabeth Greenwood (London: Merlin, 1967), 109.

23. See, e.g., Fellini, *Federico Fellini: Comments on Film,* ed. Giovanni Grazzini, trans. Joseph Henry (Fresno: California State University Press, 1988), 108–9.

24. *I, Fellini,* 104.

25. I met Giulietta Masina in Rome during the summer of 1984, while I was interviewing Fellini, and I was surprised to find her appear taller and sturdier than she seems in her films. Her height, however, was something of an illusion. She wore on the occasion extremely high heels and had her hair teased up to make her appear taller. My estimate of five feet, two inches, then, involves my attempt to correct for the illusion of her appearance on that day. In her film work, the illusion is the reverse: She is made to appear smaller than she is. Anthony Quinn has given his height at six feet, two inches. *One Man Tango,* 104.

26. Donald Costello, *Fellini's Road* (Notre Dame, IN: University Press of Notre Dame, 1983), 14.

27. Kezich, *Giulietta Masina,* 51.

28. Fellini, *I, Fellini,* 104.

29. Fellini, *La Strada,* ed. Peter Bondanella and Manuela Gieri (New Brunswick, NJ: Rutgers University Press, 1987), 183.

30. Fellini, *La Strada,* 184.

31. Fellini, *La Strada,* 194.

32. Kezich, *Giulietta Masina,* 52.

33. Fellini, *La Strada,* 193.

34. Kezich, *Giulietta Masina,* 52.

35. John Baxter, *Fellini* (New York: St. Martin's, 1993), 106. The quotation within the quotation is not cited. The observation may be Masina's, or it may be Fellini's.

36. Assistant director Moraldo Rossi has described a sudden appearance of a "phantom horse" in the headlights of Fellini's car as the two men were driving outside Rome at night. The incident is surely the "germ" from which the scene in *La Strada* comes. Most interesting, though, is how Fellini uses the piece of business to deepen the mood already present, rather than to introduce a new element of mystery. Fellini, *La Strada,* 188–89.

37. Frank Burke, *Federico Fellini: "Variety Lights" to "La Dolce Vita"* (London: Columbus Books, 1987), 46.

38. This is literally true in the sense that the sequence begins with Gelsomina, asleep in her van, being awakened by the Fool's call to her.

39. In his classic article on faces in close-up, Lawrence Shaffer makes the point that individual close-up shots need to be seen as part of the "serial record" of the face up to and following the moment in question. Here, the difference of Masina's face from what comes before and even what comes afterward is what makes the moment stand out. See "Reflections on the Face in Film," *Film Quarterly* 31, no. 2 (Winter 1977–78): 2–3.

40. Kezich, *Giulietta Masina*, 52.

41. Kezich, *Giulietta Masina*, 54.

42. Fellini, *I, Fellini*, 114.

43. Fellini has admitted a similarity between Masina's final smile and Chaplin's closing shot in *City Lights. I, Fellini*, 114. In his film, Chaplin looks slightly off camera to his left and smiles when the previously blind girl he loves sees him for the first time. The Chaplin shot is perhaps more complicated than one would suppose in that the girl learns that her benefactor is, in fact, a tramp and not a millionaire as she had supposed. The tramp, then, may be pleased and hopeful but also embarrassed when he smiles. For a discussion of Chaplin's close-up, see Shaffer, "Reflections on the Face," 4–5.

44. Two of the characters in the four movies I will treat are not actually wives in the sense of having had the legal ceremony—Melina Amour of *Variety Lights* and Ginger of *Ginger and Fred.* They are rather partners in stage teams with the male protagonists of the movies. In all the important aspects of the relationships, however, they do function as wives.

45. Fellini, "Playboy Interview," 62.

46. C. G. Jung, *The Development of Personality*, in *Collected Works*, trans. R. F. C. Hull (New York: Pantheon, 1954), 17:196.

47. An example of a widely publicized affair might be the relationship between Fellini and the actress Sandra Milo, who played in *8 ½* and *Juliet of the Spirits.* In 1982 Milo published a tell-all novel, called *Caro Federico*, that caused a stir in the press. See Hollis Alpert, *Fellini, a Life* (New York: Atheneum, 1986), 184. On the other hand, Masina herself was at one time linked by reporters with the actor Richard Basehart. Alpert, *Fellini, a Life*, 106.

48. Kezich, *Giulietta Masina*, 68, 70.

49. Fellini has put forward that one of the reasons Masina wished to play the relatively small role of Iris was that "she wanted . . . to look more glamorous and to have audiences realize that she wasn't *only* Gelsomina." *I, Fellini*, 110. Thus his problem in this sequence was to make his star both glamorous and yet not as elegant as the other guests.

50. Fellini, *Three Screenplays: "I Vitelloni," "Il Bidone," "The Temptations of Doctor Antonio,"* trans. Judith Green (New York: Orion, 1970), 200–201.

51. Fellini, *I, Fellini,* 111. In the same interview, Fellini comments further, "Personally, it was hard for me to cut so much of Giulietta's fine performance. She was so good, especially in the parts I cut. I hoped she would be understanding, because she is my wife. But she was not understanding, because she is also an actress." *I, Fellini,* 111. The scene in question exists in written form in Fellini, *Il primo Fellini,* ed. Renzo Renzi (Rocca San Casciano, Italy: Capelli, 1969), 310–12.

52. Fellini, *I, Fellini,* 155.

53. Kezich, *Giulietta Masina,* 70.

54. It is interesting to compare Masina's performance here with Anouk Aimée's performance as the deceived wife in *8 ½.* Aimée, as the wife, Luisa, watches a screen test of an actress confronting her director husband about his lack of feeling for her. Aimée is full of sharp moves and twitches as she bites her nail, smokes a cigarette, and slides down in her seat. By contrast, Masina is still, acting primarily with her eyes and rigid body, as Juliet imposes an iron reserve on her reactions to what she is seeing.

55. Fellini, "The Long Interview," in *Juliet of the Spirits,* ed. Tullio Kezich, trans. Howard Greenfield (New York: Orion, 1965), 42.

56. Masina has stated that if she personally were in Juliet's situation, "rather than letting him go, I would have split open his head." Kezich, *Giulietta Masina,* 70.

57. It seems unarguable that Fellini had Ibsen's metaphor of a doll's house in mind here. The paint is too glisteningly fresh on the house and the lawn too perfectly green for Juliet's home to be anything other than a structure of make-believe.

58. Fellini, "The Long Interview," 64–65.

59. Fellini, *I, Fellini,* 156.

60. Divorce did not become legal in Italy until 1977. Juliet might have been able to have obtained a separation and a financial settlement, but she would not have been able to remarry.

61. Alpert, *Fellini, a Life,* 294–95.

62. It was generally agreed by reviewers that Fellini's attack on tacky TV shows and commercials overwhelms the movie. The target is an easy one, and Fellini repeats his shots too often. Fellini's quarrel with television and in particular with Silvio Berlusconi's Channel 5 is discussed well by Peter Bondanella in *The Cinema of Federico Fellini* (Princeton, NJ: Princeton University Press, 1992), 221–26. Bondanella points out that the TV specials like the one in *Ginger and Fred* distort the appeal of the old stage variety shows Fellini had loved so much: "Television imitates the *variety* of the variety hall but completely distorts the individuality of the separate routines." *Cinema of Federico Fellini,* 224.

63. Fellini, *I, Fellini,* 231.

64. Millicent Marcus has demonstrated convincingly that Fellini used the TV show as a means to satirize mass communication's substitution of simulacra/impersonators for "real" people and postmodern society's easy acceptance of such

substitution. *After Fellini: National Cinema in the Postmodern Age* (Baltimore: Johns Hopkins University Press, 2002), 4–12, 185–87. Amelia and Pippo are guilty of the same postmodern crime, however, in that they impersonate a famous couple.

65. Kezich, *Giulietta Masina,* 82. For the record, the Fellinis did have a son, Federico, in 1944. Unfortunately, the son died within a few weeks of his birth.

66. Fellini, *I, Fellini,* 233.

67. Kezich, *Giulietta Masina,* 81.

68. Kezich, *Giulietta Masina,* 81.

69. Baxter, *Fellini,* 345. Masina's behavior here was quite different from that earlier in her career, when she asked only for simple lighting effects. On this film, she complained so vigorously about how old she looked in the rushes that Fellini finally changed the cinematographer to soothe her.

70. Marcus places the blame for the final breakup on Pippo's inability to say, "Amelia, I need you," which "reenacts the communication failure of their entire relationship." *After Fellini,* 196. Her point is well taken, but I would stress instead Amelia's refusal to be pulled in and used again by her partner.

6. The Comedy of Types: Early and Late

1. These films include the three Macario vehicles *Lo vedi come sei?* [Do You Know What You Look Like?], 1939; *Non me lo dire* [Don't Tell Me], 1940; and *Il pirato sono io* [I Am the Pirate], 1940; and the three Fabrizi movies *Avanti, c'è posto* [Come On, There's Room], 1942; *Campo dei fiori* [Field of Flowers], 1943; and *L'ultima carrozzella* [The Last Carriage], 1943.

2. Peter Bondanella, "Early Fellini: *Variety Lights, The White Sheik, The Vitelloni,*" in *Federico Fellini: Essays in Criticism* (New York: Oxford University Press, 1978), 224–25.

3. Fellini, *Fellini on Fellini,* ed. Christian Strich, trans. Isabel Quigley (New York: Delacorte–Seymour Lawrence, 1976), 124.

4. Angelo Solmi, in his early biography of Fellini, was the first to put forward this idea, in the course of debunking Fellini's claim that he actually traveled with a troupe Fabrizi took on the road. The more recent biographer Hollis Alpert has gone over the same ground a second time and endorses Solmi's educated guess. See Solmi, *Fellini,* trans. Elizabeth Greenwood (London: Merlin Press, 1967), 69–71; and Alpert, *Fellini, a Life* (New York: Atheneum, 1986), 68–69.

5. Fellini, *Variety Lights,* in *Early Screenplays,* trans. Judith Green (New York: Orion Press, 1971), 6.

6. Fellini, *Variety Lights,* 39.

7. Frank Burke has made the interesting observation that there is a "growing objectification" of Liliana in the movie as she moves from a spirited and stagestruck young woman to "mere decoration" in her final stage show. *Federico Fellini: "Variety Lights" to "La Dolce Vita"* (London: Columbus Books, 1987), 8–9.

8. Bondanella, "Early Fellini," 225–27.

9. Fellini, *Variety Lights*, 60.

10. In *The White Sheik,* Ivan must constantly struggle to keep his hat on his head to maintain his dignified pose, and in *The Temptation of Dr. Antonio,* Antonio will likewise struggle to regain his lost umbrella along with his lost dignity. Both Guido in *8 ½* and Snaporaz in *City of Women* don glasses when they wish to appear intelligent and adult. See Edward Murray on the subject of Ivan and his hat in *Fellini the Artist* (New York: Unger, 1985), 44.

11. The ending of the movie presages Fellini's ending for *Nights of Cabiria* in that it shows Checco on the rebound. He is on a train with Melina and other performers, heading south for another tour of provincial towns while Liliana boards a train for the sophisticated cities of the North. On board the train, Checco makes the discovery of another pretty young girl. Hopeless as his dream is, he still pursues it, and while we will certainly want to regard him as a fool who never learns, we may also give him credit for his resiliency.

12. Alpert, *Fellini, a Life,* 74–75.

13. My description of the conventional reading of the film is a generic one. It is not based specifically on any one particular essay. However, good, intelligent readings of the movies that emphasize the characters' inability to grow beyond the bounds of their types include the following: Solmi, *Fellini,* 90–93; Murray, *Fellini the Artist,* 37–47; Bondanella, "Early Fellini," 228–33; and Burke, *Federico Fellini,* 13–18.

14. *The White Sheik,* DVD (1952; Criterion Collection, 2003).

15. A double standard is certainly at work here, as in other Fellini films. Ivan is permitted to spend the night with a prostitute, while Wanda is "saved." By the same token, Guido in *8 ½* has sex with his mistress, while Juliet stops her sexual encounter with the young man in *Juliet of the Spirits* before it goes "too far."

16. Alpert, *Fellini, a Life,* 156–58. Other contributors were Luchino Visconti, Vittorio De Sica, and Mario Monicelli. Monicelli's episode was dropped from the version issued for foreign release.

17. Particularly harsh were articles by Fr. Enrico Baragli, S.J., in *La civiltà cattolica* (12 September and 15 October 1960). The gist of his argument was that *La Dolce Vita* glamorizes and spreads the immoral lifestyles it pretends to denounce.

18. Robert T. Eberwein puts the idea this way: "Fellini has depicted the paradoxical longings in the doctor most effectively by confronting him with an image that includes the only two dimensions of female sexuality Mazzuolo can imagine: woman as mother or as whore." Thus Eberwein diagnoses Mazzuolo's problem as a mother-whore complex. I prefer to speak of the unmasking of Mazzuolo's fixation at the oedipal stage, because this seems more in keeping with the narrative's drive toward an unmasking that "explains it all" and the narrative's general movement to reduce Mazzuolo from pompous adult to love-starved child. See Eberwein, *Film and the Dream Screen: A Sleep and a Forgetting* (Princeton, NJ: Princeton University Press, 1984), 117–18.

19. *The Temptation of Dr. Antonio* in *Boccaccio '70,* DVD (1962; Wea Corp., 2005).

20. As these comparisons suggest, the movie is an extremely playful one. It was Fellini's first in color, and the use of color seems to have exhilarated him. The movie is full of self-conscious references to the film medium itself, as Frank Burke has demonstrated in *Federico Fellini,* 122–25.

21. Frank Burke, *Federico Fellini,* 119.

22. There is a comic justice connected with all these spastic movements, for earlier Antonio chided a Boy Scout for stuttering.

23. Otto Fenichel, *The Psychoanalytic Theory of Neurosis* (New York: Norton, 1945), 317.

24. Fellini seems to have drawn here on the image of Gulliver on the breasts of the Brobdingnagian maids of court in part two of *Gulliver's Travels.*

25. The concept of the group as protagonist came into Fellini's oeuvre with *I Vitelloni* in 1953. It cannot therefore be considered a concept limited wholly to his later films. Yet it does seem to be one that he tended to favor more and more as his career progressed. *Amarcord* (1974) is perhaps his best-known use of the group as hero, along with the three films considered in this section.

26. Fellini, *The Clowns,* VHS (1970; Media-Home Entertainment, 1978).

27. Fellini, *Fellini on Fellini,* 121–22.

28. *Fellini on Fellini,* 124.

29. *Fellini on Fellini,* 127–28.

30. Perhaps the film *Fellini's Roma* (1972) should be mentioned here as another interesting use of the documentary form by Fellini. The film comes immediately after *The Clowns,* and many of the same generalizations I have made about *The Clowns* could be made about *Fellini's Roma.* Fellini is an on-camera narrator. He recreates scenes that help him establish those aspects of Rome that have seemed important to him, and he laments the apparent falling apart of the city into civil discord.

31. Michel Ciment, "Entretien avec Federico Fellini," *Positif* 217 (April 1979): 3. Translation mine.

32. An interesting summary of the critical debate in Italy can be found in Lorenzo Codelli's "Orchestre et Choeur," *Positif* 217 (April 1979): 11–12. Some sample American responses include Vincent Canby, "Raucous Ensemble," *New York Times,* 17 August 1979, sec. C, 13; Andrew Sarris, "Parables for Our Time," *Village Voice,* 20 August 1979, 49; and Edward Murray, *Fellini the Artist,* 233–37.

33. The notion of "utopie negative" was first applied to the movie by Codelli in "Orchestra et Choeur," 11.

34. Ciment, "Entretien," 5.

35. Fellini, *Orchestra Rehearsal,* DVD (1979; Fox Lorber, 1998).

36. Ornella Volta, "Fellini: Le Navire," *Positif* 272 (October 1983): 34.

37. The character of Edmea Tetua seems to be modeled on Maria Callas, the Greek American diva who lived for several years on the Greek island of Skorpios with her wealthy lover, Aristotle Onassis. As a soprano, Callas dominated her opera

world in the manner attributed to Tetua in the film, and after her death, the ashes of Callas were scattered on the Aegean Sea in a ceremony of state. See Arianna Stassiopoulous, *Maria Callas: The Woman Behind the Legend* (New York: Ballantine Books, 1981), 237–339.

38. Alpert, *Fellini, a Life*, 286.

39. Giovanni Grazzini, ed., *Fellini: intervista sul cinema* (Roma-Bari, Italy: Laterza, 1983), 171.

40. Volta, "Fellini: Le Navire," 32. Zanzotto had already done the poetry for the opening ceremony of *Fellini's Casanova*.

41. Volta, "Fellini: Le Navire," 34.

42. *And the Ship Sails On*, DVD (1983; Criterion Collection, 1999).

43. Sir Reginald Dongby's last name, like that of Aureliano Fuciletto, has a phallic suggestiveness. In Sir Reginald's case, however, the suggestiveness seems ironic, for he proves to be mainly a foot fetishist and a voyeur.

44. For this version of the "Moment Musical," Plenizio used electronic reproduction and rearrangement of actual sounds produced from crystal. Gianfranco Plenizio, *E la nave va; colonna sonora originale* (Notes on the Music; Milano: RAI, n.d.), A-228, 2.

45. At the funeral ceremony for Maria Callas in Chicago's Civic Opera House, the audience looked at a giant slide transparency of the soprano at the back of the stage and listened to her recording of the aria "Casta Diva" from Bellini's *Norma*. "Lyric's Salute to Maria Callas," *Chicago Daily News*, 2 November 1977, 27-B.

46. Andrea Zanzotto, "L'affondamento," in Plenizio, *E la nave va*, 2. Translation mine.

7. The Adaptations: Fellini's Valedictory

1. See, for example, Marcel Martin, *"Fellini Satyricon," Cinema 69*, no. 140 (November 1969): 55; Hollis Alpert, *Fellini, a Life* (New York: Atheneum, 1986), 245; Edward Murray, *Fellini the Artist* (New York: Ungar, 1985), 232; and Gianfranco Angelucci, "On *La voce della luna* and Other Felliniana," in *Perspectives on Federico Fellini*, ed. Peter Bondanella and Cristina Degli-Esposti (New York: G. K. Hall, 1993), 187–88.

2. Oswald Spengler, *The Decline of the West*, ed. and trans. Charles F. Atkinson (New York: Knopf, 1981), first published 1918–22; and Karl Marx and Friedrich Engels, *The Communist Manifesto*, ed. Frederic L. Bender (New York: Norton, 1988), first published 1848.

3. A similar argument could be made about *Fellini's Roma* (1972), in which Fellini shows a city at a virtual standstill, with Marxist youth contending with conservative elders.

4. The story of Fellini's dealings with the French production team and of his preparations for making *Toby Dammit* is related in detail by his assistant, Liliana Betti, in *Fellini*, trans. Joachim Neugroschel (Boston: Little, Brown, 1979), 131–53. See also

Ornella Volta, "Come è nato *Tre passi nel delirio,*" in *Tre passi nel delirio,* ed. Liliana Betti, Ornella Volta, and Bernardino Zapponi (Bologna: Cappelli, 1968), 25–28, and Alpert, *Fellini, a Life,* 196–99.

5. Betti, *Fellini,* 137.

6. Betti, *Fellini,* 132, 134, 140, 153.

7. Bernardino Zapponi, "Edgar Poe e il cinema," in Betti, Volta, and Zapponi, *Tre passi nel delirio,* 17. Translation mine.

8. *Toby Dammit* in *Spirits of the Dead,* DVD (English language, 1968; Home Vision, 2001).

9. The use of an international airport as a surreal world outside the norms of time and space occurs in Zapponi's story "Nell' aeroporto," in *Gobal,* 191–96 (Milan: Longanesi, 1967).

10. Alberto Moravia, "Documentary of a Dream," in *Fellini's Satyricon,* ed. Dario Zanelli, trans. Eugene Walter and John Matthews (New York: Ballantine Books, 1970), 27.

11. Petronius, *The Satyricon,* ed. and trans. William Arrowsmith (New York: New American Library, 1959). Arrowsmith's lucid, scholarly introduction is extremely helpful to the modern reader. Many of my generalizations about the work are derived from Arrowsmith.

12. J. P. Sullivan, *The Satyricon of Petronius: A Literary Study* (Bloomington: Indiana University Press, 1968), 34–38.

13. Erich Segal, "Arbitrary *Satyricon:* Petronius and Fellini," *Diacritics* 1, no. 1 (Fall 1971): 51–57.

14. Fellini, "Preface," in *Fellini's Satyricon,* 43.

15. Eileen Lanouette Hughes, *On the Set of "Fellini Satyricon": A Behind-the-Scenes Diary* (New York: William Morrow, 1971), 4.

16. Moravia, "Documentary of a Dream," 25.

17. Hughes, *On the Set,* 17, 57.

18. Dario Zanelli, "From the Planet Rome," in *Fellini's Satyricon,* 3–4.

19. Fellini, "Preface," in *Fellini's Satyricon,* 44–45.

20. Two scholars have already done much of the spadework in identifying classical materials in *Fellini Satyricon:* Gilbert Highet, "Whose *Satyricon*—Petronius's or Fellini's?" *Horizon* 12, no. 4 (Autumn 1970): 43–47, and Bernard F. Dick, "Adaptation as Archaeology," in *Modern European Filmmakers and the Art of Adaptation,* ed. Andrew Horton and Joan Magretta (New York: Ungar, 1981), 145–57.

21. Both the treatment and the screenplay have been published in *Fellini's Satyricon.* Additionally, Peter Bondanella has outlined the threefold development of the movie from Petronius's original work to the story treatment to the final movie in his appendixes to *The Cinema of Federico Fellini* (Princeton, NJ: Princeton University Press, 1992), 253–61. He describes the materials in each of the three works, making comparisons among the three texts now a relatively simple task.

Although I differ from Bondanella's interpretation in some of my readings of the changes, I am indebted here to his outlines of the material.

22. Jerome Carcopino, *Daily Life in Ancient Rome,* trans. E. O. Lorimer (New Haven, CT: Yale University Press, 1940), 24–26, 213–15, 226–31, and 246.

23. Cornelius Tacitus, *The Histories and Annals of Tacitus,* trans. John Jackson, Loeb Classical Library (Cambridge: Harvard University Press, 1937), 4:364–67. Bernard F. Dick suggests Seneca and his wife Pauline as models for the suicides (with the difference that Pauline survived). See "Adaptation as Archeology," 151.

24. Domenico Comparetti, *Vergil in the Middle Ages,* trans. E. F. M. Benecke (New York: Macmillan, 1895), 326–27. The first to identify this source was Gilbert Highet in "Whose *Satyricon*?," 45.

25. Fellini, *Fellini's Satyricon,* 273–74.

26. Gaius Suetonius Tranquillus, *The Lives of the Twelve Caesars* (New York: Random, 1931), 290.

27. The mood for the Garden of Delights was established in part by murals of erotic art based on copies of Persian miniatures done by artist Antonio Sordia for the film. See Hughes, *On the Set,* 146. Jean Marcadé's compendium of erotic art from the Naples area, *Roma Amor* (Geneva: Nagel, 1961), may also have provided some inspiration for Sordia's murals.

28. Apuleius, *The Transformations of Lucius, Otherwise Known as the Golden Ass,* trans. Robert Graves (New York: Farrar, Strauss and Young, 1951), 51–61.

29. Suetonius, *The Twelve Caesars,* 258–59, and Tacitus, *Histories and Annals,* 4:270–71.

30. Again Nero is the probable source for the new material, since Suetonius recounts this emperor constantly practiced wrestling with the idea of competing eventually in the public games. *Lives of the Twelve Caesars,* 278.

31. Hughes, *On the Set,* 89.

32. Zanelli, "From the Planet Rome," 11.

33. Fellini, *Fellini Satyricon,* DVD (1969; MGM, 2001).

34. William Arrowsmith points out that although homosexuality was "more leniently regarded in Petronius' time than in our own," it was still not a respectable activity and that there is a certain comic flavor to Petronius's choice to narrate his satiric vision through the vehicle of "a first-person pederast." Petronius, *Satyricon,* xiv.

35. Fellini, "Conversation with Federico Fellini," *Oui* 6, no. 1 (January 1977): 154.

36. I am indebted here to Alberto Moravia's observation that the death of the various eighteenth-century societies of Europe visited by Casanova is as much a focus of the movie as the character of Casanova. See Moravia, "Il seduttor scortese," *L'espresso,* no. 52 (26 December 1976): 90–91.

37. Alpert, *Fellini, a Life,* 244–50.

38. Giacomo Casanova, *History of My Life,* trans. Willard R. Trask (New York: Harcourt, Brace and World, 1966–71), 12 vols.

39. Frank Burke argues interestingly that Casanova is a postmodern hero in that he is Fellini's fictional rendering of Giacomo Casanova's somewhat fictional rendering of himself. Since this is the case, Casanova exists not through reference to a real "subject" but primarily through his discourse about his world. *Fellini's Films: From Postwar to Postmodern* (New York: Twayne, 1996), 224. A similar point is made by Millicent Marcus in a less polemical way: "Fellini has seen the *Memoirs* for what they are—a literary text—and has chosen to respond to them with his own admittedly idiosyncratic interpretation in another discursive mode." *Filmmaking by the Book: Italian Cinema and Literary Adaptation* (Baltimore: Johns Hopkins University Press, 1993), 209.

40. In interview, Fellini speaks of "leafing through books and documents," "looking at hundreds of paintings," and "diving into the eighteenth century" to produce the kind of documentation of place that Casanova's memoirs fail to give. Fellini, "*Casanova:* An Interview with Aldo Tassone," in *Federico Fellini: Essays in Criticism,* ed. Peter Bondanella (New York: Oxford University Press, 1978), 33.

41. This is not to say Fellini invented his final episode out of nothing. Other documents describe Casanova's plight as librarian for Count Waldstein at Dux. Fellini seems to have drawn here on Casanova's letters and an account of him written by the Prince of Ligne, uncle of Count Waldstein. See John Masters, *Casanova* (New York: Bernard Geis, 1969), 265–84.

42. Federico Fellini and Bernardino Zapponi, *"Casanova": Sceneggiatura originale* (Turin: Einaudi, 1976). A mimeographed copy of the English translation of *Fellini's Casanova* exists in the screenplay collection of the rare book room of the University of Illinois library.

43. See the Vidal papers in the University of Wisconsin–Madison film archives.

44. Alpert, *Fellini, a Life,* 250–51; Fellini, "Conversation," 154; Gore Vidal to John C. Stubbs, 11 August 1986.

45. Bernardino Zapponi, *Casanova: In un romanzo la storia del film di Fellini* (Milan: Mondadori, 1977). The novel version was published in February 1977, after the movie opened in December 1976.

46. John P. Welle, "Introduction," in *Peasants Wake for Fellini's Casanova and Other Poems,* by Andrea Zanzotto (Urbana: University of Illinois Press, 1997), xiii. Welle discusses the goddess's head and the spoken recitativo of the scene as means to transport us back to an ancient female power of a pre-Christian world.

47. This is the source Casanova himself gives in *History of My Life,* 4:78.

48. Zapponi has commented on the source for the mechanical bird. Such a bird was found among Casanova's possessions when he died. According to Zapponi, the mechanical bird may now be seen in a hall at the British Museum. Zapponi, *Casanova: In un romanzo,* 123.

49. Zapponi, *Casanova: In un romanzo,* 67.

50. Fellini, *Il Casanova di Fellini,* ed. Gianfranco Angelucci and Liliana Betti (Bologna: Cappelli, 1977), 26. Doré is a nineteenth-century artist, as opposed to the eighteenth-century Hogarth and Rowlandson. Fellini seems to draw mainly on Doré's tone, which is much darker and more overtly threatening than those of the earlier caricaturists.

51. The concept of the "unattainable lady" is advanced by Denis de Rougement in *Love in the Western World,* trans. Montgomery Belgion (New York: Pantheon, 1956).

52. Henriette, however, has been identified by editor Willard R. Trask as Jeanne Marie d'Albert de Saint-Hipolyte (1718–95) in Casanova, *History of My Life,* 3:305.

53. *Fellini's Casanova,* 16 mm (Universal, 1977), English language version.

54. The model for the character of Isabella is Voltaire's niece, Mme. Louise Denis (1712–90) in Casanova, *History of My Life,* 6:227–31, 237, 248.

55. Casanova, *History of My Life,* 6:221.

56. Marcus, *Filmmaking by the Book,* 243.

57. The original novel in Italian is Ermanno Cavazzoni, *Il poema dei lunatici* (Turin: Bollati Boringhieri, 1987), and the English language version is *The Voice of the Moon,* trans. Ed Emery (London: Serpent's Tail, 1990).

58. Fellini, *I, Fellini,* 242.

59. A portion of the story treatment has been published in Gilbert Salachas, *Federico Fellini: An Investigation into his Films and Philosophy,* trans. Rosalie Siegal (New York: Crown, 1969).

60. Fellini, *I, Fellini,* 59.

61. Fellini, "Premessa dell'autore," in *La voce della luna* (Turin: Einaudi, 1990), viii.

62. Angelucci, "On *La voce della luna,*" 189.

63. Fellini, *I, Fellini,* 247. In the quotation, Fellini mistakenly identifies the shoe as that of Marisa, Nestor's wife. I have made the correction, since it is clear Fellini is referring to Aldina's shoe.

64. Cristina Degli-Esposti, "Voicing the Silence in Federico Fellini's *La voce della luna.*" *Cinema Journal* 33, no. 2 (1994): 42, 51.

65. Peter Bondanella puts the same idea a little differently in that he, like Degli-Esposti, locates the voice *within* Ivo: "Fellini's aim is to ask his audience to consider paying more attention to their inner voices, those linked to the mysterious figure of the moon, which has always intrigued poets as a symbol of love, creativity, and poetic inspiration." *The Films of Federico Fellini* (New York: Cambridge University Press, 2002), 40.

66. *La voce della luna,* 137. Translation mine.

INDEX

Actors Studio, 141–42

adaptation, Fellini's choices for, 205–7, 211–12; sense of coldness in, 206, 223. See also *Fellini Satyricon; Fellini's Casanova; Toby Dammit; Voice of the Moon, The*

adolescence: in *Amarcord,* 71, 87–94, 104; theories of, 86–88; in *I Vitelloni,* 94–103. *See also* young adulthood or late adolescence

Adventures of the Newlyweds Cico and Pallina, The (radio show), 107, 139

Affron, Charles, 129

Agel, Geneviève, 259n21

Aimée, Anouk, 275n54. See also *Dolce Vita, La; 8 ½*

Alighieri, Dante *(La Vita Nuova),* and autobiography, 71. *See also* autobiography, theory of

All about Eve (Mankiewicz), 173

Alpert, Hollis, 39, 115

Amarcord (Fellini), 6–11, 23, 25, 27, 30–31 34, 37, 64–65, 76, 88–94, 104, 157, 222–23, 236, 238, 278n25; and adolescence, 87–94; artifice in, 10; Aurelio, 7–10, 93–94; camaraderie of adolescents in, 92–93; challenges to authority in, 91–92, 104; fantasy and play in, 88, 90–91, 104: grotesques in, 25, 27 fig. 1.7; Gradisca, 7–10, 75, 89–90, 193, 237; Lallo, 7; Lucia the tobacconist, 27–28, 89, 222; possibility of maturation in, 94; *Rex* sequence in, 6–11, 30–31; risk taking in, 88–90; shared experience in, 10–11; tracking shot to beach in, 23; Uncle Teo, 27, 93, 236

Amato, Giuseppe *(Donne proibate),* 142

Andronicus, Livius (Roman mime), 143

And the Ship Sails On (Fellini), 31–32, 187–88, 197–204; documentary quality of, 198, 200; end of era in, 197, 203–4; and Fellini's discovery of Verdi, 197; Fuciletto, 200–202; Hildebranda, 199–202; postmodern aspect of, 199; Reginald Dongby, 200–201, 279n47; role of narrator in, 198–99, 204; three operatic scenes at end of, 202–3; use of interviews in, 200; Ziloev, 200–201

Angelucci, Gianfranco, 238, 157n4

anima, 43, 46, 50, 57–64, 67, 130, 157–58, 215, 219, 227–28; as amazon, 58–59, 65: in *City of Women,* 58–59, 64–67; in *Dolce Vita,* 60–62; as Eros, 59–61, 65; in *Fellini Satyricon,* 215, 219, 222, 227–28; in *Fellini's Casanova,* 63–64, 228, 230; as spiritual figure, 59, 61–62; as mediatrix, 62–64, 222

Antonet (white clown), 189–90

Antonioni, Michelangelo, 177, 257n9

Apuleius *(The Golden Ass),* 213, 217

Aretino, Pietro *(Sonetti lussuriosi),* 226

Arieti, Silvano, on creativity, 123, 132

Arrowsmith, William, 280n11, 281n34

John C. Stubbs is a professor of English and film studies at Virginia Tech. He teaches a wide range of courses, including Italian film, American literature of the 1920s, and narrativity. Stubbs has been a Fulbright lecturer in Italy and a visiting professor at the American Academy in Rome. His books include *Federico Fellini: A Guide to References and Resources* and, as editor and translator, *Two Fellini Screenplays: "Moraldo in the City" and "A Journey with Anita,"* which won the American Association for Italian Studies Award. Among his numerous articles are essays on Federico Fellini and Orson Welles in *Literature/Film Quarterly* and *Cinema Studies*. His current project is a study of World War II situations in three generations of Italian cinema.